# THE UNITARIANS
# AND THE
# UNIVERSALISTS

# THE UNITARIANS AND THE UNIVERSALISTS

DAVID ROBINSON

Denominations in America, Number 1

**Greenwood Press**
Westport, Connecticut · London, England

**Library of Congress Cataloging in Publication Data**

Robinson, David, 1947–
    The Unitarians and the universalists.

    (Denominations in America, ISSN 0193-6883 ; no. 1)
    Bibliography: p.
    Includes index.
    1. Unitarianism—United States—History.   2. Univer-
salists—United States—History.   3. Liberalism (Religion)
—United States—History.   I. Title.   II. Series.
BX9833.R63   1985        288'.73        84-9031
ISBN 0-313-24893-1 (lib. bdg.)

Library of Congress Catalog Card Number: 84-9031
ISBN: 0-313-24893-1
ISSN: 0193-6883

First published in 1985

Greenwood Press
A division of Congressional Information Service, Inc.
88 Post Road West, Westport, Connecticut 06881

Printed in the United States of America

10 9 8 7 6 5 4

**Copyright Acknowledgments**

The author and publisher are grateful for permission to quote from the following works.

Commission of Appraisal of the American Unitarian Association, *Unitarians Face a New Age*
(Boston: American Unitarian Association, 1936). Quoted by permission of the Unitarian Universalist Association.

*Frederick May Eliot: An Anthology*, ed. Alfred P. Stiernotte (Boston: American Unitarian Association, 1959). Quoted by permission of the Unitarian Universalist Association.

James Luther Adams, *On Being Human—Religiously* (Boston: Skinner House Books, 1982). Quoted
by permission of the Unitarian Universalist Association.

Ethelred Brown, "The Harlem Unitarian Church," in the Unitarian Universalist Archives. Quoted
by permission of the Unitarian Universalist Association.

The papers of Thomas Lamb Eliot at the Reed College Library. Quoted by permission of the
Reed College Library.

To Gwendolyn, Elena, and Paul,
with love

There is a principle which is the basis of things, which all speech aims to say, and all action to evolve, a simple, quiet, undescribed, undescribable presence, dwelling very peacefully in us, our rightful lord: we are not to do, but to let do; not to work, but to be worked upon; and to this homage there is a consent of all thoughtful and just men in all ages and conditions.

—Ralph Waldo Emerson, ''Worship''

# CONTENTS

# SERIES FOREWORD

The Greenwood Press series of denominational studies follows a distinguished precedent. At the same time these current volumes improve on earlier works by including more churches than before and by looking at all of them in a wider cultural context. The prototype for this series appeared almost a century ago. Between 1893 and 1897 twenty-four scholars collaborated in publishing thirteen volumes known popularly as the American Church History Series. That shelf of books found twenty religious groups to be worthy of separate treatment, either as major sections of a volume or as whole books to themselves. Scholars in the current series have found that outline to be unrealistic, with regional subgroups no longer warranting separate status and others having sunk to marginality. Twenty organizations in the earlier series survive as nine in this collection, while two churches and an interdenominational bureau have been omitted. The old series also excluded some important churches of that time; others have risen to great strength since then. So today a new list of denominations, rectifying imbalance and recognizing modern significance, features many groups not included a century ago. The solid core of the old series remains in this new one, and in the present case a wider range of topics makes the study of denominational life in America more inclusive.

The American Church History Series was a bold attempt to link denominations together, but it was preceded and followed by isolated studies of separate churches. Many such earlier treatments harbored polemical self-justification, and later publications of this sort have continued to highlight both distinctive denominational features and apologetics. Though more recent denominational histories have improved with greater attention to primary source materials and more rigorous scholarly standards, they have too frequently pursued themes for internal consumption alone. These solipsistic orientations still set priorities for many denominational histories that yield chronologies and incremental development interesting only to insiders. Volumes in the Greenwood Press series strive to maintain the virtues of denominational history and yet to rise above past shortcomings. Each one is solidly grounded in the concrete material of specific ecclesiastical experience, but these studies move beyond parochialism. Most important, they avoid a perspective that places a single church above others in its claim to truth or norms for worship and ethics. They try to set the history of each denomination in the larger religious and social contexts that have influenced it over time. In this way, as integers and as components of a series, they try to interpret the reciprocal interaction that has occurred between different churches and the broader aspects of American culture.

One final observation about the series as a whole relates to its format. Each of these historical studies has a strong biographical focus, utilizing men and women in denominational life to underscore significant elements of progressive change. The first part of every volume takes important watershed issues that shaped a church's outlook and discusses the roles of those who participated in the events. The second part consists of biographical sketches, covering these persons and other persons who contributed to the vitality of denominational life. This format allows authors to emphasize major events germane to their subject matter while remaining sensitive to the basic human nuances that comprise the sharp particularities of history.

This book by David Robinson, Associate Professor of English at Oregon State University, is the first of the new series to appear. Its treatment of Unitarians and Universalists benefits from recent denominational scholarship and also utilizes more general studies of American intellectual and social experience. Robinson does not consider these American churches separate from or superior to European counterparts, but he uses co-religionists on this side of the Atlantic as a vantage point for observing the liberal spirit in American religion. Unitarians and Universalists, recently joined in cooperative affiliation, have often stood at the forefront of speculative and practical theological revisions. They have exemplified a dynamic questing for improvements in religious thought and for application of such advances in social action. In his interpretive chapters and sketches the author points to many instances where members of these churches championed such causes as women's ordination, human rights, and intellectual freedom. Robinson's study shows that the internal energy of religious ideas has often outmoded institutional and creedal molds. That feature is at once atypical of many other churches in this country and yet an underlying theme in all their developmental pilgrimages. The following chapters and people hold up to view a pervasive characteristic, one notable in the denominations chosen for study here and endemic to church life everywhere.

Henry Warner Bowden

# PREFACE

The historian of American religion confronts, in Sidney Mead's apt metaphor, "a vast jigsaw puzzle of events" that refuse any ultimate order. Although true of American religion in general, it seems particularly true of Unitarianism and Universalism, the most freely unorthodox of the American religious movements. Each one has deep roots in American history, with Unitarianism evolving from the original New England Puritan churches and Universalism originating in challenge to those churches. Each movement has also had a profound impact on American culture. Both Unitarianism and Universalism have more than enough historical complexities standing alone, but the merger of the two denominations in 1961 deepened those complexities by emphasizing a continuity of thought that, however real, does not explain the very different origins of the movements. Therefore, until the Civil War at the earliest, one must resist the temptation to think of a common movement of religious liberalism in America. I have thus traced in the first part of this book the early currents of two separate streams of liberal thinking, which merged only gradually.

My interest in this study arose from earlier studies of Ralph Waldo Emerson, a man who rebelled from his clerical position in the Unitarian church but not from religious liberalism. Emerson is the preeminent example of a number of cultural leaders in America who can be seen profitably in the context of the history of liberal religion in America. Although I hope my work will be of interest to Unitarian Universalists, I also hope it will provide students of American culture with another useful "angle of vision" on the problem of American cultural identity. The more such angles we have, the closer we come to the picture as a whole.

The biographical dictionary that supplements the historical essay here follows the format established in Henry Warner Bowden's *Dictionary of American Religious Biography* (Westport, CT: Greenwood Press, 1977). Bowden's aims for the biographies included in that volume were as follows: "(1) to summarize basic information on every individual as accurately as possible, (2) to incorporate vital statistics within sound interpretive judgments, (3) to present all data in a manner which stimulates further inquiry'' (p. ix). I have followed these goals in preparing the biographies included here. There is inevitably some overlap between information included in the historical essay and the biographies. Although the biographical dictionary supplements the historical essay, it is also designed to be used independently as a reference tool, research guide, and summary reminder. In the text of each chapter of the historical essay and in each biography, an asterisk has been affixed to the first mention of a name included in the biographical dictionary. There are, however, biographies of a number of individuals who are not mentioned in the text of the historical essay.

As in the *Dictionary of American Religious Biography*, bibliographic sources are included with each biography, with Part A comprising works by the individual being discussed and Part B listing references about that individual. These bibliographies are representative but by no means exhaustive, and with a few exceptions I have followed Bowden's guideline of limiting primary references to six. A table of abbreviations for standard reference works cited in the bibliographies precedes the biographical dictionary.

Choices had to be made in writing these biographies, and I expect that every student of Unitarian Universalist history will be able to specify a few names that he or she might have included. Even so, those who are included here represent the amazing and diverse vitality of the individuals who have made Unitarian and Universalist history.

## ACKNOWLEDGMENTS

My debts are many after completing this work, but it is a pleasure to acknowledge them. The deepest of them is to my wife, Gwendolyn, for her steadiness and encouragement, her occasional healthful irony, her unfailing ability to inspire me, and her love.

Many individuals have helped along the way with information and research materials, and I express my thanks to them: Joseph Barth, Lon Ray Call, Alan Deale, Philip Giles, Richard Highland, the late Munroe Husbands, Ernest Kuebler, Russell E. Miller, John H. Nichols, Rick Oiesen, David B. Parke, Pete Peterson, Alan Seaburg, Carl Seaburg, Charles Semowich, and Art Wilmot. I owe particular thanks to Conrad Wright for his thorough critique of the manuscript.

I am much indebted to Doris Tilles and the staff of the Interlibrary Loan Department of Oregon State University. Completion of the book would have been impossible without her friendly, untiring, and professional help. I am also grateful to Luella Pollock and the staff at the Reed College Library. I am grateful for research support from the Oregon Committee for the Humanities, the American Council of Learned Societies through a grant from the National Endowment for the Humanities, and the General Research Program, Oregon State University.

I also owe many thanks to the staff of the Oregon State University English Department: Diane Slywczuk, Cheryl Watt, Arlene Garren, and Margie Kickert. For further support, I want to thank Professor Dieter Schulz and the Anglistisches Seminar, Universität Heidelberg.

I benefited from supportive audiences for portions of the work at the Starr King School for Religious Leadership, Berkeley, in the fall of 1983. For guidance and many hours of editorial help, I want to thank Henry Warner Bowden. I value not only the help he gave but the friendship that evolved in the process.

# Part One
# THE UNITARIANS AND THE UNIVERSALISTS: A HISTORY

# 1
# THE UNITARIANS AND THE UNIVERSALISTS: A SUMMARY OVERVIEW

When the American Unitarian Association and the Universalist Church of America completed their merger in 1961, a new denomination was born, the Unitarian Universalist Association. Although there was much continuity between the old organizations and the new one in the merger, there was also a definite departure from the unique identities that both the Unitarians and the Universalists had developed in America since the eighteenth century. The fact of this merger, now more than two decades old, indicates the shared values of the two groups. The history of Unitarianism and Universalism in America reveals much that the denominations shared. But such a history also reveals the distinctiveness of the two movements. If they shared many liberal values, they also found different ways to express and embody those values and different groups to whom their liberal message appealed. The different sources of the stream of liberal religion should be kept in mind, for in that diversity there is a richness that needs to be remembered.

At their inception, both Unitarians and Universalists shared a common theological enemy: Calvinism. As the religion of the New England Puritans, Calvinism had deeply affected the fabric of American living and thinking. It was a vital theology, prone to different emphases and interpretations, one that was adapted in remarkable ways to the necessities of American spiritual life. But it was also a theology of uneasy tensions. In preserving the inviolability of the will of God, it seemed to many to sacrifice the will of humanity. This was most agonizingly true of the doctrine of "election" to grace, which held that God chose those who would be saved before the dawn of time, and those not so elected were powerless to effect their own salvation. It was an uncompromising system, and many began to chafe under it. In 1770 John Murray* arrived in America from England and began preaching a new message of hope. Salvation is for all; all are, in effect, "elected." This message of "universal" salvation was seized by many as an alternative to Calvinism, and Murray's message began to spread in the late eighteenth century, largely among rural and small-town populations of middling economic status. In the spread of his message, Universalism was born.

Meanwhile, another more gradual change was taking place among many of the clergy in Boston and eastern Massachusetts. Still part of the churches of the "Standing Order" of New England, established by the Puritans on a Calvinist basis, these ministers began to doubt the doctrines of Calvinism, especially that of election. They began to emphasize God's benevolence, humankind's free will, and the dignity rather than the depravity of human nature. This trend was accelerated by the religious upheavals that had begun with the Great Awakening in New England in the 1740s, the first of the great evangelical revivals that have periodically occurred throughout American history. The emotional excesses of the revival, and the threats that the many itinerant preachers posed to the established clergy, caused a reaction that forced many of the Boston-area ministers into a deeper commitment to liberal and rational theology. As this liberalism grew in the late eighteenth and early nineteenth centuries, the institutional and intellectual base of American Unitarianism was prepared. By the third decade of the nineteenth century, many of the Puritan Congregational churches began to call themselves Unitarian.

The Universalist movement developed principally in New England, with John Murray and then Hosea Ballou* taking the theological leadership of the denomination. The Universalists struggled against the system of tax support for the "established" or official churches, and their role as intellectual mavericks and social protesters, uneasy with the established order of things, has been a continuing part of their identity to the present day. Denominational organization for the Universalists remained primarily congregational, although in 1790 a national convention met at Philadelphia, and two years later the New England Convention of Universalists was formed as a separate organization. In 1803 that group adopted the "Winchester Profession of Faith," which affirmed a belief in the revelation of the Bible, the certainty of eventual salvation, and the moral imperative of good works as the essential Universalist tenets. This profession stood as the definitive description of the Universalist faith in the nineteenth century.

The Unitarian denomination emerged as a product of the Unitarian controversy of the early nineteenth century. The liberals of the day, increasingly wary of Calvinist orthodoxy, opposed those Calvinists who were trying to hold the line against departure from orthodox doctrine. In 1805 a controversy welled up when the liberal Henry Ware* was elected Hollis Professor of Divinity at Harvard over orthodox objections. Later a pamphlet debate began, culminating in William Ellery Channing's* important sermon of 1819, "Unitarian Christianity." In that sermon Channing confirmed the presence of a new theological movement, embraced the term *Unitarian*, and rallied the liberals together as a discrete theological group. Denominational reorganization was not part of Channing's vision, but nevertheless Unitarianism began to achieve institutional identity in two ways. Many of the established churches split between the liberals and orthodox, and a legal ruling over such a split at Dedham, Massachusetts, in 1820 served to give the Unitarians in many cases control of the original church buildings and properties. Hence many Puritan churches of Massachusetts became Unitarian. In 1825 the American Unitarian Association (AUA) was formed, essentially as a publishing and educational arm of the Unitarian movement. It had little power except what was given it by its constituency, but it did serve to publicize the Unitarian cause and to give the denomination a national identity.

Almost as soon as Unitarianism achieved an identity, it produced its own rebellion, Transcendentalism. This movement was most closely identified with Ralph Waldo Emerson* and Theodore Parker*, who espoused a religion of direct intuition of God, or the "One Mind" of the universe, in opposition to the more empiricist and historically oriented views of Andrews Norton* and other established Unitarians. Transcendentalism was a highly individualistic version of Unitarianism, disposed against ecclesiastical organization, and more reformist in its political outlook, within the limits of its individualism. The same sort of radical individualism in religion, although based on different philosophical tenets, would emerge later as "Free Religion" and "Humanism" in the denomination.

Hosea Ballou held the intellectual and personal leadership of Universalism in the early nineteenth century, and he pushed the concept of Universalism a step beyond Murray. For Murray, salvation was eventually assured, although suffering for many after death, for a limited time, was probable. As Ballou gradually began to see it, all punishment for sin was in the consequences of sin in this life. After death, all were saved with no period of suffering. Ballou's version of Universalism sparked a heated and at points divisive debate among Universalists in the nineteenth century. The "ultra-Universalists" followed Ballou in rejecting all future punishment, and the "Restorationists" held that limited punishment was part of the Divine plan. The difference of the major dialogues of the Unitarians and Universalists in the nineteenth century suggests the distinctions between Universalism and Unitarianism. Universalism was more closely identified with one theological position, universal salvation. Although that was a radical position for the time, in many other respects Universalism was more conservative theologically, insisting on biblical authority and the centrality of Jesus and his atonement. The drift of Unitarianism, however, was away from biblicism and the divinity of Jesus, and throughout the nineteenth century the denomination was in the leadership of the general Protestant movement away from orthodoxy and toward modernism.

The controversies surrounding Transcendentalism dominated the intellectual world of Unitarianism before the Civil War, and those controversies extended into the political realm as well, as Unitarians tried to respond to the issue of slavery. Theodore Parker, whose Transcendentalist views on theology had made him a figure of controversy, extended that controversy through his increasingly strident antislavery ideas. But by the time of the war, the denomination, like the whole nation, submerged much of its intellectual energy into the war effort. Henry W. Bellows* made an enormous contribution to the war in his leadership of the United States Sanitary Commission's efforts to upgrade medical care for the wounded. His experience in that work, and his sense of the national mood of willingness to cooperate in large undertakings, led him to form the National Conference of Unitarian Churches in 1865. It was established as a vehicle to help unite the existing Unitarian churches and to expand the movement nationally. But Bellows and others such as James Freeman Clarke* also hoped that the National Conference could gradually help Unitarianism emerge into a more general movement of liberal religion with a truly universal appeal. Many of the same hopes for a widening liberal church, universal in its outlook and appeal, also were articulated by the Universalists, who celebrated their one hundredth anniversary in an 1870 conference. Although still committed to the principles of Christian biblicism that had been articulated in their Winchester Profession of Faith in 1803, the Universalists were beginning to look beyond the strictly theological connotations of the name "Universalist." They were beginning to see that the term *Universalist* could denote the universal community of all men and women and the necessity of working toward the secular realization of that community through peace and justice on earth.

Bellows's efforts to organize Unitarianism more effectively were successful, but they did meet opposition. The radicals in the denomination, spiritual descendants of Emerson and the Transcendentalists, resisted the organization of liberal religion and suspected Bellows and others of hoping to impose some uniformity of thought or belief on Unitarianism as a condition of organizing it. They fought any establishment of a creed by the National Conference or the AUA, and some of them bolted from the denomination to form the Free Religious Association (FRA), which held its first meeting in 1867. The FRA was not a serious attempt to rival the National Conference as an organization but was a vehicle by which dissent to institutionalized religion could be expressed and the ideas of "free" religion could be spread. Octavius Brooks Frothingham* stands as the most prominent among the radicals, but Cyrus Bartol,* Francis Ellingwood Abbot,* and John White Chadwick* were also prominent in the movement. Each one had his own shade of theological belief but shared a commitment to a completely noncreedal, and largely post-Christian outlook. Frothingham's *Religion of Humanity* (1873) was one of the most important philosophical statements among the radicals. It located religious value in the evolving progress of the human race, arguing in a thoroughly nonsupernaturalistic way that God worked "*in and through human nature.*"

As Unitarianism spread from New England to the Midwest and Pacific Coast, the issues of theological modernism were also debated. The Western Unitarian Conference was formed in 1852 to organize Midwest Unitarianism. In the 1870s and 1880s it evolved into a vehicle of theological radicalism under the leadership of Jenkin Lloyd Jones* and William Channing Gannett.* At odds with the more conservative eastern Unitarianism centered at the AUA in Boston, Jones and Gannett insisted on a creedless religion tied to an "ethical basis" rather than a theological dogma. The controversies between radicals and conservatives, in both East and West, continued through the nineteenth century, but as the century closed, a harmony was achieved at the 1894 meeting of the National Conference. There the denomination unanimously adopted a declaration that "nothing in this constitution is to be construed as an authoritative test," thus declaring the denomination to be uncompromisingly noncreedal.

The Universalists were less riven with theological disputes than the Unitarians and had retained the Christian basis of their faith more completely during the nineteenth century. But in the early decades of the twentieth century the social interpretation of religion began to take a more prominent place in their thinking. The 1917 Declaration of Social Principles drafted by Clarence Skinner* and adopted by the Universalist General Convention stressed the fact that evil is the result of "unjust social and economic conditions" and called for a religion that addressed those conditions. Among the strikingly prophetic list of recommendations in the report was a call for a more democratic division of land and industry, equal rights for women, social insurance, and a world federation. For Skinner, the true Universalism was of this world; it was economic and social as well as spiritual.

Two Unitarian churchmen, Samuel A. Eliot* and Frederick May Eliot,* made enormous contributions to the institutional growth and stability of Unitarianism in the twentieth century. Samuel Eliot took the lead in consolidating the central offices of the AUA in the first decades of the century and through that consolidation helped foster the spread of the movement. After a severe dip in fortune, outlook, and morale in the 1930s, Frederick May Eliot led a renaissance of liberal religion after guiding the denomination through a thorough reappraisal in 1936.

The early decades of the century were marked by the rise of the Humanist movement among the Unitarians, an attempt to reformulate liberal theology on completely nontheistic grounds. This sparked a lively debate, still continuing in the denomination, about the nature of the idea of God and the necessity of it to religion. In one sense the Humanists, who were led by Curtis Reese* and John Dietrich,* continued the radical theological impulse that had been expressed as Free Religion or Transcendentalism in earlier periods, although the Humanists, having a distinctly empirical cast to their thinking, were inclined to be less speculative in theological matters than those earlier movements had been.

Partly in response to Humanism, but primarily in response to a more general crisis of faith in liberal thinking, another movement of criticism and analysis began in the 1930s under the leadership of James Luther Adams.* Wary of the overly facile belief in human dignity and ultimate human progress that had marked liberalism from its inception, Adams called for a revival of liberal religious principles that would focus on a recognition of the "tragedy" of human life and human progress and the necessity of active "commitment" to which such a recognition of tragedy must lead. By criticizing liberal religion at its very core, its doctrine of human nature, Adams and others hoped to revivify the active principle of liberalism that facile optimism had tended to numb in the twentieth century.

After the crisis of the 1930s, the Unitarians underwent a surge of growth after World War II, and during that period the groundwork was laid for the consolidation of Unitarianism and Universalism. Frederick May Eliot did much to prepare the denominations for the merger, although he did not live to see its accomplishment. But if the merger signified the crest of an expansionary phase, it was followed shortly by the social upheaval of the 1960s, which was reflected in a period of unrest and uncertainty within Unitarian Universalism. It may well be that that period of unrest is only starting to be superseded now. National politics, the general social disenchantment with all institutions, and demographic factors can all be said to have contributed to that upheaval. But another salient fact is that the diversity of outlook that had always characterized the denomination seemed to increase in the post–World War II period. Underneath the social stresses of the era of Vietnam, the Civil Rights movement, and the feminist movement lay the difficult question of finding a common identity within that diversity.

In the 1980s we seem to be in a period in which political goals unify rather than divide religious liberals and in which common history is starting to be seen as a sign of common identity. Politics will change, and history will come to be seen differently by successive generations; nevertheless, the act of seeing can be a bond of identity because divergent perspectives do merge on a common object of vision. As rebels against established ways of thinking, Unitarians and Universalists have always had a distinctly antihistorical temperament. Yet their very activism, intellectual and social, has been the source of a rich history. Liberals can safely look back without risking their prospective vision.

# 2
# AMERICAN UNITARIAN ORIGINS

## THE GREAT AWAKENING AND ITS DISSENTERS

Few opposed the intense revival that swept New England in the 1740s with the tenacity and vehemence of Charles Chauncy.* A serious and scholarly man, given to neither great emotion nor large ambition, Chauncy found in the Great Awakening not only a source of personal passion in his dissent to it but, even more surprisingly, a role of leadership in a movement that neither he nor anyone else in New England had contemplated. During his opposition to the Awakening, Chauncy was able to transmute his vigorous dissent into a positive set of ideas, which fall loosely into three major categories: a commitment to logic and reason in theology, a biblicism that was strict but that demanded critical and historical analysis, and an overriding concern for moral aspiration as the focal point of the Christian religion. The developing force of these ideas, as they were articulated by Chauncy and other New England dissenters to the revival, formed the basis of the movement that would, almost a century later, take on the name of "Unitarianism."

A sense of the issues at stake in the Great Awakening can be gathered from a 1742 letter of Chauncy, castigating the leaders and followers of the revival. George Whitefield, the powerful itinerant preacher who was the central figure in the movement, is described in the idolatrous terms of a man who was received by the people "as though he had been an *Angel of God; yea, a God come down in the Likeness of Man.*" His effect on his hearers was more often to produce pride in them than piety, leading Chauncy to conclude that his followers "possess a *worse Spirit* than before they heard of his Name." But within this prolonged harangue against revivalism, one of several such productions of Chauncy, there is a hint of hope, a sense that these extraordinary events may in fact "have been the Means of awakening the Attention of many; and a good Number, I hope, have settled into a truly *Christian* Temper."[1] What Chauncy considered a "truly Christian Temper" may have been far different from what Whitefield or Tennent might have conceived; his word *settled,* with its connotations of order and sobriety, gives some indication of this. But it was his effort to define and reestablish that temper, along with other like-minded New England liberals, that reveals the origins of Unitarianism in America. Its initial impulse was in fact reactionary, given the contemporary context of what Chauncy derisively called the "New Way" of the revivalists, certainly, a historical irony for a movement whose great pride has always been its liberalism. But that liberalism began to take discernible shape only after the Great Awakening drove a dividing wedge into New England Congregationalism and forced the dissenters to the Awakening to formulate a coherent stance of their own.

It should be noted that not all opponents of the Awakening were forerunners of Unitarianism. The revivals forced many ministers back to a stricter definition of Calvinism that precluded revivalism. In the South it also provoked among Anglicans the same kind of critical skepticism that Chauncy and his group represented in New England. The history of Unitarianism begins therefore with only one faction of opposers to the revival, centered principally in the Boston Congregational churches, those churches of the Standing Order that were originally founded in the Puritan migrations. There was no nominal change in these churches until well into the nineteenth century, for at the time of the Awakening, those who opposed it did so for reasons they thought were consistent with the doctrinal and ecclesiastical goals of their Puritan heritage. If anything, the opposers of the Awakening believed that the revivalists were the ones who had abandoned the beliefs and practices of Puritan congregationalism.

At the center of the controversy over the Awakening was the doctrine of conversion, or the "New Birth." It was certainly not a new concept to New England theology, since the profession of some sort of confidence in salvation was central to "visible sainthood," the open profession of faith that was a cornerstone of Puritan ecclesiastical polity. It was rather the doctrine of conversion as it was preached in the Great Awakening, and as it manifested itself in the ensuing popular religious turmoil, that was the source of controversy.[2] What was in contention can be partly inferred from some of George Whitefield's remarks about Boston during his visit there in 1740. Whitefield described Boston as "a large, populous place, and very wealthy" but characteristically found in that wealth the source of spiritual decay.

It has the form of religion kept up, but has lost much of it's [*sic*] power. I have not heard of any remarkable stir for many years. . . . There is much of the pride of life to be seen in their assemblies. Jewels, patches, and gay apparel are commonly worn by the female sex. The little infants who were brought to baptism, were wrapped up in such fine things, and so much pains taken to dress them, that one would think they were brought thither to be initiated into, rather than to renounce the pomps and vanities of this wicked world.[3]

This is shrewd observation of the sociological fact that a prosperous merchant class had emerged from the Puritan settlement that Boston had once been. There. is an indication here of Whitefield's sincere antimaterialism that lent itself so well to populist denunciations of the economic elite. Whitefield not only denounced Boston society but also charged that at Harvard "Discipline is at a low ebb," and that "Bad books [that is, works of theology with liberal or Arminian tendencies] are becoming fashionable among the tutors and students." In a general concluding lament, he suggested that many Bostonians "rest in a head-knowledge, are close to Pharisees, and have only a name to live."[4]

What Whitefield and the other revivalists hoped to do was to replace such "head-knowledge" with the heart-felt emotions of conversion, and it was expected by many that such conversions would create not only new people but a new social order and even a new millennial age. The great tool for fostering this work was fervent and emotional preaching, and there is abundant testimony to the fact that Whitefield and Gilbert Tennent in particular were extraordinarily gifted orators. But there was also something relatively new in the content, or perhaps the emphasis, of their preaching as well as in their oratorical skills. The revivalists challenged their hearers so directly with the doctrine of the New Birth that they left the clear implication that salvation was the choice of the individual. This is not a surprising doctrine until we remember that Whitefield called himself a strict Calvinist, specifically adhered to the doctrine of election to salvation, and even split with John Wesley over this very issue. Whitefield would have attributed the power of salvation explicitly to God rather than to the individual, but his very manner of presenting the necessity and possibility of the New Birth stretched Calvinism to its limits and, many thought, beyond.

Those limits had already been strained in the continuing discussions of the idea of preparation for salvation among New England theologians, and that discussion itself only indicates an inherent tension in Calvinism arising from the doctrine of the absolute sovereignty of God. If all power is attributed to God, the possibility (and the incentive) for a human contribution to the salvation process is eliminated. Because the preaching of Whitefield and the other evangelists who followed him avoided this dilemma in stressing the New Birth, it forced the hand of the opponents of the Awakening. They could, as "Old Light" Calvinists did, stress God's absolute authority, but if this doctrine seemed uncomfortable, as it eventually did to Chauncy and his colleagues, new grounds for opposition to the Awakening would have to be found. It was thus that the tendency to "Arminianism," the doctrine "that men are born with the capacity for both sin and righteousness," began to develop.[5]

Underlying these theological issues were sociological and political ones as well, for just as the Awakening drew most of its adherents from the lower classes, the opposition to it came from the Boston establishment. The theological assumptions, and at least some hint of the sociopolitical attitudes of the opposers, are set forth in Chauncy's *Enthusiasm Described and Caution'd Against* (1742), another sustained attack on the "enthusiasm," or false and misleading emotions of the revival. Chauncy wrote the sermon while an encounter with revivalist James Davenport was still fresh in his mind, and Davenport was the living example of the dangers of enthusiasm that Chauncy portrayed. He began with a careful distinction between the enthusiasm that signifies "inspiration from God," usually associated with the prophets and the apostles, and the more modern sense of it. In common usage the label enthusiast describes one who "mistakes the workings of his own passions for divine communications, and fancies himself immediately inspired by the SPIRIT OF GOD, when all the while, he is under no other influence than that of an over-heated imagination."[6] The revivalists are those who have mistaken their own ego or imagination for spirit, but the problem remains of how to distinguish between true and false inspiration. Chauncy's statement of the dilemma places the problem squarely in the center of the long-standing New England debate over the nature of inspiration; in fact, the earlier Antinomian controversy and the later Transcendentalist controversy both concern this very issue. It is in his attempt to answer this question, which comprises most of the sermon, that Chauncy offers a clear indication of what became the three previously mentioned major concerns of the liberal Christians in the eighteenth and early nineteenth centuries: rationalism, biblicism, and moral aspiration.

The depth of Chauncy's commitment to biblical religion is indicated by his putting scripture forward as the tool for distinguishing true inspiration from mere enthusiasm. After describing the nature of enthusiasm, Chauncy offered "*a rule by which you may judge of persons, whether they are enthusiasts,*" which is "*a regard to the bible, an acknowledgment that the things therein contained are the commandments of GOD.*" Those writings, given the prophets and apostles under the "Immediate, extraordinary influence and guidance" of God offer security, because the "ever-blessed SPIRIT is consistent with himself" and thus can allow no contradiction between that original revelation and some supposed private one (p. 235). Chauncy's clear position on the authority of scripture marks a good starting place for an important strand of biblical scholarship in early Unitarianism, in which Joseph Stevens Buckminster,* Andrews Norton,* and Theodore Parker* were key figures. By the early nineteenth century Buckminster had to respond to the rationalist higher criticism of the Bible emanating from Germany, but at this point Chauncy was assured that rationalism and absolute biblical authority were in no way incompatible.

That assurance was no doubt bolstered by the fact that Chauncy found a clear analogy between the disorders that Paul attempted to correct at the church in Corinth and the current religious upheaval in New England. Even in the sectarian disputes that Paul addressed, Chauncy found an antitype of those who would replace the settled clergy by placing "an undue preference of one [minister] to another." Paul was determined to check this "unchristian spirit" in Corinth, since it had "crumbled them into parties, and introduced among them faction and contention'' (p. 236). The authority of the apostle, then, is used to add weight to the opposers' complaint that the revival has fostered disorder.

Although Chauncy pointed to the Bible as the authoritative key to discerning enthusiasm, it is also clear from his discussion that the usefulness of the Bible is dependent on the rational interpretation of it. Even the example of Paul's dealing with the Corinthians reveals a kind of reasoning by analogy that requires both a serious investigation of the circumstances described in the Letters to the Corinthians, and an ability to apply such analysis to contemporary conditions. Chauncy is far from being original here, since the disposition to similar uses of scripture was central to Puritan thinking. Chauncy could, therefore, insist on the rational use of the Bible and believe that he protected an already well-established tradition from which the revivalists were departing. It was in fact their irrational ''enthusiasm'' that opened the way for his defense of rationalism, the quality that has probably become the most well-known characteristic of early Unitarianism. In the description of enthusiasm that begins the sermon, Chauncy set out reason as another locus of authority in the war with the revivalists: ''But in nothing does the *enthusiasm* of these persons discover itself more, than in the disregard they express to the Dictates of *reason*. They are above the force of argument, beyond conviction from a calm and sober address to their understandings'' (p. 232). This abandonment of reason is important, because it leaves the enthusiasts beyond the possibility of correction. Since they believe that truth has come to them from the Spirit, they take the attitude that ''they are certainly in the right, and know themselves to be so.'' Given this conviction of absolute certitude in their opinions, Chauncy depicted them as being ''not only infinitely stiff and tenacious, but impatient of contradiction, censorious and uncharitable: they encourage a good opinion of none but such as are in their way of thinking and speaking'' (p. 233). By linking enthusiasm with uncharitableness and exclusion, Chauncy cast not only a rational but a moral shadow over it, plainly suggesting that the fruits of enthusiasm are not the same as the fruits of true religion. In contrast, he later described ''real religion'' as ''a sober, calm, reasonable thing'' that ought to be judged not by the excesses of the emotions but by its moral results in the lives of those men that ''have been such a uniform, beautiful transcript of that which is just and good'' (pp. 253–54). As Chauncy's use of the Bible implied a rationalism, so his rationalism implied a willingness to judge religion by its moral results. This stress on moralism, as it evolved into an ethic of character building and self-cultivation, also became a touchstone of the liberal movement in theology. During the Awakening, the very fact of disorder and disputation, of ''all the *wildness* and *fury*, and extravagance'' of enthusiasm, seemed evidence enough that a good part of the revival was not the true work of God (p. 256). This commitment to a moral as opposed to a theological standard of judgment, combined with the biblicism and rationalism that also characterized Chauncy's attacks, mark the direction of the development of Unitarianism. At its beginning, the movement saw itself as a preserver rather than a challenger of the order of things in the church. The history of the movement concerns the gradual reversal of this self-conception.

## UNITARIAN RATIONALISM AND NATURAL THEOLOGY

The emotional excess of the revivals was the target of liberal criticism, because it differed from the rational concept of religion that crystallized in the late eighteenth century. By the early nineteenth century the Unitarian leader William Ellery Channing* would make rationalism a keystone of the Christian religion and argue in moving terms for a just recognition of the central role of reason in the religious life. In his pronouncement of denominational identity, the 1819 sermon "Unitarian Christianity," he bluntly turned aside attacks on liberal rationalism: "Say what we may, God has given us a rational nature, and will call us to account for it. We may let it sleep, but we do so at our peril. Revelation is addressed to us as rational beings."[7] Channing's statement was bold enough to rock New England at the time but was more a summation of tendencies long at work in the liberal tradition than an entirely new departure.

In an important sense, the seedbed for this rational religion was in the larger intellectual revolution of Newton, whose reputation among a good many eighteenth-century Christian thinkers is best expressed by Alexander Pope:

> NATURE, and Nature's laws lay hid in Night:
> God said, *Let NEWTON be!* and all was Light.[8]

The new science generally, and Newton in particular, held out the promise of a growing discovery of an ordered, benevolent universe, the product of a rational and benevolent God, intent on demonstrating his qualities through the perfection of nature. The new science was not the exclusive property of the theological liberals by any means; in New England it was Jonathan Edwards who seized upon it as confirmation of Calvinist dogma and a bulwark against Arminianism. But a system based on learning, reason, and order certainly had a great attraction for those skeptical of the intuition, passion, and disorder found in revivals.

The growth of natural theology in New England was not unique and was in fact nurtured by a rich speculative background in seventeenth- and eighteenth-century English theology. When Whitefield fumed against Harvard College for its preference of Tillotson and Clarke to more evangelical theologians, he put his finger on formative influences on the growth of Unitarian rationalism. John Tillotson, archbishop of Canterbury, has been singled out for typifying "the combination . . . of the rationalist and the supernaturalist," a primary founder of a tradition that included Samuel Clarke, "the most famous philosopher of his day in England." This tradition of "supernatural rationalism," which had direct impact on American liberals such as Ebenezer Gay,* Charles Chauncy, and Jonathan Mayhew,* developed the idea that natural religion is good and true so far as it goes, but it does not go far enough. Hence it needs to be supplemented by revelation that must not in any way contradict it but must be consistent with it in all of its parts.[9] The catch was in the last phrase, for the insistence that there be no contradiction between science and scripture was both the source of appeal of the tradition and a source of controversy. Clarke, for example, avoided the appearance of a contradiction between natural and revealed religion by arguing that revelation was given of God to repair the fallen state of an originally more powerful reason in humanity. In light of the corruption of reason, Clarke wrote, "there was a Necessity of some *particular Divine Revelation*, to make the whole Doctrine of Religion *clear* and obvious to all Capacities."[10] From this perspective, the Bible served to strengthen and clarify reason, not work in opposition to it, and it is clear from other of Clarke's remarks that he was much more concerned with the Deist's dismissal of scripture than with the evangelical's dismissal of reason.

Within the context established by English thinkers, New England speculation on natural theology began to thrive. One good vantage point from which to examine that tradition is one of the earlier and more important of the Dudleian lectures (1759) on natural religion at Harvard, delivered by Ebenezer Gay. His exposition of natural religion suggests the interlocking of strains of rationalism and moralism characteristic of Unitarianism, because Gay avowed to explore the "moral Obligation" that God's existence "induceth upon the Nature of Man."[11] Those obligations arise from the necessity "to render any Acts of Men, whether internal [that is, motives] or external, such as the Perfections of the Deity require" (p. 6). This stress on the perfection of God would not be out of place in Calvinist discourse, suggesting as it does a quality of awesome unapproachability. But there is another strain in Gay's discourse that points in a different direction. He suggested that humanity can aspire toward that very quality of perfection in its actions and in fact defined *religion* as the obligation to do so. To aspire toward perfection is not to achieve it, but what is important is the direction of emphasis here toward moral aspiration, which the remainder of the discourse would confirm. Gay made effective use of the analogy of the "book" of revelation by claiming, in addition to the biblical revelation, two other sources of religious knowledge: the book of the creation and "the Volume of our own Nature" (p. 6). The common assumption is that the world of external nature is the exclusive concern of natural religion, but as Gay made clear, that concern goes hand in hand with an emphasis on the moral sense, an important premise of much eighteenth-century speculation on ethics.

The structure of the lecture mirrors this concern, for Gay set for himself the dual purpose of establishing "THAT Religion is, in some measure, discoverable by the Light, and practicable to the Strength, of Nature" (p. 7). It is the first of these premises that usually characterizes rational theology; for Gay, as for most of the early liberals, the practicability of religion was equally, if not more, important. Thus although Gay offered the logical argument that God's "necessary Self-existence includes every Perfection," he offered it only in passing, as he moved to what he thought was the more important and universally apprehendable proof from experience that "the Works of God" indicate that "He is a Being of such Perfection," the nature of which obligates men and women to dedicate "the Temper of their Minds, and Manner of their Behaviour" to him (pp. 8–9). That experience is exemplified in the "Order" of the "World of Beings" that expresses God's will through the "Law of Nature." That law is more tellingly expressed, however, in "Natural Conscience," which is "the *work of the Law in their Hearts*" (pp. 10–11). The essence of the moral dimension to knowledge is "the Power of Self-determination, or Freedom of Choice," for it is here, and not simply in the making of rational judgments, that the moral law is actually fulfilled (p. 12). Gay's entire purpose had been to weld scientifically inclined rationalism with moral philosophy, and the most striking instance of this is his use of the Newtonian concept of gravity or attraction to illustrate the working of the moral sense: "THERE may be something in the intelligent moral World analogous to Attraction in the material System—something that inclines and draws Men toward God, the Centre of their Perfection" (p. 13). This pull of gravity symbolized for Gay the automatic inclination of the soul to seek the will of God in acts of "human Kindness" and of "divine Worship" or, as he put it, "a Disposition in human Nature as makes Religion agreable [*sic*] to it" (p. 15). It is on this basis that Gay claimed validity for natural religion, a basis that would continue to serve Unitarianism well into the nineteenth century.

Despite his plea for natural religion, Gay in no way wanted to displace biblical or revealed religion and the grace it promises. In maintaining that there is "no Contrariety" between natural and revealed religion, he placed himself squarely in the school of supernatural rationalism, and his explanation of the harmony between the two manifestations of religion is exemplary of that tradition: "Revealed Religion is an *Additional* to Natural; built, not on the Ruins, but on the strong and everlasting Foundations of it" (pp. 19–20).

Even though he gave a large place to nature and the moral sense, Gay was expounding a biblically based religion, with revelation helping humans to overcome what would be the sure smothering of the "innate Inclination" toward religion by a "Crowd of worldly Lusts." Without revelation, "men might have been absolutely without God in the World" (pp. 27–28). The Bible thus retained in liberal thinking the central status given it in the Calvinist tradition. It was the burden of the liberals to prove the compatibility of unaided reason and biblical truth, and often the most effective way to do this was to apply the methodology of rationalism to the interpretation of the Bible. Gay ended his address by emphasizing "the great Advantage of a liberal Education" to the ministry. Not only will the sciences yield "grand Ideas of the Attributes of God," but the study of literature will help in the "Search of the Scriptures in their inspired Originals" (pp. 32–33). The rational interpretation of scripture, an essential point of departure for liberal thinking during the Great Awakening, would continue to serve as a focus of controversy during the formative period of the denomination. Gay's articulation of it here confirmed its place in the tradition of rationalist theology.

## EARLY UNITARIAN MORAL THEORY

Gay's Dudleian lecture suggested that rationalism, even when its primary concern was the intellectual groundwork of Christian belief, carried with it a certain impulse toward moral philosophy. That interpenetration of rationalism and moralism is even more striking when we examine the unraveling of Calvinist New England's eighteenth-century orthodoxy and the growing tendency toward moral perfectionism among the Arminians who led the opposition to the prevailing orthodoxy.

The liberal attack on Calvinism took two forms, one of which is exemplified in the pastoral career of Gay in Hingham, Massachusetts. Although his sympathies were with the liberals, he chose not to introduce controversy and division in his sermons. Instead he simply ignored Calvinist dogma and preached his own form of liberal Christianity. Thus during his long pastorate, his congregation silently became liberal, abandoning the doctrines of Calvinism "without being aware when or how." [12] That such a process was possible seemed to confirm the liberals' sense that Calvinism was a corrupt engraftment on the purity of Christianity, and their resulting attitude was less that of radical innovators or rebels than purifiers and conservers of higher truth.

But Arminianism did not always take the silent method of advance, and there was open condemnation of Calvinism in New England as early as the middle 1750s. [13] In the controversy that continued into the early nineteenth century, it is important to ask how the liberals forged a positive creed from the position of rebelling nullifiers in which the orthodox placed them.

Liberals consistently attacked Calvinism on the related issues of original sin and election to salvation, doctrines that in their view undermined human moral exertion. The idea of the taint of Adam, communicated to all people regardless of their action or character, seemed to deny the possibility of the moral life; the idea of God's preordained selection of a few to salvation, regardless of their character or action, seemed to undercut the motivation for it. The liberals countered therefore with a moral system that affirmed human capability, as evidenced in the moral sense, and even those writings that did not attack Calvinism by name contributed to the liberal revolt by contributing to a positive countertheory. Jonathan Mayhew's *Seven Sermons*, preached in 1748, offers a very good sense of the developing liberal moral philosophy. Mayhew based his series on a firm rejection of all creeds and a corresponding insistence on private judgment as the necessary arbiter of religious opinion. Rhetorically, he established Roman Catholicism as his target, certainly a safe one in both Old and New England at the time, and alluded to a continuing "*inquisition*" as simply a more vicious form of paganism. But in a clear reference to recent English history, he also turned his censure on those "who punish *dissenters* and *non-subscribers*" by denying them the civil rights due them. Mayhew's ultimate rhetorical strategy became clear, however, only when he went on to link these indisputable evils to what he called "another practice akin to those mentioned above, . . . that of *Creed-making*; setting up human tests of *orthodoxy*." [14] Mayhew couched his challenge to the Calvinist orthodoxy, therefore, in the broad terms of a challenge to the very idea of orthodoxy itself, taking full advantage of the Puritan tradition of dissent from which he spoke. In opposing Calvinism on the basis of a right to private judgment, he turned part of a sacred tradition against itself.

Mayhew had, however, carefully prepared the ground of his attack and in so doing offered a work as important for its defense of individual liberty in the larger sense (an increasingly important issue in pre-Revolutionary America) as for its theological implications. The cornerstone of the whole series of sermons was an argument for human ability to make moral distinctions and act on that knowledge. Mayhew's argument aimed at both the philosophical skeptics' attempt to undermine the stability of moral truth and the Calvinists' insistence on human inability either to know fully or to act consistently on moral grounds. To establish, in his first sermon, the reality of "the Difference betwixt Truth and Falsehood, Right and Wrong," he argued for the equivalence of truth, right action, and happiness on purely naturalistic and utilitarian grounds (p. 1). But in a declaration characteristic of the belief that would sustain the liberal tradition well into the next century, he made these arguments mere addenda to the central truth of a moral "*law written in our hearts*" (p. 13).

If the moral-sense doctrine countered skepticism, Mayhew also noted that it undermined the doctrine of original sin as well: "the doctrine of a total ignorance, and incapacity to judge of moral and religious truths, brought upon mankind by the apostasy of our *First Parents*, is without foundation" (p. 38). While the Calvinists stressed incapacity, Mayhew emphasized "the dispositions and sallies of the soul towards its Creator" (p. 96). This movement of the soul is "a steady, sober, calm and rational thing," not unlike what Chauncy would have commended and not at all like "those flashy and rapturous sallies of the heart towards God" that typify the conceit of the revivalists. Religious devotion is a passion, "but a passion excited by reason presenting the proper object of it to the mind" (p. 97). But after this caution against confusing true devotion and enthusiasm, he returned to the essential truth that "real piety necessarily supposes, that the heart is touched, affected, warmed, inflamed: and not barely that we have right speculative notions concerning God" (p. 98).

As we have seen Mayhew's thought developing, this emphasis on the enkindled passion of the heart returns us to his earlier emphasis on the "*law written in our own hearts*" for moral guidance. Mayhew exemplified the tendency of the liberals to hold the idea of the moral sense in conjunction with an emphasis on individual devotionalism. Both tendencies are highly individualistic, and together they worked to magnify the importance of personal conscience and personal piety that was wholly incompatible with the stress on depravity and individual powerlessness inherent in Calvinism. In the movement of the heart toward God, the individual both followed the direction of the moral sense and increased the power and capacity of that sense. Devotionalism and moralism came together in an appealing image of the moral life, which stressed the personal cultivation that the Puritan tradition had held to be either impossible or irrelevant. But the aloof and unapproachable God of Calvinism, the concept that had rendered such cultivation impossible, now became transformed into a guide and end for that development. As Mayhew saw him, God was "perfect in all those moral qualities and excellencies which we esteem amiable in mankind" (p. 101). In the liberals' rehabilitation of human nature and possibility, even God had been affected.

In rehabilitating human nature, Mayhew and the other liberals were not asserting the actual goodness of humankind but the *potential* for goodness in human nature, a potential that, it must be stressed, had to be developed. Chauncy discussed this need for development in the context of the doctrine of conversion, or the New Birth, arguing explicitly that conversion was a process of growth rather than a blinding and instantaneous change. "If our natural powers are neglected, misimproved, and turned aside from their proper use, we become morally corrupt and sinful; but if they are cultivated and improved to our own attaining an actual likeness to God in knowledge, righteousness and true holiness, we may have now a new nature super-induced, and may, figuratively speaking, be said to be new born creatures." [15] The phrase "likeness to God" anticipates Channing's more famous sermon of that title, and the phrase calls attention to the fact that the position Chauncy and the other Arminians took here prepared the way for Channing's powerful statements of Unitarian belief in the nineteenth century. The basis of Chauncy's confidence in human ability was a "progressive capacity" in human nature, a concept very closely related to Mayhew's description of the devotional and innately moral qualities of the heart.

The extent of this Arminian refashioning of New England's intellectual world, with its new conception of both human and divine nature, is suggested by one curious later work of Chauncy, in many senses his *magnum opus*. In 1784 an anonymous work was published with the enticing title *The Mystery Hid from Ages and Generations* and the more informative subtitle *The Salvation of All Men*. The work was Chauncy's, as a number of his like-minded friends knew, who had read the work in manuscript. That they recognized it as a dangerous work is indicated by their use of a secret shorthand reference to it, "the pudding." It was a work they relished like a forbidden sweet. [16] Its danger lay in the fact that it denied the idea of eternal punishment by arguing that all souls would eventually be saved, an early instance of the doctrine of "Universalism" in New England. The argument was a dramatic break from tradition, even though this position grew logically from the premises of the moral cultivation that Chauncy and others were preaching and especially from the implication of a humanly approachable and benevolent God that was a corollary to those premises. Those who understood its implications realized that it was a death blow to Calvinism, removing the final sting from the doctrines of innate depravity and election to grace.

The heart of the argument is contained in the first sentence: "As the First Cause of all things is infinitely benevolent, 'tis not easy to conceive, that he should bring mankind into existence, unless he intended to make them finally happy" (p. 1). Chauncy elaborated this rather straightforward proposition in an opening chapter of "Preliminary Explanations," in which one important qualification is set forth: it is not punishment, but eternal punishment, that Chauncy is arguing against. "Though I affirm, that all men will finally be happy, yet I deny not but that many of them will be miserable in the next state of existence, and to a great degree, and for a long time, in proportion to the moral depravity they have contracted in this" (p. 9). The punishment of hell, as Chauncy viewed it, was itself the means to a larger end of the final regeneration of every soul, God's ultimate resource for compelling an eventual obedience when all else failed. The flames of hell therefore had the function of purification rather than punishment, and the moral life, with its possibilities of self-cultivation, extended beyond this life into the one to come.

Although Chauncy's position itself was extremely modern for eighteenth-century New England, the other notable aspect of the work is some four hundred pages of closely argued proofs that follow, based almost entirely on scriptural exegesis. If Chauncy had been led to his conclusions by purely rational analysis of the nature of God and humankind, as one suspects in considering the argument, he felt an enormous obligation to confirm that conclusion on scriptural grounds. Moreover, Chauncy explicitly denied any extrascriptural basis of his conclusion from the outset. "I had indeed no idea of the sentiments expressed in the following pages, till I had been gradually and insensibly let into them by a long and diligent comparing of *scripture with scripture*. What I therefore now offer to the world is not the result of *my own imagination*, or *wisdom*: Nor was it fetched from any *scheme of man's invention*; but *solely* from the fountain of revealed truth, the *inspired oracles of God*" (p. vi). Chauncy's declaration here, and the ponderous evidence of his devotion to biblical argument in the work itself, indicates that Arminian rationalism was having a huge impact on theological dogma in New England, although most of the changes were taking place well within the bounds of biblical religion. Rationalist methods of exegesis might be changing the nature of the biblical foundation, but as the liberals saw it, the close tie between doctrine and scripture remained unsevered.

What had been set in motion, however, were the tendencies to a theology of personal growth and moral perfectionism, evident both in the Arminians' view of human ability in this life and God's benevolence in the life to come. Chauncy's Universalism was by no means a majority opinion among New England Congregationalists, even among those who could be considered liberals. But it did set a tone characteristic of Unitarianism in its devaluation of the importance of hell and punishment in the theological scheme. Such ideas continued to be ignored, if not repudiated outright, as Unitarianism began to form a denominational consciousness in the nineteenth century. Moreover, Chauncy's Universalism gave one more unique expression to the emerging image of religious life as one of moral progress. Not only had the seeds of the characteristic doctrines of Channing been sown in the middle 1700s; they had already begun to take root and sprout.

## JOSEPH PRIESTLEY AND ENLIGHTENMENT UNITARIANISM

Although Boston and eastern Massachusetts were the cradle of American Unitarianism, and have remained its focal point, there were other Unitarian stirrings outside Boston in the eighteenth century. The most notable of them was in Philadelphia, where Enlightenment values such as reason, tolerance, and moral service gained a stronghold. Benjamin Franklin epitomized the Enlightenment spirit there, and his own description of his religious development indicates the direction of rational religion:

I had been religiously educated as a Presbyterian; and tho' some of the Dogmas of that Persuasion, such as the Eternal Decrees of God, Election, Reprobation, &c. appear'd to me unintelligible, others doubtful, & I early absented myself from the Public Assemblies of the Sect, Sunday being my Studying-Day, I never was without some religious Principles; I never doubted, for instance, the Existence of the Deity, that he made the World, & govern'd it by his Providence; that the most acceptable Service of God was the doing Good to Man; that our Souls are immortal; and that all Crime will be punished & Virtue rewarded either here or hereafter; these I esteem'd the Essentials of every Religion. [17]

Franklin's views were advanced, even for the liberals of the day, and his friend Joseph Priestley,* lamented "that a man of Dr. Franklin's general good character and great influence should have been an unbeliever in Christianity." [18] Certainly, that illustrates the difference between these two liberal leaders. But it should also be noted that Franklin's stress on a character-centered religion was much in line with later developments in American liberal religion.

In 1794 Priestley, who had been a leader among English Unitarians, came to America, escaping a dangerous situation in England. His home in Birmingham, with his library and laboratory, had been destroyed in a riot, and he was even vulnerable to charges of treason, as Earl Morse Wilbur* told us, because of his sympathy with the French Revolution. Although he came to America in hope of continuing his scientific and philosophical work, rather than church building, he did have a rallying effect on Philadelphia-area liberals. In 1796–97 he lectured in Philadelphia on religion, the first of these lectures being held at the Universalist church. This was an early instance of the shared values of Universalist and Unitarian liberals. As a result, "the first permanent Unitarian church in America''—that is, the first permanent church to call itself Unitarian—was founded in Philadelphia in 1796.[19]

Conrad Wright* has established that much of the program of the New England Arminians—the denial of election and original sin, the freedom of will, and the idea of regeneration as development—depended upon a "reshaping" of the Calvinist view of God. "They had become profoundly convinced," he wrote, "that God is a benevolent deity, whose first concern is the happiness of his creatures."[20] This realization toward which the New England Arminians were moving was the cornerstone of Priestley's theology. His own theological system, *The Institutes of Natural and Revealed Religion* (1772), began with a consideration of the nature of God, and in Priestley's view, all of God's moral character stemmed from his benevolence. "The source of all the moral perfections of God," he argued, "seems to be his benevolence. . . . Every other truly venerable or amiable attribute can be nothing but a *modification* of this. A perfectly good, or benevolent Being, must be, in every other respect, whatever can be the object of our reverence, or our love."[21] Priestley's humanly accessible God stood opposed not only to the orthodoxies of his day, but to a history of creedal "corruptions" of the genuine Christian message. Perhaps his most influential theological work was *An History of the Corruptions of Christianity* (1792), which tried to restore the purity of the Christian faith by sweeping away the dogmatic encrustations that were its corruptions.

Priestley began the discussion by considering the central issue in Christian history, Christology. He defined a *corruption* as "a departure from the original scheme, or an *innovation*" and showed how doctrines that elevate Christ to a level of equality with God, doctrines, that is, of the trinity, were just such departures or innovations.[22] The spirit of his work, then, was one of a return to first principles, a gesture of mind that has been continuously appealing to the liberal tradition. Influential Unitarian and Universalist thinkers, such as Theodore Parker and Hosea Ballou 2d,* later appealed to a version of pure or original Christianity to undercut dogma that they considered extraneous and falsifying. Priestley saw his work as part of the mission of "*reformed Christianity*," sure that "Christianity has begun to recover itself from this corrupted state, and that the reformation advances apace" (p. 7). In this spirit of enlightened advance, he argued that Trinitarianism was a late corruption of pure Christianity.

Priestley traced the corruption to the tendency of Platonic philosophers of the early church to elevate the idea of *logos* (word) from an "*attribute* of the divine mind itself" into "an *intelligent principle* or *being*, distinct from God, though an emanation from him." The wholesale identification of Christ with *logos* led to further difficulties: "Thus, since we read in the book of Psalms, that *by the word of the Lord* (which, in the translation of the Seventy, is the *Logos*) *the heavens were made,* &c. they concluded that this *Logos* was Christ, and therefore, that, under God, he was the maker of the world" (p. 28).

Priestley argued, however, that there was "nothing like *divinity* ascribed to Christ before Justin Martyr" (p. 29). He also indicated that "the early christian writers [spoke] of the Father as superior to the Son, and in general they [gave] him the title of *God*, as distinguished from the Son'' (p. 36). In a sense, then, ''the Unitarians were very numerous in all parts of the christian world'' during the earliest days of the church, and these Unitarians did not comprise a separate or distinct sect (p. 49).

Although Priestley was principally concerned to establish the superiority of God to Christ, and thereby refute Trinitarian doctrines, he was also interested in carrying his argument a step further. He wanted to establish a Socinian rather than an Arian Christology as the original faith. He wanted, in other words, to argue for ''the simple humanity of Christ'' as opposed to seeing Christ as beneath the Father, but still a supernatural being, who, in some versions of Arianism, was creator of the world (p. 48). As he saw it, there was ''no trace of the apostles having ever regarded their Master in this high light'' (pp. 86–87). In fact, Priestley went on to insist that ''the purposes of his mission'' were not beyond the capacities of a ''*mere man*,'' aided by God. ''For it cannot be said that anything is ascribed to him that a mere man (aided, as he himself says he was, by the power of God, his Father) was not equal to'' (p. 88).

Priestley's form of Socinian Unitarianism was influential in England and was not without its impact in America. James Freeman* led Boston's King's Chapel to a Unitarian stance after the Revolutionary War and was much in sympathy with the views of the English Unitarians. Priestley had some correspondence with Thomas Jefferson, with whom he shared both theological and scientific affinities, and Priestley's work proved to be a major factor in bringing Jefferson to the brand of personal Unitarianism that he adopted in his later years, although, like Franklin, Jefferson went further than Priestley in his radicalism. He called Priestley's theological works ''the basis of my own faith.''[23] In his old age he declared, ''I trust there is not a young man *now living* in the United States who will not die a Unitarian.''[24] A prophet Jefferson was not, but his version of Unitarianism, more radical and individualistic than the variety that was evolving in eastern Massachusetts, would continue to have a life of its own in America. It would not be known as Unitarianism, however, nor would it, for the most part, be institutionalized in the form of a church.[25] Thus although we must remember both the climate of religious opinion in Enlightenment America, and the stimulus of Priestley's arrival, the story of the development of the denomination remains largely a New England affair until the middle nineteenth century.

# 3
# THE FORMATION
# OF A DENOMINATION

## THE COALESCENCE OF LIBERAL IDEALS

Even while the tenets of Calvinism were being replaced by a growing liberal emphasis on individual moral development, another process was unfolding that was closely linked to it. The mind of New England, particularly that of Boston, was becoming secularized, moving into a phase of culture in which religion and religious institutions did not have complete dominance over the intellectual world. One of the ironies of the history of the Unitarian movement is that although it is religious in origin and development, one of its stronger impulses has been to break the creedal and institutional boundaries that traditionally defined religion and the church and to embody the religious sense in the secular world itself. The aesthetic and political realms have been the most frequent outlets for this impulse toward secularization, and Unitarianism has developed a close association with both literary culture and movements toward social progress.

The origins of this literary impulse can be traced to the generation of eastern Massachusetts ministers after that of Chauncy, who helped to make Boston the literary capital of America for more than half a century. Led by the brilliant young minister of the Brattle Street Church, Joseph Stevens Buckminster,* they have come to be seen as pivotal figures in the cultural history of America. Their most memorable achievements were in pulpit eloquence, where they turned the sermon into an art form, and in literary criticism and belles lettres. They are best remembered for the founding of one of the most influential early literary journals, *The Monthly Anthology and Boston Review*. But the work of Buckminster had special importance for the development of liberal Christianity, because he introduced the higher criticism of the Bible to America and used it for theological ends. Moreover, his preaching set a new tone that embodied imaginative polish and emphasized moral culture, affecting the course of both liberal congregationalism and American letters. The rise of New England's literary culture cannot be regarded separately from the development of what became the Unitarian denomination. Buckminster's career helps one begin to understand why this is so.[1]

In personal terms, Buckminster embodied many of the qualities of the age to come rather than the New England past. In his college days he passionately loved the theater, dabbled in poetry, and was attracted to the formality—the dangerous formality, many of his contemporaries believed—of the services at King's Chapel in Boston. The aesthetic sense, in other words, was strong in him, and he found upon accepting a call to the Brattle Street Church that he was in the right milieu to express and develop it. This he did most notably in his preaching, even overshadowing the eloquence of another young Boston minister, William Ellery Channing.* In the hands of Buckminster, or his contemporaries Channing and Edward Everett, or later preachers like Ralph Waldo Emerson* and Theodore Parker,* the sermon became a much more supple instrument than it had been in the hands of earlier Puritan preachers. This is in large part due to the fact that, given the liberal rejection of Calvinism, the sermon no longer had to be used to expound and inculcate oppressive doctrine. What replaced it was the need to make available the constellation of ideas that had replaced Calvinism in liberal thought: the nature and process of moral growth. Buckminster is therefore remembered as a moving and forceful preacher, not only because of his rhetorical gifts, but because he addressed directly the moral life of his hearers. Moreover, his image was transmuted to what Lawrence Buell termed "sainthood" by his tragic early death by epilepsy at age twenty-eight, when he seemed to be only at the beginning of his career. "The mourning for Buckminster was immediate and profuse," Buell noted, and the eulogizing for him continued until the Civil War.[2]

Much of his power lay in the fact that he gave vivid expression to the vision of life as a continuing process of spiritual and moral growth, which we have seen taking form in the writings of Charles Chauncy,* Ebenezer Gay,* and Jonathan Mayhew.* In the sermon "Regeneration," Buckminster tried to avoid the revivalists' extreme claims for instantaneous conversion while maintaining a fervor and hope for change.

Look back, my hearers, upon your lives, and observe the numerous opinions that you have adopted and discarded, the numerous attachments you have formed and forgotten, and recollect how imperceptible were the revolutions of your sentiments, how quiet the changes of your affections. Perhaps, even now, your minds may be passing through some interesting processes, your pursuits may be taking some new direction, and your character may soon exhibit to the world some unexpected transformation. Compare with this the spiritual regeneration of the heart. So is every one that is born of the Spirit.[3]

There is a quiet, although moving and fervent, emotion here, fostered in part by Buckminster's effective use of the implied intimacy of personal address and by the accompanying strategy of direct appeal to the minds of the readers. He invited his hearers to introspection. Moreover, he tied that appeal to the use of the biblical phrase "born of the Spirit" with the full sense of its resonance and, in this case, its power to affirm.

Although all of these factors help to enliven the passage, its real power lies in the intellectual step of comparing mental development with spiritual development—in seeing the more intangible and problematic question of regeneration in terms of the more accessible experience of intellectual growth. That growth, important as it is, is demystified somewhat in Buckminster's pointed reminder that it is continually occurring, even at the moment his words are heard. Such a depiction of intellectual growth integrates it into the events and cycles of life, removing any false association that it might have with mere bookishness or pedantry. By implication this democratization of the intellectual life applies to the spiritual life as well, even to that most fundamental of spiritual experiences, regeneration. By making it part of the organic extension of life, Buckminster wrenched the notion of conversion away from the evangelicals' association of it with extreme emotion.

But the passage is instructive in another way as well, when we consider the larger implications of the metaphorical likening of intellectual growth and spiritual regeneration. The metaphor seemed apt to Buckminster and his hearers, because they responded deeply to a vision that linked intellectual and artistic pursuits with religious and moral ones. Contemporary accounts of Buckminster and Channing usually leave one with two basic explanations for their remarkable power in the pulpit. Their moral earnestness is most important, but almost as essential is an aesthetic appeal, what was perceived to be a power and force of imagination. The moral and the aesthetic—conscience and imagination—go hand in hand, and Buckminster's suggestion that his hearers think of the spiritual life in terms of the intellectual life is based on a tacit agreement among the liberals to equate those realms. The fact was that the liberals' increasing emphasis on human moral capacity also had implications for other human abilities, including the more secular pursuits of literature and fine arts. This accounts in part at least for the fact that the cultural awakening of America, so long called for in the late eighteenth and early nineteenth centuries, finally began to take root in Boston within the general milieu of Unitarianism. The earliest expressions of these literary impulses were the launching of the *Monthly Anthology* and the founding of the Boston Athenaeum, both of which addressed American cultural weaknesses directly. There could be no growth of an independent national literary culture until there were appropriate vehicles for public discussion of literature; nor could there be any hope of intellectual cultivation without access to the contemporary intellectual discourse that only adequate libraries could provide.

The real significance of the *Monthly Anthology* was not the criticism it contained but the gesture of its production and the aspirations it embodied. Buckminster engaged in one critical skirmish in which he took the side of Thomas Gray against a staunch defender of the neoclassical ideal of Alexander Pope, but this debate occurred when the course of English poetry was being altered by William Wordsworth and Samuel Taylor Coleridge. It would be several years before Channing, Emerson, and others began to respond to them. The intellectual landscape of New England was being altered within the pages of that journal in another way, however, when one notes the biblical as distinct from the literary criticism that Buckminster expounded there. Significantly, his career reveals an increasing absorption in New Testament criticism, and he is rightly credited with being a pioneer of the higher criticism of the Bible in America.[4]

Buckminster took the lead in mastering new forms of biblical criticism, in part because he saw the opportunity to use such procedures in theological battles with the orthodox. Insofar as the higher criticism called certain parts of the canon into question, Buckminster thought that it undermined the foundations of Trinitarian doctrine and helped to establish more securely the form of purified Christianity that he believed he and his colleagues preached. But there was more than mere partisanship in his efforts, and his arguments in behalf of the newer biblical criticism are of a piece with his commitment to literary scholarship and liberal learning in general. This is most obvious in his appeal to the analogy of classical scholarship as a justification for a similar rigor in the study of the Bible. "Enthusiasts in classical literature spare no labour or expense to obtain correct texts of the immortal authors of Greece and Rome; and shall the most valuable of all antient writings, the books of the New Testament, be more incorrectly edited than the works of Homer and Virgil?"[5] Buckminster's question is cleverly designed to cut two ways. It suggests first that pagan writings have been treated with more respect and care than sacred ones and thus puts possible opponents of the critical editing of the scriptures in the awkward position of seeming to acquiesce to this state of affairs. But more subtly, it puts the considerable weight of classical scholarship and literary judgment behind such a program of editing the scriptures, forcing the opponents of such a move into a stance of anti-intellectualism. To the extent that the orthodox had a stake in defending the New Testament as they then knew it, they could take such a stance only at the risk of seeming to abandon the long Puritan heritage of academic rigor and intellectual vitality. Once again, the liberals were claiming part of the Puritan tradition and turning it against the orthodox who felt themselves to be the defenders of that faith. Controversy, which had never ceased to simmer in New England theology, was now coming to a boil.

Buckminster's grasp of the issues of biblical criticism was sound, and his greatest talent was in communicating with both lucidity and a certain urgency what was at stake in those issues. In a brief summary of the field, published in 1808, he addressed the most difficult and controversial issue of the newer criticism, that of authenticating texts. At no point did the orthodox think the sanctity of belief was more threatened than at the suggestion that the Bible need not be accepted entirely as inspired. Once such a process of questioning had begun, there might well be no end to it, and the biblical foundations of Christianity might thereby be completely eroded. Buckminster understood these grounds of resistance and was in fact sensitive himself to the inherent danger of questioning the biblical canon. He therefore distinguished between the "Received" and "True" canon of scripture, clarifying that distinction in the following terms: "The Received Canon comprehends the whole of that collection of books, which is contained in the New Testament, and which are generally received by christians, as of apostolical authority. The True Canon consists of those books only, the genuineness of which is established upon satisfactory evidence."[6] The effectiveness of such a distinction was that it allowed one to affirm the idea of scriptural inspiration, which Buckminster did unhesitatingly, but did not require that the concept be applied uniformly to every part of the New Testament. It transformed a single book into a "collection of books," each one of which must have its own authority of inspiration proven by itself. Thus to the charge that biblical inspiration was being denied or undervalued, the liberals could respond that the case was rather that they were taking inspiration more seriously than the orthodox, as their investigation of the claims to authority of individual books demonstrated.

If Buckminster's entire approach to biblical study seemed suspect to many of the orthodox, the nub of the controversy is most clearly revealed in the concluding summary of his essay. He found that "The various readings, which affect the doctrines of christianity, are very few: yet some of these are of great importance." He noted in particular I John 5:7 as a "notorious" example of the "wilful interpolations" that are most notable.[7] Although he did not quote that verse, or even allude to its content, his purpose in singling it out becomes immediately clear when one turns to its rendering in the King James version: "For there are three that bear record in heaven, the Father, the Word, and the Holy Ghost: and these three are one." The verse is an explicit scriptural endorsement of Trinitarian doctrine.

The name "Unitarian" has long suggested that the dominant idea among the liberal Congregationalists was a rejection of Trinitarian doctrine, when in fact the stress on moral culture and the corresponding rejection of innate depravity were the defining impulses of that tradition. But although there is no inevitable connection between Unitarian views of Christ and theories of moral culture, there seems to have been a "temperamental" and "historical" connection between them as they developed in New England.[8] To the orthodox, the rejection of the Trinity seemed to be the most heinous of the liberal crimes, in that it implied a rejection of the divinity of Jesus. They were therefore eager to pin the label "Unitarian" on their opponents. Channing's eventual move to accept and defend that label in "Unitarian Christianity" gave the movement its name, even if it actually obscured the movement's primary emphasis on moral development.

The liberals, however, did seem to find more basis for their emphasis on human perfection if the unquestionably human nature of Jesus were accepted, and orthodox protests notwithstanding, they thought that Trinitarian formulations of the equivalence of the Father and Son compromised the full humanity of Jesus.

Buckminster's suggestion, therefore, that such claims lacked verifiable scriptural support lent itself well to a liberal disaffection with Trinitarianism, which had been growing steadily in the late eighteenth century. The liberal agenda for the early decades of the nineteenth century became set, therefore, by several accumulating strands of Arminian thinking that grew throughout the late eighteenth century. The liberals had to persist in pushing their investigation of the bases of biblical authority, defend their rejection of Trinitarianism, and continue to mold their notions of individual moral culture into a positive theological stance. There is a real basis for their unprecedented lament at Buckminster's early death. The most promising of their leaders for the struggle was gone, but his quick transformation into New England sainthood testified to the vigor and determination of the movement he had led. By the end of the same decade in which he died, a new leader had emerged in William Ellery Channing. He was the strongest of leaders, because his distaste for that role was matched only by his iron conviction of the essential truth of what he frankly called "Unitarian Christianity."

## UNITARIAN CHRISTIANITY

If a reluctant controversialist, Channing was nevertheless a powerful one. His distaste for sectarianism in general, and theological dispute in particular, forced him to enter debate sparingly and only on grounds that seemed to him both essential and indisputable. Such a situation arose in 1815, when Channing became the central liberal spokesman in the Unitarian controversy. It was less a single and sustained debate than a series of disputes around a cluster of central issues. The most important product of this period was Channing's "Unitarian Christianity" (1819), in which he accepted the liberals' separation from the orthodox and defined the terms under which the movement would pursue an independent direction. Characteristically for the Unitarians, theological debate preceded institutional organization.

Even that open declaration of theological opinion had to be forced on the liberals. They were willing to allow their doctrines to make a silent advance, in the pattern of Gay and other eighteenth-century Arminians, but this indirect denial of Calvinism annoyed the orthodox. Although dispute had flared periodically before, the controversy did not become prominent until the Calvinists Jedidiah Morse and Jeremiah Evarts offered a challenge to liberal theology that could not be ignored. The dispute involved a biography of Theophilus Lindsey written by his fellow English Unitarian Thomas Belsham. It discussed the active presence of a Unitarian movement in England, one that looked to Joseph Priestley* as its intellectual leader. Although the origin of American Unitarianism had little to do with the English movement, there had been communication between Lindsey and James Freeman,* whose Christology was of the Socinian variety. The letters, which Belsham printed in the biography, suggested some sympathy of ideas between English Unitarians and New England liberals, (although serious differences remained) but also a reluctance on the part of the liberals to give public prominence to their dissent to orthodox doctrines. When Morse finally obtained a copy of the book from the Harvard library, where it had been quietly circulating among the liberals for some time, he reprinted the part of it revealing the liberals' connections with English Unitarianism. Morse had been long convinced of such a conspiracy among the liberals and had fought hard to isolate and separate them from the orthodox Calvinists. He had taken a leading role in opposing the election of Henry Ware* as Hollis Professor of Divinity at Harvard and then rallied the moderate and Hopkinsian Calvinists toward a joint effort in the founding of Andover Theological Seminary. In the biography of Lindsey, he thought that he "had found a book that gave him evidence that a conspiracy was afoot."[9] To make sure no one missed the point, Evarts reviewed the reprint, emphasizing what he saw as the heresy and hypocrisy in the liberals' position and suggesting that these evils were serious enough to justify their exclusion from Christian fellowship.[10]

Channing's answers to these charges thrust him into a role of leadership among the liberals, for they were brilliant rebuttals of orthodox arguments and laid the basis for the later development of a positive theology. He treated the fact that the liberals had been "accused" of Unitarianism by reversing the issue and accusing the orthodox of Trinitarianism. *Unitarianism* was widespread in Boston, he agreed, if that word simply denoted "opposition to Trinitarianism."[11] But the shades of that opposition were various, and only a very few subscribed to the Unitarianism of Belsham. The majority "believe, that Jesus Christ is more than man, that he existed before the world, that he literally came from heaven to save our race, . . . and is our intercessor with the Father" (p. 7). What does this leave exclusively to the orthodox, one might wonder. As Channing saw it, it left only the complicated problem of the separate but identical natures of the members of the Trinity, a position he was happy to let them try to defend. He avoided it by placing Jesus well above humans but well below God, by holding, as he put it, "the most exalted views of Jesus Christ, which are consistent with the supremacy of the Father" (p. 12).

Nor was it hypocrisy that had prevented them from preaching the Trinitarian doctrine but a scrupulous consistency in preaching only what they fully believed and a sincere desire to avoid inappropriate controversy in the pulpit. To launch into an attack on the Trinity would "perplex and needlessly perplex a common congregation," because it is "the most unintelligible [doctrine] about which christians have ever disputed" (p. 15). Given this position, the final suggestion that the orthodox should withhold Christian fellowship from the liberals was depicted as a shockingly un-Christian act: "let the consequences of it lie on its authors" (p. 20).

Channing's reply to Morse and Evarts spawned a series of other pamphlet wars, but he participated in them only at the beginning, saving the best of himself for works that were more broadly polemical ("The Moral Argument against Calvinism," 1820) or more pointedly affirmative ("Unitarian Christianity," 1819;

"Self-Culture," 1838).[12] "Unitarian Christianity" was one of the most immediately controversial sermons ever written in America and one of the most enduring. In it, as in his reply to Morse and Evarts in 1815, Channing was conscious that he spoke for the liberal party, and there was a general anticipation among them about his sermon that augmented its impact. Preached in Baltimore, for the ordination of the young Jared Sparks at a new congregation there, it also represented an effort to spread liberal doctrines beyond Boston, one of the signs of a growing denominational consciousness.[13]

The substance of the address reminds us that the Unitarians still saw theirs as a biblical religion well into the nineteenth century. Channing saw the essential difference between Calvinist and Unitarian Christianity as one of scriptural interpretation, with differing methods of interpretation resulting in differences of doctrine. Appealing to the validity of the higher criticism as taught by Buckminster and others, he explained that Unitarians "feel it our bounden duty to exercise our reason upon [the Bible] perpetually."[14] Reason is necessary because of the changing historical circumstances surrounding revelation and also because of the inherently symbolic character of so many of the scriptures. "Need I descend to particulars to prove that the Scriptures demand the exercise of reason? . . . Recollect the declarations of Christ, that he came not to send peace but a sword; that unless we eat his flesh and drink his blood we have no life in us; that we must hate father and mother, and pluck out the right eye; and a vast number of passages equally bold and unlimited" (pp. 368–69). No reader of the Bible could take such passages literally, but as Channing realized, once any sort of latitude of interpretation was granted, only the best resources of reason could provide a standard for interpretation. Channing's argument gained added polemical force when he turned it on the Calvinist opponents of the higher criticism, whom he found guilty of inconsistency: "None reason more frequently than those from whom we differ. It is astonishing what a fabric they rear from a few slight hints about the fall of our first parents; and how ingeniously they extract from detached passages mysterious doctrines about the divine nature" (p. 369). The issue, in other words, was not *whether* but *how* reason would be used.

Although the first part of the sermon revealed the connections between rationalism and biblicism in Channing's thinking, the concluding section, devoted to doctrine, emphasized moralism, the other major strand of Unitarian thinking. The moral dimension of these theological issues becomes clear in Channing's explanations of the "*moral perfection of God*" (p. 376), the "moral or spiritual deliverance" brought by Jesus (p. 378), and the "moral nature of man" (p. 380). He explained God's moral perfection in terms of his "parental character," thus humanizing him in a way that underlined humankind's participation in divinity (p. 377). Election and original sin, the opposing Calvinist doctrines, were thus arrayed against the emotional power of a father's love for his children. This final discussion of human and divine morality reminds us that human nature, and not the doctrine of the Trinity, was central to the Unitarian critique of Calvinism, and that the Unitarians saw complicated doctrines about the Trinitarian nature of God as unfortunate corollaries of the Calvinists' fundamental mistake about original sin and election.

The widening of Channing's perspective from the specific rebuttal of Morse and Evarts to the posture of denominational definition in "Unitarian Christianity" is a paradigm for his entire career. Moreover, his career itself is a paradigm for the Unitarian movement in its change from negation of Calvinism to radical affirmation of human nature. The year after writing "Unitarian Christianity" he authored "The Moral Argument against Calvinism," which seems superficially a narrow polemic but actually widened the basis of Unitarian thinking dramatically. He began with the same attack on the corruption of the Calvinist God, but his rebuttal led him to say that the qualities of goodness and justice "are essentially the same in God and man, though differing in degree, in purity, and in extent of operation" (p. 464). By the end of that decade (1828), he preached a sermon on human "Likeness to God," and specifically posited "the Divinity within us" (p. 293), which could render humankind "more and more partakers of the moral perfection of the Supreme Being" (pp. 293–94). It was this strain in Channing's work that appealed to Ralph Waldo Emerson and the more radical members of the generation that followed. He continued to preach a radically affirmative version of human development, even though he based it on more traditional and theologically conservative grounds than Emerson. "Self-Culture" (1838) epitomized his faith that the souls of humans were infinitely expansive if their energies were correctly channeled, and the address also revealed Channing's growing concern with the social implications of his thought. His assertion that "to raise the depressed, by a wise culture, to the dignity of men, is the highest end of the social state" had potentially unsettling social implications, as he knew (p. 36). A reformer, not a radical, he maintained faith in American institutions. But he did not ignore the fact that his theology demanded a price from those in power, and he was not reticent in pressing that debt.

From Channing, therefore, radiated almost every strand of Unitarian thinking. Although he was not unique among his Unitarian colleagues in his ideas, he was unparalleled in his expression of them. Fiercely independent as a thinker, he nevertheless found himself the representative of his generation. He thereby fulfilled Emerson's definition of genius: "to believe that what is true for you in your private heart, is true for all men."[15]

## THE DEVELOPMENT OF UNITARIAN INSTITUTIONS

The progress of liberal thinking preceded the formation of liberal institutions by a considerable degree, but that formation began to take place in the first decade of the nineteenth century. The controversy over Arminianism had been an internal dispute among the New England Congregationalists, but as the rift between the parties widened, the institutional bounds of the church began to be stretched by conflicting demands of the two parties. Theological debate had expanded to the point of denominational schism.

Not surprisingly, the first major battle of that schism, and one that has come to be widely acknowledged as a point of Unitarian origin, was a battle for control of one of the institutional foundations of New England Congregationalism, Harvard College. When the nation's oldest endowed university chair, the Hollis Professorship of Divinity, fell open in 1803 at the death of David Tappan, the process of picking a successor quickly became a contest between the liberals and the orthodox and a test of the control of the direction of the college.[16] Since Harvard stood as the major training ground for the ministry of much of New England, the outcome of this test was recognized by both sides as crucial to the entire direction of religion in New England. Liberalism had hitherto thrived within the confines of a denomination ostensibly in orthodox hands, largely because the congregational polity of the Puritan churches made orthodoxy extremely difficult to enforce. Persuasion and pressure could do very little to bring around a convinced Arminian minister who had his congregation and a few supportive colleagues behind him. Thus although losing the Hollis professorship probably would not have been a crippling blow to liberalism, the liberal victory was decisive, because it pushed the orthodox closer to confrontation over doctrine, in that they thought that an overly generous toleration of Unitarianism was in fact an abandonment of the central tenets of their faith. Control of Harvard College by liberals was, to many of them, too great a measure of toleration.

The liberal Henry Ware was eventually elected to the post, thus confirming the worst fears of the orthodox. Before the election, one orthodox writer, probably their emerging spokesman Jedidiah Morse, had tried to head off a liberal victory by warning against the possibility that "professed Unitarians" might be elected to both the professorship and the college presidency, which also had recently come open.[17] Morse's concern typified the growing sense of frustration that many of the orthodox felt as they watched their churches literally slipping away from them. Morse criticized the outcome of the election soon after, and his continuing attacks on the "Unitarians" of New England widened the battle beyond the bounds of Harvard and into the New England churches themselves. But before the pamphlet war of 1815 had broken out, the Calvinists, led by Morse, founded Andover Seminary in 1808. The move signified that they no longer thought they could further their faith at Harvard, but its results were more far-reaching than that motive might suggest. Andover initiated a formalized professional training for the ministry that challenged the informal and almost haphazard system of apprentice training at Harvard. The liberals who had won themselves a college now found themselves without a seminary. It was not the winning of the Hollis professorship, therefore, but the resulting founding of Andover that spurred the liberals to their first organizational step, the founding of the Harvard Divinity School.

The orthodox planned to insure the consistency of the traditional faith by obligating the faculty to sign a formal creedal statement every five years. To the liberals, not only the content of the creed but the idea of having to sign any creed at all, whatever the content, was objectionable.[18] Mayhew's earlier attack on creed-making had grown in importance in Unitarian circles, because such affirmations of truth seemed to suggest a finality that excluded the freest inquiry into religious questions. Thus although the formation of the Divinity School at Harvard was indeed a response to the challenge of Andover, the liberals were careful not to burden the school with any sectarian interests or to make any explicit ties between the school and their own emerging denomination.

The actual history of Harvard Divinity School is difficult to summarize, because the process of its formation was a gradual engrafting of the elements of a theological seminary on the existing college. In 1811 various members of the faculty in the college were designated specific duties in theological training by President John T. Kirkland, an act that systematized the informal instruction that candidates for the ministry had been receiving. This gave formal recognition to some important responsibilities of an already overburdened faculty, and in 1816 the Society for the Promotion of Theological Education in Harvard University was formed, primarily to raise money for needed additional professorships in Divinity. In 1819 the Harvard Corporation specifically recognized a "Faculty of Theology" and by 1826 fund-raising efforts had been successful enough for the construction of Divinity Hall. It was a somewhat gradual response to the founding of Andover, but the liberals had the existing structure of Harvard to lean upon in the interim.[19] Denominational organization was problematic for them at points, given their general reluctance to admit any sectarian motivations in their movement, but the founding of the Divinity School, however gradual, was a significant indication that they recognized the need for institutional as well as doctrinal development.

The call for the formation of the school had gained an important ally in Channing, who authored a persuasive argument for it in 1816. Channing's case for an improvement in the training of the ministry was closely linked to his conception of the role of the minister, and his argument is a good indicator of the Unitarian conception of its mission and ministry. It is in the close connection between the ministry and the people that Channing found the need for continuing improvement in the education of ministers. Although the people's connection with other professions is "transient, accidental, rare," it is "habitual" with a minister, who must "be our friend, our guide, an inmate in our families." The closeness of the pastoral tie corresponds to the central importance accorded to Christian nurture and growth in Unitarian thinking, for the duty of the minister was "to rouse us from the slumbers of an unreflecting life . . . and to engage our affections on the side of duty."[20] In a theology that stressed spiritual development through education and moral discipline, those who served as moral teachers and guides took on great importance and correspondingly heavy responsibilities.

Channing argued that in a world of expanding secular knowledge, "there is a peculiar need of an enlightened ministry," because "religion must be adapted, in its mode of exhibition, to the state of society'' (p. 280). This very assumption would later stand behind the more radical calls for an organic relation between church and society later in the century in both the Transcendentalist controversy and the Free Religion movement. Channing's enunciation of this principle reminds us how similar in some respects were the dynamics of those movements to the earlier movement that spawned them.

To the challenge of expanding secular knowledge, Channing added the threat of evangelical narrowness as a rationale for an educated ministry. ''Religious teachers there certainly will be, of one description or another; and if men of well-furnished minds cannot be found for this office, we shall be overwhelmed by the ignorant and fanatical'' (p. 280). Just as Chauncy saw reason and scriptural study the best bulwark against dangerous enthusiasm, Channing found expanded theological education the best guard against a similarly threatening and misguided fervor. ''An enlightened ministry,'' he warned ''is the only barrier against fanaticism'' (p. 280). Taking the formation of the Harvard Divinity School as the first sustained effort among the Unitarians at institutional formation, Channing's articulation of the role of the school emphasized the fragile ground that the liberals thought they were protecting—ground threatened from one side by secular rationalism and on the other by evangelical excess.

During the period of the Unitarian controversy and the formation of the Divinity School, a number of New England churches began to split over questions of orthodoxy. The heart of the Unitarian denomination was formed from these parish divisions, and although the Unitarians were to stress the need for expansion into new territory throughout the century, the base of the denomination long remained firmly in those established churches that took the Unitarian name. Such splits were not always accomplished on the friendliest of terms, and the disputes became intensely bitter when church buildings and property were at stake, as they often were. ''Which party was the real church?'' was the inevitable question when the orthodox and the liberals clashed, and the question was complicated further by the distinction within the New England Congregational churches between the ''parish'' and the ''church.'' The Puritan theocracy had made support of public worship mandatory, and a system of tax support persisted into the nineteenth century. The *parish* included ''all the male voters of the town organized to maintain religious worship, which they were taxed to support,'' and the *church* was a group within the parish, consisting ''of those who had assented to a covenant, or made a confession of faith, or professed a personal experience of religion, and who united as communicants in observing the Lord's Supper.''[21] The distinction between the two, which derived from Puritan understanding of congregational polity, became crucial when the parish and the church came to be at odds over the doctrinal stance of the minister. This is exactly what happened in 1820 in Dedham, Massachusetts. There the largely liberal parish and largely orthodox church membership split over the selection of a minister, and the majority of the church withdrew from the parish, taking church property with it. The remaining minority of the church sued for the return of the property and stunned the withdrawing orthodox majority by winning a precedent-setting case. The court ruled that that portion of the church remaining with the parish retained the property, even if a minority. The orthodox therefore could withdraw from churches under liberal leadership only at the expense of the church property, such as the communion silver and poor funds. The bitter jab of the orthodox, "They kept the furniture, but we kept the faith," expressed their sense of injustice. But for the Unitarians, the decision became a basis upon which their emerging denomination could be built.

The gradual emergence of the Divinity School from Harvard College, and the piecemeal process of church division as exemplified in the Dedham case, suggest that the Unitarians were being impelled by events toward the status of a denomination, rather than aggressively pursuing that status. Because of their position in the established churches, and their general sense that sectarianism and controversy were inevitably corrupting to the purity of Christianity, any sense of the need to organize came slowly and was resisted from within. But when Channing finally gave both a name and sense of ideological respectability to the impulse to organize in "Unitarian Christianity," the way was cleared for the formal organization of the American Unitarian Association in 1825. Even though he refused the offer of first presidency of the association, and even expressed some concern about the founding of it, Channing had provided not only intellectual leadership for it but an institutional forerunner of the association as well.[22] He had called a group of the liberal ministers of Massachusetts together in 1820 to form what came to be known as the Berry Street Conference. Although sectarian insofar as it was composed of those "who are known to agree in what are called Liberal and Catholic views of Christianity," the association carefully eschewed any narrowly sectarian interests.[23] Its stance was indicative of the liberals' tentative groping toward organization at that period.

Yet if Channing represented the caution of one generation of Unitarians in forming a denomination, that caution was not shared by some younger men, notably Henry Ware, Jr.,* James Walker,* John Gorham Palfrey, and Ezra Stiles Gannett.* These men were less concerned about the dangers of sectarianism and were increasingly out of place with no organization to promote their interests. Gannett explained the motives behind the move toward organization:

Other denominations had their societies, to which the pecuniary contributions of Unitarians might be paid, but in the management of which they were allowed to have no voice. The officers of these societies connected the propagation of tenets, which we account false, with whatever measures of general utility they might adopt. We found ourselves placed under the painful necessity of contributing our assistance to the diffusion of such views, or of forming an Association through which we might address the great truths of religion to our fellow-men, without the adulteration of erroneous dogmas.[24]

An attempt to organize a Unitarian society failed in January 1825 but was revived at the meeting of the Berry Street Conference on May 25, 1825. There the American Unitarian Association was formed, taking as its purpose the diffusion of "pure Christianity." Channing declined the offer of the presidency, which went to Aaron Bancroft, although much of the organizational and administrative work was undertaken by Gannett, the first secretary.[25]

The association was the loosest of organizations, composed of individuals rather than churches and lacking any connection to the churches except that of goodwill. Since these churches guarded their congregational polity carefully, the association never had command of many resources. Its general functions were to promote communication among Unitarian churches, to foster such missionary work in establishing new churches as it could, given its limited means, and to publish Unitarian tracts and pamphlets as a means of increasing the size of the movement. It was, in sum, a meager move toward denominational identity, but it was at least a move, and its enduring importance is that it gave an official name and home to the liberal religion that had already come into existence in eastern Massachusetts. Far more important to the well-being of Unitarianism were the intellectual efforts of a generation of ministers who had seen their liberal views take form as a denomination. Most important was the work of Channing, whose personal philosophy most exactly expressed the synthesis of the classic Unitarian period.

# 4
# THE CLASSIC PERIOD OF UNITARIANISM

## RATIONALISM AND PIETISM

The years between the formation of the denomination in the 1820s and the outbreak of the Civil War can be thought of as the "classic" period of Unitarian
history. For a few decades between the polemical war with Calvinism and the
total social upheaval caused by the war, a fragile synthesis of belief and outlook was achieved, upon which was founded the Unitarian identity. The period
is marked by a controversy of its own concerning Transcendentalism, which is
considered in Chapter 7, but the drama of that controversy, and the prominence
given it in literary history, has tended to obscure the continuity of Unitarian
denominational concerns at that time.

Such continuity as there was among the Unitarians should not be confused
with a systematic theology or a stultifying sameness of procedure. Its spirit is
best defined by Octavius Brooks Frothingham* as "a faith rather than a creed,
a sentiment more than a dogma, not sharp in outline, but full of emotion and
charged with conviction, slightly illogical perhaps, but firm,—a religion of the
heart."[1] Rationalism, in other words, goes only so far in explaining Unitarianism, despite the long-standing historical connection between them. The Unitarians used reason primarily to liberate themselves from Calvinism, and although they continued to search for rational bases for their belief, the real
grounding of their religion was in the emotions. This reliance on the emotions
or "affections" had both an inward and an outward manifestation. Inwardly,
the Unitarians of this period stressed devotionalism and religious meditation much
in the tradition of Christian pietism. By contrast, a stress on the importance of
the affections, defined in terms of duty, social responsibility, and Christian love,
focused Unitarian energies outward toward both social reform and further denominational organization.

The continuing presence of rationalism in the denomination, however, is un-

derscored in the figure of Andrews Norton,* influential both as a denominational leader and a member of the Harvard faculty. Norton has suffered the fate
of vilification by historians, largely because of his dogmatic and intemperate
attacks on Ralph Waldo Emerson.* Here, Norton's rationalism showed itself as
a reactionary force, not unlike Charles Chauncy's* reaction to the awakeners.
Emerson was no revivalist, but he represented to some Unitarians a heretical
individualism whose excesses were as dangerous as the fanaticism of the itin-
erants.

Whatever we think of Norton's attacks on Emerson, his synthesis of Unitarian opinions on biblical theology was a significant contribution to the denomination. In 1813 he assumed Harvard's Dexter lectureship in biblical criticism
after the short tenures of Joseph Stevens Buckminster* and William Ellery
Channing,* a role that made him the chief spokesman for Unitarian biblical
interpretation. From that vantage point he joined in the early controversies with
the Calvinists. His influential attack on the doctrine of the Trinity is characteristic of much of his work. The heart of his argument was that "three persons,
each equally possessing divine attributes, are three Gods." His stance was one
of firm common sense and sharp rhetorical power, with an insistence that language be used simply and responsibly. "A person is a being. No one who has
any correct notion of the meaning of words will deny this. And the being who
possesses divine attributes must be God or a God."[2] Thus the very language
of the Trinitarians themselves, if used in the ordinary way, committed them to
an opposition to monotheism. Any backing away from this equalization, and
thus individuation of the persons of the Trinity, was, as he recognized, a step
toward Unitarianism. Much the same insistence on precise and stable uses of
words would also mark his attack on Emerson later in 1838, during the Divinity
School controversy.

Although influential as both a professor and theological controversialist, Norton's major contribution to Unitarian history was his work in biblical criticism,
brought together in his *magnum opus, The Evidences of the Genuineness of the
Gospels* (1837–44). Although it was a work of grand conception and mammoth
proportion, it was at bottom a kind of tragic failure, a rear-guard action which
soon would be outmoded by trends in liberal theology. The foundation of Norton's faith, the miracles, would prove to be a stumbling block for the next generation of Unitarians, such as Emerson and George Ripley.* His angry reaction
to Emerson's dismissal of the miracles as irrelevant is more easily understood
when we remember that Emerson's Divinity School Address (1838) was delivered only a year after Norton had completed the first volume of his study. He
was a man who saw both his faith and his life's work threatened. Although the
credibility of the miracles underlay Norton's work, its immediate object was to
counter skepticism about the authorship of the Gospels that resulted from the
German higher criticism, particularly that of Johann Gottfried Eichhorn, whom
he considered representative of modern skepticism. Norton saw clearly what
Buckminster apparently did not, that although historical and critical analysis of

scripture could be a liberal tool, it could also strip even liberal Christianity of its scriptural support. Norton countered the threat of history with history itself, trying to solidify the line of biblical descent from "two individuals who were intimate companions of Jesus, eyewitnesses of his ministry, who knew the facts."[3] Both the demand for historical solidity and the reverence for the "eyewitness" account typify Norton's empiricism and suggest the gulf between him and the Transcendentalists.

But there is more to Norton's vision than cold empiricism, although he is remembered for that because those are the grounds upon which he chose to challenge the Transcendentalists. The character of Jesus is as important to Norton as his miracles, "a character to which nothing in human history, before or after, presents a parallel or a resemblance" (III, 330). To consider the depiction of this character merely a "fiction," devised by his apostles or by later writers, is "an absurdity so repulsive, that it would be equally offensive and unprofitable to dwell on it longer" (III, 334). These are not the statements of a cold empiricist but of a man of faith, battling to defend it. We may wonder whether Norton had exposed himself to skepticism so thoroughly that he fought all the harder because of the fear that exposure generated. But the fight, we must remember, had as its object the protection of an object of piety, the character of Jesus.

Although Norton made his essentially pietistic faith in the character of Jesus bear the weight of rational historicism, his contemporary Henry Ware, Jr.,* did not. If Norton is the most representative of the Unitarian rationalists, Ware, along with John Emery Abbot* and the younger Emerson, typify Unitarian pietism, a "religion of the heart" that was an important though largely unrecognized ethos of classic Unitarianism.[4] The younger Ware was not averse to rational argument and, like his father, could be a formidable controversialist, as his answer to Emerson's Divinity School Address demonstrates. But the differing personalities of Ware and Norton are suggested by Norton's attack on Emerson for abandoning the miracles and Ware's dissent from Emerson's abandonment of the idea of a personal and paternal God. To replace God the father with a mere abstraction, as Ware thought Emerson did, was to render fervent and pious morality and worship impossible. Whereas Emerson was comfortable in playing the nonrational mystic for Norton, he was decidedly uncomfortable as the antipious rationalist suggested by Ware.[5]

Although frail of health, Ware had astonishing energy, and his unflagging work touched the denomination in many areas. He was a popular preacher, even though he deemphasized the place of preaching among the pastor's duties and stressed visiting and counseling. His personal work at Boston's Second Church set a high example for the denomination, so high that he was asked to join the Harvard faculty to train young ministers in preaching and the pastoral care. He had great success as a teacher and, in that position, probably had his greatest influence on the denomination. Most of his energies as a writer were devoted to sermons and later sermonized lectures, and he was also a writer of didactic moral fiction and poetry. But his most influential work was the devotional manual *On the Formation of the Christian Character* (1831), a work that remains the fullest exposition of Unitarian pietism of the classic period.[6]

Ware's work is the best single refutation of the commonplace historical assumption that Unitarianism was a public, rational, and emotionally cold religion. Ware's purpose was to write "a book on personal religion" (p. 284) that would directly counteract the prevalent tendency to "uphold the religion of Christ on account of its general influence, its beneficial public tendency, [and] its humane and civilizing consequences." For Ware, a religion that "is concerned wholly with the state of society in general" allows an individual "to neglect the discipline of his own affections and the culture of his own spiritual nature" (p. 288). A tone that borders on the evangelical permeates the work, and the fervency of Ware's conception of the religious life is made clear in his call for an absolute humbling of the will. The Christian character is attainable "only by a surrender of the whole man and the entire life to the will of God, in faith, affection, and action" (p. 295). From a theological point of view, this is not evangelical soul winning, because Ware did not speak of any instantaneous change of character or regenerative experience. He stressed that the process of character building is lifelong, and that "its primary characteristic is a certain state of mind and affections" (p. 292). But Ware's stress on the state of mind that essentially sets the Christian apart from the world had much in common with the emotional structures of revivalism.

Such a state of mind carries with it a certain strain of other-worldliness. "You are to feel that nothing is of such consequence to you as the Christian character; that to form this is the very work for which you were sent into the world; that if this be not done, you do nothing" (pp. 294–95). In this sense Ware appears to depart from the Unitarians' traditional stress on the moral engagement of the world as a focal point for Christianity. To be sure, Ware did not intend to slight morality but to argue for the basis of morality in the dedicated mental attitude of the Christian. Moreover, he argued that ultimately "your chief business, as well as your great trial, in forming Christian character, lies in the ordinary tenor of life. The WORLD is the theatre on which you are to prove yourself a Christian" (p. 377). But Ware's final place in the tradition of Unitarian moral philosophy is innovative, in that he linked moral engagement to a base of quietist devotionalism. Although he never abandoned his concern for the outer life, he gave a fuller account of the inner life than any Unitarian before him.

## ORGANIZATION AND OUTREACH

As both an exemplar of the active outer life of the dedicated pastor, and prophet of the intense inner life of the pious individual, Ware was a rare combination of Unitarian virtues. Influential as his devotional writings were to the denomination as a whole, his example as minister and his impact on denominational organization appealed to many younger Unitarian ministers. This group had the luxury to assume that the war with Calvinism was largely over, having been fought and won by the generation before them. Their concern was less to continue theological controversy than to organize the denomination, for they realized that they had inherited a style of belief and a movement but no significant institutional basis for it. Ezra Stiles Gannett* stands out among this group, first as a leader in the move to organize the American Unitarian Association and then as a lifelong worker for denominational Unitarianism. Significantly, Gannett took Ware as "a working-model" for his activities in the ministry.[7] He shared not only Ware's religious ideals but his tendency to dangerous overwork in pursuit of them as well, as Ware himself saw in a letter of 1828: "I have long been concerned at your mode of life, which appears to be a careless, reckless throwing away of a chance for longevity. . . . For me, it is too late: for you, it is not" (p. 149).

Overwork was in the nature of the ministry in New England, but for Gannett and Ware, who devoted considerable energy to institutional organization, it was a particular problem. Gannett was "by nature an organizer" (p. 141). In addition to heavy duties as Channing's associate at the Federal Street Church, he took upon himself the organization of an almost unorganizable body, the New England Unitarians. To do so he had to overcome not only the opposition of conservative Christianity but the caution and hostility of even the most influential liberals, like Channing and Norton, who feared the sectarianism of an organized denomination. Such fears had their basis in long, bitter sectarian disputes and in a fundamental belief that organization inevitably flirted with corruption, or at least compromise, by threatening complete intellectual liberty. But to Gannett such organization, far from being harmful, was in fact absolutely necessary. At a time in which great national expansion was calling forth a corresponding outreach by the Protestant churches, the liberals found themselves lacking the necessary basis to promote their own version of Christianity. The American Unitarian Association was the response to this situation. "The name [Unitarian] which was adopted," he admitted, "has a sectarian sound. But it was chosen to avoid equivocation on the one hand, and misapprehension on the other" (p. 103).

Like almost all early Unitarians, Gannett was distinctly uneasy with the idea of exclusive sectarianism, but he saw its necessity and hoped "to make a sect without sectarianism" (p. 101). He found the name Unitarian Christianity "preferable to any other," because "it expresses the two chief points of our faith,—the unity of God and the divine mission of Christ." Even though he shared the resentment of many of the liberals at having to take any name at all, all names being ultimately confining to the most universal expression of faith, he dismissed this objection to denominational organization on realistic grounds. "Names in themselves are nothing; but as in the intercourse of life they are made to be of great importance, and as in the divisions that have rent the church of Christ it is almost necessary that we should assume some distinctive title, I wish that we might take this, which those who differ from us are willing we should have, and that we should honor it by our lips and glorify it by our lives'' (p. 116). As he pleaded with his fellow liberals to accept the responsibility to organize, so he pointed out the necessity of undertaking at times the distasteful chore of denominational assertion, rather than ''succumbing, and trembling before the breath of falsehood'' (p. 118). Lacking the sense of secure belonging within New England Congregationalism that men like Channing and Norton had, Gannett spoke for a group who felt impelled to organize precisely because they believed they were pushed out by the Congregationalists. It is interesting to find that this most active and assertive denominational organizer was beset with a deep and complicated sense of personal inadequacy, given to deep depression and self-doubt. Channing, under whom he worked at the Federal Street Church, repeatedly had to assure him of his worth and caution him against his repeated depressions and ''morbid state of mind'' (p. 147). But this fundamental insecurity had more than personal implications. The impulse to organize does not emanate from a sense of security, and what the prewar Unitarians lacked was a clear sense of their place in a rapidly changing society. This is always the case with movements of innovation in any sphere, but given the Unitarians' deep roots in New England's history, and their generally settled prosperity, the role of radical, ostracized, and potentially homeless innovators created an especially peculiar set of psychological tensions among their clergy. The drive to organize, with both its successes and failures, must be read with that context in mind.

Lacking the same impulses toward evangelical soul winning that marked many of the other Protestant denominations, Unitarians directed a large part of their expansive energies toward social reform, pioneering in urban social work as a form of expanded ministry. Joseph Tuckerman* was the man who single-handedly made such an experiment work at first, calling himself a ''minister-at-large'' who took all of the urban poor as his parish. Gannett was an active supporter of Tuckerman's activities and worked to expand them, characteristically seeking institutional support and organization for a broader ministry-at-large. Tuckerman had been appointed minister-at-large by the American Unitarian Association (AUA) in 1826, and in 1832 Gannett proposed an expanded ''Mission to the Poor in Boston.'' With Ware he helped to bring into being a separate philanthropic organization, the ''Benevolent Fraternity of Churches for the Support of the Ministry-at-large,'' becoming secretary of its Central Board. Although the primary impetus for such philanthropic organization was the growing condition of urban poverty in Boston, it is also true that this tendency to look beyond the ordinary concerns of the church was related to the declining role of the church and influence of the minister. The nobility of the effort itself belies a sense, which grew not only among the Unitarians but among many other Protestants of the period, that the problems of the nation had somehow sidestepped the influence of the churches. For Gannett, not only a new effort but a new organization was needed to meet this challenge.[8]

Tuckerman was a genuine innovator in his reform work, although like many men of original accomplishment, innovation was a by-product of his essentially pragmatic concern for ways in which he could help the poor. In his reports on his ministry, he made it clear that the ordinary means of the minister had to be modified to be effective in the new conditions of poverty. As Tuckerman found, preaching was much less important than personal visitation and counseling, and although he continued to insist that religious education was still the primary duty of the minister-at-large, that education had to be a much more personal and informal thing than it was in a parish setting. Tuckerman therefore insisted that the minister pay "constant regard . . . to the distinctive circumstances, both personal and relative, of every individual to whom [his ministry] is extended."[9] Most of all, Tuckerman learned, one must be flexible and open in the pursuit of this ministry, not bound by any accepted opinion, and he tried to impress that needed quality on the denomination as a whole.

The lack of such openness among the Unitarian middle and upper classes, whose tendency was to view the poor through a set of rigid platitudes, is forcefully suggested by the tone of Tuckerman's reports to them on his ministry. The reports are appeals not only for money but for understanding. Even though his innovative ministry expressed a deep social concern, Tuckerman was in no sense a radical, and his reports are finely balanced between arousing a concern for human suffering and assuaging the fears of the upper classes about the potential danger that the poor represented to their established interests. He depicted his own ministry as essentially a social anodyne, and in terms that would disturb many modern readers, he frankly argued the merits of the ministry as a mode of social control. The minister-at-large goes to the poor "from among those who are not poor" and is able to relieve the wants of the poor "through the sympathy of the rich, who have made him their almoner." He therefore has many opportunities "of calling forth the kindly affections of the poor toward the rich" and even of teaching "fidelity in duty, even in the poorest and lowest of all the employments of life" (p. 27). This is meant to reassure the rich who support these efforts, but it also indicates the limitations of Tuckerman's efforts. Channing had warned against ministers who went to the poor as representatives of the controlling classes, so the problem was not unrecognized among the Unitarians. But the most memorable contemporary critique of such philanthropic efforts is Henry David Thoreau's wry comment in *Walden*: "If I knew for a certainty that a man was coming to my house with the conscious design of doing me good, I should run for my life."[10]

Tuckerman was in no sense cynical in his motives, however, and fervently hoped that such a ministry, if practiced on a wide enough scale, would in fact unify the classes, even if it did not equalize property. To the extent that his theories justified economic inequalities in America, he can be blamed for failing to see far enough, as can most of his contemporaries, who, like him, were captives of a village-oriented view of what was quickly becoming an industrial economy. But insofar as he saw the facts of poverty, and attempted to be an awakener, he sounded a note of social reform that would become an increasingly important strand of the Unitarian ethos.

As an awakener, Tuckerman not only relied on his reports, but he experimented in didactic fiction, hoping to use that medium of growing popularity to make known the problems of the poor. In one sketch his fictional spokesman engages a sympathetic but uninformed member of the middle class in a dialogue about the poor, arguing that the capacity for nobility and public benefaction is not restricted to the upper classes. The depictions of physical neglect, alcoholism, abandonment, and child neglect he offered were intended to shock comfortable sensibilities, but the underlying plea is that religion be made to help "call forth in every human being that sense of the paramount claims of his own spiritual and immortal nature."[11] Tuckerman saw his ministry, then, as exemplifying the radical affirmation of the self that Channing preached. It was "self-culture" confronting the questions of social reform. If the individualism of that ideology limited its effectiveness as an organ of social change, it was also that very individualism that provided the fundamental motivation to change.

Tuckerman's efforts were most prominent, and certainly the most successful, of the Unitarian attempts at the ministry-at-large. His example did spawn other efforts not only in Boston but in New York and in the West, where they fell into place as part of a general Unitarian missionary effort. In part because Tuckerman had a real genius for what he did, and also because he worked in Boston, with the support of the established Unitarian churches, his ministry was the most effective. It is important historically not only for its concrete achievements but for its signification of a mood within the Unitarian movement. That mood can be thought of as a reformist impulse, one that militated against the social and political conservatism of the Unitarian milieu. Tuckerman exemplifies the Unitarian tendency to rethink social problems and institutions in light of a quickly changing economic landscape in America, a tendency that produced reforms in education, health and mental care, and women's rights, as well as poverty. Such Unitarian agitation was rarely if ever a threat to the established economic order in America, but these impulses to reform were the seeds of much social progress in America. This mood came to a strong focus in the abolitionist movement, which absorbed much of the reform energies of the nation in the 1850s and caused serious divisions within the denomination itself. Not only was the Civil War a national turning point, it was a pivotal moment in American Unitarian history as well. The war, and the politically divisive issues leading up to it, were instrumental in shattering the synthesis that marked the classic period of Unitarian history.

# 5
# AMERICAN UNIVERSALIST ORIGINS

## MURRAY AS UNIVERSALIST FOUNDER

The fact that Unitarian and Universalist churches merged in 1961 confirms their shared values and outlook, a confluence of interests that had been recognized since the nineteenth century. But those shared values, however prominent, can tend to overshadow the stark difference in origins between the Unitarians and the Universalists. Even though the groups shared from the outset certain premises, principally in their aversion to Calvinism, their articulation of those premises differed, as did the general ethos of the two movements. They developed in different ways, drawing from constituencies that in general differed greatly in both religious experience and socioeconomic class. The Unitarian movement was the liberalization of the established churches; the Universalist movement, like several other Protestant sects in New England, was a challenge to that very order.

Perhaps the best illustration of these differences, which were felt keenly in eighteenth-century New England, is the decision by Charles Chauncy* to delay the publication of his treatise on universal salvation, *The Mystery Hid from Ages and Generations*, partly out of fear of being linked with the founding father of American Universalism, John Murray.* Both Chauncy and Murray shared the belief that there would be no eternal damnation, but Chauncy and his fellow Arminians expressed a decided contempt for Murray. Part of it was based on Murray's continuing adherence to a Calvinist and Christocentric rather than an Arminian view of universal salvation—following James Relly, he simply "broadened" the category of the elect to include all humankind. But another important reason was that Chauncy and Murray found themselves on opposite sides of the fence in ecclesiastical politics. Whatever their doctrine, Chauncy and his Arminian colleagues remained the established clergy of New England. Murray, and most of the early Universalists, found themselves allied with the

Baptists, Quakers, independent revivalists, and other dissenting sects, who were leading the fight for an absolute separation of church and state. Even though his theological doctrines were anathema to many of the revivalists who preached Calvinist or evangelical dogma, Murray was, like them, an itinerant who felt in many cases wrongly denied access to the pulpit and to public power. Chauncy and his colleagues saw Murray and most of the other Universalist preachers not as allies in a liberal crusade against Calvinism but as part of a chaotic and threatening group of rabble-rousers who simply preached an odd version of the emotional religion they opposed. Even though they themselves were beginning to be accused of laxness in both theology and morals because of their liberal views, they saw in Murray only one who appealed to the "libertines" and "the promiscuous herd."[1]

Thus the early history of the Universalist movement is colored by a struggle both for theological tolerance and for political rights. Universalist teaching tended to evoke violent opposition from evangelical and Calvinist groups who saw the abandonment of doctrines of eternal punishment as an invitation to moral degeneracy and possibly damnation. Murray himself told the humorous story of his own attempt, before his conversion to Universalism, to save a young lady who had been "ensnared" by the "pernicious errors" of the English Universalist James Relly ("this detestable babbler"), who was later to convert him through his writings. Embarrassed by his inability to answer the young woman's arguments, he retreated in confusion. "From this period, I myself carefully avoided every Universalist, and *most cordially did I hate* them."[2] When one adds to this violent theological opposition the general mistrust of Universalist style and motives among the established churches, both liberal and orthodox, it becomes clear that early Universalist origins are a story of conflict and struggle. The embattled mentality of these early rebels must be remembered in any reconstruction of the early history of their movement.

The marked diversity of origins of the Universalist denomination makes it difficult to pinpoint a starting point for the movement. Murray has been accorded the distinction of "founder" of American Universalism, and his career as a preacher of Rellyan doctrine is the clearest link between English Universalist thinking and the American Universalist movement. The Universalist views of many of the German pietists who migrated to the colonies in the middle eighteenth century are another important strand in these origins, but there were also important indigenous roots of the movement, arising as one result of eighteenth-century evangelicalism and the general revolt against Calvinism. The Baptist movement in particular was a seedbed for early Universalism, and a good many Universalist leaders and followers, including Caleb Rich* and Elhanan Winchester,* arrived at their views by way of Baptist evangelicalism.[3] The Baptists were among the most prominent of the new sects that drew strength from the Great Awakening and leaders in the struggle against the system of taxation that supported New England's established Congregational churches. Even though Baptists were in general appalled by Universalist theology, they lent to their rebellious Universalist children a characteristic aura of populist dissent, folk authenticity, and autonomous polity.

Murray was the one of several influential contemporaries, including Rich, Winchester, George de Benneville,* and Benjamin Rush,* who began to attract some attention in the late eighteenth century for their denial of the doctrine of eternal damnation. As Universalists have been eager to point out, this was certainly no new doctrine in the eighteenth century, and the stirrings of the sentiment in America had both English and continental European predecessors. But the American Universalist church, distinctive in its institutional, although not its theological, origins, began when Universalist ideas, often of foreign origin, merged with a mood of local discontent over orthodox views of eternal punishment. Murray, who was born in England and trained in Anglican Calvinism, was also influenced by Wesleyan Methodism in his youth, and the appeal of the emotional fervor of that movement would never leave him. But he remained convinced of the doctrine of election, and after some doubt and struggle, he gained confidence of his own place among the elect. Then came the major turn in his religious development, his serious study of Relly's argument in *Union* (1749) that the death of Christ had in fact atoned for all human sin and made universal salvation not only possible but a foregone fact. Although he resisted the doctrine passionately at first, Murray found Relly's use of scripture convincing, and by 1760 he embraced Relly's Universalist ideas.

A series of personal tragedies, including an arrest for debt and the deaths of his wife and son, turned Murray to America, and even that voyage was not without problems. A storm forced his boat to make an unplanned landing at Good-Luck Point on the coast of New Jersey. But there he fell among congenial people and soon found an audience for his preaching, largely due to the sympathy of Thomas Potter, whose Universalist sympathies are traceable to doctrines of dissenting Baptist sects in Rhode Island and New Jersey. Murray preached his first sermon at Potter's church on September 30, 1770, thus launching his own career as Universalist leader and beginning one of the several early strands of the Universalist movement.

Like most of the itinerant preachers, Murray was a tireless traveler and was eventually pulled northward toward Boston, America's religious capital at the time. After preaching successfully, and fomenting much controversy, in Philadelphia (success usually equaled controversy for the early Universalists), he moved in 1772 to Newport, Rhode Island, where he tangled with two of New England's most influential clergymen, Samuel Hopkins and Ezra Stiles.[4] The nature of those debates is entirely suggestive of the two sides of the struggle that early Universalists faced. Hopkins attacked him on theological grounds, arguing against the idea of universal salvation, and Stiles battled him over access to his pulpit, denying it to him because of his lack of official clerical status. But Murray's growing reputation led a group of Rellyan Universalists in Gloucester, Massachusetts, to invite him to preach there in 1774, and thus began one of the most controversial, and significant, phases of his career.

Murray began to preach in Gloucester largely under the sponsorship of Winthrop Sargent, a prominent man of the community and leading member of the Congregational church. Almost from the beginning he was under attack from those opposed to his Universalism, but a stint as chaplain in the Revolutionary Army helped to augment his personal reputation, even if it did not render his theology any more palatable to the orthodox. In 1777 the simmering conflict in Gloucester over Murray's right to preach, even in private homes, broke into the open when members of the established church began maneuvers to expel church members who had been attending Murray's preaching. They also tried again, as they had before the war, to expel Murray himself from town. The eventual result was the formation of an independent Universalist church there in 1779 and a meeting house, on Winthrop's property, in 1780. Even though a long battle over taxation and other matters would continue to be fought, Murray, and Universalism, had established a toehold in New England, one of several foundations for the growth of the denomination.

Murray brought his Universalist ideas with him from England, but another important early Universalist preacher, Caleb Rich, suggests the native roots of the movement. Rich's Universalism evolved from an intense inner struggle over the question of salvation. He had been introduced to the questions of salvation in a Baptist church in Sutton, Massachusetts, and came under serious conviction in the late 1760s. Throughout this early period of spiritual unrest, he was tortured by the doubt that his motive in seeking salvation was a selfish fear of hell. This made even his pursuit of salvation a sinful act in his eyes. But in 1772, while he was living in Warwick, Massachusetts, he underwent several visionary experiences that gave him the assurance of salvation that he sought. Moreover, after study of the Bible he concluded that salvation was universal, but when he preached this to his Baptist brethren, he was denied fellowship in the church. Rich continued to preach Universalism, and the group of followers that he attracted in Warwick formed in 1774 the first Universalist society in America.[5]

Rich's story is notable because it suggests the inner dynamic that accounts for much of the inception of Universalism. The evangelical sensibility in eighteenth-century Protestantism often awoke fears that it could not satisfy, especially with regard to the assurance of salvation. Moreover, the tensions within Calvinism that had led to the Arminian movement in New England—the necessity of salvation pulling against the question of election to grace—could lead to Universalistic conclusions. Rich is a clear example of the evangelical sensibility, and it is worth remembering that he came to his conclusions without the influence of Murray. Universalism was beginning to sprout in the rich soil that the decay of Calvinism had produced.

## WINCHESTER AND EARLY UNIVERSALIST RELIGIOUS EXPERIENCE

One of the strongest contrasts between early Unitarianism and Universalism seems to be the nature of the religious experience at the foundation of the two faiths. Rich's mystical and visionary experiences were far removed from the Arminian rationalism of Chauncy and his liberal colleagues. For the Universalists, the word *conversion* is an important term, and it signifies the closer connection of that movement to evangelicalism in general. The paradox is that such a conversion, for the Universalist, was usually a turn away from the bases of evangelical orthodoxy, the fear of certain punishment in the afterlife. In general, Universalist converts felt the same sense of liberation from fear that evangelical converts did, except that they were able to universalize their sense of escape, while the evangelical converts experienced their salvation as intensely personal and unique. Murray's conversion, for example, seems to have been the capstone of a prolonged struggle with his soul, but Elhanan Winchester's case is perhaps more instructive of the problems of the convert to Universalism. Although not the first, or in his day the most famous, of the early Universalist preachers, his movement through the phases of Protestant evangelicalism toward Universalism is a paradigm for many early converts. His first significant religious experience was a "New-Light" Calvinist conversion, in 1769, and from there he made his way into the Baptist fold, gaining a reputation as "one of the most thorough Calvinist preachers in the country."[6] But his reading of Paul Siegvolck's (pseudonym for George Klein-Nicolai) Universalist arguments in *The Everlasting Gospel* undermined his Calvinism. "I had never seen anything of the sort before in all my life," he later remarked, and although he put the book and its idea aside for the time being, it continued to haunt him. After a period of struggle with the idea, both his desire and his belief merged in a faith that "at the name of Jesus every knee should bow."[7] This change was coming upon him in the midst of his pastorate to a Baptist congregation in South Carolina, and his own account of his situation suggests that he made his Universalist views known only after considerable hesitation, trying for a while to hold them privately and keep them out of his pulpit. While still wrestling with the issue of Universalism, Winchester moved to Philadelphia in 1780 as pastor of the First Baptist Church. As his belief in the universal restoration grew, and word of it spread among the congregation, he found himself in the center of a controversy. He was eventually pushed out of that church but took with him a part of the congregation, which formed a new church. In 1781 Winchester publicly asserted his Universalist views, and while continuing to preach in Philadelphia (1781–87) he assumed a role of leadership as a Universalist spokesman and controversialist.[8] Because of his stature as a Baptist evangelical preacher of great power (from all accounts he was a spellbinder from the pulpit), his outspoken espousal of Universalism was an embarrassment, and a cause for some concern, among the Baptists.

In his best-known work on Universalist theology, *The Universal Restoration* (1788), Winchester argued at great length that the terms *everlasting, eternal*, and *forever and ever*, which are used in scripture to describe the punishment of sinners, should be taken to signify "certain unknown limited periods" rather than a span of endless duration. Ultimately, that duration will end when all souls are "restored" in the unity of God. Winchester argued that the belief in an endless punishment "came from the Pagan theology," which posited "*two eternal principles*, ever warring against each other, and neither fully prevailing." This dualism was for Winchester completely incompatible with the Christian revelation. To hold it consistently, one had to argue that God was not the sole creator of souls. For Winchester, the promise of Christianity was that "the Kingdom of evil, and all the works of sin, Satan and darkness, shall be totally destroyed by Christ, and all things shall be reheaded in Him."[9] This was the promise of universal restoration, which was the essence of Winchester's message.

Some taste of both the experiential and evangelical basis of this early Universalist faith can be found in Winchester's preaching. The following extract from "The Outcasts Comforted" (1782)—preached to his outcast congregation in Philadelphia—resonates with that experience. Winchester preached that the Universalist position is "founded upon the plainest letter of scripture" and "is exactly according to the experience of every Christian." The word *experience* here has great significance as an indicator of the dynamics of the early Universalist movement.

For let me ask any who was ever made to experience the love of God shed abroad in their hearts by the Holy Ghost, these questions: Did you not at that time see and feel yourselves the vilest of sinners, even the most stubborn and rebellious of the human race? Did you not view the love of God infinitely full, free, unmerited and unreserved? Did you not behold in Christ an infinite fulness [*sic*], sufficiency and willingness to save all? Did you not earnestly long that all might come and partake of his grace?[10]

Such an appeal is powerful both emotionally and rhetorically. How, after all, could one deny it without exposure to charges of coldness and cynicism—or a lack of faith in the saving power of Jesus? The passage also reminds us of a certain paradox in some early Universalist thinking. The sense of depravity that many Universalists felt was the very thing that warranted their faith in the universal restoration. Original sin, in other words, was central to their vision of universal salvation. If God can save me, Winchester suggested, he can save anyone; and if he can, surely he will: "Has he taught us to do good to all? And will he not much more do good to all?"[11] Although Universalism would later develop along more recognizably Arminian lines, closer to the position of Chauncy and William Ellery Channing,* these Calvinist and evangelical roots of the movement so well expressed by Winchester help to explain its early theological distinction from Unitarianism.

The frank recognition of sinfulness forgiven suggests the major strand of controversy surrounding Universalist doctrine, its alleged tendency to encourage moral laxity. Keenly sensitive to this problem, Winchester addressed it in *The Universal Restoration*. To the charge that "the doctrine of the Restoration tends to licentiousness," Winchester appealed to experience, arguing that "benevolence, meekness, humility, forbearance, forgiveness, charity, and all goodness" are the products of the sense of a universal restoration. It is, in short, a doctrine of love, and he turned to scripture to prove that "all the law is fulfilled in one word, even in this: thou shalt love thy neighbor as thyself." [12] The optimism of these early Universalists, sometimes so full as to stun us, reaches back to the fullness of the conversion experience itself. After such a moment, what place could be left for sin?

Just as evangelical religion and pietism have many common roots, so the Calvinist and evangelical forms of Universalism that Winchester developed merged at points with a pietistic version of Universalism best exemplified in the pietism of George de Benneville. He was one of the earliest preachers of Universalism in America, having moved to Germantown, Pennsylvania, in 1741 after a fascinating but harrowing career as a religious nonconformist in eighteenth-century Europe. His father had fled from France to England under religious persecution, and the younger de Benneville, who showed a passionate religious sensibility, returned to France to preach. There he was harassed by authorities and eventually condemned to the guillotine, receiving a reprieve even while his hands were being tied at the scaffold. Upon his release from prison, he went to Germany and was influenced by the general ferment of radical Protestantism there. He also established the connections with German pietists, notably the Dunkers, which led to his invitation to Pennsylvania as both preacher and physician. [13]

During his years in Philadelphia, Winchester came to know de Benneville well. It was de Benneville who had published Siegvolck's *Everlasting Gospel*, the book responsible for Winchester's conversion to Universalism. Winchester, in turn, oversaw the publication of de Benneville's spiritual autobiography. Nowhere is the pietistic and mystical strain of Universalist religion more clearly delineated than in this remarkable text. [14] In the tradition of the spiritual autobiography, de Benneville interpreted his own life in terms of an interplay of the grimmest spiritual doubt and epiphanal moments of release, with all other outward events rendered only as peripheral details. He was haunted in early life by a vision of himself "burning as a firebrand in hell" and came to the conviction that he was damned because his sins "were too many and too great to be forgiven" (p. 75). It was another vision, this of the mediating Christ praying for his soul, that altered de Benneville's sense of sure damnation. But in that vision he discovered not only his own salvation but that of others as well. He explained this faith in his account of his inquisition on religious matters by the French authorities, who almost executed him:

They asked me many questions, but we could not agree, for they held predestination, and I held the restoration of all souls; because having myself been the chief of sinners, and that God, through Jesus Christ, by the efficacy of his holy spirit, had granted me the mercy and the pardon of all my sins, and had plucked me as a brand out of hell, I could not have a doubt but the whole world would be saved by the same power. (p. 78)

Such a passage suggests why Winchester was drawn to de Benneville. Winchester's Calvinist evangelicalism and de Benneville's pietist mysticism merged in the stress of the powerful conviction of his sin, and the even more powerful experience of conversion seemed to argue for the universality of salvation. Both Winchester and de Benneville saw themselves as representative men, elevated to the status of a kind of Adam figure for the entire race. Curiously, this elevation is based in the degree of their sinfulness, which allowed for a correspondingly impressive sense of conversion. If the "chief of sinners" has been saved, all other souls will surely follow.

The shades of Universalist belief among Murray, Winchester, and de Benneville differ slightly, and the roads by which they arrived at Universalism also differ. But all of these early leaders of the movement remind us of the evangelical and pietistic roots of the denomination. One other significant intellectual stream, in part a product of the pietist mentality, must be examined for its contribution to the movement. The pervasive millennial orientation of eighteenth-century America—especially the America of the Revolutionary period—touched the Universalist movement deeply. It was no mere coincidence that political revolt and religious upheaval were occurring simultaneously in America, but it has taken some time for historians to recognize these complex connections. In a certain sense, though, the politics of a democratic Revolution and the theology of a universal salvation were inseparable. The millennialists expected a heaven on earth established by the hand of a righteous God, working through the power of a new democratic citizen in a new world. Even though this expectation was attuned to the here and now (or the here and soon to be), and was political in its orientation, it shared the essentially optimistic faith of the Universalists, who were sure of God's ultimate power and will to save. Although the millennialism that underlay the American Revolution in no sense required an accompanying belief in universal salvation and was in fact strong among the orthodox, its worldly optimism was very compatible with the other-worldly optimism of the Universalists.

Benjamin Rush is the figure who best illustrates this convergence of democratic millennial faith and theological Universalism. He is best known as a prominent physician of the colonial period, perhaps the most important early American doctor, but his career as a thinker was not exhausted by his achievements in medicine. He was passionate about Revolutionary politics and saw in the American Revolution a promise of a new age of democracy on earth, ordained by God, to be centered in the American republic. This notion was not unusual among Revolutionary thinkers, but Rush's theological reasons for holding it suggest that the American Revolution was a product of religious faith as well as enlightenment doctrine. For him the connection between a politics of universal faith in humanity and a belief in the eventual universal salvation of humanity was inevitable.[15] Thus he wrote Jeremy Belknap in 1791:

A belief in God's universal love to all his creatures, and that he will finally restore all those of them that are miserable to happiness, is a *polar* truth. It leads to truths upon all subjects, more especially upon the subject of government. It establishes the equality of mankind—it abolishes the punishment of death for any crime—and converts jails into houses of repentance and reformation.[16]

Thus the political ramifications of Universalism went beyond the position of the members of the movement as outsiders with regard to the established church. For many the implications of universal salvation were also radically democratic.

Rush was a parishioner and ardent admirer of Winchester and in some senses might be considered his convert, even though his mind was far too original and independent to have been persuaded by one man. Like Winchester himself, he began as a Calvinist but held those doctrines "without any affection" until reading John William Fletcher's arguments "in favor of the Universality of the atonement." Winchester's preaching, plus extensive reading in a variety of Universalistic writers—he mentioned Sir James Stonehouse, Paul Siegvolck, Jeremiah White, and Charles Chauncy—made him a confirmed Universalist, although he continued to recognize the inevitability of "future punishment, and of long, long duration."[17] Rush is a most complex thinker, and to generalize about him is to invite disaster. But his range of talents and his scientific bent are suggestive of the Enlightenment, and he himself recalled in his *Autobiography* that "Armenian [sic] principles" helped pave his way to Universalism. In this sense, he stands apart somewhat from the pietism of the early movement. Yet he also told Richard Price that his acceptance of universal salvation "is founded wholly upon the Calvanistical [sic] account . . . of the person, power, goodness, mercy, and other divine attributes of the Saviour of the World."[18] This is a Christology essentially unaffected by Enlightenment rationalism or theological liberalism of the sort characteristic of early Unitarianism. But it is a Christology that affirms, on the basis of scripture, doctrines of human equality and political democracy that are generally associated with the Enlightenment of America. Insofar as Rush's disposition to Universalism is rooted in a Calvinist and Christological sensibility, he is representative of the early phase of the movement. But as an Enlightenment philosopher and proponent of the essentially rationalistic thrust of the American Revolution, he is a forerunner of a Universalism that would develop with more emphasis on the rational as opposed to the emotional bases for Universalist belief. A man of change himself, he is also representative of the direction of change within the Universalist faith.

## THE WINCHESTER PROFESSION

The first phase of the Universalist movement was rooted in evangelical piety, even when we take note of the shadings of a somewhat different personality like that of Rush. This phase was eclipsed rather quickly in the early 1800s, however, by the leadership of Hosea Ballou,* the dominant figure in the history of the church. Ballou's Universalism was by no means void of piety or emotion, but its ambience was more rational. It was in fact closer to Unitarianism. Even though his preeminence as both an intellectual and organizational leader is indisputable, it did not end the continuing presence of an evangelical and pietistic current within the denomination, one that would take on a somewhat different character as time separated it increasingly from its orthodox origins. Yet the early phase of the movement left, in addition to the heritage of Murray and Winchester, a key document, the Winchester Profession, which did help to define the denomination.

The Winchester Profession was a brief summary of the Universalist creed adopted at the 1803 meeting of the New England Convention of Universalists, in Winchester, New Hampshire. It thus takes its name from the place of the convention, not from any association with the name of Elhanan Winchester. The creed, which is notable both for its brevity and generality, can be quoted in full:

*Article I.* We believe that the Holy Scriptures of the Old and New Testament contain a revelation of the character of God, and of the duty, interest and final destination of mankind.

*Article II.* We believe that there is one God, whose nature is Love, revealed in one Lord Jesus Christ, by one Holy Spirit of Grace, who will finally restore the whole family of mankind to holiness and happiness.

*Article III.* We believe that holiness and true happiness are inseparably connected, and that believers ought to be careful to maintain order and practise good works; for these things are good and profitable unto men.[19]

The revelation of the Bible, the final restoration of all souls, and the affirmation of good works were thus articulated as the basis of Universalism, but however brief, these points are revealing under close examination. The unequivocal biblical affirmation placed the movement squarely in the evangelical tradition, a significant point when we remember that the Unitarian biblical faith, although still strong, was starting to be influenced at the period by the rise of the higher criticism of the Bible. The second article, on universal salvation, really distinguished the denomination from other Protestant movements, but it should be noted that its language is general enough to include what would become later in the century the two variant interpretations of Universalism: restorationism, or the belief in limited future punishment, and "ultra-Universalism," the belief that there will be no punishment after death. The phrase "who will finally restore'' can be read as a reference to the restoration of all souls after death, only after they have endured a period of suffering. But it also leaves room for the ultra-Universalism that Hosea Ballou would eventually propound, because it does not specifically refer to any suffering after death. The third article is less a statement of creed than a polemical device to allow the exponents of universal salvation to rebut the charges of libertinism that their abandonment of hell seemed to imply. It is an inclusion that confirms the embattled stance of the Universalists.

The history of the Winchester Profession's formulation and adoption is even more complex than its textual implications. To follow the genesis of the creed, in fact, takes one into the very tangled history of the early organizational efforts of the Universalists. Having noted the reluctance among Unitarians to take steps toward an organized denomination, certain hesitations among the Universalists are easier to understand. Like the Unitarians, they valued the "universality" of their religious sentiments and therefore resisted the segregation of sectarianism. Moreover, the fierce independence of mind that in eighteenth-century America was necessary for holding of Universalist views was also fundamentally incompatible with the inevitable surrender of autonomy that any form of organization implied. Early Universalist associations were always insistent, therefore, that any organizing or assembling be done only for mutual support and encouragement. In this "highly individualistic style of collective life," they were careful not to endanger the independence of each local congregation or of the individual members within it.[20]

Such organizations as did evolve, however, might not have done so as quickly, or perhaps might not have come into existence at all, had it not been for the external pressure of what the Universalists referred to as "clerical oppression" from the established churches. This pressure took two primary forms. First, Universalist preachers were in doubtful legal status with regard to the performance of marriages, a situation that certainly undermined one of the essential pastoral roles. But more importantly, Universalist church members in New England were also in doubtful status on matters of taxation. There the established churches were supported by a tax on the entire township in which they were located, and exemptions from this tax often came only after difficult legal struggles—struggles that required the existence of an organized and recognized church to which the exempted member had to be contributing. It was therefore the battle against unfair taxation by the established churches, and the struggle for the separation of church and state in general, that spurred the Universalists to some form of organization, and eventually of creed, as set forth in the Winchester Profession.

The first call for Universalist organization came from John Murray, who in 1783 outlined plans for annual meetings of those holding Universalist views. In 1785 the first such meeting was held at Oxford, Massachusetts, with both Murray and Winchester taking leading roles in it. But the Universalists were a hard group to organize, and, as Marini noted, by 1790 "virtually no effective cooperation existed at all'' among New England Universalists.[21] The early efforts in New England were followed in 1790 by the formation of the Philadelphia Convention of Universalists, meeting in the city that was a cradle of early Universalism. Although there has in the past been some dispute whether the meeting at Oxford or the first Philadelphia Convention should be regarded as the first national Universalist Organization, Russell Miller has definitively labeled the Philadelphia Convention "the first national organization attempted by Universalists in America."[22] The earlier meeting at Oxford, although an important signpost of the growing Universalist identity, was more a local or regional gathering than a national attempt at organization. But aside from its claim to primacy, the Philadelphia Convention also generated, with the guidance of Benjamin Rush, two documents, a "Rule of Faith" and a "Plan of Church Government," which were important sources for the Winchester Profession and for the institutional shape of the denomination. The "Rule of Faith" was essentially the same as the Winchester Profession except that it contained a much more explicit description of each member of the Trinity and is, in impression, if not in fact, a more Christologically oriented document than the Winchester Profession. The outline for church government affirmed a rigorously independent congregational polity and explicitly provided that all matters on the faith and practice of its members be left to individual congregations.[23]

Despite the fact that it took the first steps toward national organization, the Philadelphia Convention ultimately failed of being the vehicle for national Universalist organization. Both the leadership and the membership of the growing movement shifted to New England, which remains the home region of Universalists to this day. In 1792, two years after the first meeting of the Philadelphia Convention, a New England group petitioned the Philadelphia Convention for permission to meet separately, largely for reasons of convenience. Thus the New England Convention of Universalists was formed, the group that would assume actual national leadership of the movement in the decades to follow. It was this group that adopted the Winchester Profession in 1803, streamlining the earlier "Rule of Faith" into a very durable document.

The Profession did not come without some debate, however, and the surviving accounts of that debate give us revealing glimpses into the ethos of the early Universalists. The primary issue of contention was not over points of doctrine but over whether any creed at all could be tolerated by those who had suffered so much from sectarianism in the past. The man who actually drafted the Winchester Profession, Walter Ferriss, remembered a discussion "carried on with decency and with great ingenuity on both sides." But Noah Murray, a Pennsylvania Universalist, and opponent of adopting any creed, stands out in the debate:

He said much on the subject, and enlivened his pleas by quaint similitudes, drawn from calves, bulls, half bushels, etc., in which I thought he displayed more wit than solid sense, and more pathos than sound reasoning. But as he was a venerable old preacher, a man of real natural abilities, and possessed in some degree of a winning address, he was followed immediately by a number of other brethren.[24]

Another participant in the convention, Nathaniel Stacy, filled in Ferriss's account with the following details:

Mr. Murray said, in allusion to the confession of faith, "It is harmless now—it is a calf, and its horns have not yet made their appearance; but it will soon grow older—its horns will grow and then it will begin to hook." Mr. [Zephaniah] Lathe arose and replied, "All that Br. Murray has said would be correct, had he not made a mistake in the animal. It is not a calf; it is a dove; and who ever heard of a dove having horns, at any age?"[25]

What was in Noah Murray's half-bushel may be lost to us now. But his stance as an opponent of any creed, an attitude shared by a good many others, represents an independence of mind that would not be lost even as the Universalists took on a more recognizably denominational exterior.

# 6
# UNIVERSALIST THEOLOGY AND DENOMINATIONAL GROWTH

## HOSEA BALLOU AND THE *TREATISE ON ATONEMENT*

In the winter of 1804–5, only slightly more than a year after the adoption of the Winchester Profession, Hosea Ballou* wrote *A Treatise on Atonement*, the most significant theological work in the history of American Universalism. If we take the Winchester Profession to be a summary of the conclusions of eighteenth-century Universalist theology, we can take Ballou's *Treatise* as the key to denominational thinking in the nineteenth century. It was a work with eighteenth-century roots, but the direction and force of Ballou's argument made the treatise durable, even considering the short lives of theological systems.

Part of the reason for the staying power of the work was that it pushed Universalist thinking in an entirely new direction, providing an even break with the Trinitarian and Calvinist-based theologies of John Murray,* Elhanan Winchester,* and Benjamin Rush.* In his introduction to a new edition of the work, almost a century after its first publication, John Coleman Adams characterized that change in this dramatic but accurate way: "Until Ballou penned its [the *Treatise*] pages, Universalism in America was only Calvinism with a new conclusion—the old orthodoxy with a heretical outcome."[1] What Adams's remark makes clear is that in essence Ballou's *Treatise* is a wholesale attack on Calvinism. Even though attacking Calvinism was not Ballou's exclusive object, nor was it even his named opponent, his fundamental purpose was to undermine what he believed was the basis of the entire Calvinist system, the notion of the vicarious atonement of Christ for the sins of humankind. Such atonement, according to the orthodox, reconciled an enraged God to sinful humanity, or at least to a portion of humankind, and therefore made salvation for some possible. Ballou's innovation to Universalist thinking was not that he rejected the salvation of an elect few and made Christ's death a universal atonement, as Murray and Winchester did in their different ways; it was that he rejected the entire concept of the necessity of a vicarious atonement to reconcile God to humankind. His system still included a concept of atonement but a radically different one.

Although Ballou's *Treatise* was undoubtedly his greatest single contribution to Universalism, his entire career as a preacher, pastor, and theologian augmented his influence.[2] It was as a preacher that he first made his name among the new sect of Universalists in the early 1790s, for at that time the Universalist gospel traveled almost exclusively through the spoken rather than the written word. When he was ordained by Elhanan Winchester in 1794, he had already achieved some reputation as a circuit-riding preacher in New England. He had little formal education and was rustic in both dress and diction, but in addition to having developed a commanding pulpit delivery, he also had developed a sharp argumentative skill that served him well in his frequent encounters with scoffers and doubters of his new doctrines. The fundamentals of the *Treatise*, as its tone suggests, accumulated during Ballou's many early encounters with the opposers of universal salvation, when he found it necessary always to be on the attack or on the defense.

His earliest "pastorate" was in Dana, Massachusetts (1794), but the difficult conditions under which he preached typify the struggle of the early Universalists. The church paid him to preach one Sunday a month, and he divided his remaining time between other churches, farming, and schoolkeeping. Still he continued his own theological studies, finding time during the 1790s to absorb the three principal strands of influence in the *Treatise*: the writings of Ethan Allen, Charles Chauncy,* and Ferdinand Olivier Petitpierre.[3] The very diversity of these strands—deism, Arminianism, and Petitpierre's quasi-pietistic determinism—suggests a strong mind at work in original ways. Ballou was making his own use of these aids to his education, using Allen to bolster his scorn for unquestioning orthodoxy, Chauncy to satisfy his doubts about scriptural interpretation, and Petitpierre to explain some nagging problems about the nature of sin. As he molded these influences together in the fire of his preaching, he also began to develop a taste for expounding his views in writing. In 1804 he published *Notes on the Parables of the New Testament*, interpretations of the parables with Universalist implications, and then moved immediately to his systematic exposition of Universalism in the *Treatise*.

Meanwhile his pastoral career took him to Barnard, Vermont (1803), where he ministered to a group of sister societies in the area; then to Portsmouth, New Hampshire (1809), and Salem, Massachusetts (1815); and finally, to Boston, where he found a permanent home as pastor of the Second Universalist Society. Ernest Cassara has amply detailed Ballou's rising career as a preacher, and it is important to note that his expanding influence and the growth of the denomination went hand in hand. The credit is far from exclusively his, but it is true that he provided leadership at a crucial time, when no other personality of such force arose. His influence became greatest during his pastorate in Boston, which he began after the death of John Murray (although not in Murray's old church), in a move that symbolized the already accomplished change of leadership and of theological emphasis within the Universalist movement since the turn of the century. Much earlier in his career (1798), Ballou had supplied Murray's Boston pulpit during his absence, preaching doctrine different enough from Murray's to cause Mrs. Murray to voice her concern publicly to the congregation. But Ballou, although a leader in the move to liberalism, was only one of many signs that the Universalists as a whole were moving away from Murray's Trinitarian Universalism.

The break from Murray can be seen from the outset of Ballou's *Treatise*, a prolonged argument against the "infinite" nature of sin. Ballou had taken dead aim at one of the major rhetorical ornaments of orthodoxy—the assertion that infinite sin against an infinite God required an infinite sacrifice, the death of Christ, or infinite suffering, everlasting torment in hell. Ballou's strategy was to deny the infinite nature of sin by pairing it against the infinite nature of God, which he heartily affirmed. If sin were infinite, it would render the design of God "abortive" and thus deny the infinite nature of God's will.[4] A proper appreciation of the idea of the infinite, therefore, makes infinite sin impossible in a universe formed by an infinite and benevolent God, "for goodness cannot be more than infinite, neither is there a degree for Deity to occupy above it" (pp. 4–5).

To clear such ground for himself, Ballou also had to enter uncertain ground by accepting the seemingly odd conclusion that God was the author of sin. If God's will were infinite, and the existence of finite sin a fact, then that sin had been part of the will of God.

God saw fit, in his plan of divine wisdom, to make the creature subject to vanity; to give him a mortal constitution; to fix in his nature those faculties which would, in their operation, oppose the spirit of the heavenly nature. . . . But perhaps the objector will say this denies the liberty of the will, and makes God the author of sin. To which I reply, . . . that God may be the innocent and holy cause of that, which, in a limited sense, is sin; but as it respects the meaning of God, it is intended for good. (pp. 24–25)

*Sin* is therefore redefined by Ballou as a limited, immediate evil but an ultimate good, a tool of God that, although divisive in the short run, helps to create the final unity of humans and God that is the cornerstone of the Divine wisdom.

It is at this point in Ballou's argument that its affinities with the thought of the eighteenth century become clearest, particularly with that often maligned brand of eighteenth-century optimism that argued that sin is necessary to ultimate happiness. Ballou by implication argued that the elimination of sin would not ultimately be a progressive step except in the final reconciliation after death. The fall of humankind, in other words, was fortunate. "If sin and guilt had never been introduced into our system, the plan of grace by atonement could never have been exhibited" (p. 56). As Ernest Cassara has demonstrated, the primary source of Ballou's view of sin and the fall was Petitpierre's *On the Divine Goodness*. Petitpierre, an exponent of this form of optimism, had argued that God's ultimate plan for the universe was "to render mankind universally and perfectly happy." This assumption of God's benevolence, when combined with a faith in his omnipotence, led him to the assurance that "this world, formed as it is, is best adapted to the end; an end most perfect and excellent; and that it was not possible to create us in the beginning as holy and perfect as we shall be hereafter."[5]

Moreover, Ballou took another striking position from Petitpierre, a thorough determinism, and argued it with some force in the *Treatise*. Petitpierre had inferred from God's omnipotence that God "can do in, and for me, every thing that is consistent with the nature and essence he has conferred upon me" (p. 37). Ballou also recognized that absolutely free will in humankind would indeed call God's omnipotence into question and wrote that humans are determined in their choices by the objects from which they must choose. Choice, in other words, is limited by options, options that are beyond the control of humans and are ultimately the product of God. The terms of the argument are actually close to those of the great American Calvinist Jonathan Edwards, an irony when one remembers the different ends to which each thinker put his determinist position.

The goal of Ballou's system is suggested by a portion of his argument in the *Treatise* in which he dwelt on the misery of sin. Ballou warned that sin, even if "finite," is still the principal cause of human misery. "In a word, sin is of a torment-giving nature to every faculty of the soul, and is the moral death of the mind" (p. 50). This stress on the evil of sin had a secondary purpose, in defending Universalism from the usual charges of its hospitality to sin. But in the structure of the *Treatise*, a just recognition of the misery of sin was a vital prerequisite to a just recognition of the nature of atonement. Ballou's delineation of that theory of atonement is the most compelling and original part of his work. He simply stood the orthodox system upside down with the pointed question, "Is God the unreconciled or dissatisfied party, or is man?" (p. 98). For the orthodox, the answer had always been God. But for Ballou and the Universalists, God's love was secure even through human sin, and the sacrifice of Christ was a demonstration of that love rather than an assuagement of anger. As he put it, "the atonement by Christ was the effect and not the cause of God's love to man" (p. 100). It was the dissatisfaction of humans, because of the evil of sin, that made atonement necessary, and in the ordinary but powerful language for which he is noted, he explained that "atonement and reconciliation are the same," both of them "a renewal of love." Atonement is therefore made by "the power of Christ," which "causes us to hate sin and love holiness" (p. 119). It is human love for God that is renewed in the atonement, not God's love for humans.

The implications of this idea of atonement were Unitarian, and Ballou explicitly called Christ "a created dependent being" (p. 111). To demystify the atonement process even further, he argued that "the literal death of the man, Christ Jesus, is figurative; and all the life we obtain by it, is, learning what is represented" (pp. 122–23). As Ballou saw it, the atonement was a process of reconciliation that was essentially moral. There are strong parallels between Ballou's version of the atonement and the developing Unitarian theories of salvation as character formation. Ballou's variety of Universalism was far different from the more Calvinistic versions of Murray and Winchester.

Ballou thought that this reading of the atonement corrected the prevalent error of seeing God as "an enemy to the sinner," bent on endless punishment for sin, a view "that renders his character infinitely inglorious and dishonorable" (pp. 126, 128). Ballou leveled particularly harsh criticism at Samuel Hopkins's version of Calvinism (although he did not call it by name), which held that the Christian should be prepared to accept the endless misery of hell in order to keep the justice of God consistent. Although Hopkins saw this requirement as a measure of the selfless disinterestedness necessary to holiness, Ballou argued that it made the Christian life self-contradictory: "I see so much beauty and divine excellency in the justice of God that I am perfectly willing to exist, to all eternity, in rebellion against it!" (p. 129). Here is the key to Ballou's thinking: hell is not merely a place of punishment but a state of rebellion against God and against the unity of humans and God. Heaven is the accomplishment of that unity. To argue for endless punishment would be to argue for a permanent, eternal division in the fabric of the cosmos, a dualism so monstrous that it would rout any claims of the omnipotence of God. Unless one were willing to abandon God's order in the universe—the furthest thing from the mind of Christian orthodoxy—Ballou insisted that one must accept the unity of the universe and the predominant power of God's plan in it. The "consequence of atonement," as he summarized, "is the universal holiness and happiness of mankind, in the final issue of the Redeemer's process" (p. 138). It was Ballou's firm faith that that process could not be altered.

## ANTEBELLUM UNIVERSALIST THEOLOGY

Despite Ballou's influence, he by no means established a hegemony over Universalist thinking in the period before the Civil War. Even though their battles with the Calvinists and evangelicals continued, Universalists found both reason and energy to argue among themselves. As is often the case, the points of dispute reveal as much about the movement as the points of agreement. Those disputes suggest that Universalism was primarily a movement in cautious and often painful transition from pietistic, evangelical, and biblical roots to a more liberal and rationally grounded faith. The Universalists were not the only movement to suffer this trial of change, for the early decades of the nineteenth century were turbulent for Protestant theology generally. But the Universalists were in a unique position. They had arrived at an extremely modern and challenging theological position, that of universal salvation, but had done so on essentially conservative and traditional grounds. Although their leaders could defend these positions with considerable sophistication, the Universalist congregant was likely to have adopted his or her views primarily because of revulsion at the idea of endless hell and a commonsense faith that no loving father would so torture his own children. Moreover, the biblical faith of the Universalists was deep but of a different order from that of the Unitarians, who were opening the way to modernism with their scholarly researches. Ballou was a powerful polemicist with scripture and a vigorous, if somewhat fanciful, interpreter of it. But he did not have the philological and historical expertise, or the inclination to acquire it, of a Joseph Stevens Buckminster* or an Andrews Norton.* As John White Chadwick* would later say of him, "he knew his one book, the Bible, as well as any man could know it who knew no other. . . . It was not by exegesis but by humanity that he prevailed."[6]

The most telling division in Universalist opinion in the early nineteenth century was known as the "Restorationist controversy," a dispute that went to the heart of the distinguishing tenet of Universalism.[7] Although all sides were agreed that there would be no *eternal* punishment for sinners after death, opinion was unsettled on the question of a limited punishment, followed by a general restoration to unity with God. The early leaders of the movement had taken this second, or Restorationist, position in the late eighteenth century. Winchester and Rush asserted unequivocally that hell would exist for the unrepentant, and they held, like Chauncy, that its very purpose *was* to cause repentance. Murray's views on the subject were more complicated and a good deal less clear, but he ascribed to punishment after death for those who did not *believe* in the accomplished fact of the union of Christ and humans. What came to be known as the "ultra-Universalist" position arose in the early nineteenth century, however, with Hosea Ballou as the chief proponent. Sin was not punished after death, according to his view, but during life itself, and there was accordingly no punishment afterward.

As Cassara noted, Ballou was uncertain about the doctrine of future punishment early in his career, tentatively endorsing a version of it in his published debates with Joel Foster (1799). His tendency to reject the notion of punishment grew during the early decades of the century, however, and was given further impetus in 1817 when he entered into a debate, or perhaps better, a cooperative discussion, with Edward Turner. Richard Eddy* reprinted the mannerly exchange of letters between Ballou and Turner that began the discussion, and it seems clear that a major dispute over future punishment was certainly not the intention of either man. Russell Miller has suggested that Ballou wanted primarily to revive Universalist thought and discussion in the journal *The Gospel Visitant*.[8] But the issue quickly went beyond what either man had imagined it might, partly because of the centrality of the doctrine to Universalist belief and partly because of certain personal conflicts. One "restless" and "contentious" Universalist minister, Jacob Wood, a strong upholder of the Restorationist position, was willing not only to extend the controversy but to push the denomination to the point of schism over it. Wood "was a man of some talents," Thomas Whittemore* noted wryly, "but unfortunately did not seem to have the power to labor for the things that make for peace."[9]

The debate grew from the *Gospel Visitant* (extant only in 1817–18) to the *Universalist Magazine*, increasing in sharpness until the late 1820s, when feelings ran high enough among some to split the denomination. Whatever the opinion of most Universalists, and there is some controversy on this point, most felt no need to leave the denomination. But discontent was high among some of the Restorationists, and a small group of ministers and laypersons banded together to form the Massachusetts Association of Universal Restorationists in 1831. Under the leadership of Adin Ballou,* a distant relative of Hosea, and Paul Dean,* the Restorationists met separately until 1841.

The ultimate impact of the Restorationist controversy on the Universalist denomination was small. The movement to secede seemed an extreme step for most Universalists, even those who held Restorationist views. As Russell Miller has noted, "scores of Universalists . . . if not the majority" felt comfortable in holding Restorationist views "without feeling either the necessity or the desirability of renouncing their Universalist ties."[10] The general consensus of Universalist historians, in fact, is that Restorationism did indeed become the dominant view of the denomination during the nineteenth century. The controversy retains a large place in Universalist history because of Ballou's role in it and because Ballou's disciple Thomas Whittemore, himself one of the major controversialists, believed it was so important. Moreover, the controversy is amply documented, having provided one of the most important occasions for written expression by early Universalists.

The controversy was central, however, to the development of Ballou's theological ideas, for in the course of it he came to firm opposition to the doctrine of punishment after death, even of a limited sort. As noted above, he had wavered on this question before, and he indicated a tendency to favor the doctrine of punishment when he proposed the exchange with Turner for the *Gospel Visitant*. "Though at first thought it might seem that the two who are to conduct this investigation, should be of opposite sentiments on the subject to be argued," he wrote Turner, "on more mature consideration a thought suggests itself, that the enquiry would be more likely to be kept free from improper warmth or injudicious zeal, were the parties of the same opinion, than if they were of opposite sentiments."[11] The implication is that Ballou knew Turner's position in favor of limited punishment and shared it, although he offered Turner his choice of sides. It was during this debate that, as Ballou later said, he "became entirely satisfied, that the Scriptures begin and end the history of sin in flesh and blood."[12] When the dispute expanded in the early 1820s to the *Universalist Magazine*, Ballou was a confirmed ultra-Universalist and leading thinker for that position within the denomination. Ballou's controversial writings on future punishment culminated in 1834 with the publication of *An Examination of the Doctrine of Future Retribution*. This work stands as Ballou's most important work after the *Treatise*, and it can be said to complete the theological system that the *Treatise* began.

The denial of suffering after death was accomplished in Ballou's system by his insistence on the natural and more immediate suffering that sin causes in life itself. He had taken that position in the earlier *Treatise*, and it was only an extension of that idea, and the reinterpretation of certain passages of scripture, that brought him to the stance against future punishment. The whole tendency of his theology had been naturalistic, and it was a logical step to insist on the natural evil of sin rather than supernatural punishment. Chadwick noted that Ballou's *Treatise* "anticipated the full-grown expression of Channing's thought on all its principal lines." But Chadwick's equation of Ballou's later stand against future retribution and the thought of Ralph Waldo Emerson* is even more revealing. Emerson expounded a law of "Compensation" (1841), which posited that "you cannot do wrong without suffering wrong." For Emerson, as for Ballou, it was an "immense concession" to assume "that the bad are successful; that justice is not done now."[13] As Ballou had earlier put much the same point, "the only fear which can be sure to prevent crime, is the fear of committing it; and therefore, that sin itself ought to be considered as the greatest evil, and the evil most to be dreaded."[14] Although Emerson was finally more naturalistic in his questioning of a personal Deity and his disregard for the Bible, it is testimony to Ballou's freshness to see his position in the light of thinkers such as Channing and Emerson. Ballou, however, never abandoned his commitment to a biblical basis for truth.

## THEOLOGY AND DENOMINATIONAL IDENTITY

As we have seen in tracing the development of Unitarianism, the identity of a rebelling sect is fragile. That fragility exists in large part because of the necessarily defensive posture that the movement requires and the sense of exclusion that such a posture brings with it, even when the "exclusion" is desired. The Universalists, even more than the Unitarians, faced this problem of identity. Their rejection of an endless hell was seen as even more radical than the Arminian positions of the Unitarians, and this theological radicalism was compounded by problems of legal status and of social class. Universalist theology not only served the function of religious speculation but also augmented the denomination's sense of identity. Because the Universalists' views on universal salvation often resulted in their exclusion from the Christian mainstream, any precedent for their views in the history of Christian thinking was a welcome source of confirmation.

Hosea Ballou 2d's* *Ancient History of Universalism* (1829) is most properly seen in this context of the denomination's struggle for identity. It was a work in which Ballou, a grandnephew of the elder Ballou, painstakingly traced the existence of Universalist ideas among the fathers of the early Christian church, finding precedent there for contemporary American Universalism.[15] Ballou's study had a polemical purpose, as did almost everything the early Universalists wrote, but its importance is perhaps greater when we consider the psychology of such historical thinking. Although the initial rebellion of a movement requires a certain disdain for history, as it is manifest in the tradition and authority of an established church or creed, the maturing of a denomination is inevitably accompanied by a yearning for history. The new path that has been struck seems easier to travel with a sense of precedent, and the deeper in the past these precedents can be found, the surer the sense of identity that the denomination forges. History functions as a kind of guarantor of universality, affirming the unquestionable humanity of a creed or movement. It is thus no surprise that Ballou's history had a strong impact on the Universalists' sense of themselves. The work was followed in 1830 by Thomas Whittemore's *Modern History of Universalism*, which had been planned as a companion volume to Ballou's. With the movement in America half a century old, the search for history had begun in earnest.

Although polemic in purpose, Ballou's book did not try to overemphasize the presence of Universalism in the early church. In fact, through A.D. 190, the first period he studied, he found "but few indisputable traces either of that doctrine [universal salvation], or of its opposite" (p. 19). This objectivity actually lends credence to his argument, for the reader comes to see eventually that the lack of a stress on endless punishment is as significant, if not more so, than the lack of an articulated Universalist position. The controversies over Universalism and the general acceptance of a doctrine of endless hell were later engraftments onto Christian history. Their historical relativity separates them, therefore, from essential Christian truth.

The relevance of this early period of Christianity to Ballou's contemporary world is brought out in an implied comparison between the modern Universalists and the early Christians. The "number of *professed* christians" was small, he wrote, and generally "composed . . . of the lower classes of people. The rich and the noble were, for the most part, attached to the ancient forms and institutions." Moreover, the Christian religion was "novel" and as a result "was not, indeed, very well understood by the public at large; nor did it escape considerable misrepresentations among its particular enemies" (p. 24). Surely it is not hard to read in this description the protest of the Universalists against social exclusiveness and entrenched power or the complaint that their religion was misrepresented by the orthodox as an invitation to debauchery without consequences.

The real father of Universalist thinking for Ballou was Origen, who in A.D. 230 published his *Of Principles* "in which he advocated, at considerable length, the doctrine of Universal Salvation" (p. 85). Before Origen's work, the general opinion of orthodox Christians was that there would be "a future state of suffering," but the idea was little pursued beyond that: "whether it were endless, or would terminate in annihilation, or whether it would result in a general restoration, were probably points which few inquired into" (p. 83). Origen's doctrine, as Ballou read it, grew out of his more general conception of the preexistence of all souls. All souls were created at once, before the creation of the material universe. Their embodiment was a kind of disciplinary state of existence, related to the possible degeneration that they underwent as a result of the exercise of their free will. But they remained equally free to develop their potential for good, and at length, all would find their way to restoration.

Curiously, Ballou found no evidence that Origen's Universalism was attacked from A.D. 254 to 390, even though his works had "the severest scrutiny" in that time (p. 147). Even when they attacked him, his critics did not object to his Universalism. Persecutions of Origenists did exist around A.D. 400, but they were less significant to the early fate of Universalism than the rise of Augustine as the leading theologian of early Christianity. As Ballou saw him, Augustine was "the father of the present orthodox system of total depravity, irresistible grace, and sovereign, partial election." This system, existing in Ballou's day as orthodox Calvinism, became "a more fatal check [on Universalism] than even the decision of a council would have imposed" (p. 256).

Why did such a system prove so decisive in arresting the growth of Universalism? The political power of those who supported it, and the enormous influence of Augustine, had some bearing on this. But Ballou also saw an intellectual reason at work involving the idea of a limited election to grace. If it was assumed, as Origen and many other early Christians had, that God wanted salvation for all, it was much easier to accept the idea that such salvation would be achieved. But if God was portrayed as wanting "to save a part, and a part only, and at the same time abandon the rest to certain and complete ruin, the doctrine of endless misery stood on its own proper and substantial foundation, the divine counsel" (p. 257). Ballou recognized that the idea of universal salvation was inextricably linked to the idea of God's benevolence and that election, in undermining the notion of his benevolence, made the idea of endless hell plausible. Thus in the early conflict of the ideas of Origen and Augustine, Ballou identified what he saw as the nature of the dispute between Universalism and Calvinism. The condemnation of Universalism by the Fifth General Council of the church in 553 was therefore an ecclesiastical coda to a theological turn of events that began with the use of the Augustinian system (p. 296).

The influence of Ballou's historical work can be seen in Thomas B. Thayer's* *Theology of Universalism* (1862), termed by Russell Miller "the most thorough and systematic treatment of Universalist theology before the Civil War." Thayer's aim was, indeed, for comprehensiveness and systematization, and he hoped to establish that "Universalism is not a confused collection of doctrinal fragments, . . . but a system of divinity."[16] He noted his indebtedness to Ballou's *Ancient History* in the text, quoting it often, and the sense of historical continuity established by Ballou complements well the theological unity for which he argued. Thayer himself had published an earlier work of historical theology, *The Origin and History of the Doctrine of Endless Punishment* (1858), in which he argued that Oriental, chiefly Egyptian, sources had been the point of origin for the doctrine of eternal damnation, and the doctrine was by implication a pagan corruption of the biblical tradition. His *Theology of Universalism* is strongly grounded in scripture, but its major premise is one shared by almost all Universalist writers—the benevolence of God precludes the possibility of endless punishment. "Everywhere the soul of man is reaching out toward a Deity, in Whom is embodied this perfection of wisdom and goodness, of justice and mercy" (p. 12). With this premise, Thayer could go on to argue that "Divine Justice adapts its punishment to the condition and needs of the offender, measuring them so exactly to the purpose aimed at, that no mistakes are ever made here" (pp. 81–82). Punishment for a purpose means punishment for reclamation, not retribution, and it thus excludes endless punishment as a possibility.

Like the elder Ballou and Petitpierre before him, Thayer entertained the idea of determinism, and although he was loath to deny human freedom of will, he placed the freedom of God before it. "In our anxiety to assert the freedom of man's will, we must not forget that God is free as well as man; free to choose, free to work. . . . But if a man can so abuse his freedom as to defeat the purpose of God, then God is not free; *he* cannot do as he pleases!" (p. 51). An individual is not free, in other words, to thwart God's will and go to an endless hell, for even sin itself, which Thayer recognized as the product of God, has a purpose that is ultimately educational. "This condition [the sinful world] was not ordained for its own sake . . . but as a means to a beneficent and glorious end, as a school wherein we are to be taught and trained for a higher sphere of life and action, both in the present and in the future" (p. 20). Most Universalists would have agreed with this doctrine of life as a probationary state whose end was spiritual education and character formation. It was a point of shared emphasis with the Unitarians (Thayer quoted Channing in the work) whose stress on cultivation of the soul was a version of this doctrine. By the end of the century this doctrine would in fact be shared by most American Protestants, a kind of hallmark for the modernist and Humanist tendencies of liberal theology. The work of Thayer and other Universalist and Unitarian theologians was not only beneficial to their denominations but was gaining a wider audience in American Protestantism as a whole.

Although the contributions of Hosea Ballou 2d and Thayer enlarged the discourse of Universalism in the early nineteenth century, Thomas Whittemore's more popular *Plain Guide to Universalism* (1840) is perhaps a more revealing source of information about the common concerns of the Universalist laity. Whittemore was the most prominent disciple of Hosea Ballou, converted to Universalism and led into the ministry by him. He staunchly defended Ballou's "ultra-Universalist" position in the denominational controversies, but perhaps his most important work was his constant publicizing of Universalist ideas, of which his *Plain Guide* is a good example.

In that work Whittemore defined *Universalists* very simply as "those who believe in the eventual holiness and happiness of all the human race, as revealed to the world in the Gospel of the Lord Jesus Christ."[17] The definition included those Restorationists who believed in limited future punishment, as well as those like Whittemore who thought that all punishment for sin was in this life. More than half of Whittemore's roughly three-hundred-fifty-page text is comprised of discussions of individual biblical texts, a fact that amply demonstrates how immersed the Universalists were in biblical sparring with the orthodox. As if that evidence were not enough, Whittemore avowed the Universalists' commitment to biblicism unequivocally: "The primary question with the Universalist is, *what has God revealed in his word?* To this standard we bow implicitly. The true sense of this book is the only true orthodoxy we know of" (p. 252). Thus it was the marshaling of supporting texts, and the refuting of those that suggested endless punishment, that drew much of the intellectual energy of the early Universalists.

Whittemore also devoted some discussion to the refutation of objections to Universalism, one of which was the inevitable fear that belief in the lack of an endless hell would be an invitation to sin. Here he articulated the position, which he derived principally from Ballou, that sin is indeed punished. That punishment, however, "is not delayed until the future existence, but . . . it is swift, sure, and inevitable; . . . sin goes hand in hand with woe throughout its whole duration; . . . it is itself *hell*, into which the sinner cannot plunge, without feeling its flames and torments" (p. 262).

Whittemore's fervor, and the general sense of pietism among the early Universalists, is revealed in the distinction he offered between "positive" and "negative" Universalists. The negative Universalists merely give the idea of universal salvation intellectual assent and are not moved into action by it. But what Whittemore hoped for was converts of the positive sort who "embrace the doctrine with a *living* faith." Such Universalists, as he described them, "not only believe it [Universalism], but they *feel* it; they love it; it is the meat and drink of their souls." This felt faith is perhaps the strand that links Universalists to the pietist strain in American Protestantism, where religion is a thing of the heart and not the head. That such feeling produces "a constant and ever-active desire that others may be brought to the knowledge of the truth" also suggests the connections between Universalism and the broader evangelical ethos of American Protestantism (p. 279). Alienated from that tradition by their rejection of the dogma of eternal hell, the Universalists still exhibited many of the same gestures of feeling and faith. Like the Unitarians, they were theological rebels, but in terms of religious sensibility, they retained for much longer than the Unitarians the emotional sensibility of evangelical Protestantism.

One of the best exemplars of this evangelical sensibility was Universalism's greatest missionary, Quillen H. Shinn,* a leader later in the nineteenth century. Shinn's roots were southern, and his style was that of a country evangelist. He preached the Bible (much of which he knew by heart), and as one hearer remembered, he "won his audiences by reciting Scripture rather than reading it." "While demolishing the endlessness of punishment," he continued, "he never failed to impress on sinners that there was no escape from punishment." [18] It is not surprising to find, then, that Shinn was skeptical of the currents of modernism in Universalism late in the nineteenth century: " 'Liberal Christian' is a term I do not use," he said. "I despise it because it usually means one who believes more in some heathen philosopher than in Christ" (p. 125). Much of this attitude arose from what Shinn perceived as the practicalities of church building and spreading the Universalist gospel, and he was caustic about young preachers who were too enamored of their intellectual gifts and their modern views:

I often wonder what they [young ministers] mean when they use Liberal Christianity as a substitute for Universalism. It needs defining. It may mean infidelity. It usually means nothing. It is a mirage. When we get to it it is gone. Brethren come down out of the vapors. Walking the milky way is unprofitable. Universalism is the great name and Universalist preaching is a great need in the Universalist church. (p. 117)

As his style was molded by evangelicalism, Shinn's labor for Universalism was evangelical as well. He took a number of pastorates in the 1870s and 1880s, many of which were church-building experiences, and became a full-time missionary in 1891, acting independently at first and later gaining some support from the Universalist General Convention. His talents and energies were distinctive, and his career makes clear the populist roots of Universalism.

# 7

# THE TRANSCENDENTALIST CONTROVERSY

---

## THE REJECTION OF SUPERNATURALISM

With his health in danger from overwork at Boston's Second Church, Henry Ware, Jr.,* obtained the help of a younger colleague, a personally shy but publicly eloquent young man, Ralph Waldo Emerson.* Emerson's father, William, had been an influential Boston pastor of the liberal school, and when he died (young Waldo was only eight), Joseph Stevens Buckminster* preached the funeral sermon. With Ware destined for the newly created chair of pulpit eloquence and the pastoral care at Harvard, in a mistaken attempt to find a less stressful vocation, Emerson was being groomed for the pastorate of a historic church, recently revitalized under Ware's dedicated and energetic pastorate. There Emerson was ordained in 1829, but by 1832, after the death of his young and beloved wife, Ellen, and a period of intellectual unrest, he resigned his pastorate and embarked for Europe. Whether or not his parishioners attributed the resignation to grief, they did know that Emerson had made what was to them an unacceptable demand: he had asked to be excused from administering the Lord's Supper. With some regret they had accepted his resignation, and it seemed that a promising pastoral career had come to an abrupt end.

In fact Emerson's resignation was only the beginning of his new career as lecturer, essayist, and poet, a career that brought him to be the fountainhead of American literature. But his resignation also signaled the stirrings of a movement of rebellion within the Unitarian denomination, called by its supporters the "new views" or "absolute religion" and by the opposition "Transcendentalism" or, more bluntly, "infidelity." Transcendentalism became the popular (and confusing) label for the movement whose fundamental ideas Emerson would later insist were "the very oldest of thoughts cast into the mould of these new times."[1] To some Unitarians the ideas were instead new and dangerous, and their willingness to comment on those dangers in forceful terms caused the

Transcendentalist controversy. It was more than just another of New England's theological disputes. Part of its importance is attributable to the stature of Emerson and to a lesser extent to individuals of the ability of Theodore Parker,* George Ripley,* Orestes Brownson,* Frederic Henry Hedge,* and James Freeman Clarke,* all Transcendentalists of great accomplishment and influence. These essentially religious leaders were joined by literary talents such as Henry David Thoreau, Margaret Fuller,* and Jones Very to create an epoch of central importance to American literary history. But a further importance has been argued by Perry Miller, who saw in the movement a reflection of "a crisis of the spirit and of the nation."[2] To Miller, the Transcendentalists represented idealistic youth in revolt against materialistic age, a drama that has been repeated frequently in American life. The Transcendentalists gave a uniquely forceful expression to that revolt.

Miller made another point of importance about Transcendentalism when he pointed out that the movement was primarily "a religious demonstration."[3] Noting the general lack of cohesion among the group, he argued that the one unifying factor among them was an aversion to the Unitarianism they knew in their youth. Miller insisted on this interpretation in part as a corrective to an excessively literary sense of the movement, flowing out of an increasing interest in the poetic achievement of Emerson and Thoreau. It was an important corrective, one that has since set the tone of Transcendentalist historiography. It was, in fact, more important than Miller probably knew, because its upshot has been to call into question Miller's fundamental assumption of a "revolt" or "rebellion" by suggesting a continuity between Unitarianism and Transcendentalism that is often overlooked in the descriptions of the conflicts between them. His sense of the religious nature of Transcendentalism carries the implication that the Transcendentalist controversy, although it had many larger implications, was at bottom a Unitarian dispute. It was in fact a cluster of several distinct disputes, each triggered by a provocative text, a challenging articulation of the new views that in the eyes of the conservative Unitarians demanded a rejoinder. Ripley, Emerson, and Parker in turn were the authors of the controversial texts, and in each case their argument had specific reference to central questions within the current Unitarian discourse. Emerson's and Parker's texts were also addresses delivered at ceremonial occasions within Unitarianism, further dramatizing the conflict. Emerson's Divinity School Address (1838) was delivered before a graduating class of young men trained for the Unitarian ministry at Harvard Divinity School, and Parker's *Discourse on the Transient and Permanent in Christianity* (1841) was delivered as the sermon for Charles Shackford's ordination.

But these two major Unitarian manifestoes were preceded by a somewhat less dramatic, but nevertheless important review article by George Ripley. Ripley had been a student of Andrews Norton* and shared Norton's concern with questions of biblical accuracy and authority, although his studies in the early 1830s were to take him far beyond the position of Norton on the importance of the biblical miracles. In 1836 Ripley reviewed the English Unitarian James Martineau's *Rationale of Religious Enquiry* for the *Christian Examiner*, the foremost Unitarian journal of the day and one in which Norton had had a major role since its inception. The position as organ of Unitarian opinion gave its contents a large role in denominational definition and identity—at least it did so in the eyes of many, including Norton. So when Ripley broached ideas that seemed dangerous to Norton, their appearance in the *Examiner* only exacerbated the problem. Norton's attack on Ripley, which is analyzed below, was, as William Hutchison saw it, a protest not only against his ideas but against their vehicle of expression. Norton believed he was defending the Unitarian name as well as criticizing false ideas.[4]

We can surmise that the "danger" of Ripley's comments in the review was related to the inflammatory power of his rhetorical attack on the "prevailing systems of theology": "It is hard to imagine a study more dry, more repulsive, more perplexing, and more totally unsatisfactory to a scientific mind, than theology, as it is presented in the works of by far the larger part of English writers on the subject." This was no attack on Norton or his theology by name, but it was an attack by implication, and Norton was shrewd enough to realize it. It was an expression of restlessness and a plea for nourishment that was not being provided by the established thinkers. "It is no wonder," Ripley continued, "that the heart is pulverized, that the freshness of life is exhausted, under their influence."[5] Norton responded to this and later attacks, notably in Emerson's Divinity School Address, with real fury. But as Ripley's language here reminds us, there was emotion on both sides.

If Ripley's attack on the "prevailing systems of theology" was an oblique attack on Unitarian thinking at the time, his indictment of Christian "mythology" was a more direct challenge to Norton and to the supernatural rationalism of established Unitarianism. He characterized the development of human thought as a process of "purification" in which theology lagged far behind: "Astronomy has been separated from astrology, chemistry from the search after the philosopher's stone, medicine from the incantations of magic; but between theology and mythology, a sharp line of distinction yet remains to be drawn" (p. 130). This set of polarities associated theology with superstition and primitive ignorance, but more directly, it touched a raw nerve in theological discourse, the validity of the supernatural elements of the Bible, especially the miracles of the New Testament and the resurrection and divine nature of Christ. If mythology included the supernatural aspects of primitive religion, might it not include also the supernatural elements of Christianity? Did purification mean a reduction of Christianity to pure naturalism? Ripley was not prepared to go this far yet, but this was certainly the direction of his thought.

What was clear was that Ripley was completely unwilling, however, to use the reports of supernatural acts such as miracles as a basis for Christian faith. He argued instead that a belief in miracles depends on faith and not faith on a belief in miracles. "If, then, a firm faith in Christianity may be cherished independently of miracles; . . . and if there be great difficulties in the proof of miracles, without a previous conviction of the divine authority of him who is said to exhibit them, we hold it be an unsound method to make a belief in them the essential foundation of Christian faith, or the ultimate test of Christian character" (p. 131). Even though Ripley went on specifically to note that he had "not been inclined to controvert the truth of the Christian miracles," his attitude rendered them a largely irrelevant side issue in theological thinking and in religious faith (p. 131). In minimizing the importance of miracles, he had rendered Norton's entire critical enterprise futile.

Norton responded with a letter to a Boston newspaper impugning Ripley's scholarly competence, hardly the best grounds on which to do battle. But the battle was on, spurring Ripley to expand his views in more detail in *Discourses on the Philosophy of Religion* (1836). That same year Emerson, who had by now launched a career as a lyceum lecturer, published his first book, *Nature*. Emerson did not here concern himself with the question of miracles, but it can be said that his entire procedure rendered them irrelevant. He developed his argument out of the context of eighteenth-century natural theology but expanded that tradition with an element of quasi-mystical religious experience and an idealism gauged toward his overriding concern with moral development. Out of this amalgam Emerson extracted a theory of "correspondence" in which nature and the mind are seen to be reflective versions of each other, each in turn reflecting the universal mind of God. This correspondence of nature and mind had its moral uses, especially in its suggestion of the dynamic and evolving character of the soul. In a system such as Emerson's, it was the ordinary course of nature that was endowed with divine significance, and a supernatural miracle was simply an intrusion on this process. A belief in miracles was not only unnecessary but obstructive to the religious life.

*Nature* was a controversial book, attracting criticism from another of Harvard's Unitarian spokesmen, Francis Bowen.* Because it existed not only in the realm of theological discourse but also as a statement of secular philosophy and even more importantly as a poetic effusion, the work was not as central to the controversy within the Unitarian camp as his Divinity School Address two years later. Here the occasion, an address before Divinity School graduates groomed for the Unitarian ministry, was all-important. Not only did Norton sense the public importance of such an address and measure out his public censure accordingly, but Emerson did as well, being keenly sensitive to social and political nuances despite his disdain for the social world. A few months before the address he recorded in his journal a meeting with some Divinity School students "who wished to talk with me concerning theism." Emerson's growing denial of the fatherlike, personal God of Christianity, still dear to most Unitarians, was coming to be well known by now, and he had some hesitation to enter dialogue on this sensitive topic.

I went rather heavy-hearted for I always find that my views chill or shock people at the first opening. But the conversation went well & I came away cheered. I told them that the preacher should be a poet smit with love of the harmonies of moral nature: and yet look at the Unitarian Association & see if its aspect is poetic. They all smiled No. A minister nowadays is plainest prose, the prose of prose. He is a Warming-pan, a Night-chair at sick beds & rheumatic souls; and the fire of the minstrel's eye and the vivacity of his word is exchanged for intense grumbling enunciation of the Cambridge sort, & for scripture phraseology.[6]

Emerson was politic enough not to make his language this inflammatory in his public address the next July, and in fact the reader who goes to the text of the speech expecting to find the basis of controversy will be puzzled at first to find only Emerson's praise of the "refulgent summer" and his unassailable commendation of the religious sentiment. But the audience left the address with other words echoing in its collective mind: "I think no man can go with his thoughts about him, into one of our churches, without feeling that what hold the public worship had on men, is gone or going. It has lost its grasp on the affection of the good, and the fear of the bad" (CW, I, 88). This was more than just a sociological observation; it was an indictment of the clergy from which Emerson had withdrawn. Any doubt about that was confirmed by the remark that "tradition characterizes the preaching of this country; that it comes out of the memory, and not out of the soul; that it aims at what is usual, and not what is necessary and eternal" (CW, I, 87). In a frank indictment of his colleagues, all the more searing because it was aimed at a generation coming to take a place among them, he admitted, "On this occasion, any complaisance, would be criminal, which told you, whose hope and commission it is to preach the faith of Christ, that the faith of Christ is preached" (CW, I, 84).

To this direct challenge both to the competence and faith of the Unitarian clergy Emerson added certain doctrinal remarks that came to be the controversial focus of the address, even though we may suspect that the remarks on Unitarian preaching may have burned more deeply at the moment. Expanding on the position he had developed in Nature, he rejected the biblical miracles in strong words: Jesus "spoke of miracles; for he felt that man's life was a miracle. . . . But the very word Miracle, as pronounced by Christian churches, gives a false impression; it is Monster. It is not one with the blowing clover and falling rain" (CW, I, 81). Monster is an accurate term from Emerson's perspective in that it denotes a departure from nature, but its graphic and pejorative qualities made it more than an expression of dissent on an abstract theological issue. Moreover, Emerson added to this attack on miracles a denial of the personal authority of Jesus. Although there was much of praise and reverence for Jesus in the address, Emerson also warned against worship of his person rather than his principles: Christianity "has dwelt, it dwells, with noxious exaggeration about the person of Jesus. The soul knows no persons" (CW, I, 82). To have suggested that any reverence for the person of Jesus could be "noxious" was to court attack. Emerson appeared later to show genuine surprise at the controversy he stirred and was unwilling to engage directly in the debate that followed. Having made his point, he preferred to move on. But the

Divinity School Address marks the point at which the rift between the two parties of Unitarianism became unbridgeable. It was not only Emerson's arguments but the power of his language—both to inspire and to enrage—that widened the chasm to such extremes.

Norton responded with a blistering assault on all forms of "The New School in Literature and Religion" that is remarkable both for its unabashed anger and the breadth of its targets. After a wholesale indictment of almost the entire Romantic movement, he singled out Emerson's address less for doctrine than for its "ill-judged and indecorous" language.[7] Norton the linguist was ever aware of the nuances of phraseology, and Emerson's slighting of the clergy, as we have seen, was by no means overly subtle. But Norton feared more deeply the poetic license with which Emerson approached sacred subjects. "The words God, Religion, Christianity, have a definite meaning, well understood. . . . We well know how shamefully they have been abused in modern times by infidels and pantheists; but their meaning remains the same; the truths which they express are unchanged and unchangeable" (p. 196). To appreciate the above passage, we must imagine the sneering weight that *infidel* and *pantheist* carried in the 1830s; we must also sense the alarm that plays just under the surface of the confident assertions of Norton. There is an implied plea for support in his insistence on the solid and commonly understood meaning of the very abstractions—God, religion, and Christianity—that Emerson and Ripley were redefining so radically. Norton was alarmed, because he understood that Emerson's whole strategy was simply to alter the shape of the discourse by redefining the whole theological enterprise. Feeling the ground move under him, Norton was grasping for life. His major counterattack, a discourse before the Divinity School alumni in 1839, attempted to expose *The Latest Form of Infidelity*. Less centered on language than doctrine this time, it defined that infidelity as the denial of "the miracles attesting to the divine mission of Christ." Those miracles he deemed necessary because of his conviction—and here was the philosophical kernel of the dispute—that a person "cannot pretend to attain, by his unassisted powers, any assurance concerning the unseen and the eternal, the great objects of religion" (pp. 210–11). To Emerson, and to a greater or lesser extent his Transcendentalist followers, the intuition of the soul was the only possible source of any religious knowledge.

It was on different grounds that Emerson's address was answered by his once senior colleague at the Second Church, Henry Ware, Jr. Ware was concerned less about the question of miracles than what he saw as Emerson's abandonment of a personal God for an abstract concept. His sermon *The Personality of the Deity* argued that a sense of a fatherlike God was essential to religious faith and human morality. Ware's talent for persuasion is clear in the sermon, especially in his emotionally charged comparison of an individual without belief in a personal God to a child raised without parents in the impersonal institution of an orphanage. Yet even Ware's invitation to respond to the sermon could not move Emerson into direct controversy. Already set on a new career as lecturer and essayist, he would not allow himself to be distracted from what he saw as the more important work that pressed him.[8]

If Emerson believed his mission was beyond the church, many of his followers did not, and their persistence within the Unitarian denomination permanently altered it. Even though he had denounced the clergy as it stood, Emerson himself had advised the young Divinity School graduates to remain within the church to breathe new life "through the forms already existing" (*CW*, I, 92). Theodore Parker, who heard the speech with great satisfaction, took Emerson's call to heart, and his determination to pursue Transcendentalist ideals within the institutional framework of the Unitarian church led to a further crisis in the controversy. Parker's crisis in fact was perhaps more significant for Unitarianism itself, precisely because it forced an evaluation of the denomination's identity.

## THEODORE PARKER: TRANSCENDENTALISM WITHIN UNITARIANISM

In the 1830s and 1840s Parker began to distinguish himself for radical views in three areas: biblical criticism, theology, and politics. His early interest, and one that he never abandoned, was scriptural study. In his intense study of biblical history and languages, which began at Harvard, he came to doubt direct inspiration of the scriptures and other positions held by the orthodox. Committed firmly both to the moral life and to religious experience, he found less and less support for his faith in the Bible. As a result he was pushed toward a more naturalistic view of religion, a perspective that allowed him to hold on to what he thought was the valid core of Christianity while discarding the unnecessary and often obtrusive trappings of the church. His complaint, like Emerson's, was against "historical religion," and he crystalized these views in the enormously controversial sermon *The Transient and Permanent in Christianity*. Although Parker admitted that "religious forms may be useful and beautiful," he believed that "an undue place has often been assigned to forms and doctrines, while too little stress has been laid on the divine life of the soul, love to God, and love to man."[9] Those forms and doctrines were the transient things of Christianity; "the divine life of the soul" and its manifestations in "love to God, and love to man" were the permanent things. Stated thus abstractly, there seems little that is objectionable in Parker's view. Even after he had spelled out the details in the sermon at an ordination service attended by a good many Unitarian ministers, there seemed to be no alarm within the denomination. Parker insisted that doctrines and systems of theology were the most transient things of religion: "nothing changes more from age to age than the doctrines taught as Christian, and insisted on as essential to Christianity and personal salvation" (p. 122). But in these doctrines he included the sacred authority of the Bible and the divine nature of Christ; thus he entered controversial ground. The doctrines "have nothing to do with Christianity except as its aids or its adversaries;

they are not the foundation of its truths." In a further linguistic distinction, he called such issues "theological questions, not religious questions" (p. 131). For Parker, theology was transient, religion permanent. The object of his preaching was to direct his listeners to the "absolute value" of religion, which "never changes" (p. 146).

In perhaps the most forceful and, to many, shocking passage of the work, he showed how dispensable the notion of a divine Christ was to him:

If Jesus had taught at Athens, and not at Jerusalem; if he had wrought no miracle, and none but the human nature had ever been ascribed to him; if the Old Testament had forever perished at his birth,—Christianity would still have been the Word of God; it would have lost none of its truths. It would be just as true, just as beautiful, just as lasting, as now it is; though we should have lost so many a blessed word, and the work of Christianity itself would have been, perhaps, a long time retarded. (p. 131)

Parker's insistence that systems and doctrines were inconsequential justified the Unitarian rejection of Calvinism and the liberals' struggle for more modern views of the Bible. This perhaps helps to explain the lack of immediate criticism that his sermon drew. But to suggest the potential equivalence of the pagan Greeks and Jesus was to take a step too far. Still, Parker's daring might not have sparked open controversy had not three non-Unitarian ministers, with more conservative views, published the gist of the sermon in several orthodox journals. As Conrad Wright noted, they wanted "to smoke out the Unitarians and find out whether Parker would be disavowed by his fellow liberals," and all in all, they succeeded admirably.[10]

Parker's fate in the aftermath of the sermon has been amply narrated. In an 1843 meeting of the Boston Association of Ministers, an essentially Unitarian body, he was asked directly to withdraw because of his theological views, particularly his rejection of the miracles and the divinity of Christ. Parker saw the issue as one of free speech and refused to withdraw because of his passionate dedication to the ministry. Unable to persuade him to withdraw and unwilling to force him out, the association let the matter drop, leaving it to individual pastors to refuse to exchange pulpits with Parker if they found his theology dangerous. A good many of them did refuse, and Parker, still adamant in retaining his Unitarian identity, became something of a martyred outcast and, as a result, a hero of conscience and freedom in Unitarian history. Perry Miller's shrewd analysis of the whole episode, although taking note of a certain relish that Parker had for the role of martyr, attributed a large significance to the episode as a test of the American liberal tradition. Parker challenged the liberals' commitment to the ideal of noncreedal thought and open expression, grounds that underlay their own revolt against Calvinism. If liberalism passed this test, however narrowly, by refusing to excommunicate Parker, Parker also demonstrated what Miller termed the "concealed terror within the assurance of progress," the self-devouring nature of an impulse that must always destroy itself to go beyond itself.[11] Parker had taken the tools handed to him in the liberal tradition—the use of reason in biblical interpretation and skepticism about dogmatic systems of theology—and had used them against that very tradition. He was in fact extending liberal principles, but he found himself at odds with the liberals and threatened by the very system that had nurtured him. By going beyond the intellectual boundary of many of his colleagues, he found himself alone and felt his isolation keenly. "Nothing is secure but life, transition, the energizing spirit," Emerson wrote, which is to say that change itself is the only permanence (CW, II, 189). Parker embodied that energizing spirit, but his own mixture of assurance and insecurity suggests the high price it exacted. The energy that he had to muster to reject and even attack the very tradition that nurtured him had to be more than matched with the energy to declare himself still part of that tradition.

If Parker embraced the Unitarians, it cannot be said that they returned the compliment. Although they did not exclude him from fellowship, he "suffered nearly complete ostracism from his Unitarian colleagues because of his theological views."[12] The Parker episode sent shockwaves through the denomination and even moved the American Unitarian Association (AUA) to flirt with creedalism. In 1853 AUA adopted a declaration affirming among other things a belief in "Jesus Christ, the everlasting Son of God, the express image of the Father, in whom dwelt all the fulness of the God-head bodily, and who to us is the Way and the Truth and the Life." But the statement, although officially adopted, was for the most part forgotten later in the century.[13] The statement represented less a desire to enforce a rigid doctrine than an attempt by most Unitarians to disassociate themselves from Parker's heresies.

## THE SOCIAL CONTEXT OF TRANSCENDENTALISM

Underlying Parker's theological struggle was a political one, and although he was one of the more dramatic of the political reformers, the political question itself permeated the entire Transcendental movement. If it was a "religious demonstration" and a phase of Unitarian development, the movement also had an inextricably political element that colored both of these other parts of its character. Transcendentalism stands at the turning point in American life when moral questions began to resolve themselves into political ones.

John White Chadwick* noted the more than coincidental fact that Parker preached his first sermon against slavery in 1841, the year of his sermon *The Transient and Permanent*.[14] That overlapping of religious and theological radicalism emphasizes the way that the "new views" of Transcendentalism reached into politics as well. Slavery and its abolition, finally including the Civil War, became the dominant political issue of Parker's day. Just as it divided the country, it also divided the Unitarian denomination. One of the first significant antislavery tracts was Lydia Maria Child's* *Appeal in Favor of That Class of Americans Called Africans* (1833), which helped move William Ellery Channing* to throw his influence into the antislavery cause. Channing's *Slavery* (1835) signified his entry into that cause, but his views, which alienated Unitarian conservatives, failed to satisfy the radical abolitionists. Channing's development in the late 1830s and early 1840s from cautious criticism of slavery to more radical condemnation of it was painful for him, given his general distaste for politics. While O. B. Frothingham* attributed his general caution to the "dictates of natural feeling and Christian charity towards the masters," Andrew Delbanco more convincingly found its source in the more complex refusal of Channing to externalize evil through the antislavery cause.[15]

For Parker, a farm boy whose milieu was far from aristocratic, the slavery issue was more pressing. He and Channing stand as representatives of different strands of antislavery that Conrad Wright discerned among Unitarian ministers—the immediate abolitionists, influenced by William Lloyd Garrison, and the gradualists, disturbed by slavery but distanced for a number of reasons from abolitionist politics. Another more cautious and conservative group also existed among the Unitarians who opposed slavery but were even more reluctant to make the political commitment to stop it.[16] These divisions within the denomination reflected its history and social position. As a denomination of the more prosperous, the Unitarians had much interest in social order and stability. But the New England conscience, so much a part of the movement's history, militated against that conservatism when it faced the repugnant immorality of slavery. Finally, the call for self-cultivation and moral growth that was the theological distinction of the movement lent itself readily to the appeal to uncompromised human freedom and dignity that the antislavery movement embodied. When northern sentiment was generally enraged after the Fugitive Slave Act of 1850, Unitarian opposition to slavery was pushed into its most active phase. When fugitive slaves legally had to be returned South under the provisions of the law, the issue confronted northerners most explicitly, for here they felt direct complicity in the sin. "This is not meddling with other people's affairs," Emerson wrote in his journal. "This is other people meddling with us." He called it a "filthy enactment" and added, "I will not obey it, by God." In one of the most dramatic cases, Parker and the young Unitarian radical Thomas Wentworth Higginson* were involved in a failed attempt of civil disobedience in 1854 when the escaped slave Anthony Burns was captured in Boston and returned into slavery. Both Parker and Higginson were indicted, but not convicted, for their part in the incident.[17] The strife surrounding the whole slavery question made Parker an even more controversial figure than his theological positions had already done.

Although slavery was undoubtedly the great political question of the time, the era was marked by a general social upheaval, a questioning of all settled political views and classes. The Transcendentalists were on the cutting edge of these reforms as well, because Emerson's call for the full development of the latent divinity of the individual often found itself on a collision course with the political establishment. Orestes Brownson, who became Unitarian under the influence of William Ellery Channing, but ultimately converted to Catholicism, tried to push beyond the doctrines of self-culture of Channing and Emerson to an analysis of American society that posited class conflict and fundamental economic inequity as basic problems. Channing's nephew William Henry Channing* criticized Emerson directly for lacking a broad enough interpretation of self-culture and redefined the concept to mean the development of humanity in a collective sense. He had gained early experience in the ministry-at-large in New York, following Joseph Tuckerman's* example in Boston, and continued efforts toward social reform by preaching a form of Christian socialism aimed at communal reorganization of society.[18]

George Ripley was perhaps the most notable of the Transcendental social reformers in the 1840s because of his leadership in the famous communal experiment at Brook Farm. Ripley hoped that a community "would permit a more simple and wholesome life, than can be led amidst the pressure of our competitive institutions."[19] Based on an ideal of self-development secured through a social setting that combined manual and mental labor, the experiment embodied the highest ideals of Transcendental social reform—unless one counts Thoreau's commune of one at Walden Pond. In a strict sense Brook Farm was a failure, because it did not remain a permanent way of life for its members, collapsing after an existence of five years. But its fame while it existed, and growing fame since, attest to its importance as an act of social criticism if not an accomplishment of social reform.

The three decades before the Civil War also saw the flowering of the movement for women's rights, which partook of the same general air of reevaluation and reform. If the general goal of self-development gave impetus to the antislavery cause, it had an explosive effect on women for much the same reasons. Here the ideal of self-development bumped into the iron restrictions of custom, legal inequalities, and male self-interest, forcing both a philosophical rethinking of the sex roles and a political assertiveness to try to change them. Julia Ward Howe,* the author of "The Battle Hymn of the Republic" and a leader in the suffrage movement after the war, was brought into sympathy for abolitionism through hearing the sermons of Parker. Parker was also a supporter of the women's movement, and although not entirely without masculine biases, as she portrayed him, he was "the first minister who in public prayer to God addressed him as 'Father and Mother of us all.' "[20] Emerson's coeditor on the Transcendental journal the *Dial*, Margaret Fuller, made the chief theoretical statement of American feminism in a *Dial* article that was expanded into *Woman in the Nineteenth Century* (1845), a work that convincingly compared women under the existing social circumstances to slaves. Fuller also led a notable series of "Conversations" for women in Boston in the 1840s that aimed to bring women's intellectual powers into open exercise and display. American feminism lost a powerful voice when Fuller died in a tragic shipwreck in 1850. Her work is discussed in Chapter 10. Elizabeth Palmer Peabody* was less radical in her feminist views than Fuller, or at least did not articulate them as directly, but she served as an example in Unitarian circles and among the Boston literati of, to adjust Emerson's phrase, "Woman Thinking." Her mentor was William Ellery Channing, whom she served as secretary and intellectual confidante, and she also had a close relationship with Emerson and the Transcendental educator Amos Bronson Alcott. Her great skill was her ability to serve as a conduit of people and ideas.[21]

It is not difficult to see in the reforms of the antebellum period the same political issues that continue to face us. It is also true that the ideology underlying these changes still persists: the quest for personal development and satisfying social relationships and for a society that will make that development possible. In other words, we live today with the issues that rose to the surface in the ferment of Transcendentalism. The breadth of these issues takes us beyond the scope of Unitarian institutional history, but that very fact argues for the central importance of the battles being fought within it. Certainly, it affirms Perry Miller's sense that Theodore Parker's fight was America's as well, that the agony of the Unitarian denomination in the 1840s was also that of American liberalism as a whole. The war into which almost all of the energies of the antebellum period eventually flowed had a profound impact both on those reform movements and on the Unitarian denomination itself. Organization, self-definition, and the nature of liberal faith all pressed Unitarianism with redoubled urgency in the late 1860s and 1870s. At that point, Unitarianism entered a new phase of its development.

# 8
# LIBERAL RELIGION
# AT MIDCENTURY

## THE "SUSPENSE OF FAITH"

With the Civil War the course of American society changed drastically. Into that war much of the crusading idealism of the immediate postwar period was poured, and as "The Battle Hymn of the Republic" reminds us, that contest was seen by many as a holy war. But when we consider the "Gilded Age" of political corruption and the robber barons after the war, it is easy to suppose the war was a sink into which much of the nation's moral energy flowed, to return, if at all, only much later in the century. The details of the protracted debates over ethics, theology, and politics in postwar America belie this assumption, but there is unquestionably a change of course in American culture at midcentury—a point at which American idealism had to seek new grounds for itself and therefore take on new forms. The recent historiography of the period has also interpreted the Civil War as more than the preservation of the political union of the states. The war was both caused by and in turn helped to cause a powerful ideological consensus. It was, for the North at least, a culminating episode in the American myth, and it therefore submerged reforming idealism into the larger cause of the destiny of the nation.[1]

Unitarianism was profoundly affected by these changes. Abolitionism had struck its deepest roots in New England soil, and Unitarians had their share of leadership in that movement, even though the denomination as a whole was far from radical on the slavery issue. The fact was that some Unitarian leaders had sensed the changing direction of American culture before the war's conclusion. The Transcendentalist controversy, particularly as it spilled over into the politics of antislavery, was in a sense an early indication of cultural upheaval. But more pervasive, even though less tangible than the Transcendental rebellion, was the general sense of religious unease felt throughout Protestantism. The liberals found that the price of their freedom was to feel this uncertainty first, and some among them believed that the test of their freedom was to face it directly. To Henry Whitney Bellows,* the most prominent figure in postwar Unitarianism, it was important to admit that "a great and painful indefiniteness of opinion" about the Christian life existed "among thinking men of all sects— secretly in most, openly in many, and characteristically in our liberal Body."[2]

Bellows's place in Unitarian history is that of a "churchman," rather than a theologian or a preacher.[3] He took a firm grip on denominational affairs after the Civil War, pushing a national organization and a sense of renewed evangelical purpose on Unitarians, who had been notably lacking in exactly those elements in their makeup. But Bellows's activities as an organizer, forming an important episode in Unitarian history, are better understood in the context of his articulation of the midcentury situation of American Protestantism, what he termed the "Suspense of Faith."

Bellows's analysis of that dilemma came in the form of an address to the alumni at Harvard Divinity School in 1859, an occasion comparable to that of Ralph Waldo Emerson's* Divinity School Address in 1838. If Emerson rocked the denomination with a call for radical individualism, Bellows seems to have been almost as disquieting in arguing for a renewal of commitment to institutionalism—to the church in a traditional, although not a confining or conservative, sense. That Bellows was, in the words of Walker Donald Kring, "almost 180 degrees different" from Emerson points up the major issue that would face the denomination in the late nineteenth century—the place of the church.[4] The legacy of Emerson and Theodore Parker,* a legacy of individualist noncreedalism, was still very much alive, as the existence of the Free Religious Association later in the century suggests. Bellows represented a position that opposed that legacy largely on the grounds of a belief in centrality of the church to the religious life.

Bellows's contemporary, and sometime opponent on theological issues, John White Chadwick,* recognized him accurately as a "Channing Unitarian," but one who, unlike William Ellery Channing,* possessed a "denominational consciousness and sectarian zeal."[5] His ministry in New York had been impressive, and his emergence as a Unitarian leader is notable in part because he did not hold a Boston pulpit. Bellows's career is thus a reminder that the boundaries of the denomination were moving beyond New England rapidly in this period.

Almost every commentator on Bellows has recognized the importance of "The Suspense of Faith" to Unitarian history, for it stands as one of those rare documents that captures the spirit of an age.[6] To Bellows, as to Emerson earlier, the audience and the occasion were uniquely suited to a call for a general change of direction in the religious life of the denomination. For Bellows, that change was necessitated by an "undeniable apathy in the denominational life of the body." Even though there had been a general growth in Unitarianism, he asked his audience to recognize that "with general prosperity, in short, there is despondency, self-questioning, and anxiety."[7] The strength of Bellows's address, however, is his insistence that this phenomenon of doubt is not unique to the Unitarians but is a general condition of Protestantism and even a central fact of nineteenth-century culture. In Bellows's view, Unitarianism had put itself in the vanguard of Protestant development and therefore experienced earlier and more directly the nineteenth-century crisis of faith. "The underlying principles of and sentiments of the Unitarian body have turned out to be the characteristic ideas and tendencies of the religious epoch we live in. Protestantism produced us, not we it" (p. 9).

Bellows's phrase "suspense of faith" aptly captures that crisis of faith, for the word *suspense* vibrates uneasily between two related but importantly different meanings. On one level it suggests a pervasive mystery about the object of faith, an unsettling lack of clarity in the contemporary conceptions of God, Christ, and the church. But more deeply, it hints at the complete suspension of any faith and the frightening possibility of the negation of the religious sensibility. There are indeed high stakes here, he implied, for a temporary upheaval of faith can easily become a permanent cessation of it. It was Bellows's belief that this would not be the case, however, for he went on to argue that the religious crisis of midcentury could be discerned in the broadest terms as part of a dialectical movement in history and thus a necessary stage in religious development.

Bellows located the cause of the suspense of faith first in the general secularization of modern culture. "Political and democratic life, literature, and the public press" were all working toward "emancipating the community from bigotry and superstition," a role formerly performed by the church (pp. 5–6). This secularization was complemented by the general liberalization of Protestantism, which evolved as it faced the challenges of "science, philosophy and literature," all of which were "creating substitutes for religion" (p. 16). But more importantly, Bellows argued that the "universal" reason for the pause in faith was the conclusion of a cycle in religious development that had emphasized the "self-directing, self-asserting, self-developing, self-culturing faculties." It was the end of the era of the self, and the movement that had culminated in Channing's and Emerson's calls for self-culture and self-reliance now had to give way to another trend of development. The era had been liberating, but now, as Bellows explained, "we are weary of the toil it has thrown on us; the speculation, inquiry, and self-sustaining energy we have put forth under its compulsion." But it is not wholly out of weariness that the age has paused: "having achieved our freedom, we know not what to do with it; having cultivated our wills, consciences, and intellects to the utmost at present possible, they cry out for objects that they do not find" (pp. 22–23).

What follows such an era of self-assertion? Bellows argued that it must be an era of institutions, a period when the emphasis on self-development can translate itself into more permanent terms through an investment in the church. Institutions are "the only instruments, except literature and the blood, by which the riches of the ages, the experience and wisdom of humanity, are handed down" (p. 37). In taking this position, Bellows set himself against the leading tendency of Unitarian thinking since the 1830s and also set the terms for the major debate in the next decades: pure individualism versus denominationalism. He specifically criticized "the Emersonian and transcendental school" for its valuation only of "the egoistic" movement of humanity: it was "Protestantism broken loose from general history, taken out of its providential plan, and made the whole, instead of the part" (p. 24). The self required fulfillment in the church; without it, Protestantism became a religion of chaos and risked its very identity as religion.

Like Emerson, Bellows had not been afraid to take a controversial stand, but he was surprised at the vigor of the reaction that followed. He had touched a nerve in the thinking of many Unitarians, who were "stunned and outraged by Bellows's ideas," even though much of their concern can be attributed to misunderstanding.[8] Bellows had ended the address with a call for "a new catholic church," using the term in its broadest sense, with no intention of meaning the Roman Catholic church. Even so, the very term itself, particularly in the context of Bellows's call for a turn away from individualism toward institutionalism, left him open to suspicion of high-church sympathies, and he had to assure friends and parishioners alike that the denominationalism he was preaching did not amount to Episcopalianism or Catholicism. What it did represent was Bellows's opening salvo in a campaign to put the Unitarian denomination on what he thought was sounder organizational footing. That campaign took shape in his organization of the National Conference of Unitarian Churches in 1865, just as the Civil War closed. The war itself had a direct impact on Bellows's work, for his role in the United States Sanitary Commission had thrust him into a role of national prominence and had bolstered his confidence as an organizer and administrator. Through his work for the Sanitary Commission, and the organization of the National Conference that flowed from it, Bellows began to translate his call for "a new catholic church" into reality.

## THE NATIONAL CONFERENCE

The outbreak of the war had caught the North unprepared both militarily and psychologically. In the confusion of its opening months, that absence of preparation showed itself most glaringly, and most tragically, in the lack of organization or facilities to care for the sanitary and medical needs of the troops, particularly the wounded. Walt Whitman, who found a war vocation for himself as nurse to the wounded, described the battlefield hospitals he found after the Battle of Fredericksburg (December 1862) as "merely tents, and sometimes very poor ones," with the wounded lying on ground frozen hard, "lucky if their blankets are spread on layers of pine or hemlock twigs, or small leaves." A later commentator pointed out that at the war's inception, the problems were even worse: "Enlisted men travelled miles in cattle cars; they lacked even the crudest accommodations for human comfort; they found no preparations to receive them at their destination. . . . The disease rate was beginning to rise, but the government was helpless to provide adequate precautions."[9] The crude conditions of the camps, where disease and infection were rampant, was startling to many in the North, and private efforts began to be made to remedy the situation. The Sanitary Commission, which became the focus of this concern, grew out of an Aid Society in New York that included some parishioners of Bellows. He took an active role early in its formation, but his real commitment was awakened when he visited Washington and was able to see the actual conditions of the camps and the unconcern of military and government officials. He then took on the difficult task of leading the Sanitary Commission, a role that required him to be public conscience to the military authorities, political infighter, administrative strategist, public orator, and fund raiser on a large scale.[10]

The importance to Unitarian history of Bellows's work for the Sanitary Commission was that it gave him a greater national exposure and a deeper involvement with organization on a national scale. Indeed, it thrust him into a role of national leadership. Bellows translated that experience directly into the formation of the National Conference in 1865. That was not an easy task, even for a man of Bellows's skill and prominence, because the idea of a national denominational organization ran afoul of the strict congregational polity of the Unitarian heritage. Moreover, it brought the divisive question of creed to the forefront, for many Unitarians thought that a national organization could be established and operate effectively only on the basis of a statement of common belief. Yet such a statement was adamantly opposed by the growing group of radicals in the denomination, many of whom were in the process of abandoning the Christian tradition entirely.[11]

Bellows's general preference was for the statement of a creed, but his real interest was in forming an effective national organization, and he thought the question of a creed was insignificant by comparison. He thus found himself between the conservative creedalists and the radicals in the negotiations for the conference, hoping to develop an organization with as much direction and focus as possible but unwilling to sacrifice even a loose unity to a doctrinal position that was too confining. His position at the time of organizing the National Conference, then, typified his description by Conrad Wright* as "an inveterate middle-of-the-roader" whose tendency was generally to seek compromise rather than confrontation and to stress pragmatic organization over fine points of doctrine. Bellows recognized that a good many others shared his pragmatic orientation and referred to this group as the "Broad Church men," which included Edward Everett Hale,* Frederic Henry Hedge,* and James Freeman Clarke,* all men of intellectual stature and influence. That the group was not composed of hidebound conservatives should be plain from the Transcendentalist orientation of Hedge and Clarke, whose views are discussed in detail later in this chapter. But they departed from Emersonian Transcendentalism in a commitment to the church as an institution. It was on this ground of denominational interest that they met Bellows and Hale, who were less Transcendental in their theological positions. Bellows described his original plan for the National Conference as "a scheme for reorganizing the whole denomination on the basis of *work*, not of creed." [12] It was vitally important to him that Unitarians not allow scruples about creed and doctrine to prevent them from undertaking the task before them.

Although some of the most conservative elements of the denomination opposed Bellows because of their desire to retain an inviolate congregational independence, the major opposition came from the radicals, notably Octavius B. Frothingham,* Francis E. Abbot,* and W. J. Potter,* who saw the issues involved in a very different light. Having for the most part followed Emerson and Parker in a pursuit of absolute religion that went beyond the confines of Christianity, they saw the organizational plans as a threat, because they feared that any organization would have to be made on the basis of a Christian tradition that they considered confining. More will be said later about their position in theology, but the initial meeting of the National Conference in 1865 revealed much of what the radicals feared in Bellows's organizational drive. They objected to the phrase "the Lord Jesus Christ" in the preamble to the constitution, because the phrase was "hostile to freedom," as Frothingham later remarked. [13] In fact, they came to see the entire organization in the same way. This dispute over terminology suggests the theological sensitivity of the denomination at this point in its history. Bellows was tolerant, to be sure, and understood the nuances of belief involved, but he was temperamentally unable to see them as serious enough to block his hopes for organization. Frothingham, on the other hand, was too dogmatic in his radicalism to see any possible compromise for reasons of mere institutional growth. Schism was almost inevitable.

But a major split did not occur at the 1865 convention, nor was the split that came the following year serious enough to impair any of Bellows's plans. He was able to draw together a large, representative body of Unitarian clergy and laymen and institute permanent machinery to assure the continuance of the organization. He had been able to defeat a potentially divisive move by conservatives to establish a creed too narrow for many Unitarians. He was pleased with these results, even though the convention had refused to call itself, as he had hoped, the "Liberal Christian Church of America," a title that signified Bellows's hopes for its universality. The more important goal had been accomplished, and as Kring noted, Bellows was surprised to find the denomination "so practical, so Christian, & so willing & anxious *to work on a larger scale*." [14] Problems would soon arise, however, in the dissatisfactions of Frothingham and others, and these problems led to the formation of the Free Religious Association. But the radicals' general distrust of institutions assured that their group would pose no serious threat to the new National Conference.

## WESTERN EXPANSION: THE MIDWEST

Bellows's move to unite the Unitarian denomination on a national basis was partly an attempt to embody his vision of a new "catholic" church. But it was also a response to the fact that Unitarianism was in an important phase of growth, principally in the states west of New England. Bellows organized the National Conference on the basis of combined lay and clerical representation of individual churches (each to be represented by the minister and two laypersons), a system that would bring more influence to the proliferating congregations of the Midwest and the Pacific Coast. He had been well aware of this growth and indirectly had played a part in it by sending Thomas Starr King,* the denomination's greatest western missionary, to the newly organized San Francisco church in 1860. Bellows and many other Unitarian leaders saw the West as both an opportunity and a serious challenge. Like everyone else in America, except the Native Americans, they saw the enormous potential for growth that the West represented. But the Unitarians, whose efforts at missionary work lagged significantly behind those of the Trinitarian, evangelical denominations, also saw that their eventual fate depended upon efforts in the West. Not to expand beyond New England and New York would mean parochial irrelevancy for the denomination. Such a fate to a movement that had always considered itself a vanguard would have been worse than death. Charles Briggs, who as secretary of the American Unitarian Association had toured the West in 1836–37, summarized the challenge aptly: "The destiny of our country, the destiny of Unitarianism is to be decided in the West."[15] The Universalists, although smaller and perhaps less expectant about the destiny of their denomination (although not of their ideas), experienced a similar mixture of attitudes toward the West. Success there could make or break their denominational identity.

It was in the West that the closeness of the two groups, which was always clear to sectors of both denominations, became more apparent. Western expansion of both sects arose from two sources. Transplanted New Englanders who wanted to keep alive their native religious tradition provided the most dependable congregations for both Unitarians and Universalists. A more volatile, but potentially more promising, source of expansion was the converts or "come-outers" from evangelical or orthodox churches. Liberal religion was sometimes their destination but at other times only a stopping-off point in their religious development. These sources of membership, along with the different, and usually much thinner, cultural climate of the West, gave western Unitarianism a distictive identity. Its relationship with the Unitarianism of Boston was not without its strains.

Although it is tempting to generalize about the western expansion of liberal religion with a few broad sweeps, the truth is that it involves hundreds of individual stories. The growing awareness of the importance of the West became most intense to the denomination in the late 1830s and early 1840s, the very time in which Transcendentalism, Parkerism, and political turmoils were causing painful splits. Demands were being made on a denomination unsure of its own stability and direction. Moreover, the calls for help were scattered and their circumstances differed. But one need seemed almost universal: ministers. The Unitarians had some difficulties in supplying their pulpits in New England, but it took a real commitment to move into the new western settlements. There a minister often had to organize as well as serve a congregation. Travel was difficult, pay was low and often uncertain, and the liberal minister worked in an isolation that was often debilitating. These factors, combined with a good measure of love of home, perhaps explain the complaint of Augustus H. Conant of Illinois that "they who have come West to labor as missionaries have left their hearts and hopes in New England." [16] Western Unitarians came slowly to understand that although missionary help from Boston had its place, their best hope was from ministers of their own growth and training.

Meadville, Pennsylvania, was one of the earliest western outposts of Unitarianism because of the leadership of Harm Jan Huidekoper,* a convert from Dutch Reformed Calvinism. Huidekoper brought some of the brightest of the Harvard Divinity School graduates to Meadville as preachers and family tutors. His dedication to liberal religion and his material generosity led to the founding of Meadville Theological School there in 1844. The mission of the school was to provide pastors for the West, and the hope was that the seminary would help to remove the major obstacle to western missionary work. [17]

Among the early exponents of Unitarianism to the Midwest, two men deserve particular attention. James Freeman Clarke,* who went to Louisville in 1833, was destined to play a large role in denominational affairs throughout his life. William Greenleaf Eliot,* who went to St. Louis in 1834 and spent his life there, also had an influential career. Eliot was much more conservative theologically than Clarke and was never the scholar or author that Clarke was. But he exemplified the role the minister could take in building not only the churches but the civic institutions of the West. Eliot regretted that his busy life of pastoring and community building never left him time for authorship—"my time . . . is all broken up in little pieces"—and Clarke envied Eliot as a "man of action, who can translate thought into life, who can root it in institutions." [18] But the two of them show the range of possible accomplishment and the special problems of Unitarians in the West.

As a student at Harvard Divinity School in the early 1830s, Clarke was among an extraordinary group of young ministers that included Eliot, Christopher Pearse Cranch,* and William Henry Channing.* Clarke demonstrated intellectual leadership in his early immersion in German literature, a passion he shared with Hedge, Margaret Fuller,* Emerson, and Parker, and thus he imbibed Transcendentalism at the outset of his career. But like Hedge, he also combined Transcendental philosophy with a strong commitment to the church, a subject we will examine later in this chapter. The strength of that commitment is best seen when we consider the choice that he faced after divinity studies: a New England pastorate, which would have assured his continuing study and intellectual contacts, or a western outpost. Clarke's decision was to go West, and he created there for several years his intellectual milieu almost single-handedly.

He had, as he recalled, several reasons for that choice, but they all seem to indicate a sense of the challenge of the West. Although "harder at first," it promised eventually "a wider field of activity and influence." A New England parish, he believed, would cause him "gradually [to] subside into routine," but the West would leave him "free to originate such methods as might seem necessary and useful." But more telling is his conviction that "if I could make converts in a community where my belief was unpopular, I should be convinced of its adaptation to human needs, and so be able to speak with more strength of conviction" (Clarke, p. 50). Clarke's explanation aptly summarized the conditions of Unitarian expansion. The West did represent an area of freedom and experiment, a place where the New England tradition weighed less heavily—hence the vigorous presence of radicalism in western liberal religion. But the price of that freedom was a severe crisis of confidence, in which the survival of liberalism could at times seem threatened. It was a crisis that manifested itself both in the life of the denomination and in the private spiritual experiences of its ministers, as Clarke's remark about his own "strength of conviction" indicates.

Clarke accepted a call to Louisville in 1833, where he soon formed a close relationship with two other western Unitarians, Ephraim Peabody, who arrived at Cincinnati in 1832, and Eliot, who followed Clarke's example by going to St. Louis in 1834. Clarke's memories of the experience of going west still speak to us vividly—stagecoaches overturning on rutted roads, a jumble of human types both refreshing and disconcerting to the new preacher, the raw ugliness of a frontier town so different from the settled East, and the astonishing forests of sycamore and beech. He first suffered fear with his new preaching duties, and discouragement with his small congregation, and thought his "efforts were wholly ineffectual." But he also felt secure in a "freedom of the mind" and noted the absence of "prescriptive manners . . . cant phrases and solemn phraseology" among the western clergy, which made "such preaching as in every way surpasses Eastern oratory" (Clarke, pp. 61–80; 101–3).

Clarke made his way as a minister well enough, although his most significant work was his editing of the *Western Messenger*, a periodical intended to diffuse Unitarian opinion in the West. The journal has gained lasting fame, however, as a literary and not a theological journal, for it bore the poetical stamp of Clarke and of his coeditors, Cranch and W. H. Channing. It was the first periodical to publish poetry of Emerson and remains an important part of the Transcendentalist movement for its defense of his controversial addresses in the late 1830s. But if Transcendental, it was also adamantly Unitarian, for Clarke and Cranch refused to admit that Unitarianism was not Transcendental. Cranch would follow Emerson in leaving the ministry and pursuing the culture of art, but Clarke remained uncompromisingly a minister, a Unitarian, and a Transcendentalist.[19]

Clarke left Louisville in 1840 after much soul searching, thinking, apparently, that the West would be served better by another kind of talent and that other duties called him. There are also some indications that Clarke regarded his western career as a failure, and his return to Boston was in some sense a retreat. As Elizabeth McKinsey found, despite "his success in Boston, Clarke carried with him a sense of regret, buried deep within," for the loss of his early hopes in the West.[20] But even though he spent the rest of his career in Boston, he was an example to others who shared his missionary zeal. Eliot, who followed him west, presents a different paradigm of western Unitarianism, for he was a missionary who stayed and stayed emphatically, playing a central role in the development of St. Louis and Missouri. During Eliot's last year at Harvard, Clarke had gone to Louisville, and Eliot's letter to him in 1834 shows how he looked to him for advice and encouragement: "Say decidedly 'You can succeed,—you have the requisite ability,' and if I know myself, I will come. The self-sacrifice, though it sometimes comes over one like a cold hand on the heart, in general means nothing at all." If Eliot's attempt at self-assurance here seems to reveal more of his doubt than his desire, he added a declaration that would set him apart from Clarke and most other missionaries: "if I come, I come to remain, and to lay my ashes in the Valley of the Mississippi" (Charlotte C. Eliot, p. 15). Out of such tenacious dedication, Eliot's ministry arose, one of the strongest in the West.

He went west with his Harvard training and the full weight of the Unitarian tradition—ordained at Channing's Federal Street Church, with Clarke, William Henry Furness* of Philadelphia, and Henry Ware, Jr.,* participating in the ceremony. But one telling early experience shows the distance between that tradition and the West into which he came. His first congregation of thirty listeners in St. Louis dropped off to nine after a few weeks when they discovered that the Unitarianism that Eliot preached was not "anti-Christian" or "in special antagonism to all other churches." Although Unitarian missionaries might be prepared to face physical discomfort, isolation, and indifference, few expected to be received as anti-Christs or listened to out of a hope for titillating novelty. Eliot persisted, however, and by the end of a year had some two hundred members.[21]

The direction of Eliot's career in St. Louis was indicated soon after his arrival, when he addressed the Franklin Society there on the formation of literary institutions in the West. Seeing danger in what he thought was the universal motivation for western settlement—making money—he urged a renewed attention to "religion and learning" as safeguards of the new society. Stewart Holbrook remarked on the "fanatical respect for education" that most New Englanders brought with them to the West, and perhaps this is nowhere truer than in the case of the Unitarian ministry. Eliot translated his missionary ideals into educational and philanthropic ones as well, and it can be said that religion and education, rightly conceived, were almost synonymous for him.[22] He worked as school-board member and president at a period when public schools had to be started almost from nothing. He led in the forming of the Western Sanitary Commission during the Civil War, a western counterpart to Bellows's work in the East. But more notably, he led the founding of Washington University, hoping to create there a western university as the pinnacle of his faith in education. The formation of a western university was in a certain sense always a declaration of independence from the East. For Eliot it was also an embodiment of eastern or, more specifically, New England Unitarian values that sanctified above all else the progressive growth of the mind and spirit. Such values were, as we have seen, intensely inner directed, incapable finally of any institutional embodiment. But as the church was to the growth of the soul, so was the university to the growth of the mind. These two processes of growth, moreover, were overlapping to a great extent, so mental and spiritual progress came close to being one and the same.

Even though the university was the secular embodiment of Eliot's religious ideals, he was not willing to accept secularism as religion, and he maintained a relatively traditional and Christologically centered faith throughout his St. Louis ministry. This alienated him from the currents of radicalism and change among the western Unitarians, but Eliot saw himself much in the tradition of William Ellery Channing, the man whom he had considered his pastor in Boston. He stands in many ways as a representative "Channing Unitarian," steadfast in the supernatural rationalism that Channing embodied. The schism in western Unitarianism that developed around issues of "Free Religion" is treated in more detail later, but Eliot was in consistent opposition to cutting Unitarianism away from what he considered the Christian tradition. That theological stability served him as a basis for church building and helps explain the strength of his career's focus in St. Louis.

## WESTERN EXPANSION: THE PACIFIC COAST

The same challenge that faced Unitarians and Universalists in the Midwest was also present on the Pacific Coast, except that the distances were much greater and the country newer and rawer. The church in San Francisco, a bedrock of Pacific Coast Unitarianism, offers some sense of the challenge in its checkered early history. Charles Farley, the first Unitarian preacher there, apparently went west to hunt gold, but he soon found himself preaching to Unitarians there, staying only about six months before returning to the East in 1851. For the next decade the congregation had a series of other ministries that lasted one to five years—not the sort of stability conducive to growth.[23] The experience of San Francisco's church in its early years thus suggests that the general problem of western Unitarianism, an adequate supply of preachers, was even more exaggerated in the Far West.

The history of the San Francisco church, and the entire history of Unitarianism in the region, was changed dramatically, however, by the coming of one man, Thomas Starr King. King had remarkable talent and exceptional energy, and he went to California at a crucial point in its history, just at the outbreak of the Civil War. As both a Unitarian leader and a political figure, he left his mark on the state.

King's career also demands our attention for a reason other than his pioneering work in the West. Originally, he was a Universalist, son of a Universalist minister, and trained in part by Hosea Ballou 2d.* But he ended his career in Unitarian pulpits, becoming one of the most notable Unitarian pulpit orators of his age. Throughout his career King refused to acknowledge any significant differences between the denominations, seeing them as varieties of a larger liberal faith that encompassed them both. As a Universalist minister, he affirmed the important place of Unitarianism in liberal religion, and as a Unitarian, he refused to accept any severance of his ties with Universalism, maintaining connections with both groups. He sensed in his career both the tendency of Universalism to narrow dogmatism and the danger in Unitarianism of social exclusiveness, but he saw each movement as a particular historical manifestation of the liberalism that seemed to him the promise of the future of Christianity. When commenting on the difference between the two in 1858, he related the now famous anecdote of the Universalist minister who summarized a dispute with his Unitarian colleague in these words: "The Universalist . . . believes that God is too good to damn us forever; and you Unitarians believe that you are too good to be damned."[24] In his insistence on embracing both traditions, and excluding neither, King was a forerunner of the unity that Unitarians and Universalists eventually achieved.

The roots of his combined Universalist and Unitarian heritage can be seen in his early education, which was based in the Universalism of his father. But he was also exposed to Unitarian influences in the preaching of Channing and the lectures of Harvard's James Walker* on the philosophy of religion. After the death of his father, when his family's narrow circumstances became even more difficult, he kept school in Medford, Massachusetts, there meeting Hosea Ballou 2d, who became not only his tutor but his fast friend. Ballou gave King the only formal training he would have for the ministry, other than Walker's lectures. It was really King's own voracious appetite for reading and discussion that constituted his course of preparation. But only a few years later, in 1847, he was lecturing on Goethe before the demanding audiences of Boston and Cambridge, with impressive results. Walker's memorable comment on the lecture summarized its reception: "it was not merely remarkable that so young a man should have given such a lecture," he said, "but that anybody should have done it" (Frothingham, pp. 93–94). King, now a Universalist minister in Charlestown, was beginning to establish a reputation in Boston both for pulpit eloquence and for intellectual accomplishment.

Meanwhile he was being pulled into the Unitarian orbit, both by his intellectual inclinations and the practical opportunities available there. In 1843 he had declared that "the Unitarian party, as a whole, understand themselves better, and are doing a nobler work, than the Universalists." He went on to specify his complaint against "the miserable dogmatism" of his denomination, which used the doctrine of universal restoration as the only criterion for judging a person and his or her creed. Thomas Whittemore's* criticism of Channing for failing to take a Universalist stance on restoration was mentioned specifically by King as evidence of the paucity of Universalist attitudes. King was beginning to feel that his rapidly developing intellectual needs could be better met through Unitarianism. In 1848 he accepted the pastorate at the Unitarian Hollis Street Church in Boston, saying that he had long preached "the distinctive feature of Unitarian theology" and assuring his Universalist congregation that the move was in no way caused by a "change in religious views" (Frothingham, pp. 48, 102–4). He saw practical opportunities in Boston Unitarianism and accepted them on his own terms, with no alteration in the direction of his theological development.

The Hollis Street Church was a challenge to King not only because of the superficial change in denominations but because the church "had been torn apart by the temperance and antislavery issues" and was at the point of collapse. But King brought to the pulpit there qualities that made a successful rebuilding possible, and the church grew to be five times larger. King, meanwhile, was making himself "nationally famous" as a preacher.[25] His oratorical gifts played a large role in this success, but he was also a tireless worker and a remarkably engaging personality. Theologically and politically, he was progressive without being radical, much in line with Bellows. Few radicals could have had prolonged success with an established church such as the Hollis Street. But King's efforts also exhausted him. He had ended his Charlestown work in near collapse, brought on in part by the financial necessity of lecturing in addition to preaching. It remained financially necessary for him to continue lecturing in Boston, and in 1859 he began to look for a change of situations. Through the offices of Bellows, he chose the San Francisco church. Although Bellows supported him in the venture, he had actually advised him to take another, more secure situation in Cincinnati, knowing that the San Francisco church was "tottering," although it had promise. Still, King decided for San Francisco with the apparent hope that its remoteness would relieve the temptation to continue lecturing. Nothing could have been further from the truth.[26]

King's brief career of four years in the West can be quickly summarized. He stabilized and began rebuilding his church and again found his lectures in demand. As war broke out, and California was forced to choose its allegiance, King became the most notable spokesman in the state for the northern cause. He was instrumental in assuring California's decision not to secede. Both the intensity of his effort and his ready wit are revealed in a letter about his speaking engagements during his campaign for the Union: "Tonight . . . I am to speak in a village with the sweet name of Deadwood, and to-morrow at the very important and cultivated settlement of Rough and Ready. Scott's Bar wants me; Horsetown is after me; Mugginsville bids high; Oro Fino applies with a long petition of names. Mad Mule has not yet sent in a request, nor Piety Hill, nor Modesty Gulch; but doubtless they will be heard from in due time" (Frothingham, p. 200). This new brand of essentially political lecturing revealed him to be a superb stump orator and made him as much a political as a religious leader, an identity that he maintained during the war in fund-raising for the Sanitary Commission. He was even touted for the Senate in 1862 but had no interest in a full-time political career.[27] His friendship with Bellows, even over this great distance, continued to grow as he aided him in his war effort.

If King brought the message of the Union to California, he also brought Unitarianism to the West Coast, engaging in missionary efforts outside San Francisco that were building blocks for the future. King was indeed a Unitarian pioneer in the West, and his untimely death from diphtheria in 1864 cut down his effort while still green with promise. Bellows himself came to San Francisco for six months after King's death, to preach in his church and raise money for the Sanitary Commission. This is evidence both of Bellows's regard for him and his recognition of the importance of King's western work. Bellows stayed until he secured a hand-picked successor, Horatio Stebbins,* who was minister there for thirty-five years.

One of King's lecture tours in 1862 had taken him north through Oregon and Washington to Victoria, British Columbia. There he saw firsthand the new territory that he had commended to another young minister, Thomas Lamb Eliot,* some two years earlier. Eliot, the son of William Greenleaf Eliot, had gone west for reasons of health in 1860 and met King in San Francisco. He was set on the ministry, in his father's example, but a remark of King's seems to have focused his direction even more sharply: "The Pacific Coast claims every man who has ever seen it and is willing to sacrifice himself to it," King told him. "Remember that any one that has seen this coast has got to come back. There's Oregon."[28] Eliot indeed came back, settling in Portland in 1867. There he began one of the most important Unitarian ministries on the West Coast.

Like his father, Eliot excelled as a church builder, pastor, and community leader rather than as a dramatic orator like King. He was a bedrock of stability for Unitarianism in the West, providing the denomination with a secure base of operations in the Northwest. In this and many other respects, his career mirrors that of his father in remarkable detail. He went west with missionary intentions and lived his life out in the first pulpit he accepted. Like his father, he remained moderate theologically, keeping his distance from the Free Religion movement and looking to Boston Unitarianism for his support. He also devoted himself to cultural and educational activities, serving Portland as superintendent of schools and leading the city in the formation of its library and art museum. Like the older Eliot, his crowning achievement was the foundation of Reed College, which the bequest of one of his parishioners made possible.[29]

When these parallels to his father's career are noted, it is not surprising to find his father's example playing an early role in his decision to go west. His deliberately missionary sense of vocation is clear in this letter to his father, written a year before he went to Portland:

I long for an experience such as yours in some way off point, where I may grow with the people. As a young man; with peculiar advantages and facilities, it seems as if I am suited for *this* and no other work. Your *name* alone is a stronghold for any missionary; and my chief concern, next to my duty to God, is not to demean that privelege. Somehow I can find no one half so ardent as I am about it! If I speak of Oregon, they speak of hardship and distance and selfsacrifice! As if it were any to me—and not rather the most selfish choice I can make.[30]

Given the isolation of Portland in the 1860s, it is not hard to see what Eliot meant by "hardship . . . and selfsacrifice." But the "selfishness" of his choice can be understood in much the same way: the very newness of the place made it an arena of opportunity. Eliot could indeed "grow with the people" and participate in community development in ways that would have been impossible in the more settled and developed East. It was not a choice for one who wanted to direct his energies exclusively to scholarship or preaching. But it was the appropriate route for a builder like Eliot, who hoped to see his theology take shape in institutions and see those institutions form the basis of a community. Such patient building was the living out of his father's admonition to "stick to your post and let your influence be cumulative."[31]

But Eliot's persistence in church and community building is more than just a mirror of his father's career, for his work sprang from a deep sense of the role of the church in the spiritual life of humankind. Although Eliot often preached individualism and self-culture much in the tradition of Channing and Emerson, he also recognized the loneliness and isolation that shadowed the independent self. In the notable sermon "Spiritual Sympathy" (1869), he acknowledged that most individuals experience a secret "unrest" based in their "longings for a better life."[32] What distressed Eliot was not the fact of this restlessness and dissatisfaction but "*the difficulty of expressing to another these inward thoughts.*" The tragedy of life is not that there are trials, disappointments, and dissatisfaction but that there is so little sympathy among fellow sufferers of the same malaise. "There seems to me no sadder truth than this, *that men should live on*, year in, year out, dreaming that they must stand alone."[33]

It is for this reason that Eliot saw an important place for the church as a means of relieving this crushing isolation. "The bond of the church is this," he wrote, "the *brotherhood of man*—Sympathy."[34] He went on to define the church as "*a fellowship of striving souls*," a definition that attempts to balance the competing claims of individual aspiration and communal sympathy. Formed in the tradition of self-culture and the expansion of the soul that Channing preached, Eliot was sensitive to the dangers that an exclusive reliance on the self could bring. Without denying the fundamental claims of the self, he tried to temper them with a call to a potential unity available in the church. It is in this light that his long pastoral career, and even his long career of public service, can best be understood.

## THE BROAD CHURCH GROUP

Nineteenth-century Unitarianism was influenced most profoundly by a group that could be called neither radical nor conservative but took a theological stand molded from elements of both of these camps. It has been called the "Broad Church" group because of its commitment to the growth of a diversified denomination.[35] James Freeman Clarke and Frederic Henry Hedge are the foremost examples of the group, although these men speak for the attitudes of a wide group of Unitarian laypersons and clergy. Influenced in their early development by the Transcendentalist movement, Hedge and Clarke developed an intuitionist view of religious truth, that rejected mere biblicism, church authority, or religious tradition as a source of religious authority and located it instead in the direct revelation of God to the soul or the indwelling of God within the soul. This was the doctrine of Emerson, and both Hedge and Clarke were associates of Emerson in the early and controversial phases of the Transcendental movement. The Transcendental Club, the loose and informal group that met in the middle 1830s to discuss the "new views," was in fact familiarly known as "Hedge's Club," because its meetings occurred when Hedge was in the Boston area.

But both Hedge and Clarke departed from Emerson in some important ways, and it is these departures, as much as their initial agreements, that mark their eventual importance to Unitarianism. Each man had a temperamental difference from Emerson, which helps to account for the different direction of his career. Hedge was more cautious, reserved, and a more thorough scholar than Emerson. Clarke was more irenic in temper and much more given to peacemaking, always hoping that pragmatic compromise among warring factions would make further constructive work possible. Although important, these personal traits should also be seen in the context of a larger intellectual commitment by each man to the workings of the church. In this respect, they were closer to the vision of Bellows than to that of Emerson. Although they expressed this commitment in different ways, it was this sense of the church's importance, and of the related significance of the historical continuity that the church represented, that explains their impact.

The early interest in German literature that Hedge and Clarke shared with Emerson, Parker, and Fuller marked them as Transcendentalists. Clarke's conduct of the *Western Messenger* during his years in the West and Hedge's contribution to the *Dial* also secured their respective places in the radical ferment of the time. But even in this early phase of their careers, each man exhibited a marked commitment to church renewal as well as to intellectual reform. Clarke's missionary work in the West is a clear example of this, as is his later return to Boston to found the Church of the Disciples in 1841. Although still a Unitarian, Clarke's vision of what the church could be is revealed in his model of the Church of the Disciples as a "free church," one that could lead the way to a unified and universal Protestant church that would come together less on the basis of theological doctrine than on the basis of a common practical service to humanity. Francis Greenwood Peabody* described the impression of unity that Clarke's church had given him: "The whole company was, as it were, one family—a realization of primitive Christianity."[36] Clarke hoped that it would not be "coincidence of opinion" that bound the church together but "coincidence of practical purpose" (Clarke, p. 155). Although he could be eloquent on theological issues, and although his output of religious writing was enormous, he always moved with very practical ends in mind.

Like Clarke, Hedge was immersed in his church commitments from the outset of his Transcendental studies. Among the Transcendentalists, Hedge defended the AUA in preference to a reorganization of the church on different grounds, and he took an increasingly wary view of Emersonian attitudes toward the church as he increased his own involvement with his first pastorate in Bangor, Maine.[37] Clarke increasingly took on the role of denominational leader, becoming AUA secretary in 1859 and playing a leading role in the formation of the National Conference after the war. Hedge became a professor of ecclesiastical history at Harvard and thus remained close to the intellectual life of the denomination. But both of them also offered statements of theological positions that added much to the dialogue of liberal religion in the late nineteenth century.

Hedge's characteristic blend of views can be seen in his *Reason in Religion*, a volume devoted to reconciling the competing claims of faith and reason. In his definition of revelation, the basis of religious knowledge, Hedge made his Transcendentalist perspective clear. "Revelation is not external, but internal. Internal in the first instance; then, in a secondary sense and degree, it may become, as personal or ecclesiastical authority, external."[38] The statement is characteristic in its balance. Although Hedge insisted on the primacy of personal or internal revelation, he also left room for ecclesiastical authority, which had played such a strong role in Christian history. Hedge always maintained a historian's respect for the power of the past and emphasized continuity as well as change as an essential element of religion. For Hedge, the fundamental internal revelation of God to the soul was supplemented by secondary forces, primarily the church. These internal and external sources of revelation fostered a process of spiritual growth that was the essence of the religious life for Hedge. "The operation of God's spirit in the regeneration of a human heart but unfolds a life-germ inborn in that heart, and is therefore a natural process, as much so as the growth of an apple or an apple-tree" (pp. 27–28). This is the center not only of Hedge's doctrine but of nineteenth-century Unitarianism. Hedge's description of regeneration as natural growth, even to his use of a metaphor of organic growth from nature, links him with Channing, Emerson, Parker, and even some later radicals who were committed to a view of religion as a process of organic evolution. But Hedge was willing to go further to note that revelation often left itself embodied not in mere passing insight but in religious tradition and institutions. All traditions, he argued, even if they become "hardened and sapless with the lapse of time," still serve to "attest some former inspiration which flooded the soul, as the fossil-shell on the mountain-side attests the swelling of the waters in some foregone spasm of the globe." Thus, for Hedge, "the fruit of revelation is tradition" (p. 66). He argued for the necessity of tradition in a denomination whose principal spokesmen had focused on the necessity of change and whose best minds had tended to reject tradition altogether. In an 1864 address Hedge used the metaphor of organic growth, which we noted earlier in a different context:

Whoever would build permanently must build on the past, he must take the foundation which is given him in the institutions and ideas of the Church, whose offspring he is. He must graft himself on the old stock, and know that he bears not the root, but the root him. It is easy, I say, to deny; a small modicum of talent is required to assail and repudiate existing beliefs. But the true reformer accepts existing beliefs, and unfolds the truth that is in them into new and nobler forms of faith.[39]

Hedge's defense of tradition and ecclesiasticism was particularly effective, because Hedge based it in essentially radical intuitionist doctrine. Hedge called his position "enlightened Conservatism," but it is wrong to think of him exclusively as a conservative, given his sympathy with the new views that Emerson and the Transcendentalists espoused.[40] But it is important to remember his sense of responsibility to recognize and defend the place of history and institutions in the religious life.

Hedge's call to permanent building, and his recognition that the true builder senses his dependence on the church, would have struck a responsive chord with Clarke. Although he was more an experimenter and reformer than Hedge, Clarke remained solidly committed to progress through the expansion of existing institutions. He shared Bellows's dream for the growth of Unitarianism into a universal church and believed that, ultimately, the liberalization of Christian doctrine could serve as the basis for a truly universal religion. His influential study in comparative religion, *Ten Great Religions*, embodies this sense of a universal human quest for a central religious truth, although Clarke upheld the ultimate comprehensiveness of Christianity as a key to realizing this universal impulse.[41]

Some sense of his vision of the church can be gathered from his remarks at the organization of the National Conference in 1865, at a key point in Unitarian history. Sounding a note of solace and compromise amidst the potential divisiveness of the factions at the conference, Clarke argued that theological names, and even theological beliefs, were secondary to theological action. Specifically noting the radicals present, those who would eventually launch the Free Religious Association, Clarke argued that "so long as we have work to do in which we agree, we can cordially unite" (Clarke, p. 266). This is the same basis on which he worked in the Church of the Disciples, a pragmatism that refused to recognize the boundaries of philosophical parties.

Hospitable as he was to the radicals, and radical as he himself was on many issues, theological and social, Clarke still opposed the Free Religion movement as a movement away from the church. His criticism of its weakness is characteristic of his own intellectual values, for he dissented from it not on philosophical but on pragmatic grounds. "Free Religion sacrifices the motive power derived from association and religious sympathy for the sake of a larger intellectual freedom. The result is individualism. It founds no churches, but spends much force in criticizing the Christian community, its belief, and its methods."[42] It is an anomaly to hear one of the founding voices of New England Transcendentalism, whose touchstone was individualism, now criticizing that central doctrine. But as Clarke believed, pure individualism was "incapable of organized and sustained work" in philanthropy and moral reform, and those were, for him, the ultimate criteria of a philosophy. Generous to orthodox and radical alike, Clarke still took a position of criticism of both groups, although his criticism was always couched in an invitation to forget minor differences in favor of the larger work.

Clarke was a talented religious writer, one whose concerns seem remarkably representative of denominational thinking during his life. His previously noted *Ten Great Religions* summarized the liberal impulse to explore comparative religion, and he also articulated other central concerns of the movement, such as the impulse to personal development that he explored in his lectures on *Self-Culture*. But it is his articulation of the "Five Points" of Unitarian belief that stands as perhaps his most enduring intellectual contribution to Unitarianism, the most nearly expressive creed that the denomination formulated in the nineteenth century.[43]

Clarke articulated his version of Unitarian belief as a contrast to the Five Points of Calvinism—Absolute Decrees, Atonement by Christ for the Elect only, Original Sin, Effectual Calling, and the Perseverance of Saints. These points he considered a theology of the past, noting that they are "as remarkable for what they omit as for what they assert." Those omissions he proposed to remedy by stating the Five Points of "the theology of the future." Characteristically, Clarke did not limit this theology to Unitarianism but implied that its appeal would be universal in the future of humanity. Its essentials, without Clarke's fuller explanations, follow:

1. The *Fatherhood of God*
2. The *Brotherhood of Man*
3. The *Leadership of Jesus*
4. *Salvation by Character*
5. The *Continuity of Human Development* in all worlds, or the *Progress of Mankind* onward and upward forever.[44]

It should be noted that Clarke retained the sense of a personal God as primary in the new theology. This is far different from the cold sovereign of Calvinism, but the fatherly personality of God is "the source of the purest piety." Jesus is retained as essential to the theology of the future, although Clarke saw his religious significance to be that of a teacher or leader rather than a supernatural being. The final points on character and human progress are perhaps the most influential of Clarke's assertions, because they retain and extend the basic Unitarian emphasis on self-culture and personal growth and also sanctify that process with an optimism that for many defined the unique piety of liberal religion. The significance of the final emphasis on progress also grows when we consider, later in the study, the reaction against that notion among some twentieth-century thinkers.

Ultimately, Hedge and Clarke represent a continuity within Unitarianism between the intellectual ferment of the denomination's radicals and the day-to-day building of church organizations. In both cases their liberalism was a constant test of whether the long gap between speculative ideals and practical reality could be bridged, and they consistently affirmed that it could be. For Hedge, the power of tradition and, for Clarke, the necessity of labor were the keys to bridging that gap. For both men, the institution of the church was the place where ideals were translated to reality.

# 9
# FREE RELIGION AND THEOLOGICAL RADICALISM

## THE FREE RELIGIOUS ASSOCIATION

The formation of the National Conference signified a rising mood of ecclesiasticism among Unitarians, and the immediate success that the organization had in raising funds for several educational and philanthropic causes was further testimony to that mood. But at the outset of this increasing organizational push, a countersentiment was building, hints of which had been revealed in the radicals' opposition to the creedal language in the constitution during the 1865 convention. Even as Henry W. Bellows* and the other leaders of the National Conference began to put the wheels of their new organization in motion after that meeting, the radicals retired to lay a plan of action. Their first notable activities came a year later in 1866 at the second National Conference meeting in Syracuse. There, under the leadership of Francis Ellingwood Abbot,* they attempted to get the convention to disavow any "common creeds or statements of faith" and declare itself a thoroughly nonsectarian organization. They also proposed to change the name to the National Conference of Unitarian and Independent Churches, thereby explicitly affirming the right of many member congregations to identify themselves outside the Christian fold.[1] They lost this battle, and after the defeat, the radicals began to plan an independent organization, free from both Unitarian and Christian creeds or controls. Their defeat at the Syracuse convention, therefore, led directly to the formation of the Free Religious Association.

These radicals, "splendid gadflies and dissenters within the denomination," were not very influential as church builders or organizers.[2] Their importance was in the intellectual stimulus that they provided to the denomination. Although in an immediate sense they had few followers, they were an advance guard, generally ahead of the religious thinking of mainstream Unitarianism and thus fighting an often frustrating battle. But the direction of their thinking—

away from supernaturalism toward science, away from theism toward Humanism, and away from ecclesiasticism toward social reform—charted important directions in denominational development in the twentieth century.

Something of their state of mind in 1866 can be gathered from O. B. Frothingham's* description of their loss at Syracuse as a "virtual exclusion" from the National Conference.[3] Bellows's organizing attempts had the look of a demand for conformity to them, and the general insistence on confirming the Christian roots of the organization seemed to them reactionary in the light of current theological and scientific developments. The radicals were "modernists," dedicated to the "adaptation of religious ideas to modern culture."[4] Although Bellows was far from being a radical himself, his clear description of the "suspense of faith" in liberal circles is a telling reminder of the milieu from which the leaders of the Free Religion movement emerged. Culture, as Bellows recognized, had taken the lead from theology in directing human affairs, and it was therefore to forms of culture that people increasingly began to look with religious questions.

Science was, without question, predominant among these cultural forms, and nineteenth-century theology was riven by its encounter with the rise of science in a new form—evolutionary naturalism. Because of its openness to the scientific perspective, liberal theology was affected first and perhaps most deeply in this confrontation. It is a coincidence of some significance that Bellows's description of the "suspense of faith" was delivered in 1859, the same year that Charles Darwin published his *Origin of Species*. Darwin's theory would not have its full impact until after the war, but already in the earlier half of the century, science had made significant inroads into theological thinking. The evolutionary theories connected with the work of Darwin and others were the principal evidences of the challenge of science to accepted patterns of belief, for they called into question the doctrines of God and of human immortality, which Abbot pinpointed as the key religious questions of the era (or perhaps of any era).[5] Did the development of one species from another through the process of natural selection leave any place for a creative and concerned God in the cosmos? Did not the close kinship of human being and beast that this theory suggested make it difficult to maintain faith in an immortal soul that separated humanity from the other animals? Many Unitarians who thought that the rational attack on Christianity would cease with biblical criticism and modification of some supernatural aspects of Christianity were dismayed by the far-reaching implications of the rapidly accumulating discoveries of natural science.

The reactionary rejection of Darwin among the fundamentalists is the most widely remembered outcome of the conflict between science and religion, but in the liberal tradition the response was not opposition but a concerted effort to make religious use of the evolutionary theories. Looking back on the period of Darwin's first impact, John White Chadwick* remembered that Darwinism at first "seemed the wreck of our high faith in human nature," but in fact, "it has proved its grandest confirmation."[6] In this attempt to transform evolution into a doctrine that supported religion, the liberals were intensely aware of thinkers such as Herbert Spencer, who also tried to draw philosophical conclusions from evolutionary thinking. Spencer, whose dominance in English and American philosophy after the war was unparalleled, had great appeal, because he seemed to fit the scientific evidence of Darwin and others into a larger cosmological pattern, one that many of his readers believed could yield theological implications. But the liberals were not completely unprepared for the Darwinian revolution. The Transcendentalists had propounded a cosmological view that stressed process and evolutionary development, and Ralph Waldo Emerson,* most notably among them, had developed his ideas out of a close encounter with science as early as the 1830s. Evolutionary theory did not ruffle him at all, and his patient and even eager acceptance of science would be matched by the most important Unitarian thinkers of the generation after his.[7]

The Free Religious Association had little significance as an institution except in serving as a rallying point for the radicals. Individualists as they were, they made the organization a limited one, hoping to diffuse Free Religion as an idea or a state of mind rather than as an institution. After the defeat of the dissidents' attempts to amend the constitution in Syracuse, Cyrus Bartol* invited a small group to meet at his home. Bartol had not been at the convention but was in close contact with many who were. His purpose for the meeting, as he explained to Abbot, was to form "a band of *disciples of the Spirit*" from among those who were "theologically shut out" of the Syracuse convention. Clearly, Bartol hoped that a more general movement toward the religion of the "Spirit," which he preached, would result, and he took these actions even though they seemed to run counter to his good friend Bellows's hopes for the future of the National Conference.[8] Although Bartol felt alienated from the drift of Unitarianism toward denominationalism, he eventually became disaffected from Free Religion itself when he felt it had abandoned this commitment to spiritual or intuitive religion. But at this point the radicals, although not in complete agreement over the direction to take, were united in their opposition to the National Conference and organized if for no other reason than as an act of independence from it. After further meetings under Bartol's aegis, a growing list of supporters and sympathizers emerged, including Frothingham, Emerson, and Bronson Alcott. The organization then held its first public meeting in May 1867. Stow Persons estimated the highest membership figure to have been only about five hundred nationwide, although in fairness to the radicals, they would have been the first to admit that membership and organization were not high on their list of priorities. The diffusion of ideas was important to them, however, and for this reason the *Index*, a journal founded by Abbot in 1870, was more successful during its span of sixteen years. To the extent that Free Religion was the embodiment of Tom Paine's dictum that "my own mind is my own church," the *Index* was not only the most successful but perhaps the only form that the movement could consistently take.[9]

The presence of figures like Emerson, Bartol, and Alcott in the Free Religion movement suggests the close affinity that this later form of radical religion had with Transcendentalism. It is clear that Theodore Parker* was a central influence on prominent later radicals such as Frothingham, John Weiss,* and Thomas Wentworth Higginson*; Frothingham and Weiss both wrote biographies of Parker, and Weiss succeeded him in his pastorate in Boston. Nor is it surprising to find that Emerson, by then more a venerated sage than a controversial radical, addressed the first public meeting of the Free Religious Association in 1867. More importantly, there were also significant continuities of thought between the two movements. Their uncompromising individualism is the most notable, and in both cases a firm sense of the immanence of God in the human soul underlay that individualism. The stress on growth, energy, and development— or on progressive evolution, as it would come to be seen by the later radicals— was also central to both movements. In both cases this self-reliance came into conflict with a Unitarianism that could neither go as far in its faith in the self nor abandon the structures of the church.

Although these continuities both of men and ideas are important, it must also be remembered that the world of the 1870s and 1880s was far different from the 1830s, and that this difference was inevitably reflected in the development of Free Religion. Whatever shared assumptions the radicals had, the pressure of the era's intellectual direction forced a split among them, one that Abbot recognized and defined in an 1871 article in the *Index*.[10] To his mind, Free Religion could be divided into the "intuitional" and the "scientific" schools. The intuitional school extended the assumptions of Emerson and Parker, and the scientific school broke with its Transcendental heritage over the source of religious knowledge. Abbot, the leading spokesman for the scientific school, fought to put religious thinking on the firm ground of "science" or rigorously logical thinking. Dismissing Emerson's faith in an inner revelation of God that amounted to an innate religious knowledge, he hoped to strengthen faith by holding it up to the same scrutiny and open analysis that had brought about the scientific revelations of the age. Others like Frothingham, although hospitable to scientific inquiry, continued to look to the human self for religious knowledge, but they found that humanity embodied religion less as individuals than as a race. The story not only of Unitarian theology but of the general direction of nineteenth-century American thinking can be discerned in these schools.

## FREE RELIGION: THE INTUITIONAL SCHOOL

In his important exposition of Free Religion, *Radical Problems* (1872), Bartol included a dialogue with a "friend," a thinly disguised version of the debate he had been carrying on with his real friend Bellows. Personally close but theologically at odds, Bartol and Bellows parted intellectually on the place of Christianity in the religious nature, a split that characterized the more general divergence of the radicals from Bellows's conception of a universal Protestantism. The central idea of the radicals was that the "Spirit takes in all," Bartol wrote. "My friend says, The Spirit is born of Christianity. I answer, Christianity of the Spirit. He says, Spirit is an abstraction. I say, A reality. He says, The gospel covers the ground. I reply, Neither actual nor ideal. I stand within the Christian lines, the lowest private in those ranks. But I look out to the origin and end of the march. There are greater words than Christian,—the Divine Humanity, the image of God in the soul of man."[11]

Bartol's definition of the radical position as an affirmation of "the image of God in the soul of man" is clearly Transcendentalist in origin.[12] That image of the God within was the source of religious truth, a truth available to the mind innately or intuitively, unmediated by scripture, reason, tradition, or any other force. "We have seen [God], though the sight fade the next moment for ever away. One beholding is pledge that to behold him we are made. Somehow the spirit in us, seeing and seen, ours and his, must be everlasting spectator of the eternal spectacle" (Bartol, p. 55). Such Emersonianism, in some ways a relic of the spent phase of Transcendental enthusiasm, was also at the basis of the modernist radicalism of Bartol and other intuitional radicals. It was this sense of unqualified individual power or perception that gave to the radicals their focus of resentment against institutional religion, their attitude of putting up with the church as at best a necessary though unsatisfactory compromise with material life. Bartol characterized Emerson as a man who "was not important to the Church till he left it to become such a figure as to make his judges the world's benefactors" (Bartol, p. 65). In this ironic inversion of Unitarian history, Andrews Norton's* attacks on Emerson benefited the world not because they were true but because their falsity forced Emerson further from the church to a place where he could think and speak more clearly. Thus Emerson's turn to the literary life actually contributed to the evolution of the church by freeing an original thinker from ecclesiastical hindrances.

Emerson's development from Unitarianism to Transcendentalism can be thought of as an illustration of Bartol's general conception that "Free Religion is an unfolding of previous forms" or an "organic evolution" in which doctrines of the past gradually assume newer and larger significance in the light of the present. The principle was illustrated for Bartol in a friend's description of his spiritual development: " 'I spell my God with two o's and my devil without a d' " (Bartol, p. 103). Bartol, himself a minister, was in no way hostile to the church and recognized that "faith must be nourished by scriptures and institutions." But the nurture that those things could provide had to be kept in perspective, because faith was "congested when they become ends instead of means" (Bartol, p. 214). As a result, he observed, "it is not strange those who can abide nothing but reality choose to be unchurched, and that thoughtful persons fall away from ordinances and tests" (Bartol, p. 154).

What sustained faith such as Bartol's was pure individualism, a Protestantism of the most extreme sort, which insisted that the soul's access to God was utterly unmediated. It insisted, finally, that God and the soul were inseparable. Yet if the radicals gladly claimed Emerson as their spiritual ancestor, they also tended to view him as a pure poet or thinker, inspiring because unsullied by the world, but troubling also for that very reason. A more tangible if somewhat less poetic example to them was Theodore Parker, whom they venerated not only for his Transcendental spiritualism but for his direct involvement in political reform. Emerson's individualism carried with it an aloofness that Parker's battling engagement in the world counterbalanced. Frothingham's characterization of Parker in the biography that stands as his homage to him indicates his image in his radicals' minds: "A reformer by instinct, readily kindled into indignation at the thought of evils he never saw, the daily communication with evil in its concrete forms moved and roused every energy in him. His gravest charge against religion was not its superstition, but its inhumanity." [13] That the word *inhumanity* rings strongly in this passage is no accident, for Frothingham was the most prominent American exponent of what he called the "Religion of Humanity." Frothingham's book of that title (1873) was the most influential statement of Free Religion, and it is best understood as the radicals' reformulation of intuitional religion after the pure individualism of Emerson ceased to be sustaining.

Frothingham's point of departure in the book is his belief that "the spirit of God has its workings *in and through human nature*." [14] Although in many senses this is a thoroughly Emersonian sentiment, Frothingham's departure from Emerson becomes clear when we realize that he emphasized God's workings through human nature collectively rather than individually. Although for Emerson, the single soul at its most private moment was the vehicle of God, for Frothingham, the human race in its most public achievements was divine. There is "no progress to the race," Emerson wrote. "Progress belongs to individuals and consists in becoming universal." [15] For Frothingham, individual progress was possible only within the larger context of the human species in general. History revealed "the persistent effort of organic human nature to come at its prerogative of self-government; and a new outbreak of glory accompanies each new effort" (Frothingham, p. 24). It is in these glorious outbreaks of human power and self-sufficiency that Frothingham saw a divine hand, a perspective that both objectified religious experience and legitimized the expression of the religious impulse in the social world.

Seen in this way, a religion of human progress had affinities with Bellows's insistence on the importance of institutions in religion. But Frothingham, one of Bellows's sharpest critics, rejected what he believed was the inherently conservative nature of institutions, which always carried with them the weight of the past. The key to his vision was its future-mindedness, its insistence on constant striving. The most striking illustration of this was his ability to turn the Victorian crisis of belief in God into an occasion for celebration. Admitting the insolubility of the problem of God's existence, a surprising concession to agnosticism, Frothingham labeled this unknowable God a "hidden God," whose inaccessibility is actually a positive spur to human nature. Such a conception of God "strengthens because, while it kindles the imagination and exalts sentiment, it leaves will and endeavor free." Unburdened by the present God of Christian tradition, a person is thus able "to do his own work, without interference from spectres. The intruding God mars his own best creation" (Frothingham, pp. 53–54).

Frothingham's concessions to modernism here illustrate the distance many of the radicals were willing to go to free themselves from binding tradition. In pulling away from those limitations, they often found themselves also cut loose from the security of faith, but even that could be a positive turn of events for Frothingham: "In *honest* doubt is all the live faith that exists. . . . The spirit of truth manifests itself in the form of doubt. . . . Doubt is the evidence of a live mind. The creeds mark the point which mind has reached and where the mind rests. Doubt is the tingling of new vitality in the brain, the movement of fresh waves of spiritual power" (Frothingham, pp. 317–18). The key to this outlook is the unquestioning belief in progress, the tendency to see all movement as positive. Nowhere is Bellows's admission of weariness at the demands made by the suspense of faith more directly challenged than in Frothingham's praise of the hidden God and the doubting mind.

## FREE RELIGION: THE SCIENTIFIC SCHOOL

The spirit of the scientific school of Free Religion is best indicated by Francis Ellingwood Abbot's claim that "Science is . . . destined to be the world's true Messiah."[16] Even though he recognized the "disrespect for venerable ideas" that characterized modern science, he thought that this was an aberration of its youth, which with time and patience would be overcome. He was referring to the already notable hostility between science and religion, the fear with which theologians viewed scientific advance, and the contempt with which scientists treated religious questions. For Abbot, this was a particularly painful dichotomy, because he believed that elements of the future of human progress were held in both camps. Religion, because of its concern with human spiritual destiny, asked the right questions. But science, because it was "neither more nor less than *human knowledge*, in all its various branches and departments," was the only force ultimately capable of providing answers (p. 114). Theologians therefore had to overcome their fear of science and accept the fact that statements of faith would have to be treated like other scientific questions. Scientists would have to come to see that larger questions of religion were worthy of their attention. Abbot admitted that "the present attitude of science towards ideas of God and Immortality is that of pure indifference," but he saw signs of change, and perhaps more importantly, he thought that the growth of science would inevitably lead it in the direction of religion. "Science will at last take into its own hands interests which are now somewhat contemptuously abandoned to the care of priests" (p. 114).

Behind this commitment to rationalism, this willingness to place the fate of religious knowledge in the hands of science, was a strong faith that science would finally confirm religious faith and set it on the right track. It was Abbot's conviction that "the final answer of science will but deepen, fortify, and exalt our human Faith in God . . . [and] strengthen and purify and elevate our human hope of Immortality" (p. 115). At the beginning of his career Abbot's faith was deep enough to allow him to commit it to science, which he saw as the new vehicle for religious knowledge. Much in the mold of William Ellery Channing,* he refused to admit that reason and the deepest religious truths were in any sense contradictory.

Abbot criticized the intuitional school of Free Religion for its failure to take its faith in science far enough. By locating the source of religious knowledge as somehow beyond logic, and by further associating that knowledge with a separate "faculty of intuition," the intuitionists left themselves, he believed, in a vulnerable position, unable to deal frankly and convincingly with the problem of atheism. When confronted with someone "devoid of the idea of God," or one who has the idea of God and denies it, the intuitionist can either refuse to believe the sincerity of the person or posit a lack or misuse of his or her religious faculty. In either case, intuitionism tends toward a "pride of spiritual aristocracy" that reveals "some relics of dogmatism" still lurking in the basis of religious faith (p. 114).

Despite his declared willingness to trust science explicitly, Abbot had his own problems with some of the forms that the science of the day took. In 1868, almost three years before his article on scientific and intuitional Free Religion, he had engaged some troubling issues raised by Herbert Spencer's *Principles of Biology* (1866).[17] In tackling Spencer, he was confronting the philosophical hero of the period and challenging the drift of Darwinism into Social Darwinism. He admitted that he could not "echo the unintelligent, because undiscriminating, praise which has been lavished on this philosophy by enthusiastic admirers," and his essay was an attempt to separate the valuable from the misleading in Spencer (p. 420).

Spencer's major accomplishment was his ability to bring all phenomena under the single idea of evolution. "The development hypothesis," Abbot argued with prescience, "will probably take rank in the end with the accepted truths of science," and Spencer's acceptance and extension of it only confirmed its centrality (p. 379). But Spencer based his extension on grounds that were finally unjustifiable, by positing mechanisms as the means of evolutionary development. With his usual skill at telling discriminations, Abbot divided the schools of evolution into the mechanists and the vitalists, taking his stand as a vitalist and attacking Spencer as a mechanist. As Abbot defined the two camps, the vitalists held the "specialty of vital [or living] phenomena" that generates evolutionary change from within, and the mechanists saw evolution as the exclusive result of outer effects producing mechanical alterations in organisms. It is not difficult to see what Abbot thought was at stake here. To preserve a sense of the unique inner directedness of living things was also to preserve a sense of divinity in the universe, a divinity that revealed itself in the workings of the evolutionary process. It was Abbot's bid to accommodate religion to science by seizing on the scientific discovery of evolution as an essentially religious perspective.

He brought this perspective together most notably in *Scientific Theism* (1885), a book that he believed was the crystallization of years of thought on the change that science had introduced into religious thinking.[18] Abbot worked toward his own philosophical position by considering and refuting two opposed tendencies in modern thought, idealism (which he labeled "phenomenism") and mechanism. The book's title was headed by the phrase *Organic Scientific Philosophy*, which indicates these two complementary aspects of his thought. He embraced the scientific method, with its insistence on a knowable external world, and rejected nineteenth-century idealism, which limited knowledge to the subjective perception of the individual and therefore led to solipsism. He insisted that the external world must be seen as a living organism rather than a machine and thus opposed the Spencerian tendency to see natural evolution in purely mechanistic terms.

The mistake of idealism is that it "takes the Appearance wholly away from the universe and puts it wholly in consciousness, thereby annihilating the very experience which it assumes to explain." Idealism in attempting to account for experience actually denies it and "reduces itself to mere gibberish" in the attempt. Abbot instead argued that the principle of "the *Infinite Intelligibility of the Universe* is the corner-stone of scientific Theism" (Abbot, pp. 124–25), by which he meant a universe always open to the probing of the human mind. Abbot hoped here to avoid the necessity of admitting any unknowable fact in nature while still preserving the possibility of human forays into an ever-available mystery. Behind this position is his worried rejection of the Kantian claim that the external object, the "thing in itself," is always unknowable. Abbot thus set himself against the Kantian and Hegelian idealism that were prominent in the philosophy of the time. But closer to home, he also rejected the Transcendentalism of Emerson and his later intuitionist followers. Transcendentalism, as Emerson plainly defined it, was "idealism as it appears in 1842."[19] For Abbot, the universe is infinitely intelligible, because it continually opens up before the queries of the mind. Such a universe is an evolving one, and Abbot saw clearly that it was this conception toward which evolutionary thought was tending. Although the battle over evolution was not completely resolved, Abbot believed that its final result would be "the permanent and universally recognized establishment of the conception of the *System of Nature* as an *Infinite Organism*" (Abbot, p. 166). For Abbot, the infinite intelligibility of the universe necessarily meant an organic conception of the universe. The only possible alternative, the mechanical conception as he found it in Spencer, failed to satisfy the necessary demands because of its denial of teleology. Even the notion of a machine implied a purpose, or a teleology, Abbot argued, and "since both the machine and the organism necessarily presuppose teleology and are equally inconceivable without it, the mechanical theory of evolution utterly breaks down: *its denial of teleology is its suicide as a philosophy*" (Abbot, p. 190). Although he attacked mechanism on logical grounds, it is clear that his reaction is based in emotion: the dead lifelessness of the machine seems unable to nourish the religious sensibility as the implied life of the organism can.

The result of Abbot's rejection of idealism and mechanism was a view of the universe as a self-evolving, conscious entity, both "real" by scientific standards and "alive" as an organism is. The end of the universe is the "*Eternal Teleological Process of the Self-Evolution of Nature in Space and Time,*—in a word, the *Infinite Creative Life of God*" (Abbot, p. 202). It is a more detailed working out, more cosmic in scope, of the same progressive or evolutionary impulse in humanity on which Frothingham based his work. Although it still leaves a central role for humanity as the perceiving part of this evolving life, it places that impulse, which Frothingham would have affirmed, into a larger scenario of universal evolution. That such a view left little room for a "personal" God and had little need for traditional Christian doctrine was of small concern to Abbot. That a conception of God had been preserved, in a universe that was far from cold and lifeless, was the important fact.

Although Abbot was unquestionably the intellectual leader of the "scientific" school of Free Religion, his public presence was equaled by that of John White Chadwick, a man who forged his own synthesis of religion and evolution, but who did so with more attention to the issues of Christian thinking that he was modifying. Chadwick worried about the drift of modern thought, and the question he posed in *The Faith of Reason* (1879) was one that nagged most of the liberals of the day: "Supposing that these tendencies go on and ultimate, will there be any thing left to mankind that can properly be called religion?"[20] Like Abbot, Chadwick could not be satisfied with the faith in intuition that had sustained Frothingham and Bartol. Such intuitions "do not enjoy the high repute to-day which they did formerly," he remarked with understatement. "It begins to be doubted whether there are any such intuitions," he pointedly added. As insistent as Abbot about the location of truth in experience, he affirmed that necessary truths of the sort that the Transcendentalists might have attributed to intuition were actually arrived at "by observation and experiment and reflection" and "do not inhere in the mind as such." Thus the religious intuitions are in fact "products of ancestral and race-experience organized in us." They are "the flower of an hereditary experience, whose roots are buried in an immemorial past" (pp. 83–84).

Chadwick's purpose, therefore, was to appropriate the model of evolutionary change and apply it to religious experience. What he called the "God-idea" developed anthropologically with humans, and "natural selection operated here [in the God-idea] as in the physical world" (p. 91). Chadwick's was a developing God, a figure of process and growth like the "hidden God" of Frothingham or the evolving self-creator of Abbot. Chadwick located the origin of religion as the primitive "expression of man's awe and wonder in the presence of his own mysterious life" (p. 58). For Chadwick, religion was fundamentally a person's sense of "his relation to the universe itself," a relation based in mystery but sustaining for the very fact that mystery suggested presence perhaps more effectively than a presumed certainty of faith could have (p. 40). Like Abbot, Chadwick posited a self-evolving quality in God that linked him to an organic rather than a mechanistic model: "God is no builder, no architect, no infinite mechanician. A rose upon its stem in June is a more adequate symbol of his unfolding life than any Christopher Wren or Michael Angelo. From within outwards, not from without inwards, is the procession of the Holy Spirit" (p. 114). It was on these terms, then, that he and others found evolution to be a sustaining rather than an undermining force, even though that knowledge came after some struggle.

## THE WESTERN ISSUE

This radical tendency toward religion as an ethical system, with a drastically altered conception of God and a growing distance from the doctrines of Christology, had a very large impact on Unitarianism in the West. George Willis Cooke described the "distinctive attitude of freedom" in the West as the result of "its fluctuating conditions, and the absence of fixed habits and traditions," factors that were supplemented by the congregational freedom of Unitarianism.[21] Actually, the Western Unitarian Conference, which had been formed in 1852 as a focal point for those Midwest churches, was organized on a conservative basis doctrinally, largely due to the influence of its first president, William Greenleaf Eliot.* Eliot had not only stressed missionary activity as a primary goal of the organization but tied that activity firmly to an acceptance of the supernatural character of Jesus and the fact of his miracles.[22]

Eliot remained an influential man in western Unitarianism, as did his son Thomas Lamb Eliot,* whose sympathies were also relatively conservative. But the elder Eliot's leadership in the West was eclipsed after the war by that of Jenkin Lloyd Jones* and William Channing Gannett,* who became the standard-bearers for the radical religion that flourished in the West. After the Civil War they led the Western Unitarian Conference on a largely independent course from the more conservative East, and throughout the period there continued to be tension between western radicals and the New England conservatives associated with the American Unitarian Association. This tension was not healed until the National Conference of 1894. The drive of Jones, Gannett, and other radicals was to organize western Unitarianism on an "ethical basis"—not to require any statement of theistic belief of those individuals, ministers, and congregations accepted as Unitarian. The principle of association was to be ethical, lying in the shared commitment of all congregations to personal moral growth and social improvement. In this goal Jones and Gannett had much success, but also met opposition, both from eastern Unitarianism and from a number of westerners—Eliot, Jasper Douthit,* and Jabez T. Sunderland* the most prominent among them—who insisted on a theistic basis for Unitarianism.[23]

Jones is a remarkable, colorful figure in Unitarian history, a man like Theodore Parker who was likely to inspire either intense admiration or deep suspicion among those with whom he associated. He was reared on a frontier farm in Wisconsin, to which his parents had emigrated from Wales in the 1840s, when Jones was an infant. Despite very limited means, he made his way through Meadville Theological School and then had early pulpits in Winnetka, Illinois, and Janesville, Wisconsin. While at Janesville he began important work in children's religious education and published *The Sunday School*, a periodical termed by Charles Lyttle "original and surprisingly modern" in both its nondogmatic content and its method.[24] Although an effective pastor and an exceptional pulpit orator, Jones's real gift was as an organizer, and in 1875 he was elected missionary secretary of the Western Unitarian Conference. This allowed him three months a year away from his pastoral duties to travel the region, preaching and organizing Unitarian societies. The creation of the position was itself an assertion of western independence from the AUA. Funds for missionary work that had gone to the AUA were now kept in the Western Unitarian Conference to support Jones's work. Jones's work went well enough that in 1880 his appointment as missionary secretary became full time, and he moved to Chicago as his headquarters. There he reorganized the Fourth Unitarian Society as All Souls Church in 1882 and stayed in Chicago until his death in 1918, having become by then "the oldest settled minister of any denomination in Chicago."[25]

Jones was deeply a westerner (the Midwest still representing the West in Unitarian circles), but his close associate William Channing Gannett had gone west with a rich family tradition of Boston Unitarianism. His father, Channing's associate and successor at the Federal Street Church, had, as we have seen, been a founder of the AUA and one of the leaders of the denomination. But Emerson and Parker, as well as Channing, were key intellectual influences on the younger Gannett's formative years, and his radical sympathies were made clear in his early membership in the Free Religious Association. His later close associations with the radical figures Jones and John White Chadwick further deepened his place in the radical cause. Like most of the radicals, Gannett watched the activities of the National Conference with suspicion. In his excellent study of his commitment to noncreedal religion, William H. Pease showed that events in the late 1860s "nearly drove Gannett out of the church," and he wrote to Chadwick with talk of forming a new organization.[26] In fact, his career took the different form of a battle to preserve noncreedalism and a radical presence in western Unitarianism and in the denomination as a whole. With Jones and others he edited *Unity*, a periodical that became the voice of radical western Unitarianism. He had significant ministries in St. Paul, where he went in 1877, and later in Hinsdale, Illinois, and Rochester. He also had a gift for poetry, which he employed in hymnody, and, as we shall see, was the author of one of the most memorable descriptive statements of liberal theology.[27]

Jones, Gannett, and other "*Unity* men," as the western radicals came to be known, had established "Freedom, Fellowship, and Character in Religion" as their motto. It was as notable for what it omitted as for what it included: no mention of God, Christ, the church, or the Christian tradition. The word *free-dom* spoke pages of noncreedalism; the word *character* suggested ethics as the basis, and perhaps the sum, of religion. Yet there were dissenters, the most notable of whom were Douthit and Sunderland. Both of these men chafed under Jones's leadership, hoping for a more theistic orientation for the Western Conference. Douthit represented the variety of frontier Unitarianism that did not lean toward radicalism but was decidedly Christian. He was born near Shelbyville, Illinois, a portion of southern Illinois in which he found himself in the minority because of his comparatively liberal theology and his abolitionist politics. He was attracted to Unitarianism for the freedom it gave him to preach but was seriously concerned about what he saw as the move of the denomination away from a belief in God and Christ. He has been described as "a horse-and-buggy missionary preacher in a region where a rugged Calvinism prevailed," and although he fought the Calvinism, he also fought hard to preserve a Christian basis in liberal religion.[28] His periodical *Our Best Words* was a conservative rival to Jones's *Unity*. Sunderland, who had a Baptist background before becoming Unitarian, also shared Douthit's concern about the loss of the Christian identity of Unitarianism. He had ministered in Chicago, where he knew and worked with Jones, and later moved to Ann Arbor, Michigan, before he took over from Jones the role of secretary of the Western Conference in 1884. It was clear that he hoped to use his new office to counter the nontheist identity that Jones had given the Western Conference and push it toward a clearer affirmation of its Christian history and connections. He emerged as a leader of the conservatives after the 1882 meeting of the Western Conference, where he had attacked the motto "Freedom, Fellowship, and Character in Religion" as inadequate.[29]

There followed attempts at conciliation by the *Unity* men—they had briefly allowed him to work with *Unity*, and the Western Conference supported his effort to move into closer cooperation with the AUA. But on the question of a required theistic affirmation, a creedal statement, there could be no agreement. The Western Conference had, in 1875, declared itself firmly noncreedal: "The Western Unitarian Conference conditions its fellowship on no dogmatic tests but welcomes all thereto who desire to work with it in advancing the kingdom of God."[30] That statement had been a conscious response to the developments in the National Conference in the 1860s and 1870s and to the controversial exclusion of William Potter's* name from the Unitarian Yearbook in 1874 (the Yearbook controversy) because of his refusal to label himself a Christian. That action may well have been welcomed by many conservatives and seized upon by radicals as proof of the AUA's intolerance, but as Conrad Wright* noted, it was based on at least a measure of misunderstanding between Potter and George W. Fox, the AUA assistant secretary. Still, it increased the mistrust between the radicals and the major portion of the denomination. The *Unity* men wanted above all to hold the line on this noncreedal position, while Sunderland and

Douthit found it a genuinely worrisome indication of the lack of a Christian faith.[31] This issue came to a boiling point at the 1886 meeting of the conference, for which Sunderland prepared one of the better-known tracts in Unitarian history, "The Issue in the West."

Sunderland realized the implications of the radicals' stand, particularly as it concerned ethics, and pressed the issue of the sufficiency of such a basis for religion:

The issue is not whether we shall make much or little of ethics. All are agreed to put as strong emphasis upon ethics as possible, as Unitarianism has always done. The question is, whether we do not stand for ethics with a *plus—ethics and also something else*, namely, belief in God and Worship—these as being both of them important in themselves, and also being something without which ethics itself loses its highest sanction and impulse.[32]

Theism was the real issue, as Sunderland saw it, for to abandon the idea of God was in fact to abandon religion itself. Seeing that the definitions of radical and conservative were quickly shifting, so that theism was beginning to be associated with conservatism, Sunderland proclaimed his own radicalism but insisted that such radicalism was dependent on God: "It is as a radical that I hold that no religion which does not believe mightily in God . . . can ever get much of a hold upon men" (p. 34).

It was principally this sense of the centrality of theism that led Sunderland to agree with others that if the radicals "continued to push their efforts to remove Western Unitarianism off its theistic basis the inevitable result must be reaction and very likely a split." His purpose, as he perceived it, was to "avert the calamity which I have foreseen" by calling on those opposed to the drift to Free Religion to unite with as clear a purpose as the radicals had (p. 6). The object of their efforts would be an affirmation "that the body has always been, and still is broadly Christian," and the corollary to that affirmation—and this posed a more serious issue—was that "our ministers should not ordain, . . . our fellowship committees should not recommend, . . . [and] our churches cannot without disaster call to or maintain in their pulpits men who are known to be devoid of these essential faiths." These faiths, as he characterized them, were "the simple fundamentals of Christian theism" (pp. 30–31).

Sunderland's arguments professed to head off an inevitable split but in fact caused one. The delegates of the conference failed to see the dangers that he outlined here or were reluctant to push their views to the point of seriously threatening the conference. Gannett saw the pamphlet as an attempt to exclude from fellowship "those who do not take the names Christian or Theist" and urged a denial of its position. The result of the debate at the conference was an unequivocal rejection of any sort of creed, and in June of 1886, having been rebuffed in their attempts to swing the Western Conference in a more conservative direction, Sunderland and others formed the Western Unitarian Association, clearly hoping to link themselves more securely to what they considered the mainstream of eastern Unitarianism at the AUA.[33]

Sunderland, because of his position as the AUA's western secretary, succeeded in bringing the controversy to the East, and the "western issue" soon
became a national one. The sympathies of the AUA were clearly with the
Christian theists of Sunderland's shade, but it could neither force nor maneuver
any change from the Western Conference. The ensuing conflict did, however,
lead to one important statement of principles by Gannett, which the Western
Conference adopted in 1887 as a nonbinding explanation of its theology. "The
Things Most Commonly Believed To-day Among Us" has been recognized since
as one of the most moving and accurate statements of faith among Unitarians—
it held, according to Lyttle, "everything excellent in Unitarian history and belief." [34] It is also a masterpiece of rhetorical balance and linguistic strategy.
Gannett's statement revealed more clearly than any comparable one the situation of Unitarianism as the century came to a close.

> We believe that to love the good and live the good is the supreme thing in religion:
> We hold reason and conscience to be final authorities in matters of religious belief:
> We honor the Bible and all inspiring scripture, old or new:
> We revere Jesus and all holy souls that have taught men truth and righteousness and
> love, as prophets of religion:
> We believe in the growing nobility of Man:
> We trust the unfolding Universe as beautiful, beneficent, unchanging Order; to know
> this Order is truth; to obey it is right, and liberty, and stronger life:
> We believe that good and evil inevitably carry their own recompense, no good thing
> being failure and no evil thing success; that heaven and hell are states of being; that no
> evil can befall the good man in either life or death; that all things work together for the
> victory of Good:
> We believe that *we* ought to join hands and work to *make* the good things better and
> the worst good, counting nothing good for self that is not good for all:
> We believe that this self-forgetting, loyal life awakes in man the sense of union, here
> and now, with things eternal,—the sense of deathlessness; and this sense is to us an
> earnest of a life to come:
> We worship One-in-All,—that Life whence suns and stars derive their orbits and the
> soul of man its Ought,—that Light which lighteth every man that cometh into the world,
> giving us power to become the sons of God,—that Love with whom our souls com-
> mune. This One we name,—the Eternal God, our Father. [35]

Gannett was not only poetic but deft with words for practical reasons as well.
The statement does all it can to make room for as many shades of belief as
possible. It ends with a very significant reference to "the Eternal God, our
Father," a phrase necessary to accommodate the majority of Christian theists
in the conference. But the significance of that phrase is suggested by Charles
Lyttle's omission of it, perhaps by error, from his *Freedom Moves West*, a book
with decidedly radical and Humanist sympathies. Without that final phrase, it
is possible to define *God* as a force of Life or as "that one with which our souls
commune"—a wide enough definition to accommodate many Humanists. But
even with the final phrase, God is presented as a name for things that one might

prefer to call by some other name without such traditionally religious connotations. Clearly, the statement reflects the growing concern over the concept of God in liberal religion, one that would flower in the next century as the Humanist-theist debate. Two of Gannett's affirmations, however—"the growing nobility of Man" and "the unfolding Universe"—would have been welcomed by conservatives and radicals alike, for they summarized the intellectual tendency of the whole movement, from the beginning of the century to the end.

Gannett's statement was important, as Conrad Wright noted, for providing "the doctrinal or ideological basis for reconciliation," and that reconciliation came at the 1894 meeting of the National Conference.[36] There, as part of the business of reworking the constitution, a new preamble was adopted by a surprisingly unanimous vote. Not only did the vote signify the skill of statement of the resolution, but a new mood in the denomination, brought on in large part by the emergence of a younger generation with concerns other than creedal dispute.

The Conference of Unitarian and other Christian Churches was formed in the year 1865, with the purpose of strengthening the churches and societies which should unite in it for more and better work for the kingdom of God. These churches accept the religion of Jesus, holding, in accordance with his teaching, that practical religion is summed up in love to God and love to man. The Conference recognizes the fact that its constituency is Congregational in tradition and polity. Therefore, it declares that nothing in this constitution is to be construed as an authoritative test; and we cordially invite to our working fellowship any who, while differing from us in belief, are in general sympathy with our spirit and our practical aims.[37]

There are ambiguities in this statement as well. Each individual may make what he or she will of the phrases "the Kingdom of God" and "the religion of Jesus." But there is also an unmistakably pragmatic tone to the declaration and a social orientation that befits such pragmatism. The declaration stands not only as a summing up of the past but as an indication of the social challenges and responses that Unitarianism would begin to manifest in the coming century.

# 10
# LIBERAL RELIGION AND SOCIAL REFORM

## ADIN BALLOU AND THE UNIVERSALIST SOCIAL CONSCIENCE

In 1870 the American Universalists celebrated their centennial with a large convention at Gloucester, Massachusetts. Such anniversaries are prone to lead to a reevaluation of the past and a projection of future hopes, and this process was a significant part of the Universalist centennial.[1] But one event at the centennial is particularly worthy of note for what it reveals of Universalist theological development during the nineteenth century. After considering the adequacy of the Winchester Profession of Faith, adopted in 1803, the convention voted not to change or modify the profession in any way. When this fact is put against the enormous changes that Unitarian thinking had undergone since that date, it becomes a significant indication of a fundamental difference between the two traditions. The varieties of Transcendentalism and Free Religion that had been so important to Unitarian theological development made much less headway in Universalism. The explicit affirmation in the Winchester Profession of the "Old and New Testament," the "one God," and the "Lord Jesus Christ" were all divisive issues, at best, for the Unitarians; yet the Universalists continued to hold them with much less controversy and uneasiness.

In one sense this suggests a certain theological stagnation within Universalism, although one may also view it as a consistency that was lamentably lacking among Unitarians. But it was true that the Universalists continued to link their identity to one central and defining doctrine—the salvation of every individual. Unitarianism, on the other hand, focused on a defining attitude or gesture, the unremitting analysis and constant reformation of all doctrine. This lack of change in the basic theology of Universalism also reflects a different attitude toward speculative theology in that tradition. The threat of hell and eternal damnation brought out the defining tenets of Universalism in the late eighteenth century. This was a much more tangible issue than the questions of predestination and innate depravity that spurred the early Arminian theological formulations in the Unitarian tradition. This defines an important area of difference in the two groups. In the nineteenth century theology was more speculative for the Unitarians but more pragmatic for the Universalists.

If the Universalists were reluctant to move beyond the theological tenets of the Winchester Profession, they expended considerable intellectual energy in two other areas—their conception of their place in Christian history and their sense of the structure and mission of the church. Indeed, these impulses were various enough to pull Universalism in several directions simultaneously throughout its history, rendering it, in the opinion of George H. Williams,* "a much more complex movement than American Unitarianism."[2] Much of the impetus for the search for a historical past that predated the American movement can be traced to Hosea Ballou 2d's* *Ancient History of Universalism*. Ballou's linking of Universalism to the earliest forms of Christianity, an attitude that was readily accepted by the denomination generally, gave to the term *Universalist* a secondary meaning that grew in importance as the nineteenth century ended. In this secondary meaning, *Universalist* came to refer not to the fact of salvation for all but to the all-inclusive quality (or potential) of the Universalist church. It referred to a hoped-for universal unity this side of the grave, as well as the other.[3]

The Universalists therefore took a large interest in defining themselves as the descendants of the earliest Christians, and this attempt "to write itself into early Christian history," as Williams put it, was an expression of the denomination's attempt to expand its identity.[4] The tendency to universalize themselves also helps to explain another important aspect of the movement, its millennialist expectations for human progress, and a corresponding sense of tension or opposition to the social world as it exists. If they thought they were representatives of the earliest Christian past, and therefore inheritors of a movement that revolutionized the course of history, they also felt themselves called to help usher in that next revolution that the millennium represented. Although in some cases the millennialism was closely tied to American expansionism, there was a significant element of social activism in the movement that set itself in opposition to American social reality, as against any social reality that failed to reflect what they considered the will of God on earth.[5] Thus social rather than theological ferment was the distinguishing mark of Universalism in the nineteenth century.

Adin Ballou* is an important representative of this Universalist social conscience. An ardent abolitionist and communal reformer, he also founded the utopian Hopedale community. Although Ballou's principal place in Universalist history was as a social reformer, he was also part of the Restorationist faction of the denomination that dissented from Hosea Ballou's* belief that there would be no punishment whatever in the afterlife. This theological position is an indication of his religious temperament, for there remained in him much of the evangelical piety that had formed his religious character. Early in his life he had regarded all Universalists "as anti-religious in spirit, anti-Christian in doctrine, and practically no better than Deists."[6] Even though he was won over to Universalism under the influence of Elhanan Winchester's* arguments and his own reading of scripture, his surrender to that faith was intensely painful: "I wept, prayed, and reviewed the ground I had gone over again and again till I was well nigh distracted. I could not eat, drink, sleep, or appear like myself. I grew pale, and wore an anxious, sickly look, to the serious concern of my wife and friends, who knew nothing of the conflict that was raging within me."[7] Although the principles of Universalism finally won this battle within Ballou, it is clear that he was a man who approached such questions with a deadly earnestness and unbending honesty. Thus, although he could be persuaded of the final restoration of all souls, he could not be brought to the ultra-Universalist position of Hosea Ballou. He came to resent what he thought was the overbearing dominance of that view in the movement and sounded his dissent most notably in a sermon preached at Medway, Massachusetts, in 1830: "The Inestimable Value of Souls." Attacked by Thomas Whittemore* as a regression from ultra-Universalism, it set Ballou's course as a rebel even within his rebellious new sect.[8]

Ballou's inability to give up all sense of a future punishment was consistent with the communal ideals of Hopedale, where a biblically based Christian perfectionism was the dominant ethos. As Ballou described it, the founders of Hopedale realized that "we must not only preach but live by what we had received as truth, or else renounce it as impracticable."[9] Those truths pushed them toward a stance of common ownership of property and nonresistant pacifism, ideals that they believed could be pursued only as a group set apart from the social mainstream. Hopedale lasted fifteen years in its original form (1841–56), a good record for such experiments, although its ending, characteristically, was the result of a financial failure. In a modified form, the community existed until 1868. Even so, as Ballou himself later realized, the value of the experiment was in what its members learned—it was "a school of valuable experience" to them, even if we suspect that the experience, at least at the end, was harsh.[10]

Like another communal experiment, Brook Farm, Hopedale has seemed to gain in significance despite its practical demise. In both cases the communes remain valuable indicators of the beliefs of the period—beliefs strong enough to make men put their lives and fortunes on the line to test them. George Ripley* made Brook Farm a Unitarian or Transcendentalist version of Hopedale, and the contrasts of the two experiments are instructive. Hopedale was more political, and Brook Farm more educational in goal. Hopedale was more pietistic and certainly more biblical; Brook Farm was artistic. Just as Brook Farm began in 1846 to transform itself into a different enterprise—a phalanx modeled on the principles of the French Utopian Charles Fourier—a fire crippled it financially. Hopedale persisted a decade longer, but by then most of the nation's moral energy was focused on the coming war.[11]

The most notable characteristic of Hopedale was its affirmation of nonresistance, a philosophy that Ballou articulated in his most important work, *Christian Non-Resistance* (1846). For Ballou, the doctrine was "as ancient as Christianity, and as true as the New Testament," and he found its sanction in Matthew 5:39: "Resist not evil." After making some careful distinctions about the extent of this injunction, Ballou paraphrased it as "Resist not personal injury with personal injury."[12] He recognized the far-reaching implications of this reading of the scripture, and as he explained it, we can see why he felt compelled to withdraw from society to be able to live up to it. "It bears on all mankind, in every social relation of life. It contemplates men as actually injured, or in imminent danger of being injured by their fellow men; and commands them to abstain from all personal injuries either as a means of retaliation, self-defence, or suppression of injury."[13] Aside from the personal moral obligations that this stance implied, it also severely restricted the range of relations that one could conscientiously maintain with government. Moral obligation and political dissent went hand in hand for Ballou. Only "absolutely uninjurious" resistance can be offered to any threat, and these "benevolent resistances," which help promote "safety and welfare," are a duty.[14]

Although Ballou based his position on Scripture, he worked hard to provide both philosophical and pragmatic justifications for it. "All-perfect, independent, self-sustaining, unswervable love—DIVINE LOVE—is the principle from which Christian non-resistance proceeds."[15] Such was the principle, most Universalists would have affirmed, on which they anchored their belief in the universal salvation of all souls. The same loving God who would draw all souls to him also commanded a moral enactment of that love by humans. But even more telling is Ballou's insistence on "the essential efficacy of good, as the counteracting force with which to resist evil."[16] There was more than a sacrificial attitude behind Ballou's stance. Convinced that force is not only evil but finally inefficient, he saw a consistent application of nonviolence as the key to a general social reformation. Indeed, the living out of such principles "would immediately usher in the Millennium"—an event that he knew was promised. Humanity, he pleaded, needed only to redeem that promise.[17]

## FEMINISM AND REFORM

During the early nineteenth century another group, the largest of the oppressed classes, began to assert its own claims to its potential. Women began to move toward their liberation, and the religious community, in some significant ways a point of origin for that movement, also began to feel the effects of it. The liberals, bound to premises that helped to set the demands for change, again found themselves near the center of that ferment.

It is somewhat easier to see the connection that existed between literate Unitarianism and the women's movement, for the commitment to education and the opportunities for it in that tradition could provide the seeds for change in women's development and thus in their conception of their role. That this was indeed the case has been established in much recent work on the origins of American feminism. According to Ann Douglas, a process of "feminization" was transforming the entire culture, a process fostered by a close connection between the liberalizing aims of Unitarian and other liberal Protestant theology and the sentimentalizing aims of much popular women's writing.[18]

Yet if those same conditions did not exist to as great an extent among the Universalists, other factors made that tradition equally hospitable to the women's movement. The very iconoclasm of the Universalists and their loose structure and tradition of experiment slackened certain oppressive ties on women that remained tighter in other traditions. The feminist roots of American Universalism can be traced to a prominent source—Judith Sargent Murray,* the wife of the denomination's founder John Murray.* An author and early advocate of sexual equality, Murray's attitudes are typified by this ringing polemic from an essay of 1790: "Yes, ye lordly, ye haughty sex, our souls are by nature *equal* to yours; the same breath of God animates, enlivens, and invigorates us; and that we are not fallen lower than yourselves, let those witness who have greatly towered above the various discouragements by which they have been so heavily oppressed."[19] Murray's strong defense of woman's nature also shows a close and natural recurrence to theology to support the arguments for their equality. Women were eager to meet the religious sanctions of their oppression with a religious justification for their liberation. To point to this real although limited hospitality to women's rights in Unitarianism and Universalism is by no means to imply an easy acceptance within them of feminism. The Unitarian theological school at Meadville, for instance, refused to accept the application of Olympia Brown* for admission, because its "trustees thought it would be too great an experiment."[20] Brown, who later became a leading feminist reformer, persisted in her efforts and was admitted to the Universalist school at St. Lawrence University, but even there her pursuit of training was by no means easy. By 1870, one hundred years after the sect was founded, only fifteen women had been Universalist preachers in America, and that record was, by the standards of the day, a good one.[21] The danger of dwelling on the progress of certain women and their ideas of equality is that the difficulties of scores of others may be forgotten. But both Unitarianism and Universalism do leave us with some impressive women's stories, a few of which may indicate the larger nature of American feminism.

Such an inquiry must begin with a consideration of the "cult of domesticity," a locus of ideas about the nature and place of women that thrived in the early nineteenth century. Insofar as this ideology identified the home as the place of women and argued for women's fulfillment through domestic expression, it can be taken as a regressive attempt to keep women "in their place." Yet curiously, it was not as antifeminist as it at first seems, for its thrust was to provide an identity to women and even a certain measure of independence and control over their lives. In the fictional depictions of this cult in women's fiction of the time, Nina Baym even found a "pragmatic feminism" and noted that the pattern of the fictions is a young woman's growth from dependence to self-reliance. The home was a somewhat restrictive sphere, as later feminists came to recognize, but that it was a sphere for women at all was important in the 1820s. On these grounds, it is easier to see why Nancy F. Cott found that feminism historically depended on "the ideology of domesticity." [22]

There is perhaps no better example of female achievements within this sphere than that of Lydia Maria Child,* a woman whose intellectual and spiritual roots were in New England Unitarianism. [23] She was not a minister or theologian— the times precluded that as a possibility for her—but she participated in the theological education of her brother Convers Francis,* the Unitarian minister in Watertown and later professor at Harvard Divinity School. Francis was an associate of Ralph Waldo Emerson's* and sympathizer with the Transcendentalists, much in the center of the theological and literary currents of the day. When he assumed the pastorate of Watertown after his studies at Harvard, Lydia came to live with him, and there launched her literary career as a novelist, author of books of domestic advice for women, and an influential writer on abolitionism. By the middle 1830s she was by one estimate "the best-known woman writer in America." [24]

Child is best remembered historically for her contribution to the abolitionist cause. Her *Appeal in Favor of That Class of Americans Called Africans* (1833), which influenced William Ellery Channing's* *Slavery* (1835), has been mentioned earlier. Thomas Wentworth Higginson* said that Child's book made an abolitionist of him. Later she became editor of the *National Anti-Slavery Standard*, a more moderate reform publication than William Lloyd Garrison's *Liberator*. But before publishing her antislavery work, Child had published *The Frugal Housewife* (1830) and *The Mother's Book* (1831), both full of advice for women in their domestic roles. Domestic though the books were, it is not hard to find in them the "pragmatic feminism" that Baym found in the novels of the era. Child, for instance, warned that in the education of daughters, "the greatest and most universal error is, teaching girls to exaggerate the importance of getting married; and of course to place an undue importance upon the polite attentions of gentlemen." She also lamented the "absence of *domestic education*" among American women, seeing the usefulness of practical education as one means of promoting the individual self-reliance and happiness of women. [25]

In discussing women's rights, Child focused on the irony that men were unable themselves to live out much of the advice they gave to women. "It would seem indeed," she wryly remarked, "as if men were willing to give women the exclusive benefit of gospel-teaching." But the issue of women's place she by no means took lightly: "That the present position of women in society is the result of physical force is obvious enough; whosoever doubts it, let her reflect why she is afraid to go out in the evening without the protection of a man." Nor do manners or the refinements of the lady's and gentlemen's role make up for this predicament: "This taking away rights, and *condescending* to grant *privileges*, is an old trick of the physical-force principle." It is odd then to hear

Child confess "that much of the talk about Women's Rights offends both my reason and my taste." What she seemed to feel was at stake here was a necessary female identity and connection with the home, one that, rather than shrinking as women were liberated, would instead grow to absorb the male role as well. "The nearer society approaches to divine order," she wrote, "the less separation will there be in the characters, duties, and pursuits of men and women."[26] Given her conviction of the centrality of home and family, this meant a larger domestic identity for men as well as a larger independence for women.

Child was a pioneer who deserves a better remembrance, but her contemporary Margaret Fuller,* a pioneer in a different and more radical fashion, is already coming into such a remembrance—a large and growing body of historical and interpretive studies of her life and work. Fuller, like Child, was raised in a Unitarian milieu and made close early friendships with James Freeman Clarke* and Frederic Henry Hedge* during their own theological studies. Later she formed a close friendship with Emerson, one of the most important of such relationships in American intellectual history. Even though she attracted and impressed all of New England's better minds, her life was a struggle and a search, and her only lasting vocation was her mind. Even in that she suffered, the victim, in some senses, of an education by her father that was as much revenge upon her for her sex (although perhaps an unconscious one) as a gesture of his belief in sexual equality. She described her father as "a man of business, even in literature," and remembered the severity and pressure of his teaching, which in her early childhood left her exhausted, overstimulated, and "a victim of spectral illusions, nightmare, and somnambulism."[27]

Yet Fuller was an extraordinary woman and was unwilling to give up her intellectual development even if she came to recognize her father's mistakes as a teacher. Her single goal was intellectual and spiritual development: "*Very early I knew that the only object in life was to grow*" (*Memoirs*, I, 133). Child would have readily accepted such a doctrine, but Fuller exemplified it in a different and more challenging way by focusing her energies on what was then regarded as an essentially male realm. She was an early student of Goethe and wrote one of the more influential American appraisals of him in 1841. She was first editor of the *Dial*, the periodical that for four years (1840–44) stood as the key expression of Transcendental thought. In 1839 she organized and conducted a remarkable series of conversations for women, public dialogues designed to address the condition and prospects of women. Perhaps most important, she wrote *Woman in the Nineteenth Century* (1845), a challenging assessment of the powers of women and an argument for their full social and intellectual equality. The book has been called "a landmark in the history of women's rights," and Fuller argued that the development of the full potential of women was necessary to the continued progress of society as a whole. "I think women need, especially at this juncture, a much greater range of occupation than they have, to rouse their latent powers."[28] This insistence that women's development is dependent upon an increased range of choices for life differs in emphasis, if not in fundamental assumption, from Child's. If Child had the ear of more of her contemporaries because of her domestic and pragmatic version of female self-reliance, Fuller, ahead of her time in several ways, has come to be seen as an important early crusader for an enlarged sense of woman's identity.

Fuller seemed to find herself only by leaving America for Italy, where she took part in Mazzini's struggle for independence in the late 1840s. By then she had married and seemed to be finding both personal fulfillment and an arena of action commensurate with her intellectual growth.[29] On her return to America in 1850, she died in a shipwreck within sight of land. Her legacy, large as it is, was only beginning to take shape.

Child and Fuller represent notable examples of the presence and accomplishment of women in nineteenth-century Unitarianism, and they are paralleled by two others, Mary A. Livermore* and Olympia Brown, among the Universalists. Of these four, only Brown was an ordained minister, although the other three women had the closest of connections, through male friends or relatives, to the pulpit. All of them stand as examples of intellect that had to make its own way in the world. Child, Fuller, and Livermore found in authorship a profession, although that is the loneliest and most insecure of them. For Livermore, however, authorship was in many senses a by-product of a primary commitment to lecturing. The same vital and growing lyceum network that largely supported Emerson as a public speaker also welcomed her, as she began to lecture as part of her work for the U.S. Sanitary Commission during the war.

Livermore had married a prominent Universalist minister, Daniel P. Livermore, who edited the denominational journal *New Covenant* in Illinois.[30] She wrote much for that journal, and although she always advocated the extension of women's rights, her experiences in working for the Sanitary Commission sharpened her sense of injustice and made her an advocate of women's suffrage. The change was not easy for her, because it involved a fundamental revision of her faith in the paternalistic benevolence of men. "I had been reared and had lived all my life among the best and noblest men; my estimate of men in general was a lofty one; and my faith in them was so strong, that I firmly believed it was only necessary to present to them the wrongs and injustice done to women, to obtain prompt and complete redress."[31] Livermore's work in the political organization that the Sanitary Commission was undertaking convinced her, however, of the naiveté of her faith. "I saw how women are degraded by disfranchisement, and, in the eyes of men, are lowered to the level of the pauper, the convict, the idiot, and the lunatic, and are put in the same category with them, and with their own infant children. Under a republican form of government, the possession of the ballot by woman can alone make her the legal equal of man, and without this legal equality, she is robbed of her natural rights" (p. 480). Thus Livermore joined the suffrage movement when it began to grow again after the war, and her lyceum career centered around her advocacy of what she termed "the great awakening of women" (p. 491). Her most popular lecture, "What Shall We Do with Our Daughters?" (delivered more than eight hundred times in twenty-five years) began with Livermore's account of her first reading of Fuller's *Woman in the Nineteenth Century* and the promise that it seemed to hold for a new age for women. The "air of repression, of limitation, of hindrance, of disability, of gloom, of servitude" that had clouded the history of women finally seemed to be lifting in the nineteenth century (p. 616). Although she understood the slow working of such historical processes, Livermore thought that a significant difference would be felt by the generation of women following her own. Thus, she argued, " 'what shall we do with our daughters?' is really the sum and substance of what, in popular phrase, is called 'the woman question' " (p. 619). The substance of her lecture was little more than what a modern reader would recognize as common sense. Protect the physical health of women as a first step toward promoting their mental and moral development. Provide them a range of training and options for employment, including not only domestic training but technical, business, and managerial education, and provide the moral and religious instruction that "underlies and permeates all other training when it is wisely and judiciously given" (p. 628). But such common sense, when it pertained to women's education, was at a premium in the nineteenth century, and Livermore faced "unfavorable criticism" as she began. "But I was so confident that I was right, that I received it without reply, and continued to say what I believed ought to be said" (p. 492).

Although a central part of her career, Livermore's lecturing took place amidst a host of other activities, primarily organizational and administrative duties for the women's rights movement. She represented the more moderate wing of nineteenth-century American feminism and combined her crusade for suffrage with work for reform in temperance, race relations, and church organization. Her vision was one of progress, and a millennialist thread holds her various activities together. She envisioned an approaching "great, grand time" that promised social justice and equality.[32]

One sign of that justice was the career of Olympia Brown. Brown was among the first American women to receive denominational ordination (1863), an important step in women's access to authority and roles of decision making. Brown was a determined woman, a skillful preacher and organizer, and she also had a keen sense of denominational politics. She needed all of these qualities to secure her ordination, as she recounted the steps in the process.[33] After a brief stay at Mount Holyoke, she completed her education at Antioch, one of the few colleges committed to coeducation. It was at Antioch that Brown decided to enter the ministry. Her major reason was compelling and suggests how closely linked were her theological vision and her sense of social justice. While at Mount Holyoke she had been confronted with a disturbing version of hell-and-damnation orthodoxy, a shock to her, since she had been raised on the teachings of Hosea Ballou, whom her mother admired. Challenged by the demands of that orthodoxy, Brown worked out her own sense of liberal religion in opposition to it. In the more liberal atmosphere of Antioch, she gradually formed "the determination to be a preacher,'' still largely in the spirit of rebellion from evangelical Protestanism. "Ever since my experience at Mt. Holyoke I had been anxious to tell the truth about the doctrine of endless punishment. I vainly supposed that if people could only be told that there was no such thing as everlasting punishment as it was then literally preached, they would be rejoiced'' (p. 26).

Brown recognized that ordination was important to her mission. She had been influenced by Antoinette Brown (Blackwell),* a preacher who lacked official recognition from a denomination and "therefore did not have the authority or influence which ordination should give" (p. 26). So she decided to seek admission to the Universalist Theological School at St. Lawrence University, realizing that her preparation at Antioch would not be enough to win her ordination. To the credit of the president of St. Lawrence, Ebenezer Fisher,* she was admitted. But in accepting her, Fisher noted that "he did not think women were called to the ministry." It is a measure of Brown's determination that such a response did not dissuade her, as Fisher apparently thought it would. "I leave that between you and the Great Head of the Church," he had written her in conclusion. "This, I thought, was just where it should be left," was Brown's reaction, and a surprised president and faculty found themselves soon undertaking, without great enthusiasm, the education of a woman for the ministry (p. 27).

Brown had to be as careful and persistent in obtaining ordination as in pursuing her education. While at St. Lawrence she established a reputation for her preaching in northern New York and took that reputation, along with an invitation to assume a pastorate in the area, into the meeting of the ordaining council in 1863 and won her case. Once the fact was accomplished, even President Fisher, who had not supported her in her search for ordination, took part in the ceremony. With some charity, Brown remembered these hesitant male pioneers and experimenters who helped her win ordination: "They took that stand, a remarkable one for the day, which shows the courage of these men" (p. 30).

The beginning of Brown's career was not easy. The most important of her early churches, in Weymouth, Massachusetts, was in a sad disarray when she took it over, but the congregation was progressive, and she found there the support and opportunity she needed to launch her career. She stayed there six years and followed it with ministries in Bridgeport, Connecticut, and Racine, Wisconsin. But she wrote, "As the years passed by it became more and more clear that I must give myself more to the suffrage work" (p. 62). This commitment to the women's rights cause led her to resign her pastorate at Racine in 1887. In a sense that change of career directions was actually a fulfillment of a life whose direction had been toward liberation. The weight of what she considered regressive religious belief was oppressive, as was the weight of sexual discrimination. Her career was a battle against both of them.

## THE SOCIAL GOSPEL AND THE ETHIC OF INDIVIDUALISM

At the turn of the century, both Unitarianism and Universalism had their part in a more general movement within Protestantism, the social gospel. The social gospel stressed the relevance of Christianity to the socioeconomic realm and demanded that Christian ideals be realized in the economic relations between individuals and classes. Even though it emerged into the forefront of Protestant thinking at the end of the century and stood in many senses as a challenge to the tradition that spawned it, it was, as Sydney Ahlstrom remarked, "anything but new." It was instead a kind of culmination of many of the tendencies toward social action that had been evident within parts of American Protestantism since before the Civil War. What seemed to bring these tendencies to the forefront with so much force late in the century were the economic upheavals of late nineteenth-century American life. The labor unrest of the late 1890s was the single most important cause of the movement, because that conflict directly challenged the complacent optimism of many Christian thinkers. The rise of an uncontrolled laissez-faire capitalism accentuated the moral and ethical implications of economic power, and those issues were dramatized in the labor disputes. The period following the Civil War was one of enormous economic and geographic growth for the nation but also one of scandal, strife, labor unrest, and mounting agrarian and urban problems. The social gospel addressed those issues, combating with a message of compassion, hope, and reform the increasingly unfair distribution of the nation's wealth and what Ahlstrom noted as the Puritan legacy of "the American's basic contempt for poverty."[34]

Given the history of social concern that we have noted in the Unitarian and Universalist tradition, it is not surprising to find within that liberal tradition one of the theoretical pioneers of the social gospel, Francis Greenwood Peabody.* Born in the heart of the Boston Unitarian tradition (his father was the minister at King's Chapel in Boston), Peabody's real intellectual maturity came when his Unitarian sensibility was enriched by his study in Germany during the 1870s with the German theologian Friedrich A. G. Tholuck.[35] Peabody later recalled his earlier studies at Harvard Divinity School caustically: "It had been a disheartening experience of uninspiring study and retarded thought. The fresh breeze of modern thought rarely penetrated the lecture-rooms, and a student found the intellectual atmosphere unexhilarating to breathe."[36] But Peabody's studies in Germany, particularly his experiences under the guidance of Tholuck, convinced him that theology could engage the problems of the contemporary world. Although he set out to be a parish minister and treasured the experience he had as a minister in Cambridge, Massachusetts, he found his health too precarious for the demands of the parish. In 1880 he decided to leave the ministry. "I was, as it then seemed, demoted to temporary duty in the Harvard Divinity School." But this "calamity," as he thought, "turned out . . . to be an opportunity,'' and Peabody found an important place for himself in his long career at the Divinity School (Peabody, p. 117). There he was a pioneer in the study of social ethics, impressing upon his students the theological importance of ''the social question.'' His book *Jesus Christ and the Social Question* (1900) became one of the milestones of the social gospel movement and of twentieth-century liberal religion.[37]

Part of the power of Peabody's volume was its frank recognition of the changing circumstances of the age and their effect on its spirit. Not only is the present age given a peculiar mission, he wrote, ''but there is added a distinct consciousness of that mission.'' He defined that consciousness as ''a burdening sense of social mal-adjustment'' and further specified that it is this ''social question'' that ''gives its fundamental character to the present age.'' The root of that sense of maladjustment was ''the contradiction between economic progress and spiritual ideals,'' the great cost in social injustice that the rise of industrial capitalism had caused (pp. 2–3).

Peabody went on to specify two other aspects of the modern temper that set it apart. The ''degree of radicalism'' and ''scope of reconstructive purpose'' of the age ''practically create a new situation'' (p. 5). What he meant in outlining this first unique aspect of modern thinking was that the three institutions that ''appear to support the fabric of modern civilization—the family, private property, and the State''—were now under serious questioning and even attack (p. 7). In addition to this radicalism a second aspect of modern thinking made it, for Peabody, a unique phase of human history. ''Whatever aspect of it we approach, we find the discussion and agitation of the present time turning in a quite unprecedented degree to moral issues, and using the language and weapons of a moral reform. The social question of the present time is an ethical question'' (p. 9). The significance of this fusion of the political and ethical categories is enormous, for Peabody had come to the recognition that in the modern age, moral questions often are political. Thus he argued that ''the social question, which on its surface is an economic question, issues in reality from a sense of wrong'' (p. 10). In distinction from some forms of radical analysis, which would give primacy to the economic category, Peabody argued that the modern social consciousness is fundamentally an ethical expression.

Given this ethical quality in the reform impulse, Peabody found an anomaly in the fact that the church was alienated in large part from this consciousness. The reform spirit that he discerned was essentially secular. ''It is not enough to say that the socialist programme is indifferent to religion. It undertakes to provide a substitute for religion'' (p. 19). This was, for Peabody, one principal problem to be faced by the Christian community. To bring about a reunion of religion and social reform would not only be to give the church a renewed place in human affairs; more importantly, it would restore to the religious spirit its direct connection to its ethical imperative. A theology alienated from ethical expression was, for Peabody, a doomed enterprise. For him, the social gospel was an antidote to this alienation.

In terms of his social views, Peabody was hardly a radical. There is no call in his work for an overthrow of the social order. Even the violent labor conflicts of the 1890s, which transformed the outlook of many Protestants, did not persuade Peabody that the relation between labor and capital was inevitably one of warfare. The "prevailing industrial warfare," he argued, "is not an antagonism which is inherent in economic life. In fact, it is at bottom not an economic antagonism at all" (p. 271). Like the social protest movement itself, Peabody found the labor movement an expression of moral outrage rather than economic war. The workers, who "find themselves the agents in producing wealth of which they obtain but an insignificant share, . . . cry out with passionate indignation as against a grievous wrong" (pp. 271–72). It was not the production of industrial wealth, or even the ownership by individuals of the means of production, that caused the problem. It was the unjustifiable distribution of the wealth that violated the moral sense of justice.

As the title of his book indicates, Peabody hoped to bring the character of Jesus to bear on the modern social question, and it is in this attempt that we begin to see his social position develop. He did not attempt to impose an ancient order on a modern condition, for he recognized that in the Gospels there was no systematic social plan. "Jesus was, first of all, not a reformer but a revealer; he was not primarily an agitator with a plan, but an idealist with a vision" (pp. 77–78). He was, in fact, unsystematic to the point of inconsistency, at least to one who tried to draw a rational and orderly set of sociopolitical attitudes from his teachings. Jesus's method was the "case-system," an empirical and inductive response to social and moral problems as he found them (p. 88). His goal was never political but stayed within the bounds of a much more limited personal sphere, where personality itself was an answer as well as a method. "The communication of vitality, the contagion of personality, the transmission of character,—these are the ends he seeks, and these are possible only through that individualization of teaching which marks his ministry" (p. 90).

When Peabody turned then to the existing industrial order, he was constrained to recognize that no "specific instructions concerning the form of modern industry shall be derived from the teaching of Jesus" (p. 273). In an age in which both ardent free-enterprise capitalists and socialists of various kinds had been eager to find support or justification for their views in Jesus, Peabody insisted that the message of the Gospels continued to be personal, resistant to any attempts to impose systematic politics on it. Peabody's was a liberal view, one that sought change and accommodation within existing structures, although it was not necessarily wedded to those structures. Such accommodation could be achieved, he thought, through a revitalization of the goal of service. The example of Jesus, finally, was one of service through self-sacrifice. His power derived from his surrender of himself, and this was an example, personal in essence, that had social implications. "The law of service which he announces for his disciples is not a wholly unknown principle in the world of competitive trade. It governs the organization of industry regarded as a whole, and it tests great numbers of individual lives even when they are unconscious of its judgment" (p. 321). Peabody's idea of service was an almost direct appeal to the rich and controlling classes for a more responsible stewardship of wealth. It envisioned a benign form of capitalism, but a capitalism nevertheless, one infused with an ideal of worth measured by one's impact on others. "Here is a test which any man may apply to his own business life. Am I, in my own place and degree, moved by a spirit of service?" (p. 322). Even by the standards of his day, this was cautiously progressive economic theory, and among the leaders of the social gospel, his positions were firmly moderate. But his strength and importance was in his recognition of social problems, for on that score he did much to advance the dialogue of the period.

Peabody did not abandon the individualism that had marked Unitarian thinking from the Arminian movement on. But he did turn that individualism against the tendency of the nineteenth century to identify personal development and evolutionary optimism with the expansion of American business and economic interests. In him we see the ethical individualism of Unitarianism, and of American culture in general, made into an instrument of self-criticism and social change. Peabody insisted that the profoundest lessons of Christianity are personal, known and taught only on an individual basis. But the substance of those lessons is self-sacrifice, the channeling of personal development into an ethic of service to others. The follower of Jesus "sanctifies himself for others' sakes, and there is given to him unanticipated effectiveness for social service" (p. 358). Peabody was thus able to extend the Unitarian ideology of self-development into the arena of social service, a widening of that perspective, although not a break with the past. The call to social involvement as a means of self-development has, since Peabody's day, become a central part of the Unitarian ethos.

The legacy of Peabody was the conviction that matters of ethics and politics were inseparable. That legacy was exemplified in the career of John Haynes Holmes,* a leader in pacifist and reform causes in the early twentieth century. Holmes had been educated at Harvard College and Divinity School, where he had courses from Peabody and began to imbibe the social imperative of the day. He assumed duties as the junior minister at the Church of the Messiah in New York in 1906 and set the tone of his career in the ministry with his insistence upon the preacher's duty to speak out on social issues, invoking the example of Theodore Parker* as a model for the Christian minister. He found, as Peabody had, that the economic injustice of the industrial age was a central concern of Christian ethics, and in a sermon on Christianity and socialism, he argued that the "brotherhood" that socialism represented was "the religion of Jesus." He also developed a close friendship with progressives such as Socialist party leader Norman Thomas and American Civil Liberties Union founder Roger Baldwin.[38]

In 1912 Holmes published his definitive statement of the political imperative of religion, *The Revolutionary Function of the Modern Church.*[39] It was a plea for a renewed life in the church, which Holmes thought could only be achieved on the basis of "modernism." By this he meant a religion completely free from "the supernatural and the miraculous" (p. 5). But he also meant more. He called for "a movement of 'modernism' in the world of action as well as in the world of thought," one that would move the church directly into the sphere of social action (p. 11).

The basis of this active modernism was the movement of religion away from a concentration on the individual alone, to a fuller sense of the social nature of every individual. Liberalism, specifically the Unitarian movement, had not yet altered the fact that in the Christian tradition the individual was central. The liberals had replaced the old emphasis on salvation with a new emphasis on "nurture, education, cultivation," a movement that signified a fundamental faith in human nature (p. 24). Although Holmes recognized this central feature of liberalism as "an absolute break with the whole theory of salvation in both its Catholic and Protestant forms," he also believed that, in another respect, the continuity of the Christian tradition had remained intact (p. 22). "In other words, Liberalism is at one with Catholicism and Protestantism in seeing in each individual nothing but an isolated personal entity, having little or no vital connection with anything or anybody external to itself" (pp. 28–29). Thus the doctrine of self-cultivation of the liberal tradition did not address the social problems of the individual. "The Liberal seeks to save himself by culture, education, and development as an individual; and he seeks to save other people in the same way as individuals" (p. 34).

The essential fact of modern life, however, was that this individualism had been proven wanting. Holmes saw the theory of evolution (especially as interpreted by Herbert Spencer), with its stress on environmental determinants to identity, as one refutation of the concept of inviolate individualism. He saw the complexity of modern social organization as another. These factors suggested "that, strictly speaking, there is no such thing as an individual at all; that what seems to be an isolated personal entity . . . is in reality a social creature" (p. 38). Holmes's most effective support was the argument made by Jane Addams in *The Social Application of Religion* concerning the vulnerability of women and families in urban tenement conditions to forces beyond their control. Addams's demonstration that social conditions dictated the fulfillment of the individual, or the lack of it, was for Holmes ample proof that "the problem of life to-day is no longer the problem of the individual but the problem of the society which environs the individual and determines the conditions of his life" (p. 66). This pressed on him a new definition of the individual: "The individual is an epitome of the society of which he is a member" (p. 71).

From this notion of the socially determined individual, the new function of the church was not hard to deduce. Holmes concluded, following Theodore Parker, that the church "must grapple at first hand with the conditions of society" (p. 170). Therefore, the motivations and the conditions for membership would have to be essentially different. The nature of that difference is indicated in one passage of particular eloquence by Holmes. Its flavor is distinctly utopian:

In the past, the church has been regarded as a more or less passive witness of salvation; in the future it will be regarded as an active agent of salvation. In the past, it has been the body of those who have been saved from the evils of the world; in the future it will be the body of those who are saviours of the world from the evils which assail it. In the past, it has been a place of refuge, where men could flee for safety; in the future it will be an armoury, where men may come to arm themselves against "the rulers of the darkness of the world." (p. 177)

These principles of religion as social change, and the church as the agent of that change, had been set in motion, as we have seen, during Holmes's ministry in New York. By 1918 Holmes's reputation as a leader of the radical wing of liberal religion had grown large enough that upon the death of Jenkin Lloyd Jones* he was offered Jones's role as director of the Abraham Lincoln Centre in Chicago, a social service organization that Jones had forged as an expression of his own social vision.

Although Holmes decided to stay in New York, the offer in Chicago gave him the chance to lead the Church of the Messiah into a new identity as a congregation much in the mold of the Free Religion movement. The church dropped "Messiah" from its title, ended pew rental, and eliminated a covenant as a requirement for membership. It was renamed the Community Church, symbolic of the direction that Holmes was leading it—from liberal Christianity to a religion of social concern. In Holmes's view the reformulation of the church was "the logical completion and perfection of the liberal movement in modern religion" for three reasons: it "(1) shifts the basis of religion from God to man; (2) moves from the individual to the social group as the center of religious life; and (3) accepts the community in place of the denomination as the unit of spiritual integration."[40] This affirmation of Humanism, rejection of individualism, and embracing of secular social life as the sphere of religion were indeed the major thrusts of twentieth-century liberalism, as Holmes declared.

By far the most significant social stance that Holmes took was his pacifism, a stance brought to dramatic climax in World War I. Holmes had felt the injustice of the European War at its outbreak, but by 1916 he developed a belief in consistent nonresistance that extended to all wars, a position articulated in his book New Wars for Old.[41] Holmes argued that all human progress could be explained as "the restriction of force within ever narrower and narrower bounds and the expansion of love to ever wider and wider areas" (p. 114). He found the origin of nonresistance, as Adin Ballou had done, in Christ's charge, "Resist not evil." Holmes defined this charge as the resistance of specifically human evil (not the hostile forces of nature). By resistance, Holmes argued that Christ meant that one should not repay evil with evil or force with force. What measures would then be left to the nonresistant? Holmes listed three, in ascending order of importance: passive resistance, the use of reason, education, or persuasion; and the use of love and service to others. "To forgive, to serve, to love supremely—to meet injury with service and evil with good—this is at once to conquer every difficulty, stay every peril, and win mankind" (p. 137).

Holmes recognized the chief objection to his position: "Is not the consistent non-resistant a suicide?" (p. 211). But, again, like Ballou, he insisted on the practical efficacy of the principle of nonresistance, calling it "the only force that is practicable" (p. 219). This did not mean, for Holmes, that the principle "will never fail under any circumstances" (p. 222). He was too much a realist to expect that. But he did insist that in the longer view its results would be more practical than force. For Holmes, nonresistance was founded on the working of two spiritual laws—"that like always produces like" and "that the spirit is always superior to the flesh" (p. 259). Thus force will, overall, result in force, and love will result in love; conscience and right, the things of the spirit, will finally win over material force. It is no surprise that Holmes became "a foremost American interpreter of Gandhi's views." He discovered Mohandas Gandhi's example and writings after he had worked to his pacifist principles, but he saw in him a modern-day Christ, one who vindicated the rightness and practicality of the nonresistant position. In a sermon in 1921, which did much to awaken Americans to the importance of Gandhi's work, Holmes declared him to be the "greatest man in the world," although he did so with as yet only a slim knowledge of Gandhi's career. But the analogy with Jesus that he saw was central to Holmes's sense of Gandhi's importance and turned out to be prophetic: "When I think of Gandhi, I think of Jesus. He lives his life; he speaks his word; he suffers, strives, and will some day nobly die, for his small kingdom upon earth." Holmes would later say that "my real life as a teacher began with Gandhi," and it can also be said that Gandhi's reputation in America began with Holmes's sermon.[42]

Holmes had published his idea of nonresistance after the war had begun but before America's entry into it. That entry was a severe test for him, leaving him the choice of abandoning his views or of standing "as pacifist and heretic" against the overwhelming war sentiment. The dilemma was particularly acute because of his relation to his church—could his people accept a minister opposed to the war effort that most of them supported? Holmes took his stand against the war in 1917: "When or if, the system of conscription is adopted, I shall have to decline to serve. If this means a fine, I will pay my fine. If this means imprisonment, I will serve my term. If this means persecution, I will carry my cross."[43] Holmes's courage was rewarded by the support of his church, based not on an agreement with his opposition to the war, but on his right, as minister of a free church, to speak as his conscience dictated. He stands as a central exemplar for the pacifist voice within liberal religion, a minority voice, but an influential part of the liberal social conscience.

No discussion of liberal religion as a social venture could overlook the contributions of Clarence Skinner,* Universalist leader both as a minister and educator and a man who, as Alan Seaburg put it, "may prove to have influenced Universalism as deeply as did the great Hosea Ballou."[44] An associate of Holmes in many endeavors, Skinner's importance to Universalism was his leadership in the denomination's move from a conception of Universalism as a theological doctrine to a broadened notion of Universalism as a working philosophy aimed at securing the universal harmony of all individuals on earth. His commitment to social religion is exemplified in his appointment in 1910 to serve as secretary of the Universalist Social Service Commission, which was followed by his appointment as professor of applied Christianity at Crane Theological School, associated with Tufts University. His early pronouncements in that position were intended to demonstrate the social implications of Universalism, seizing on the implications of the word *brotherhood* as a guide to a transforming social vision. That expansion of the notion of brotherhood was in fact part of a long process by which Universalism was evolving from Christian sectarianism to universal religion.

A more official pronouncement of this developing social vision can be found in the 1917 Declaration of Social Principles and Social Program, which was written by Skinner and adopted by the Universalist General Convention. The declaration rejected the idea of "inherent depravity" in humans and argued instead "that mankind is led into sin by evil surroundings, by the evils of unjust social and economic conditions." Its call was for the establishment of a democracy, "not only an inherent right, but also a divinely imposed duty." A long list of specific social recommendations included a call for "democratization of industry and land," equal rights for women, guarantees of free speech, prohibition, "some form of social insurance," and work toward a world federation. The prophetic nature of these recommendations is today striking. The report concluded with this "program for completing humanity":

*First:* An Economic Order which shall give to every human being an equal share in the common gifts of God, and in addition all that he shall earn by his own labor.

*Second:* A Social Order in which there shall be equal rights for all, special privilege for none, the help of the strong for the weak until the weak become strong.

*Third:* A Moral Order in which all human law and action shall be the expression of the moral order of the universe.

*Fourth:* A Spiritual Order which shall build out of the growing lives of living men the growing temple of the living God.[45]

It is significant that the final point here places the order of life before the spiritual order. This certainly indicates the movement of Universalism toward a conception of universal social democracy or brotherhood, rather than an otherworldly religion.

In a comparison of the social outlook of Peabody and Skinner, James D. Hunt noted that despite many points of similarity, Skinner's was ultimately a more radical outlook than Peabody's. That Skinner was a generation younger than

Peabody accounts in part for the difference. Peabody stressed stewardship, the responsibility of those who owned wealth to see that it was equitably distributed. His was a philosophy of philanthropy and service. Skinner was inclined to take the more radical stance that inequalities in ownership of goods should be eliminated. In a 1945 book called *A Religion for Greatness*, Skinner outlined a "radical religion" based upon a "vital, meaningful relationship between the self and the universe," a religion that he thought of as "Universalism" in a modern sense.[46] That this new Universalism had economic implications is made clear by Skinner's definition of "economic universalism" as a mode of organization "wherein the maximum numbers of human beings would be creative participators in the wealth of the world" (p. 43). Such an economic vision was one component of Skinner's larger call for a global unity in which individual nation states, while maintaining their identity, would "be integrated with a larger political whole, global in its extent" (p. 80). Ultimately, the "social universalism" that Skinner proposed is one that is both integrative but radically democratic—democratic in the sense in which Skinner defined it: "the organization of society with respect to the individual" (p. 103). If this vision seems to contradict the movement away from individualism that we noted in Peabody's writings, it should be said that for Skinner, individualism can only be preserved through the pursuit and accomplishment of this social universalism. The self, in a sense, has to be lost to the larger social vision in order to be saved. Only through the system of progressive global integration and economic equality that Skinner outlined can there be a complete organization of society in terms of the individual. Skinner recognized the necessity of having to sacrifice individual means of action to group solidarity in order to achieve an end that is ultimately individualistic.

Skinner's call in this book for global integration as the ultimate expression of Universalism had its roots in an earlier book that defined both the nature and future of liberalism, *Liberalism Faces the Future* (1937).[47] There he defined the "starting point" for liberalism as "belief in man," a sense that "at the core of human nature is a something sound and good" (p. 57). The liberal affirmation of human nature rests on a confidence in human intelligence, an "inherent moral capacity to choose the right" and a "social ability to meet the difficulties of shifting and confusing social forces" (p. 59). For Skinner, this human social ability was a paramount consideration in any social or religious theory, and the challenge of modern thought was to find a way to make effective "the innate urge to socialization which resides in social groups" (p. 61). For Skinner, the unity that social cohesion promises is central to any hope for individual freedom: "there is a natural, in fact, inescapable, connection between freedom and unity" (p. 74). As Skinner put it, in discussing individualism, it was necessary to see "the difference between necessary and enough." Individualism was indeed "necessary," but it was not "enough." (p. 97). A larger view was required that demonstrated that individual fulfillment arose within a social context.

# 11
# THE HUMANIST DEBATE

## THE HUMANIST MOVEMENT

The articulation and general acceptance of William Channing Gannett's* "Things Most Commonly Believed To-day Among Us," even though it explicitly avowed a form of theism, can be seen to mark movement away from theism in some Unitarian circles. This movement accelerated and gained prominence in the rise of the Humanist movement in the first three decades of the twentieth century. Although Gannett's declaration was clearly conciliatory toward the majority of theists in the denomination at the time, it left open a distinctly naturalistic interpretation of religion, noted earlier. A "God" that could be thought of as "that Love with which our souls commune" was not necessarily a supernatural or transcendent being or even a being at all. God might be thought of simply as a name or symbol for the aspiring religious sensibility of humanity. If this religious sensibility was not necessarily tied to a transcendent being, it might be thought of more precisely as an expression of the human personality itself, and religion might well be redefined as a purely human enterprise. Such was the drift of thought that eventuated in the Humanist presence in Unitarianism, the denomination's "most vital and distinctive theological movement since Transcendentalism."[1]

But any rejection of theism was decidedly a minority viewpoint in the late nineteenth and early twentieth centuries, especially in the East. James Freeman Clarke,* who is perhaps the best guidepost to the Unitarian sensibility during his age, argued for the necessity of a belief in God to any expression of religion: "Until some idea of God enters the mind, religion is impossible. It is a confusion of terms to define religion as a longing after the Infinite, or as an attempt at self-development, or as the sense of obligation, or the like."[2] For Clarke, religion had to remain centered in God rather than humanity, although that focus on God was certain to lead to human expression and growth. Minot

J. Savage* similarly argued that "in the true use of language, remembering that it is symbolical and only shadows forth the infinite reality, we may say that we can rationally believe that God is conscious, personal, and good."[3] Both Clarke's and Savage's theistic affirmations reveal a certain linguistic consciousness that suggests that many theists feared having the idea of God defined into inconsequence or even nothingness. As when Ralph Waldo Emerson* and others mounted their attack on the belief in the divinity of Jesus, the linguistic substructures of theological belief threatened to melt away.

We have already noted the fear of Jabez T. Sunderland* and other western conservatives that the concept of God was losing importance in Unitarianism. The "western issue" was only a prelude to the twentieth-century debate of Humanism, one that, although it involved different participants and phraseology, actually involved many of the same issues. Although its roots were deep in the theological ferment of the nineteenth century, the Humanist movement took shape in the second decade of the twentieth century through the developing theological positions of Curtis W. Reese* and John H. Dietrich.* The two of them met in 1917 when the Western Unitarian Conference was convened at Reese's church in Des Moines. Reese was calling for a "Democratic" approach to theology, one that upset all hierarchy, even that of God. Eventually, the label "Humanist" came to characterize his views, as well as those of Dietrich and others, largely because that term provided such an effective rhetorical contrast to theism.[4]

Dietrich and Reese were two of the most active individuals in Humanism; in fact, there might not have been a movement without them. They brought not only ideas but a proselyting zeal and an enormous organizational energy to the movement. Moreover, they shared a striking similarity of intellectual background, which helps explain their zeal. Both had simple beginnings as farm boys, Dietrich from Pennsylvania and Reese from North Carolina. Both began their ministries in more theologically conservative denominations before moving into Unitarianism. Dietrich ministered in the Reformed church, beginning his career in Pittsburgh in 1904, but he soon became a figure of controversy because of his liberalism. He was tried for heresy and removed from the ministry in 1911; thus forced from his denomination, he became a Unitarian and took over the church in Spokane the same year. As a Unitarian he thrived, moving to Minneapolis in 1916 where he remained for the rest of his active ministerial career.[5]

Curtis W. Reese was raised a Southern Baptist and preached from 1908 to 1913 in Baptist pulpits while attending college and the Southern Baptist Theological Seminary in Louisville. Impressed by the higher criticism of the Bible, which undermined his biblical faith, he evolved intellectually toward Unitarianism and eventually declared his change of faith in 1913, taking over a Unitarian Church in Alton, Illinois. From there he moved to Des Moines, having notably successful ministries in both cities, and eventually to Chicago as secretary of the Western Unitarian Conference in 1919.

These parallels are notable because they are more than coincidence. The radical impulse that pushed Dietrich and Reese beyond their more conservative backgrounds would also lead them to test the boundaries of Unitarianism. In fact, the third figure usually included in the leadership of Humanism, Charles F. Potter,* was a Baptist minister to begin with. Potter converted to Unitarianism in 1914 in a similar pattern of growing doubts about his traditional faith and attraction to the freedom of thought within Unitarianism.[6] These men represent a challenge that the denomination had to face increasingly in the twentieth century, especially in the West—to provide an institutional home for many who outgrew their previous one, "come-outers" from other denominations who were not committed to Unitarianism by birth or tradition but saw in it something they could not find in another more conservative faith. That Dietrich and Reese were not of New England origin, and that they ministered in the West, is also significant. By the early decades of the twentieth century, the intellectual preeminence of Boston to the denomination could no longer be assumed.

After this meeting in Des Moines, Reese and Dietrich both began to gain prominence in Unitarian circles and to diffuse their Humanist version of religion. One of the earliest and most controversial Humanist pronouncements was Reese's address to the Harvard Summer School of Theology in 1920. The fact that the address was given at Harvard added to its significance; like Emerson's Divinity School address, it might never have had the impact it did without that setting. Moreover, a version of it was published in the *Christian Register*, the principal denominational periodical at that time, thus expanding its impact. The spirit of Reese's address was communicated in the opening sentence: "Historically the basic content of religious liberalism is spiritual freedom."[7] The operative word of the sentence is "content." As Reese phrased it, freedom is not the attitude, the stance, or the gesture of liberalism but its content. In other words, there is no content to liberal belief in the ordinary sense of a set of accepted beliefs or truths or in the sense of a creed, even an unofficial one. That initial rejection of creed, stated as an affirmation of freedom, led Reese to argue that "Liberalism has insisted on the essentially natural character of religions" (p. 883). For Reese, the ultimate goal of liberal theology was a purely naturalistic faith, which he saw emerging in the Humanist movement.

Reese did offer a formal definition of liberalism, which serves well as a working definition of Humanism, even if it does not encompass all of liberalism. It reads as follows: "Conscious committal and loyalty to worthful causes and goals in order that free and positive personality may be developed, intelligently associated, and cosmically related" (p. 883). The reference here to religion as a process of personality development should by now be familiar. What makes the definition notable however is that Reese holds such development to be the result of a prior commitment to "worthful causes." It is through this social engagement that the personality is allowed to develop, a turn of thought that in itself is significant comment on the place of self-culture in Unitarianism. Reese found self-culture, pursued as an end in itself, to be a potentially hazardous diversion of energy away from social connection.

Reese directly stated that "the outstanding characteristic of modern liberals, and indeed of all modern thinking, is the evaluation of personality as the thing of supreme worth" (p. 883). Such personality had to be free of the pull of institutions, which often had to be "outgrown, and . . . like the hull of a chrysalis, be burst asunder and left only to mark an epoch past" (p. 883). But he also stressed "the essentially interdependent nature of human beings" and called for a principle of "radical good-will" to help usher in a united world. "The coming order," he wrote, "is a world order" (p. 884). In the order that he envisioned, democracy would be the operative principle. For Reese this meant not only a political democracy in the sense in which we usually understand it but a spiritual democracy as well. He rejected the "monarchic view of religion" (p. 883) that placed God in the role of master and humans in the role of slaves and envisioned instead "a religion that would not be shaken even if the old thought of God were outgrown" (p. 884). It was principally this implied rejection of God that "alarmed" many at Harvard, as Lyttle reported. Reese's statement showed clearly that Unitarianism had not yet completely resolved the "western issue" of several decades before.

As the implications of Reese's speech and other Humanist expressions reverberated through the denomination, William L. Sullivan* articulated one form of the resistance to Humanism. Sullivan had begun his ministerial career as a Roman Catholic priest but was forced out of his denomination by Pope Pius X's condemnation of modernism. Sullivan went on to a brilliant career in the Unitarian ministry, gaining particular prominence for his power of pulpit oratory. In the 1920s he was one of the most influential defenders of theism in the denomination. His debates with the Humanists reached a dramatic height when in 1921 he shared the rostrum of the National Conference at Detroit with Dietrich in what was essentially a Humanist-theist debate. Sullivan had hoped that the debate would result in the adoption of a statement affirming a belief in God, but the sympathies of the delegates were so clearly against such a statement (although the conference was not necessarily nontheist) that the plan was not offered.[8]

In a *Christian Register* article setting out his position just before that convention, Sullivan attacked both the Humanist rejection of God and other related attempts to formulate an idea of an evolving, or a less-than-omnipotent, God. "God, No-God, Half-God" was his title, a phrase whose striking absurdity was meant to call derision on those who abandoned, or even modified, traditional theism. For Sullivan, the notion that "a man who worships the Eternal is a servile person" deserved ridicule, and he satirized the nonauthoritarian God who would presumably replace the monarch as "the Big Democrat whom we are to clap upon the back with an equalitarian 'Howdy do, Camarado!' "[9] Sullivan's attack certainly has rhetorical impact, as this example suggests. Moreover, his sense of offense at the linking of theism and servility or feudalism has a certain justification, given the implications of Reese's choice of symbolism. But this sort of symbolic name calling on both sides did little to clarify the issues. Sullivan's "Big Democrat" image would be remembered much longer than his final grounds for his theistic affirmation, grounds that much more deserved to be heard. "Therefore amid the transiency and suffering necessarily involved in finiteness we look to the Eternal Perfection, knowing that . . . He will lead [our souls] at last to . . . union and communion with Himself" (p. 776). The Humanism of Reese and the theism of Sullivan arose from distinctly different senses of the world. Reese saw the coming of the new world order and the necessity of working toward it. Sullivan saw the transiency and suffering of earthly life as a permanent condition and stressed God as humankind's only relief from it. Unitarianism has continued to be split between these views, although the debate was never so agonizing as during the 1920s. Curiously, the principal spokesmen of the debate, Dietrich, Reese, and Sullivan, were all come-outers, converts to liberal religion who found support for their searches within the denomination and seriously influenced it with those searches.

Undoubtedly, the most famous statement of the Humanist position was "A Humanist Manifesto," which was drafted in 1932–33 by Roy Wood Sellars and signed by a number of influential intellectuals including Dietrich, Potter, and Reese. Its fifteen propositions attempt to summarize "the radical changes in religious beliefs throughout the modern world." Addressing the theistic question first, the manifesto characterizes the universe as "self-existing and not created" and defines *religion* as "those actions, purposes, and experiences which are humanly significant." Religion, in other words, is human life, and "the end of man's life," for the Humanist, is "the complete realization of the human personality."[10]

The manifesto is an admirably succinct presentation of Humanism, but a fuller sense of the movement, especially during its flourishing decade of the 1920s, is presented in the 1927 volume *Humanist Sermons* edited by Reese.[11] In his preface to the volume, Reese sketched an outline of Humanism, distinguishing it from materialism, positivism, rationalism, and atheism and then emphasizing three defining aspects of it. Humanism affirmed "that human life is of supreme worth" and that human nature is an end in itself, not a means to any other goal. Humanism was also committed to the use of "human inquiry" as a way to "understand human experience," an affirmation of the basically scientific and antisupernaturalistic impulse of the movement. Finally, it represented the most complete "effort to enrich human experience" (pp. x–xv). Reese placed his emphasis on progress, both of the individual and society.

Reese's affirmations tell us much, but not all, about the ethos of the movement. He was careful to stress that the existence of God is not denied by Humanism, but perhaps more important than an explicit theological position was the antimetaphysical mood of the group that he communicated. God was, for them, even worse than dead—God was ignored. Their revolt was not only away from belief in God but away from concern with theological speculation. In a later essay on Humanism, Reese noted that "the Humanist regards the universe as the given and is not likely to speculate unduly on either the beginning or the end of things cosmic.''[12] Yet there remained in Reese's affirmations a stress on development, growth, and culture, a strand of thought shown by all Humanists, which served not only as a bond of kinship among themselves but a link to the entire Unitarian tradition from Charles Chauncy* to Henry Bellows* and Octavius Frothingham.* ''The primary concern of Humanism,'' as Reese tellingly put it, ''is human development'' (Reese, p. xiii).

Like proponents in the Free Religion movement, the Humanists were convinced that the acceleration of change in the modern world would necessarily change religious faith. They saw themselves less as innovators of a new faith than as men working to preserve the essential elements of religion in the face of radical change. John Haynes Holmes* argued that the key to the change is that ''the supernatural is everywhere giving way before the natural,'' and in that process of giving way, religion is crumbling (Reese, p. 13). ''Our religion is going—no doubt of that!'' Holmes admitted, as if playing to the worst fears of modern Christians. His qualifications to this admission, however, caught the essence of the Humanist stance of optimism in the face of upheaval: ''But is it not going in order that religion itself, in some perfect and absolute sense of that word, may truly come?'' (Reese, p. 13). The pursuit of religion in a perfect and absolute sense is the quest that Ralph Waldo Emerson, Theodore Parker,* Frothingham, and others undertook. Holmes and the Humanists shared with them a conviction that the new and important in religion could rise only out of the ashes of the old religion.

What plagued the Humanists was the worry, often articulated by opponents or skeptics of their movement, and we could presume by members of their own congregations, that Humanism lacked something sustaining to the spirit. Insofar as Humanism was aimed at an uplifting of that very human spirit, this was a worrisome charge indeed, one that they took up with due seriousness. Charles H. Lyttle, who later contributed to the historiography of the movement, recognized that the most serious charge against Humanism was its ''impoverishment of religion through loss of faith in a personal God and in life after death'' (Reese, p. 28). What did it have to offer in compensation, he asked? Because of ''the critical realism of the modern mind,'' he argued, the satisfaction of Humanism is ''not only equal to the old but . . . better than the old'' (Reese, pp. 28–29). His sense of the requirements of a modern faith tallies with that of Frederick May Eliot,* who saw an advantage in the Humanist's ''opportunity for complete sincerity in his religious life. . . . He may not believe very much, as measured by orthodox standards,'' Eliot noted, ''but what he does believe he believes with his whole mind'' (Reese, p. 188). For Lyttle, the experience of reaching back to the great minds of the past provided ''the elements of personal communion and inspiration in religion'' that belief in a personal God once supplied (Reese, p. 31). That very inspiration of humanity itself could assuage our fear of the grave by affirming our connection with a great and ongoing human tradition. Such immortality, for Lyttle, did not appear to be of the personal sort but lay in the ''perpetuation of mutual ideals directed toward the future's nobler morale" (Reese, p. 34). This may have seemed cold comfort to many, but at least such comfort as there was here could not be so readily undermined by modern doubts.

This acute sense of the demands of the present age that marked Humanism was balanced by a historical sense that is also important to the movement. Part of the reason that the Humanists insisted that religion was facing a turning point was their historical judgment that the present age was unique. But in another sense they saw themselves enacting a human drama of which the past had ample precedent. Lyttle's call for spiritual experience through a vision of history exemplified the furthest reach of that sense. His argument that the fear of Humanism as a thief of religious value "is an old fear, periodically recurring in history, and receiving but slight vindication" would have been readily accepted by the group (Reese, pp. 34–35). Even more revealing is Dietrich's argument that Humanism, far from something new, "is merely an expansion, and a more rigorous application of Unitarianism" (Reese, p. 102). Quoting William Ellery Channing's* pronouncement in *Slavery* that a person "is an end, not a mere instrument or means," he claimed the denomination's chief saint on behalf of the Humanists: "And this doctrine which Channing preached one hundred years ago is seized upon by certain followers of Channing today and made the basis of a religion" (Reese, p. 102). "Channing Unitarianism," the label in the nineteenth century for the Christian and denominationally oriented wing of Unitarianism, is here seized and turned upside down.

Dietrich was aware that in doing so he was violating certain historical facts, but his point was that the direction of Channing's thought, if not its final resting place, was toward Humanism. But to make his point, a certain discrimination was necessary to indicate the gap between Channing and the twentieth-century Humanists. Dietrich went on to make that distinction in these terms: "Even Channing rested his idea of the dignity of man upon the thought that he had within him the germ of the idea of God. . . . But our idea of the glory of humanity is not based on any reflected glory" (Reese, p. 104). Dietrich's claim of Channing for the Humanist movement was countered in Francis Greenwood Peabody's* 1930 address to the Harvard Divinity School on the one-hundred-fiftieth anniversary of Channing's birth. Channing was a Humanist, Peabody admitted, but he was also more than that. As Dietrich had done, he recognized an essential difference: "His ground of confidence in the dignity of humanity was in his conviction that human life had in it the marks of divinity," Peabody argued.[13] Peabody found an incompleteness in Humanism, an unwillingness to ask the questions that theism took up about the nature of existence.

It is fitting that Channing should serve as a meeting place for these divergent views, for there had been keen competition to claim his authority within the denomination from the moment of his death. The basis of his "Humanism" helps bring into focus the difference between Humanists and theists at this point. For Channing, and for many theists, human nature retained a glory because of its connection with God, or its "Likeness to God," in his memorable phrase.

For the Humanists, the values concentrated in God, although not necessarily lost, were cut loose from any transcendent or supernatural context and grounded in human nature alone.

That there were important differences between the Humanists and theists is unquestionable, but it should not be imagined that the camps were so rigidly divided that there was no overlap in outlook. Frederick May Eliot's contribution to *Humanist Sermons* stressed the contribution of Humanism to the "inner life," a contribution that Eliot could recognize even though he was a theist. Eliot called for an evaluation of Humanism and indeed of all religion on the practical grounds of its contribution to "that mysterious, indefinable, but nevertheless intensely real thing," the "soul" (Reese, p. 185). Recognizing that "orthodox Christianity" had in the past worked to sustain men and women in a day-to-day faith, Eliot now saw that same role being fulfilled by Humanism, by offering an honest faith. Eliot knew that there were many "who are afraid to face the facts about their own beliefs lest they lose their faith altogether. . . . Such people are building their faith upon the sand" (Reese, pp. 188–89). Better a more limited, yet sounder faith than one that reaches beyond its capacity to support itself honestly, Eliot believed. Only a solid faith can provide the ground for human action and inner growth, which constitute the religious life.

## THE REACTION TO HUMANISM

As one of the most influential Unitarian leaders of the twentieth century, Eliot's hospitality to the Humanist movement was an important factor in the acceptance of that position within the denomination.[14] Eliot recognized in Humanism a potential for translation into the life of action that justified it. "The really important thing about these people [Humanists] is that they care, and care tremendously, for human values. It is moral passion that provides the dynamic for their intellectual efforts and their homiletical endeavors."[15] Given the extensive commitment that Reese, Dietrich, and Potter made to social reform, it is evident that Eliot understood the dynamic of the movement well. Even so, he demurred. That pause of his, again amplified in significance because he made it, is worth exploring as an important counterpoint to the Humanists, one more representative than the more impassioned opposition of William L. Sullivan or, earlier, Jabez T. Sunderland.

Eliot took his stand as a theist with a full knowledge of the problematic nature of the word *God* and a frank recognition that the word itself was only a symbol. Yet for Eliot, this was the important fact about it, for religion was a process of constructing symbols and acting under them. Symbols were the means by which the individual came into contact with religious reality, and "God" was the most potent of all of them. He described his belief in God as an affirmation of "three great experiences": "a moral imperative [which] is real and inescapably important"; a conviction of "a rational order within and behind the universe"; and a sense of a purposive, rather than accidental, existence for humanity. In none of these cases might one be constrained to use the word God, but the word symbolized "the reality that I believe exists behind the deepest convictions of my own mind and heart" (pp. 260–62). God, then, anchors a sense of a moral, orderly, and purposive world in a sustaining reality. For Eliot, the word passes the test of pragmatic usefulness that measures any theological concept.

But what of its problems? Is it precise enough, or isn't it weighted down with the dogmatic baggage of too many Christian centuries? Eliot found in those very objections to the use of "God" important reasons for its acceptance. "We need somehow to get our basic convictions so deep down into our lives that they will govern our actions at those moments when there is no time to think, and the best way to do that is to give them expression in symbolic forms which are colorful and rich in emotional appeal. We need symbols that will reach down deep into our souls and make their power felt in the innermost recesses of our personality. . . . The word 'God' is such a symbol" (pp. 262–63). Again it is the ability of the symbol to "govern our actions" that was crucial for Eliot. He recognized the fact that the word in some cases could be a stumbling block, and this accounted for his great sympathy for the Humanists, who he thought shared with him the fundamental beliefs that he symbolized as God. Still, he saw that an intelligent and open use of the word had the potential to enrich the religious experience of many Unitarians who had grown beyond any conventional use of it. He was firm in his conviction that everyone had discovered, in whatever form, "something to which he would give the name of sacred reality." Those discoveries of the sacred "have for you the value of something supremely great, and they exercise over you an authority that brooks no question and tolerates no disloyalty. For you, then, those sacred realities are what you mean by God" (p. 263). Eliot's theism was not, therefore, a return to traditional theology, which many Unitarians had abandoned. It was the revivification of a religious symbol central to the Christian religious experience but a revivification on grounds that were very nearly compatible with Humanist naturalism. Far from seeing God as a supernatural or superstitious obfuscation of the essence of the human religious experience, as many of the Humanists did, Eliot saw God instead as a tool for deepening and multiplying that experience. Nor did theism, for Eliot, imply a turning away from the human realms in favor of the divine. God was a lens by which one could focus a vision of the world, an evidence of the firm reality of our being here.

Throughout his discussions of God, Eliot conveyed the sense that human beliefs, human actions, indeed human life itself, needed the grounding or stability of a sense of transcendence. Humanity was impoverished, in fact, if it did not recognize a mode of existence beyond its own. This tendency to look beyond, or as Eliot put it, "behind" human nature, marks an unquestionable difference of sensibility between him and the Humanists. It also suggests the very point at which the Humanist movement would be attacked in this century. That point was the adequacy of human nature as a sustaining vehicle for religious belief and ethical action.

That critique had begun to formulate before Eliot's demurral and was in fact given its most memorable statement even before Humanism emerged as a movement. William Wallace Fenn's* critique of "Modern Liberalism" in 1913 assailed the liberal tradition for its failure to "bear the weight of the tragedies of human experience."[16] Fenn, himself a Unitarian and later dean of the Harvard Divinity School, voiced his objection to liberalism "from within" the tradition, focusing on that aspect of it that seemed to him hardest to maintain. It was not the attack of conservative opponents, who thought that a lack of Christology was liberal religion's weakness, that worried Fenn. It was the sense that liberal religion was somehow an inadequate explanation of life that was deeply troubling to him. Fenn's critique now seems at points a telling comment on Humanism, which was not yet an explicit force in Unitarianism, because Humanism was of a piece with Transcendentalism and Free Religion as an extreme gesture of the characteristic liberal affirmation of human nature. The Humanists could not embrace the philosophical idealism or the tendency to metaphysical speculation of those earlier phases of liberalism, but that only placed the weight of their reliance more squarely on human nature itself.

Fenn's sense of the shortcomings of liberalism is best summarized in one memorable sentence: "Does not its amiable faith in inherent goodness appear but ghastly mockery when confronted by the facts of life?" (p. 516). To him, those grimmer facts were apparent not only in the potential violence of the world surrounding humans but in humans themselves. "And what of human sin? Here more than anywhere else the weakness of Modern Liberalism shows itself." Thus the liberal estimate of human nature, and its corresponding faith in progress, was "too jocund" (p. 516). Levity, even a levity born of the sincerest optimism, was hollow in its contrast with life.

As William Hutchison noted, the importance of Fenn's critique was increased by its appearance just before World War I. "Less than a year after its publication, an unexpected war gave a fairly sharp twist to the kaleidoscope through which world views and theologies were perceived."[17] This change in intellectual tone that was heightened by the war only increased during the twentieth century, occasioning in some theological circles the rise of neo-orthodoxy, which tried to take full account of both the tragedy of human life and the sinfulness or limitation of human nature. This challenge caused no major exodus from the liberal camp—modernist views of God and the Bible had made too many inroads for any sort of "return" to the old faith. But it did spur a general mood of reevaluation of the basis of liberalism. One of the more important of these analyses came from James Luther Adams,* a man whose attempts to reground liberal theology have made him a key Unitarian spokesman in the twentieth century.

Addressing the American Unitarian Association in 1941, when World War II underscored the very weaknesses in liberalism that Fenn had noted, Adams summarized the evolution of liberal theology in the twentieth century as a process of reassessing human nature. Although he noted a long list of reasons why the "reputation" of human nature could change from age to age, the most telling of these reasons was "the profound change in the historical situation." [18] Modern history had simply belied the optimism of the past. For Unitarians and Universalists, that change was especially wrenching, because so much of the ethos of both movements had been tied up in James Freeman Clarke's evocation of "the progress of mankind onward and upward forever." "Since the turn of the century," Adams wrote, "some religious liberals have greatly altered their attitude toward the older ideas of growth, progress, and perfectibility" (pp. 44–45).

For Adams, the change in attitudes could be understood through the emergence of two terms, tragedy and commitment, which were lacking in the older liberalism but very much a part of the liberalism of the future. By tragedy, Adams meant more than the simple failure of human plans or the cruelty of fate. Tragedy arose when "the perversions and failures of history are associated precisely with the highest creative powers of humanity." Tragedy, for Adams, carried with it a deep irony, for history did not, curiously, negate the very potential for progress that the older liberalism had emphasized. Instead, history seemed to draw tragedy out of that very progress. "The very means and evidences of progress turn out again and again to be also the instruments of perversion or destruction" (p. 49).

Adams's insistence on tragedy as a condition of human life was a reaction to the overly rationalistic tendency of past liberalism to see unity and progress in all things. Still, pessimism should not be the result of this recognition, according to Adams. In fact, it is closer to the truth to say that his insistence on the recognition of tragedy was in fact a battle against pessimism, for he recognized how easily disillusionment could arise when one's theory about life and one's experience of it were too much at odds. Although the sense of tragedy might chasten our self-regard, Adams hoped also that it might enkindle our moral commitment. "The decisive quality of a personality is its commitment, for the basic commitment determines the self and its interests, instead of being determined by them" (p. 54). In one sense Adams was struggling against the confident stress on the self and its cultivation, which had defined liberalism. But as the above remark demonstrates, this struggle was in a larger sense an attempt to revive that very tradition. Only through commitment, a purposive direction of energies to some goal that transcended the self, could the self achieve its identity. To say that "commitment determines the self" rather than vice versa was indeed to admit that the self or, more broadly, human nature, was perennially in a state of flux. Adams understood that an "element of commitment, of change of heart, of decision, so much emphasized in the Gospels, has been neglected by religious liberalism, and that is the prime source of its enfeeblement" (p. 56). The language is patently revivalistic, in keeping with Adams's Baptist background. The vision, however, is modern, forged out of the prag-

matism characteristic of early twentieth-century thought, which placed definition and identity in a secondary and derivative role to action. A liberalism was
doomed that clung to faith in progress without a sense of building that progress.
For Adams, that faith in progress had to arise in the very process of one's commitment to achieve it.

A similar critique of liberalism was emerging from a different source, the
history of American intellectual life. That intellectual life had a significant part
of its beginnings in New England and grew out of developments in New England theology; moreover, the richest age in American literary and philosophical development, the decades preceding the Civil War, coincided directly with
the evolution of Unitarianism from Calvinism. As Martin Green put it, "the
history of nineteenth-century Boston is also the history of the American mind
in this period."[19] Perry Miller was the leader of these studies, and although he
was a professional critic and historian, and not a Unitarian himself, he nevertheless addressed a central question in liberal religious circles in 1942, when
he addressed the Unitarian Ministerial Union at King's Chapel, Boston.[20] Adams
published Miller's essay in his *Journal of Liberal Religion* (where his own essay "The Changing Reputation of Human Nature" had appeared), a fact that
further emphasized a coalescence of views about the liberal tradition that had
emerged in the 1930s.

Miller noted the "devastating analysis" of liberal optimism that had been
leveled "by the most sensitive of our poets and the most profound of our nov-
elists." Along with modern scientists, they had challenged that tradition "to
make good the claims they have been so long advancing for the inherent dignity
of man." Yet this was by no means an exclusively intellectual problem: "now
two or three dictators and several thousand bombardiers have brought the challenge directly home to us, where face it we must" (p. 44). What the tradition
had to face, Miller believed, was a certain emptiness within the concept of "individualism" as it had evolved in this century. Although Unitarianism had
preoccupied itself with the process of liberation from creeds and dictated belief,
it had not enlivened that freedom with the substance necessary to make it meaningful: "after [Unitarianism] had made men free to choose, what did it leave
for them to choose?" (p. 42).

Miller, who was the leader in the revival of Puritan studies in this century,
contrasted this empty liberalism with the Puritanism from which it revolted. Although few, he realized, could entertain Puritan doctrine seriously now, it had
to be admitted that it was a theology equipped to explain "the more terrible
moments of human life" (p. 36). Even though the tradition of individualism
for which Channing and Emerson were great spokesmen had its roots in the
individualism of the Puritans—in the final stress they placed on the moral responsibility of the individual—that individualism was of a different quality from
the modern variety. "The individual could be free only *for* ends, not *from* ends,
and his liberty was achieved only upon terms" (p. 43). What Miller suggested
by this distinction between "freedom for" and "freedom from" was a quality

of commitment, to use Adams's term, which had somehow evaporated from the notion of freedom as it evolved into the twentieth century. Individualism had come to mean, all too often, irresponsibility to any larger whole, to any enterprise larger than the self. Whenever such commitment is stripped from individualism, the value of individualism becomes nil, and the tradition reaches a dead end.

Self-criticism is often a prelude to growth, and that would prove to be the case with Unitarianism. Even as the intellectual tradition of liberalism was being criticized, the denomination was undergoing a thorough institutional reappraisal as well and laying the grounds for what it hoped would be a major expansion. That institutional history is examined in Chapter 12. But other signs of both self-examination and renewal of purpose could be found in the intellectual sphere. In May 1943 a group calling itself the United Unitarian Advance proclaimed "The Faith Behind Freedom," a document that attempted to address the dwindling basis of faith in liberalism, which both modern society and the terrors of the war had brought to the fore. "Many beliefs, once confidently held, have crumbled with the coming of the modern age: others are falling now before the fury of the storm."[21] The document could serve as both a plea for renewal of faith to liberals and a potential refuge for more conservative believers who found their faith eroding. At its center was the affirmation that "Freedom grows from free religion, that only a free religion can be universal, and that every other freedom is based on freedom of the mind." By linking the military struggle against Fascism to a more universal struggle of all liberal religion against any mental restraints, the declaration moved in the direction of reasserting an essential moral commitment in liberal religion. The ultimate goal of the war, then, could be perceived as a move toward the transformation of the world into "a single, free community." This meant that liberalism was primarily committed to "a world of liberation not only from war but from the tyranny of hate and greed, and from the barriers of race and class." Such a world also implied "a better regulation of the world's prosperity."

Here, then, at perhaps the darkest hour both of modern history and of liberal belief came a call for renewal that promised to reconnect the splintered individualism of the twentieth century to a larger crusade of universal unity. Here also was a key moment in what can be seen as the growing imperative to social reform within liberal religion. By the time of World War II, moral issues had become political issues. From that moment, liberal religion was to find a large part of its sense of commitment in its attention to social justice.

One more contemporary note might be added to this discussion of the fate of individualism in the liberal tradition—that the problem, or the issue, is still very much alive. After the war, one of the directions that Unitarianism took in its quest for expansion was the Fellowship movement, a plan by which the American Unitarian Association granted both recognition and aid to lay groups of religious liberals. Nowhere, perhaps, does the spirit of individualism, and in many cases the spirit of social commitment, exist more purely than in these fellowships. But on the other hand, nowhere does the problem of balancing the demands between organization and individualism show itself more keenly, since the pattern for these groups is very often one of struggle. The very existence and continued health of these fellowships, many of which grow into churches, but many of which do not, points to a continuing felt need for corporate worship, or perhaps "fellowship," as part of the experience of religion.

The questions that are posed by the liberal tradition of self-reliance, questions that the Unitarian Fellowship movement very often brings into focus, have recently been examined from a historical perspective by Conrad Wright.* Wright has been a leader in a revival of Unitarian historical studies that have emphasized the native origins of American Unitarianism and have stressed the previously overlooked importance of men like Henry Ware, Jr.,* James Freeman Clarke, Henry Bellows, Samuel A. Eliot,* and Frederick May Eliot, who were theological moderates but institutional innovators and builders. Wright identified Thomas Jefferson and Ralph Waldo Emerson as examples of the extreme individualism that has been a hallmark of liberal religion. Although Jefferson's religion was of the rational variety, and Emerson's more mystical, the religion of each man was "individualistic and privatized," so much so that their views "can yield no rationale for religious fellowship in general or the Church in particular."[22] Such a persistent strain of individualism in liberal religion, which can be traced into the twentieth century, may help to account for the relatively small size of Unitarianism and Universalism. But what disturbed Wright was that this individualism is an ideology with definite historical boundaries, which has flourished in modern thinking in part because of economic and social conditions: "individualism is a response to a fairly sudden favorable alteration in the balance between population and resources, given a particular state of technology" (p. 11). If individualism is a response to such conditions, he asked, is it not also subject to threat when those conditions change, as current population trends suggest that they will? "What I am concerned to suggest," he noted in summary, "is that the value system that liberals have taken for granted, and have always assumed will be vindicated by history, is in need of overhaul along with everything else" (p. 13).

There is an element of speculation in these predictions, as Wright readily admitted, but also a disturbing ring of truth, both for liberal religion and for Western culture in general. Is there not, in his association of individualism with economic conditions, at least a suggestion of why Unitarianism in particular has appealed to a more affluent group than many other religions? In conclusion, he suggested a reemphasis on "commitment and discipline" as necessary to the church; a "rediscovery of worship as a corporate act"; a "rejection of the narcissism" of certain movements in recent culture, with a corresponding attempt to define ourselves through relations with others; and finally, a renewed sense of the use of individualism for "critical" (or dissenting) rather than purely creative or expansionary ends (p. 17). All of these suggestions are aimed at balancing the individualistic strand within liberal religion, which the post-Vietnam years had again brought out. In this sense his critique of the tradition stands much in the line of Adams and Miller, for it refuses to look with optimism on the unaided potential of the private self or even to locate within that self the ultimate criterion for religious value—at least not within a self that is cut off from a more complete religious body.

The nature of Wright's argument suggests that maintaining a balance between freedom and commitment within liberal religion continues to require attention. There is a dialectic at work here, both historically within the denomination and in some sense within the soul or psyche of each member. There is no worship without religious experience, but religious experience is incomplete without the experience of worship. To maintain this dialectic becomes, in a sense, the religious discipline of every religious liberal.

# 12
# LIBERAL RELIGION
# IN THE MODERN AGE

## ADMINISTRATION AND CHANGE

Because of both the spiritual commitment to individualism that has marked liberal religion from the first, and the inherited structure of congregational polity of the earliest New England meetinghouses, the Unitarian church has had a persistent problem with organization as a national body. There has been a continuing resistance among local churches, ministers, and laypersons to the buildup of any centralized authority within the denomination. Universalists have been similarly unyielding in their commitment to congregational autonomy. In a recent history of the institutional growth of the American Unitarian Association (AUA), Virgil E. Murdock summarized those organizational difficulties under four categories: (1) a "lack of commitment to associative action"; (2) "theological and political controversies"; (3) the organization of "special purpose organizations outside the association"; and (4) a "failure of the A.U.A. to centralize its power locus."[1] These persistent problems have rendered the denomination's institutional story one of periods of organizing zeal followed by declines into controversy, apathy, or rival splinter-group activity. The two moments of organizational push in the nineteenth century can be identified roughly as the formation of the AUA in 1825, led by Henry Ware, Jr.,* Ezra Stiles Gannett,* and others, and the organization of the National Conference in 1865 by Henry W. Bellows.* In the twentieth century the organizational periods can be said to begin with Samuel A. Eliot's* assumption of the role of AUA secretary in 1898 and Frederick May Eliot's* election as AUA president after the 1936 report of the Commission of Appraisal. In the last three cases a strong leader, Bellows or one of the Eliots, was instrumental in the organization of the denomination.

Although the fact of this tendency to decentralization is undeniable, it is by no means universally accepted that this is a tragedy, or even a problem. Many Unitarians came into the denomination to escape churches where power and authority seemed to them too centralized. Moreover, the commitment to spiritual freedom, the hallmark of liberalism since William Ellery Channing's* day, in one sense demands a certain skepticism toward organization and an ultimate reliance on the self.

In the previous chapter, this problem was discussed as a theological one. To see it as an institutional problem is also enlightening, and it brings us first to a closer examination of the career of Samuel A. Eliot, a man who lived out his conviction that liberal religion had to pay closer attention to its organizational basis to survive and prosper. For Eliot, that organizational basis was the AUA, and his greatest contribution to Unitarian history was in transforming that institution into one that could answer the needs of the Unitarian movement in the twentieth century.

In a concise and accurate piece of self-characterization, Eliot expressed his sense of purpose in contrast to that of his good friend but sometime opponent in denominational affairs, William Wallace Fenn.* Fenn, he said, "was primarily interested in the root of things, the fundamental motives, the basic convictions, . . . while I was more concerned with the application in the life of the community of principles he expounded so eloquently."[2] The "life of the community" is a key phrase for understanding Eliot's work. In the sense that "commitment" became a watchword for Unitarians in the early decades of the century, Eliot's form of commitment was to engender fuller life in the liberal community. Such life was possible only if organized Unitarianism could support its existing churches and institutions and expand as well. Convinced that the message of liberal religion was relevant to the needs of the Midwest and West, places where it had taken only a slim hold, or none at all, his general plan was to secure the New England base of the AUA as a launching place for expansion. Although a Bostonian's Bostonian (his grandfather was mayor of Boston, his father president of Harvard), he had seen through early ministerial work in Seattle and Denver that the liberal message did indeed have an audience outside New England. "There are thousands of intelligent people who are wholly alienated from the churches and who, because they have never heard of a rational religion, imagine that they have no religion at all" (pp. 74–75). On this point, his sense of the Unitarian future was wholly correct, since converts from more conservative churches have continued to be an important basis of Unitarian growth.

But to secure the base of that expansion in the AUA, Eliot faced some fundamental problems when he began his first term of service on the Board of Directors in 1894. Loosely run, and without a firm sense of direction, the AUA simply lacked the strength to lead any expansionary effort. It had been formed in a missionary spirit in 1825 and had taken on responsibilities primarily in publishing and church extension. It existed originally as an organization of individual members, not of churches. When Bellows organized the National Conference, based on the principle of church membership, that body became a more representative and, in that sense, a more legitimate spokesman for Unitarianism. As Murdock put it, the National Conference "was in effect the legislative arm of the movement while the Association [the AUA] could be said to be the executive arm."[3] A major change occurred in 1884 when the AUA began to accept churches as well as individuals as members. The National Conference was finally absorbed into the AUA later in 1925, but the earlier change meant that "from 1884 the Association was, in fact, an association of churches."[4]

Eliot's entry onto the AUA Board of Directors marked an alteration of direction for it. He pushed for policy change that ended the practice of deficit spending, covered by the use of endowment funds, and replaced that practice with a "pay-as-you-go policy." His leadership qualities emerged quickly, and he became AUA secretary in 1898. This was the chief administrative post of the denomination, but Eliot realized that it did not have what he thought was the necessary strength for effective administration. In 1900, therefore, the AUA reorganized to give him the title of president, a role as both the ceremonial and administrative head of the denomination.[5]

Eliot's centralization of the administrative functions of the AUA was not carried out as an end in itself. Underlying his efforts was a conviction that the future of liberal religion was dependent on a strong base of operations. His essential concern was for church extension, and his earlier work with growing churches in the West was in fact a prelude to his constant travel and speaking on behalf of Unitarianism. His methods got results, as David Parke's summary of his accomplishments indicates: "The Association's endowments had increased twelvefold, from half a million to six million dollars. The staff had grown from four to twenty-five persons. The church building loan fund had granted almost 300 loans to churches without losing a dollar."[6] All of these statistics attempt to quantify a sense of vitality within Unitarianism during Eliot's years, one that is all the more notable because of the perceptible malaise into which the denomination began to slip after his return to the parish ministry in 1927. The major evidence of that malaise is the report of the Commission of Appraisal in 1936, a report that did much to set the agenda for the denomination in the years that followed. But the very call for such reappraisal suggests the feeling of decline within the denomination after Eliot's retirement.

Such decline is perhaps inevitable in the wake of strong leadership, but it was felt acutely by many liberals in the 1930s. It should also be remembered that Eliot's leadership was not without some opposition. William Wallace Fenn originally opposed his election as AUA secretary because of his opposition to Eliot's financial proposals and his general fear that his strong executive abilities would "shift the traditional balance of power between the central organization and the churches, in favor of the former." Later, John Haynes Holmes* opposed Eliot's reelection because "the A.U.A. had become a business organization and had ceased to be a spiritual force."[7] These expressions of discontent, although they were not significant obstacles to Eliot, clearly show that his reenactment of the Bellows role still aroused the same opposition. In other words, the liberal resistance to institutional authority continued.

Eliot's resignation, followed as it was by the economic catastrophe of the 1930s, the rise of Fascism in Europe, and the prolonged uncertainty about religious values typified in the Humanist controversy, led to the dark night of the soul of American Unitarianism. Its result was significant—not only was the report of the Commission of Appraisal drafted, but Frederick May Eliot was elected to the AUA presidency. This "Unitarian renaissance" stands as the denomination's most significant institutional moment in this century, as profound a change as Bellows's organization of the National Conference after the Civil War. James Luther Adams* was a central figure in that renaissance. The idea of denominationwide reassessment originated in large part with him, and as a member of the commission, he had influence upon its recommendations.[8] For Adams, the vitality of liberalism depended on a continual process of reexamination: "As liberals, we assume that liberalism like any other movement, can remain alive only through 'coming to itself,' through repentance and return. Only where there is a sincere recognition of incompleteness and failure, only where there is a recovery of depth, breadth, and length, only there is the authentic spirit of religious liberalism to be found. Hence, the liberal expects to hear over and over again: liberalism is dead; long live liberalism."[9] This sense of a return to ultimate foundations to find renewed vigor is very much the spirit of the report of the Commission of Appraisal. "Have we sufficient faith in our own future," the commission asked, "to warrant us in undertaking the arduous task of making ourselves fit to survive?" This question, basic as it seems, was not entirely rhetorical. A majority of Unitarians might well answer the question no, the commission admitted. "There are a great many discouraged Unitarians today, and many disheartened Unitarian churches." Moreover, there is a "dangerously low" level of morale, so low that "effective planning and action" was threatened.[10] The report, then, is both self-analysis and a plan for action—it is both "repentance" and a call for "return," to use Adams's terms.

The heart of the report was a list of seven recommendations that are important guideposts to the denomination's sense of itself in the middle 1930s. There was a call for larger cooperation with other denominations, including the Free Church Fellowship, an organization that was exploring means of cooperation and unity among liberal churches, especially the Unitarians and the Universalists. This recommendation also included a call for further international cooperation. The second recommendation suggested "decentralization of administrative practice" within the denomination and heavier reliance on "local and regional responsibility." Clearly, one of the legacies of Samuel A. Eliot's leadership had been centralization, and with that tendency came an inevitable drift toward bureaucracy. The commission hoped to reverse this trend not only with an emphasis on local responsibility but by recommending "recurrent self-examination" within the denomination. A third recommendation was to increase the efforts "to discover and train leaders," a response to the denomination's worrisome loss of ministers. The commission also recommended a periodic effort "to formulate . . . the major arguments and disagreements within the denomination." Could Unitarianism say what it stood for without violating its long tradition of resistance to a creed? Yes, the commission thought, "*if both agreements and tensions were set forth*" and if these listings were explicitly labeled "tentative." In fact, the commission itself offered just such a list:

### Unitarians Agree

1. —in affirming the primacy of the free exercise of intelligence in religion, believing that in the long run the safest guide to truth is human intelligence.
2. —in affirming the paramount importance for the individual of his own moral convictions and purposes.
3. —in affirming that the social implications of religion are indispensable to its vitality and validity, as expressed in terms of concern for social conditions and the struggle to create a just social order.
4. —in affirming the importance of the church as the organized expression of religion.
5. —in affirming the necessity for worship as a deliberate effort to strengthen the individual's grasp of the highest spiritual values of which he is aware.
6. —in affirming the rational nature of the universe.

### Unitarians Disagree

1. —as to the expediency of using the traditional vocabulary of religion, within a fellowship which includes many who have rejected the ideas commonly associated with such words as "God", "prayer", "communion", "salvation", "immortality".
2. —as to the wisdom of maintaining the definitely Christian tradition, and the traditional forms of Christian worship.
3. —as to the religious values of a purely naturalistic philosophy.
4. —as to the adequacy and competency of man to solve his own problems, both individual and social.
5. —as to the advisability of direct action by churches in the field of social and political problems.

The fifth and sixth recommendations of the report dealt with two matters of central importance to the week-to-week life of individual churches, worship and religious education. The commission argued for the crucial importance of both activities and called for renewed emphasis on both. It gave its support to "the experimental spirit in worship" of which it believed there were many signs among churches. It also proposed the establishment of a Department of Education, to which the denomination should give explicit recognition and material support for the continual development of education programs. In its last recommendation, the commission stated, "religion that does not express itself through action in human society is not in any true sense religion at all" (p. 14). The element of social action had to remain part of the tradition of Unitarianism, although there seemed to be a general recognition by the commission of the problems and dangers of entrusting this function to a single department or agency. The commission urged that social action, on both the local and national level, be genuine and fully representative of the group's convictions.[11]

Although the report did serve as a focus for new energies, thus becoming a turning point for Unitarianism, its effects were not so easily assimilated. This is especially true of what can be called its major, though indirect, result, the bringing of Frederick May Eliot's leadership to the forefront of the denomination. Eliot, minister of Unity Church in St. Paul, Minnesota, and grandson of William Greenleaf Eliot,* had headed the commission and thus found himself in a delicate position after the publication of its report. It was, in many senses, a critique of the current AUA administration, headed by Samuel A. Eliot's successor Louis Craig Cornish.* Frederick May Eliot thought that he could not therefore accept the AUA presidency, for which many people supported him, without seeming to taint the objectivity of the report. As Carol R. Morris showed in her intriguing study of Eliot's eventual election, he explicitly requested that the AUA Board of Directors not consider him for the presidency, largely on the grounds that his candidacy would cast doubt over his motives in working for the commission. Only after some very sensitive persuasion by the chairman of the nominating committee, Leslie T. Pennington, and an unequivocal expression of support from the board and many others was Eliot persuaded to accept nomination for presidency. Despite the fact that the election was contested, and that controversy arose over Eliot's sympathy with Humanism, he assumed a commanding and vigorous leadership of the denomination in 1937.[12]

Eliot was troubled by the questioning of his theological legitimacy, not only because of his commitment to intellectual freedom within the denomination, but because of his clear sense of the liberal tradition's history of evolutionary change. He called Unitarianism's ability to unite those of very different views its "chief glory," and went on to make this wry observation: "One of the most interesting aspects of our history is the process by which the radicals of one generation have come to be regarded as '100% Unitarians' by succeeding generations. The truth of the matter is that we are a church in which growth is not only permitted but encouraged—growth in thought, growth in sensitiveness to moral values, growth in courage to put religion to work in the world."[13] Certainly, this sense of the centrality of growth and development calls William Ellery Channing, Ralph Waldo Emerson,* James Freeman Clarke,* John White Chadwick,* and others to mind, placing Eliot in the mainstream of a tradition that he well understood. He recognized the importance of growth to the liberal's delicate balance, and he set out to foster that growth as denominational leader.

Eliot characterized the time of the report of the Commission of Appraisal in these frank terms: "Unitarians suddenly awoke to the realization that a long period of neglect of organizational matters had brought the denomination to the verge of collapse" (p. 60). His sense of the seriousness of the movement's problems is notable, for it was in that spirit of concern that he undertook leadership. Like Henry Ware, Jr., Henry W. Bellows, and James Freeman Clarke,

Eliot combined an intellectually sophisticated religious vision with a genius for pragmatic organization. It was an exceptionally appropriate moment for such a combination. Samuel A. Eliot had been well able to get things done, but he was weaker in his ability to inspire others with his vision. Louis Craig Cornish, his successor, did much to increase Unitarianism's vision of its international place and mission, but he lacked Samuel Eliot's executive ability.

Frederick May Eliot insisted that liberalism had to retain its faith that "human reason and good will can transform the world" (p. 19). Yet he understood the warnings about facile optimism that William Wallace Fenn, James Luther Adams, and Perry Miller had raised. Writing in the *Journal of Liberal Religion* in 1943, the year after the appearance of the articles of Adams and Miller discussed earlier, Eliot argued for an "idealism, grounded in positive faith in man," (p. 21), but an idealism that "is neither romantic nor naive." Such a faith avoids those pitfalls by rejecting the prevalent attitude of the liberal past, "that what is good will inevitably and almost automatically win its own way" (p. 23). In the past, optimism such as this had never seriously entertained the possibility of "the final defeat of truth and the complete destruction of liberty and justice" (p. 24). It therefore lacked the essential motivation to action, the possibility of the ultimate failure of all humane ideals. Only when this sense of defeat and death is real, Eliot thought, and only from the position of fragility and undeniable mortality can liberalism begin to change the world in a meaningful way.

It is not hard to see how this faith in progress through responsibility coincided with Eliot's belief in God, which we discussed earlier. Eliot thought that we needed a concept of God to give us full access to those fundamental beliefs that dictated our actions. God was a basis upon which we could act, and the possibility of progress demanded action. But Eliot's vision also made a central place for the church as an institutional repository and protector of liberal values. In 1935, during what he identified as the crisis point of the Unitarian denomination, Eliot defined the liberal as one who "is resolved that in the realms of the mind and of the soul there shall be no compulsion, so far as he can prevent it; and he believes that the best way to promote this end is to create and maintain such institutions as can be made to serve human purposes in a wholly free spirit" (p. 72). In the Emerson who viewed institutions as a threat to liberty and the Eliot who viewed them as a protection of liberty lie the two opposing poles of liberal belief.

It is important to note that Eliot was a convinced churchman, because only a believer in institutions could have guided the denomination as successfully as he did in the late 1930s and 1940s. He believed that the liberal church was the best of all institutions for protecting the liberal spirit and noted its complete opposition to any form of mental or spiritual coercion. "Such a church is a company of seekers, and the bond which holds them closely together is their common confession that what they seek is still beyond them" (p. 72). There is a necessary unity in the group, but it is a unity that in no way hinders the essential element of growth. In fact, the thread that all members of a liberal church have in common is their need to grow, their sense of not having finally arrived at a point of fulfillment.

Eliot was well aware of the difficulties that the idea of the church had faced in the liberal tradition. In a 1937 commencement address at Meadville Theological School, very soon after he had assumed the AUA presidency, he examined those difficulties as part of a larger analysis of what held the church together. The skepticism about the nature of the church, which he voiced in order to refute, is a succinct summary of the persistent problem of freedom and commitment, and it certainly suggests the remarkable sympathy of mind that characterized Eliot as a thinker. It seemed as if he could not only understand but actually experience the force of an argument, even if he finally opposed it: "In other words, there cannot be such a thing as a free church, because there is something inherent in the very nature of liberalism that destroys the possibility of institutional loyalty. Liberty is a disintegrating force. Freedom leads to more and more extreme individualism, in thought and conviction and conduct. The inevitable end-product is anarchy. The very term 'free church' is a contradiction in terms'' (p. 95). For Eliot, this seemingly impossible contradiction was resolved by two strands within liberalism that made possible the unity necessary to the life of the church. Eliot termed these strands ''common memories and common practices—the things we do together as members of a free church, and the things we all remember in connection with our church'' (p. 103). These agencies can be thought of as the liberal future and the liberal past, as action and tradition. In Eliot's view, and this despite his own version of theism, the liberal creed was actually the cumulative memory of past action. That memory was itself constantly being adjusted because of the obligation to common action that binds the liberal church together. Creedless though it was, Eliot's version of the church did include reverence for a past heritage that contained a measure of theological belief and dogma. Even a liberal who believes he has gone beyond William Ellery Channing's Christology or Hosea Ballou's* biblicism can still find value in the common memory of the example of integrity and growth that these men set. For Eliot, the liberal church must first be going somewhere. But it must also remember where it has been.

This vision, and the steps of leadership that he took to implement it, made Eliot ''a symbol of renewed vigor for Unitarianism.''[14] Signs of that invigoration emerged in a number of places, most of which reflected the agenda of the Appraisal Commission's report. Under the leadership of Ernest Kuebler* and Sophia L. Fahs,* the New Beacon Series in children's religious education was launched in 1937, reflecting the report's call for a rethinking of education and a reemphasis of it. The Unitarian Service Committee was formed in 1940 to meet the calls for social action that were becoming ever more pressing in light of the rise of Fascism. These efforts took on at times an international scope, also helping to fulfill the call for the denomination to take a stand as an international body.[15] Except for the commission's own formulation of theological agreements and disagreements, Eliot did little officially to clarify Unitarian theology, perhaps, as Robert Hemstreet suggests, because of the potential divisiveness of the Humanist-theist controversy that had flared up during Eliot's election. But in 1943, under the directive of a program for expansion, A. Powell Davies* drafted a new set of five principles that were accepted by the AUA not as a creed but as "a basis for Unitarian Advance."[16] This pragmatic basis of the acceptance of the report should be noted. The five principles are as follows: "Individual freedom of belief; discipleship to advancing truth; the democratic process in human relations; universal brotherhood, undivided by nation, race, or creed; and allegiance to the cause of a united world community."[17] Hemstreet's comment that the principles were all "methodological" and avoided even the mention of God, Jesus, or Christianity is pertinent here. It seems that only on the basis of method, and not of content, could a liberal statement of faith exist.

Progress toward merger with Universalism was also much slower than the language of the report might have suggested, and it must be acknowledged that this goal was controversial within both denominations. Each denomination recognized the rationale and possible benefits of merger, but each also understood the cost in unique identity that merger might bring. In the troubled 1930s and during the war, simple survival was often a priority. In 1939 Eliot looked forward to "the uniting of our two denominations into 'The United Liberal Church of America' " and argued that "if liberal religion is to play a real part in working out the destiny of democracy in America, it is imperative that our efforts be concentrated and not scattered."[18] The merger question therefore remained a major item of the agenda of Unitarianism during the Eliot years, even though its accomplishment would not come until the presidency of Eliot's successor, Dana M. Greeley.*

The call for greater freedom in forms of worship and the call for increased local responsibility were pursued by Eliot's administration, but at least a part of the fulfillment of those goals came from a source not anticipated at the time of the report. The Fellowship movement, launched in 1948, created a constituency of lay-led church groups. This was a liberal religion of the grass-roots variety, intensely local and of necessity very often innovative in worship style. Eliot hit upon the idea of such fellowships in a moment that was characteristically one of "action" and "memory." Pondering the question of how to sustain churches that had shrunk below the level of maintaining a minister, Eliot discovered an earlier experiment in "Unitarian Lay Centers," since forgotten within the denomination. Although the concept was revived to help save existing churches that were fading, under the guidance of Lon Ray Call* and Munroe Husbands* it turned out to be an excellent vehicle for encouraging interest in Unitarianism among groups not yet strong enough to form a church. In the period 1948–58, one of great numerical growth for Unitarianism, the number of people who joined fellowships accounted for one-third of the denomination's increase.[19]

In 1954, four years before his unexpected death, Eliot noted a steady progress within Unitarianism over the preceding twenty years. His retrospective view of those decades is important, for it reveals Eliot's own sense of how the denomination turned itself around during the years of his leadership. Unitarianism had substantial growth in both church membership and numbers of churches or fellowships after the war. Although all American churches showed a growth, the Unitarian expansion was notably large. Eliot also found a corresponding renewal of spirit in Unitarianism, a fact of more importance than numerical growth. "Within the last twenty years there has been a quiet but steadily growing determination within the Unitarian body to find a practical solution to the basic problem of combining its traditional faith in the values of individualism with at least a minimum of efficient organization." Such determination required "compromise," a word with "an ugly and repellent sound in Unitarian ears." Still, for Eliot, such compromise as might be necessary for institutional survival would ultimately protect the individualistic core of the liberal faith. Such progress in cooperation was being made, as Eliot saw it. "The denomination has pulled itself out of the decline—in numbers, in organizational strength, and in morale—that was so threatening a score of years ago." Eliot listed the Unitarian Service Committee and the Beacon Press as evidences of this turnaround, but he also added the advances made toward merger with Universalism as a major sign of progress. The recent formation of the Council of Liberal Churches (1953), a step toward the combination of some administrative functions of the two denominations, was cited by Eliot as perhaps "one of the most important events in the history of American Unitarianism." [20] His sense was clearly that much had been done but that the next challenge, and one of great importance, was the accomplishment of Unitarian and Universalist unity.

## UNITARIAN-UNIVERSALIST MERGER

The merger of the American Unitarian Association and the Universalist Church of America was completed in May 1961, and through that merger the Unitarian Universalist Association was founded. Although the merger was the fulfillment of an idea that had been alive in the two denominations for more than a century, it was not easily accomplished, nor did it alter the fact that two distinct religious traditions had been consolidated. Consolidation is an act aimed at the future; there can be no consolidation of the past. As Russell Miller reminded us, our sense of the accomplishment of the merger may alter our view of history, which in some respects reveals "deep differences of theology, class configuration, philosophy, behavior, and attitudes which cannot be easily overlooked or minimized." [21]

We have noted the momentum toward merger within Unitarianism at the end of Frederick May Eliot's administration, but the antecedents to merger in both denominations dated well before Eliot. These conditions should be noted with Miller's caveat about a too-easily-assumed inevitability in the outcome always in mind. That the union had been discussed for more than a century before it was completed is perhaps the most convincing testimony to the difficulties inherent in it.

What the two movements had in common, and what eventually brought them together, was their liberal doctrine. In the eighteenth and early nineteenth centuries that meant first a rejection of Calvinism and, ultimately, of evangelical Protestantism generally. The benevolence of God and the worth and dignity of human nature were the common cornerstones of that rejection, although there were shades of difference and emphasis in these shared values. But beneath these common ideals, there were also significant frictions. The Unitarians grew from the established or "Standing-Order" churches in New England, those officially sanctioned by the government and supported by taxes. The Universalists were emphatically disestablished and with other groups like the Baptists fought vigorously to break the hold of the "official" churches in New England. This distinction points to further differences between the groups in social class, economic power, and resulting education. Hosea Ballou himself noted the educational differences that rendered most Universalists "little better than barbarians when compared with the graduates of Harvard College and other polished literati." Indeed, Henry W. Bellows, whom Miller identified as one of the earliest proponents of Unitarian and Universalist unity, identified the difference in social class as the greatest barrier to that unity.[22] Complicating this class difference were internal problems in both organizations. Many Unitarians in their early history found it hard enough to think of themselves as a sect or denomination, much less to consider merging with another such sect. The Universalists, always with a sense of struggle and persecution, felt compelled to battle for their own identity and right to exist, a battle that was threatened by merger with the richer and more influential Unitarians.

In a curious sense it was only after each denomination began to achieve the security of an independent stature that the arguments for unity began to emerge. Bellows secured Unitarianism as a denomination, but he did so, it should be remembered, as part of his search for a much more universal church. His organizational push was at least in part antisectarian. In this sense Bellows was part of a general current within both groups that was flowing toward a definition of religion and of the church on truly universal grounds. Part of this current can be seen in the broadening hospitality among the liberals toward the religions of the world, as best exemplified in the early studies of non-Christian religions by Lydia Maria Child,* James Freeman Clarke, and Samuel Johnson.*[23] The confirmation of a universal religious sense or capacity in humanity that these studies began to offer, even with their Christian perspective, helped to advance the notion of a universal liberal religion embodied in a universal nonsectarian church. The first obvious step toward such a church seemed to be the combining of forces sympathetic to liberalism, most prominently the Unitarians and Universalists.

In the late 1850s, as Miller reported, Henry W. Bellows spoke positively of an eventual Unitarian and Universalist merger, noting that social rather than theological differences seemed to be the major obstacles to union of that time. When his project for Unitarian awakening, the National Conference, had its first meeting in 1865, there was discussion of union with Universalists, and a committee of correspondence was formed to explore cooperation and unity between Unitarians and other liberals.[24] Little resulted from these efforts with respect to merger, but the very gestures were significant as an indication of the universalizing impetus in Unitarians. Moreover, such gestures grounded future discussion of merger in history; they made the possibility of union less a new idea than part of a long-unfinished portion of the liberal agenda.

There were other expressions of the antisectarian impulse among the liberals of the day. James Freeman Clarke's free-church experiment, The Church of the Disciples, was an attempt to move beyond ordinary sectarian boundaries, even though Clarke himself remained one of the most solid contributors to Unitarian denominational growth. Thomas Starr King's* transition from Universalist to Unitarian, and his insistence on maintaining loyalty to both traditions, is a more personal example. But perhaps the universalist tendencies of Unitarianism reached their zenith in the career of Jenkin Lloyd Jones,* the leader of the western radicals. Jones had consistently pushed his religion away from both theological and institutional confinement. In 1882 he launched another free-church experiment, the Church of All Souls in Chicago. Although Unitarian in affiliation, it was a Unitarianism of the radical variety that Jones had espoused in the West. The church's Bond of Union reveals the radical and nonsectarian thrust of the experiment: ''We join ourselves together in the interests of Morality and Religion, as interpreted by the growing thought and purest lives of Humanity, hoping thereby to bear one another's burdens and promote Truth, Love and Righteousness in the world.''[25] Yet such a free church was only part of Jones's attempt to universalize liberalism. One of the most notable achievements was his central role in the World Parliament of Religions as part of the World's Columbian Exposition of 1893 in Chicago. Jones arranged to bring together a large representation of the world's religious leaders in a meeting that bespoke a brotherhood that could transcend theological and cultural differences.[26] It was one of the most notable expressions of the growing hunger among Unitarians for international cooperation, an impulse that would continue to grow in the early decades of the twentieth century. The Humanist movement, in many ways the intellectual descendant of Jones, Octavius Brooks Frothingham,* and other radicals, would keep this universalist impulse alive within Unitarianism. The dilemma that this at times presented is worth noting. Although the sense of world purpose was one of the fuels to a Unitarian missionary effort, that very impulse was not sectarian in the ordinary sense. The very notion that compelled Unitarians to send their word abroad would also prevent their conceiving of their work as merely denominational extension. The missionary enterprise for liberals was less that of persuasion and conversion than a seeking out of shared values and an emphasis on cooperation and unity on an equal basis.

Although much of our attention has been focused on the Unitarian approach to merger, many of the same trends toward universalizing liberal religion were also at work among the Universalists. Even at the Universalist Centennial celebration of 1870 there was a disposition to seize upon the sense of "Universalism" as the universal world religion. Foreign missionary efforts began soon thereafter, and the Universalists were further moved toward an interdenominational position by the efforts of Jenkin Lloyd Jones and the World Parliament of Religions. As George H. Williams* noted, this sense of Universalism as a universal world religion "would become the dominant strand in the denomination" by the middle of the twentieth century.[27] One of the clearest statements of that view of Universalism was offered in 1949 by Brainerd F. Gibbons, who would later become a president of the Universalist Church of America. Ernest Cassara saw Gibbons's statement as a prime example of a conception of Universalism "whose future lay beyond Christianity."[28]

A new type of Universalism is proclaimed which shifts the emphasis on universal from salvation to religion and describes Universalism as boundless in scope, as broad as humanity, and as infinite as the universe. Is this Universalism's answer: a religion, not exclusively Christian or any other named brand, but a synthesis of all religious knowledge which passes the test of human intelligence, a truly universal religion?[29]

Yet there were complications to this movement, for it represented a fundamental change of identity for the Universalists. One of the most salient facts of Universalist history is the gradual erosion, through the nineteenth century, of the movement's distinctive message of universal salvation. Unlike the Unitarians, who had defined themselves largely on the basis of a theological method or approach, rational religion, the Universalists had based their identity on the doctrine of salvation to all. This doctrine, moreover, was formulated in direct opposition to Calvinist ideas of the election of a restricted few to salvation. As Calvinism waned, and as Protestantism liberalized itself generally, the centrality and distinctiveness of the Universalist position faded as well. In one sense this pushed the denomination toward the new sense of "universal" that we have been considering. But in another sense it impeded the theological development of the movement, because it meant that to reformulate the questions of salvation in more modern terms was to abandon the original tradition of the denomination.

Complicating this issue was the foundation of biblicism and the centrality of Christology to Universalism. Neither the movement away from a scriptural basis of faith nor the abandonment of a faith in Jesus made as much headway within Universalism as within Unitarianism. In a sense this is to say that Universalism remained more conservative, but it might be more accurate to say that Universalists continued to draw liberal conclusions from their traditional bases of faith. Hosea Ballou, for instance, had come to more radical conclusions respecting the afterlife than Channing; yet Ballou had worked more strictly from the Bible. Even though the traditional elements of Universalist faith did not exclude them from liberalism, these elements did stand as a barrier to Unitarian and Universalist union. George H. Williams detailed considerable Universalist opposition to merger in the 1890s because of a perceived difference in the relative authority given to Christ in the two traditions. That perception was keyed to the radical presence and the Free Religion movement within Unitarianism. It is not surprising, therefore, to note that there was a movement for merger not with the Unitarians but with the Congregationalists in the early part of the twentieth century. This did not materialize, but the study of the possibility, and negotiations toward it in the 1920s, probably helped increase the Unitarians' sense of the appropriateness of further cooperation with the Universalists.[30]

Yet there was a continuity between the older Universalism of the salvation of all people and the newer conception of the universal church. That continuity is perhaps best seen in the work of Clarence Skinner,* the dominant figure in modern Universalist thinking. Skinner found in the idea of "brotherhood" the fundamental connection between the older and the newer Universalism. "Faith in the transforming power of Brotherhood is growing great," he wrote in 1915. "The idea of the Universal Brotherhood is the great social dynamic of the twentieth century. Sometimes it is dynamite. It fires our hopes, builds our dreams, unfolds before us the Messianic vision of an imminent Kingdom of heaven on earth." Skinner located this essentially utopian idea of the transformation of the world in a faith in human dignity that was for him the essence of Universalism.

And Universalism inspires this faith not only because it teaches the divine origin of all men, but likewise because of its belief in the common destiny of humanity in all times and in all stations of life. Universalism triumphantly holds to the universal salvation of all mankind. It believes that all human souls are children of God with a spark of the divine in their nature, and that eventually, after the varied experiences of this world and the next, those souls will reach a perfect harmony with God.[31]

What Skinner saw in the older Universalism was the sense of human solidarity, which he thought marked the modern imperative toward social transformation. "Never was there such a bold proclamation of brotherhood" as the old assertion of universal salvation. "It is the largest, most astonishing evidence of the new social consciousness."[32] On this basis, then, Universalists could both stand within their unique tradition and formulate an identity that led forward, equipping them with an ideology for the modern age as well. Insofar as this ideology denied the limits of sect, it made the union with Unitarians a more logical extension of the essential impulse of Universalism.

Such an emphasis on the social nature of Universalism was also reflected in one important official pronouncement of the denomination, the "Bond of Fellowship" adopted in 1935. Although the statement itself eschews any "creedal test," it clearly hoped to capture a reigning sense of purpose among Universalists. It interpreted that purpose as "to do the will of God as Jesus revealed it and to cooperate in establishing the Kingdom for which he lived and died."

This is clearly a kingdom on earth, and it illustrated, in Ernest Cassara's phrase, "the extent to which Universalists had melded into the social-gospel Protestantism of the day."[33] By this time, the conscience that rebelled against Calvinist election in the late eighteenth century had become a conscience in rebellion against social injustice in the twentieth century.

It was during the 1930s that the first concrete step toward merger was made in the formation of the Free Church Fellowship. AUA president Louis Craig Cornish was an important figure in the formation of the organization and served as its first president, an action much in keeping with his general dedication to a broadening of Unitarianism into an international, universal movement. The Free Church Fellowship was conceived as a federation of all liberal churches that would act to provide an ecumenical structure under which unified action could be taken. Although it hoped to attract liberals from all over Protestantism, its essential support was from the Unitarians and Universalists. Perhaps because of the difficulties of the times, in which the denominations were themselves having difficulties in self-maintenance, the organization never grew or prospered. Even though the future of the fellowship would belie those predictions, the Appraisal Commission Report of 1936 saw in the organization "a real possibility of substantial progress" toward closer ties among liberals and called for further efforts toward realizing the goals of the fellowship.[34]

A more substantial act of organization and one that could be regarded as the first actual phase of merger was the formation of the Council of Liberal Churches in 1953. In the background of that act, as Dana M. Greeley suggested, were Frederick May Eliot's speeches on behalf of Unitarian-Universalist unity in 1947. The formation of the council actually merged the administrative functions of religious education, publications, and public relations of the two denominations. This was followed by the appointment of a joint commission on merger headed by William B. Rice,* and finally in 1959, by a joint biennial conference of Unitarians and Universalists in Syracuse, New York. On the basis of the consensus that emerged from that meeting, which was affirmed in plebiscites in both denominations, merger was completed in 1961, with Dana M. Greeley elected as the first president of the Unitarian Universalist Association.[35]

As the two denominations moved toward merger the debate about its advisability intensified. Although it seemed from one point of view a wise combination of resources that would expand the capacities of both groups, others saw the move toward merger as a dissipation of energies that would be better spent on local problems or within existing denominational channels.[36] As the 1959 meeting of the Joint Delegate Assembly at Syracuse revealed, there were still deeply felt differences about the religious orientation of the two denominations, differences both within and between the denominations. In a draft of the new constitution for the Unitarian Universalist Association, there was considerable debate over one portion of a statement of Purposes and Objectives. One version had been included in an original "blue book" issued by the commission in August: "To cherish and spread the universal truths taught by the great prophets and teachers of humanity in every age and tradition, immemorially summarized in their essence as love to God and love to man.'' But as the assembly began, the commission revised the statement: ''To cherish and spread the universal truths taught by Jesus and the other great teachers of humanity in every age and tradition, and prophetically expressed in the Judeo-Christian tradition as love to God and love to man.'' The specific affirmations of Jesus and of the Judeo-Christian tradition in the second version of the statement emphasize the problem of identity within the denominations that have already been discussed. To what extent is Unitarian Universalism part of Protestant Christianity? To what extent is it beyond Christianity, standing as a new universal religion? This was the most hotly contested issue in the conference, for it touched the always sensitive area of definition and creed. After an apparent consensus had been reached on the first version of the statement, the one lacking the Judeo-Christian references, the Universalists reconsidered their decision and offered this version: ''To cherish and spread the universal truths taught by the great prophets and teachers of humanity in every age and tradition, immemorially summarized in our Judeo-Christian heritage as love to God and love to man.'' While deleting the reference to Jesus, this version of the statement did retain a reference to ''our Judeo-Christian heritage.'' When the Unitarians suggested a change from ''our'' to ''the,'' it was accepted. But this slight variation in wording, and the importance attached to it by the delegates, indicated the problems not yet resolved among the Unitarians and the Universalists. Perhaps more importantly, however, the eventual merger plan was overwhelmingly ratified by the individual churches and then by the American Unitarian Association annual meeting and the Universalist General Assembly. All issues had not been resolved in every mind, but an undeniable consensus had been achieved on the merger of the denominations.[37]

## UNITARIAN UNIVERSALISM: THE CONTEMPORARY ISSUES

What was the condition of the new Unitarian Universalist Association (UUA) after merger was achieved, and how has the organization evolved since that time? These are difficult questions to answer historically, for temporality is the focus of the historian, and definitive judgments come, if they ever do, only at some distance from events. It seems safe to say, however, that the past two decades have been trying ones for liberal religion not because of the merger of the two denominations but because of other social and political events that have had a direct bearing on the message of liberalism.

There was a considerable amount of self-searching in the denomination before and after the merger, an assessment of identity that in a sense followed the precedent of the Unitarian Appraisal Commission of 1936. On the eve of merger the AUA set out to assess itself as *The Free Church in a Changing World*, and the report of the six commissions established to carry out the assessment was published under that title in 1963.[38] One thing of particular significance to an understanding of Unitarian Universalism that emerged from the report was the sense of enormous diversity of theological opinion within the movement. The second commission, which reported on "Theology and the Frontiers of Learning," found "six major theological emphases among us," which are usually "interfused in individuals and coexist in groups" rather than existing in any "pure form." These emphases follow, with the title given by the commission and my own brief paraphrase of the definition of these positions:

1. *Christian Liberalism.* The Christian tradition is viewed in the light of reason and informed by "contemporary understandings of myths and symbols."
2. *Deism.* The natural order of the physical universe, revealed in science, is used as a guide for understanding and action.
3. *Mystical Religion.* The basis of religion is an experience of mystic oneness with the Divine.
4. *Religious Humanism.* The basis of religion is the use of the natural resources of humankind to create a better and more meaningful life.
5. *Naturalistic Theism.* The process of creativity, "only in part controlled by man," and operating within the bounds of nature, is the basis of religion.
6. *Existentialism.* The human condition is one of both isolation and "radical freedom," and human integrity is the product of decisions made within that context. (pp. 25–26)

Such diversity as this, even allowing for the fact of significant overlaps (say, between deism and naturalistic theism or religious Humanism and existentialism) has continued to be a salient fact of contemporary liberalism. Although the content of religious belief varied widely, the commission saw a greater consensus on the form or "style" of liberalism, which they summarized under four categories: (1) "this-worldly concerns," (2) "strong ethical responsibility," (3) "deep commitment to democracy," and (4) a belief that "true community is religiously based" (pp. 26–27). For the commission, this diversity of content and similarity of style suggested the possible emergence of a new theological vision, which was to be greatly desired as an affirmation of a cohesive denominational identity. "But a new imperative is laid upon us now. Can we generate a dynamic religious belief which fits with and draws its strength rationally from the present frontiers of learning?" (p. 41). What the report seemed to suggest was a pattern of increasing religious pluralism, but a simultaneous need to discuss consensus, or identity, within that pluralism. Forcefully stated by Paul N. Carnes in a concluding commentary, here is that need: "For religious liberalism has little to meet the challenge of today's need, or win our own personal need, if all it offers is a casual 'Join us and you can believe anything you want to'—as if religious convictions were to be left to such ephemeral judges as whim and wish!" (p. 162). If pluralism has remained a fact of the denomination since the 1963 report, so has this desire to forge a consensus not for the purpose of conformity or standardization but for the sense of identity that such a consensus would suggest.

This study of the denomination begun before the merger was followed by another study after the merger, which was based on a survey of current denominational opinion on a wide variety of subjects. The survey was carried on by a Committee on Goals appointed by the UUA Board of Trustees in 1965. Their report was submitted in 1967, and a more extensive analysis and interpretation of the data of the survey was published in 1973 by the committee's chairman, Robert B. Tapp. "The aim of this project," as Tapp described it, "was to sketch a profile of the 'typical Unitarian Universalist,' to measure any regional differences that might exist within the denomination, and to ascertain if there were any noteworthy differences between existing churches that had been experiencing rapid growth and ordinary churches."[39] Based on a final sample of 12,146 questionnaires from eighty churches and fellowships, the survey gives us some sense of the nature of the denomination in the middle 1960s—after merger and before most of the political upheaval of the late 1960s.[40]

The survey revealed a religion overwhelmingly composed of converts, those who were not born into Unitarianism or Universalism but who arrived there either from a background of a different faith, or of little or no religious affiliation. Only 10.6 percent of the respondents were born Unitarian or Universalist; only 12.1 percent had Unitarianism or Universalism as the family religion during childhood (p. 239). Thus Tapp concluded that "the central element in the UU experience is the conversion experience," although it is one far different from that of "revivalistic Protestantism." It is a slow process, stretching often from childhood to adulthood, usually based on the experience of a university education. As Robert Tapp noted, this is more "a deconversion process" than a conversion process in the ordinary sense of the term (p. 199). Tapp suggested three phases of this process: first there was "the deconversion stage, the dropping-out of the older religious identification," followed by a second phase of assimilation of "new values," and finally, a third phase that occurs "when, and if, for some reasons, these new identification-values become institutionally grounded," or in other words, if the "convert" elects to join a Unitarian Universalist church (p. 200). That there are many people outside the denomination who reach the second but not the third phase, that values change but institutional affiliation often does not, is one of the more significant suggestions that Tapp makes in discussing the formation of what he labeled "post-traditional" religion (p. 200).

Other names for this process come readily to mind. "Maturation" rather than conversion or deconversion might seem a more appropriate label. A Channing or an Emerson might call it "self-cultivation." Other students of the sociology of religion would see in it the general patterns of "secularization." The major question for the future of Unitarian Universalism, however, is the transition from Tapp's second phase to the third phase. It is the role of the church in the process of changing values. Hence the relevance of the recent UUA advertising slogan, "Are you a Unitarian Universalist without knowing it?"

What did the survey reveal of the attitudes of the denomination? There was an uneasy relation to the traditional terms or structures of Christian religion. Although only 2.9 percent of the respondents believed God a "supernatural being," 23.1 percent chose to see God in Paul Tillich's terms as "the ground of all being." But 28.0 percent saw God as "an irrelevant concept" and 1.8 percent saw God as an actually "harmful" concept. The largest percentage (44.2 percent) took the middle ground of agreeing that " 'God' may be appropriately used as a name for some natural processes within the universe, such as love or creative evolution" (pp. 222–23). Certainly, this is a wide range of opinion, confirming the 1963 report's sense of diversity in the denomination. But it is difficult to determine whether the categories of choice, or the very act of having to choose from among different articulations, may not seem to accentuate divisions. In many senses the liberals' insistence on creedlessness has been an insistence on the right of personal formulation of religious concepts, which are in a large measure beyond the reach of empirical enumeration. Other results of the survey did confirm the movement of the denomination away from the bounds of traditional Protestantism. Very few (10.5 percent) classed immortality as part of their belief; a majority (56.9 percent) would not define their religion as "Christian" (p. 226). Although 11.2 percent preferred the denomination to move closer toward either "liberal Protestantism" or "the ecumenical movement within Christianity," a large majority preferred a movement toward "an emerging universal religion" (36.7 percent) or "a distinctive humanistic religion" (52.0 percent) (p. 236). As a further indication of theological direction, 79.4 percent of the respondents indicated a belief that modern science "strengthens liberal religion" (p. 224).

Converging with this hope for the evolution of a new religion, universal or distinctively humanistic, and this corresponding valuation of science, the respondents also expressed an overwhelming belief that "there has been progress in the history of human civilization" (95.2 percent). The "growth of science and knowledge" was the most frequently chosen support for this belief (p. 226). Tapp saw this as the idea of "greatest unanimity" among Unitarian Universalist beliefs.[41] Certainly, it calls to mind James Freeman Clarke's famous fifth point of Unitarian belief—"the progress of mankind onward and upward forever"—and affirms it even after the searching questions that contemporary life and belief had put to that faith. The forward-looking thrust of liberal religion seems confirmed by that response. Moreover, the survey confirmed what the liberal tradition had always assumed of itself—that its members were more likely to be oriented toward social action and political change than others. Tapp noted "consistent relationships between posttraditionality and liberalism" with regard to questions of "war, demonstrations, and conscientious objection," issues of rising importance in the middle 1960s (p. 102). Liberal religion and liberal politics, in other words, seemed to have some connection.

To understand further the denomination since merger, one should also note the pattern of denominational growth and decline. James M. Hutchinson's analysis of this pattern in the last three decades is revealing. The expansion of membership that marked the postwar period and the 1950s ended in the late 1960s. In 1968 membership was 148 percent of the 1950 membership, but at that point a sharp decline began, to 124 percent of 1950 membership in 1972 and 114 percent of membership in 1978.[42] This pattern was common in other Protestant denominations and probably reflects some demographic patterns of the postwar baby boom. Those children were reaching college age, and the pattern of family church attendance and membership is probably reflected in these figures. But it seems that there is more than demographic coincidence in these figures. In the 1960s liberal values came under attack, an attack as severe as that of the 1930s. Moreover, there was a correspondingly intense pressure of politicization of the churches. The results of the Goal Committee's Survey did reveal a predilection to social action in the denomination. But it also brought out a split between the majority of "post-traditionals" and more conservative members about the role of the church in social action. Divisiveness and disagreement over ultimate goals is not the most conducive atmosphere for church growth.

Even deeper issues may be reflected in this decline, however. It should be remembered that the Vietnam War and the rise of civil rights activism took place as the nation attempted to move into the era of the "Great Society." The liberal agenda of the times confronted the simultaneous rise of the very issues, the war, racial equality, economic justice, and sexual equality, which were undermining faith in the liberal institutions attempting to carry out that agenda. This political situation by no means exempted the churches, to which many Unitarian Universalists looked as an institutional vehicle for approaching these problems. One of the denomination's most significant crises of the late 1960s was the wrenching struggle over black empowerment. In 1967 a Black Unitarian Universalist Caucus (BUUC) was formed to seek social change and challenge the problem of racism in American society. In 1968 the General Assembly, in an emotional meeting at Cleveland, voted to support a Black Affairs Council (BAC), sponsored by the BUUC, with an appropriation of $250,000 annually for four years. David B. Parke has called the decision "incomparably the most important event in the history of our movement since the end of World War II."[43] The decision had substantial support at the General Assembly—72 percent of the delegates supported it—but the plan also met with resistance in the denomination. In 1969, a new group emerged with a different philosophy of handling the denomination's response to racism. The Unitarian Universalists for Black and White Action asked for recognition, in Donald Harrington's words, "of the continuing legitimacy of the integrationist approach."[44] It was clear that the 1968 decision had not settled the debate about how the denomination should combat racism. In 1969 the General Assembly reaffirmed the 1968 commitment to BAC, but by a narrower margin. In 1970, the crisis reached its peak. As Parke recounts it, "In January 1970, the UUA Board of Trustees, responding to a devastating shortfall in income, cut back the allocation for the Black Affairs Council. Charging racism, the Black UU Caucus terminated the Black Affairs Council's affiliation with the UUA and with it any hope of further denominational funding."[45] Emotions continue to be felt over these events, and the intellectual issues involved here are far from being resolved. But as some commentators have noted, the issue of black empowerment is connected to the question of the class-bound nature of liberal religion as it is manifested in Unitarian Universalism.[46] In this respect the denomination mirrored, in an agonizing way, the larger issues of race and class as they surfaced in American society in the late 1960s. To what extent should a local church be the vehicle of political opposition? This was not so clear to many, and even activist churches ran the danger of discovering a paralyzing political impotence in expressing their dissent. Many others outside the church felt this powerlessness as well, a fact that suggests a widespread liberal crisis of faith that could be particularly debilitating to religious liberals. This crisis of faith, rooted in politics, but a politics that had become the central moral issue of the day, certainly helps to account for part of the faltering of the denomination after merger.

This is not to say that political involvement by the churches led directly to a membership decline. Hutchinson noted "considerable evidence" against a direct correlation of these facts, suggesting that this analysis of church decline because of social action had been overemphasized.[47] My sense is that the decline was partly a result of a shifting cultural attitude toward all institutions, including the church. It is no accident that the Vietnam era was superseded by the "me"-oriented, or narcissistic, 1970s. When institutions lose the trust of people, people must fall back on the self. The liberal church, because of its already existing ambivalence about an individual's surrendering of autonomy to a group, was sure to suffer this loss of faith in some form. But it is notable that as of late 1983, denominational growth appeared to be on an upsurge, reversing the trend of decline.

In discussing these political questions, I am calling attention to what has become an increasingly engrossing concern in contemporary Unitarian Universalism. Even after the era of the Vietnam war, the related question of nuclear armament has recently emerged as a central issue for liberals. The issue of women's rights has also been a pressing one, resulting in the call from the 1977 General Assembly to "put traditional assumptions and language in perspective, and avoid sexist assumptions and language in the future."[48] Valerie C. Saiving's 1978 Dudleian lecture expounded the concern about the need to find alternatives to the sexist nature of thinking arising from the Western philosophical tradition.[49] The "network of unconscious and semiconscious presuppositions about the wider context within which *all* experience occurs" is, in Saiving's view, "an implicit metaphysics" whose premises "are shaped by patriarchal structures and modes of thought" (p. 13). For Saiving, one of the results of rethinking those assumptions is a recognition of a series of dichotomies in Western thinking, including "creator and creature, humanity and nature, mind and body, reason and emotion, activity and passivity, self and other, subject and object, individuality and relatedness, life and death" (p. 18). These dichotomies have been related in our tradition "with the dualism of male and female" (p. 18), establishing a structure of "dichotomy and domination" (p. 26) that is destructive to the realization of the full potentialities of life.

These political issues which have gripped liberal religion force two other questions to the forefront, questions that have deep roots in the history of the denomination. These questions concern the nature and necessity of a theological vision in liberal religion and the concept and function of the church in liberal religion. We might articulate the first question by asking whether one can specify a difference between liberalism and religious liberalism in contemporary culture. This isolates the concept of religion and asks for a definition of it, pulling us back to the theological underpinnings of modern liberalism.

The Humanist movement in liberalism, the continuing growth of secularization in modern culture generally, and the evidence of a pervasive "post-traditional" outlook in Unitarian Universalism all suggest that "theology" has increasingly moved to the background in liberal religion. Certainly, no one can assume that liberal theology carries the implicit assumption of a God or "Theos" as the word suggests. More fundamentally, the pluralism of liberal religion can threaten a disconnectedness or isolation, a situation articulated by Ronald Clark as the absence of a "Great Code":

And the UU recognizes, after being sidetracked time after time, that *there is no Great Code in our church.* There is no universal, understood way to say, "For the next immediate interlude of time I wish to speak of something of supreme importance—of supreme seriousness" so that one is certain that the responses will be in tone with the intent.[50]

This sense of an absence, the feeling that, in Robert Hemstreet's words, "at the present time, our movement has no recognizable theological shape" is a painful difficulty for many religious liberals.[51] It must be said, however, that codes or shapes or definitions represent limits, which might coexist uneasily with the very pluralism that is so attractive to many Unitarian Universalists. We are, as always with this tradition, enmeshed in the dilemma of creed and freedom or, as the problem takes shape now, in the conflict between definition and unlimited pluralism.

What are the fundamental theological alternatives available to religious liberals? It should first be said that at this period there is no exclusively Unitarian Universalist theology, just as there is no Methodist or Episcopal or other exclusively denominational theological mode in contemporary Protestantism. A diverse set of theologians and philosophers, including Alfred North Whitehead, Paul Tillich, Martin Buber, and Pierre Teilhard de Chardin, have had an influence on Unitarian Universalist thinking, and the whole of Protestant, Catholic, Jewish, or secular theological speculation remains available, as well as potent non-Western influences such as Buddhism. The four figures whom I have named have had powerful influences on all Christian thinking. But two others have been notably influential to twentieth-century religious liberalism, Henry Nelson

Wieman* and Charles Hartshorne.* They have been called the leaders in the school of process theology, and they shared several common emphases of that mode of thinking, whose key exponent has been Whitehead, a philosopher who influenced them both. But their methods and assumptions differed as did their ultimate philosophical systems, and in the nature of that difference there is an indication of the available directions for contemporary liberal theology. Wieman represents the attempt to ground the notion of God in empirical reality, and Hartshorne continues the tradition of speculative rationalism in defining the idea of God. This generalization should not overlook either Wieman's commitment to rational speculation or Hartshorne's sense that God "is in some fashion a universal datum of experience." But the general direction of Wieman's thought is empirical, as Hartshorne's is rational.[52]

As Wieman described his philosophical outlook, much of his work was devoted to recasting the direction of religious speculation. "Increasingly I am convinced that religious inquiry is misdirected when some presence pervading the total cosmos is sought to solve the religious problem. It is even more futile to search infinite being which transcends the totality of all existence."[53] This would seem at first to put Wieman in line with the school of naturalistic thinkers opposed to metaphysics entirely, a stance in some senses typical of Curtis Reese's* articulation of Humanism in the 1920s and 1930s. But in fact Wieman asserted that the result of this sort of thinking "is not necessarily the kind of humanism which claims that man can transform himself by setting up the proper ideals and devoting himself to desired goals" (p. 4). The most important aspects of our personality and behavior seem to be beyond the reach of conscious will. Wieman thus posited the need for "creative transformation operating beyond the control of conscious volition to save from evil," a process conventionally termed "grace" (p. 4). The source of that creative transformation or, as perhaps Wieman would put it, the *fact* of that creative transformation can be termed God. In an earlier writing, Wieman referred to the "growth of meaning in the world" as "God at work in our midst." This growth of meaning was neither "supernatural" nor "outside human life," but it was "ultrahuman." The distinction was for him important.

The human individual *undergoes* this growth; but he does not cause it. The intelligence cannot do it because it is the very intelligence itself that grows. The individual undergoes this growth as sunshine, air and earth undergo transformation into a scarlet poppy. Men can do more than the poppy. A man can seek out the conditions that are required for this growth and for its greater abundance. Above all, he can yield himself in blessed abandon to the transforming power of it. But he undergoes it; he does not cause it.[54]

Thus for Wieman the religious life can be thought of as the continuing attempt to "yield" to the process of growth, or creative transformation, or creation of meaning. It is a process whose sources are ultimately beyond the individual and can be located in a person's social interchange with his or her environment (both natural and social).[55]

Theology is thus the attempt to clarify this process of growth or, to give Wieman's insistence on empiricism its full weight, to analyze the events that constitute this growth. All theology must be grounded therefore in human life or, more specifically, in the actions or occurrences of an individual life. Increasingly wary of abstraction during his career, Wieman understood well that empiricism required specification and that theology had both to begin and end in concrete events. Hartshorne similarly emphasized the process of growth or creativity, and his entire philosophical program in fact can be interpreted in terms of underlying metaphor of "creativity," a version of the idea of the universe as process developed by Whitehead. As Hartshorne articulated this view, "there is a sense in which every individual creates and could not fail to do so while existing at all. *To be is to create.*"[56] The only limiting factor to this universe of creative process is that the creativity (or being) of one individual is limited by the creativity of another. Such limits insure the positive, rather than destructive, nature of the universe and save it from formless chaos. Since creativity determines existence, and the limits of other entities insure creativity, it can be said that it is the limiting effect of others on an entity that enables that entity to exist at all. This means that the nature of reality is fundamentally social, that existence itself is the product of a social relationship.[57]

The implications of this view of reality for Hartshorne's doctrine of God were enormous. God stood as the supreme example of the creative process, a position that led Hartshorne to differ strongly with the traditional view of God as changelessly perfect. "Perfect" Hartshorne argued that God was, but that perfection did not consist of changelessness. Traditionally, God's perfection had meant that God contained, and had therefore exhausted, all value and could not therefore be surpassed by any other in value. Hartshorne argued that although God could not be surpassed by any other, God could be self-surpassing. God could, in other words, change or grow. God contained all *possible* value, but possibility could change and God could therefore grow.

Otherwise expressed, let us define perfection as an excellence such that rivalry or superiority on the part of other individuals is impossible, but self-superiority is not impossible. Or again, let us say that the perfect is the "self-surpassing surpasser of all."[58]

Moreover, Hartshorne's emphasis on the social nature of reality also resulted in interesting new implications for the concept of God. In traditional terms, individuals were limited by their relationships, so that a perfect or unlimited God must be unchanged by the creation, radically free from it. In Hartshorne's view, medieval theories of God posited that "God knows all things, but in such fashion (it was held) that there is zero relativity or dependence on God as knower, and maximal dependence in the creatures as known" (p. 8). God, in other words, exists beyond relativity to the world. For Hartshorne, though, relativity constitutes value, because of the social nature of the world. God is therefore completely relative; God's being changes in relation to the world, and the completeness of the relation is the measure of God's perfection. Hartshorne posited a knowing or personal God, who knows in the sense that we know, but whose knowledge includes our own in its comprehensiveness. Although God's knowing "must not be absolutely different from our knowing," it differs in being "all-inclusive" while our own "is fragmentary, as our whole being is fragmentary."[59] It is on the question of God as "knowing" in a personal sense that Hartshorne and Wieman disagree most clearly. Wieman remains closer to pure naturalism, and Hartshorne finds a central place in his system for a God whose knowledge surpasses and includes our own.[60]

The rationalist and empiricist alternatives that Hartshorne and Wieman represent with respect to theology do not, however, address the second vital concern of contemporary religious liberalism, the doctrine of the church. The pull toward privatism has always been strong in the Unitarian tradition—Ralph Waldo Emerson is certainly the key example of this—and that pull has not lessened in this century, especially in light of the general cultural movement toward secularism. That the movement needs, however, "a doctrine of the church" has been consistently noted in opposition to this tendency.[61] In the 1963 report of the Study Commission on the Church, this concern was expressed with some force:

There is a tendency to dismiss matters of organization as "mere administration." But such considerations often raise questions of the most fundamental character. When we deal with church government or polity, we are dealing with people and how they ought to be related to one another. It makes a difference whether we organize our churches autocratically, democratically or in some other way. The decisions we make in administrative matters may play a part in determining the kind of church we are to have in the future.[62]

The strongest contemporary version of a doctrine of the church has been the writing of James Luther Adams on the "voluntary association." Clearly, such associations include many types of organizations other than churches—political interest groups, social organizations, charitable associations, and others—but as Adams argued, the history of such organizations is tied to that of the church, and the function and importance of such organizations in contemporary society casts light on the function and importance of the free church.

The essential characteristic of such organizations is "voluntaryism"—an adherence to the rule that "the member may in principle freely join an association, and he is free to withdraw from membership."[63] Similarly, Unitarian Universalists have affirmed the sense of their organization as a "free church," one in which "the individual is central. In him all authority is rooted. Accordingly such authority as the church possesses rests on the consent of the individual members."[64] What Adams has persuasively argued is that such associations are not only a result of an open or democratic society; they are in a real sense the protectors of such a society. The freedom of association grounds freedom and gives it form and meaning. "Freedom in this *institutional* sense," he argued, "distinguishes the democratic society from any other."[65] Seen in this light, the voluntary association becomes an essential mode of "commitment" for the individual. It is both a means of expressing and enacting the free choice that makes an open society.

Adams saw "that in the history of Christianity the first expression of voluntaryism appears in the primitive church, a voluntary association," and further noted the rich development of these organizations in late eighteenth- and early nineteenth-century society, often with close connections to the church (p. 63). The Missionary Society of Connecticut and the American Bible Society are examples of the several organizations he named that are "new, specialized voluntary organizations," formed "as instrumentalities to carry out the task of persuasion" (p. 69). For Adams, the rise of this principle of voluntaryism around the turn of the eighteenth century was "an organizational revolution" associated with the rise of modern industrial society. It is especially significant in the shaping of American religion, for voluntaryism "functions as a creative principle by making way for free interaction and innovation in the spirit of community" (p. 77). As Adams pointed out, William Ellery Channing noted this creative aspect of voluntary association. That it has functioned as a central tenet of the liberal church needs to be repeatedly recognized and repeatedly affirmed.

The hope that the voluntary principle offers to the free church is the achievement of what Adams called "independence and interdependence," or "the achievement of unity in variety" (p. 77). That is, the hope of voluntary association is the creation of a community that does not compromise the autonomy of its individual members. In voluntary association lies the solution to the dichotomy of individual and group responsibility that has marked the history of liberal religion in America. If this solution seems utopian, one thing should be remembered. Its achievement is not a static or stable thing. Voluntary association is a principle of action; its achievements are those of process. Association happens for a purpose, in order that an action may be undertaken—worship, organization, education, or other corporate activities. In this sense the nature of voluntary association is certainly not alien to the metaphysics of process that inform the work of Hartshorne or Wieman. "A special demand confronting the churches, then," Adams concluded, "is the demand for the information of reformation—the reformation of the voluntary principle" (p. 88). In whatever shape the liberal church continues, its continuance will have been the result of this voluntaryism becoming a mode of personal religious expression.

# NOTES

## CHAPTER 2

1. See Richard Bushman, ed., *The Great Awakening: Documents on the Revival of Religion, 1740–1745* (New York: Atheneum, 1970), pp. 116, 117–18, 120. For biographical information on Chauncy, see Edward M. Griffin, *Old Brick: Charles Chauncy of Boston, 1705–1787* (Minneapolis: University of Minnesota Press, 1980). On the Arminian reaction to the Great Awakening, the standard study is Conrad Wright, *The Beginnings of Unitarianism in America* (1955; rpt. New York: Archon, 1976).

2. The Great Awakening is discussed most thoroughly in Edwin S. Gaustad, *The Great Awakening in New England* (New York: Harper and Brothers, 1957); and Alan Heimert, *Religion and the American Mind: From the Great Awakening to the Revolution* (Cambridge: Harvard University Press, 1966).

3. George Whitefield, *George Whitefield's Journals (1737–1741)*, ed. William V. Davis (Gainesville, FL: Scholars' Facsimiles and Reprints, 1969), pp. 474–75.

4. Ibid., pp. 463, 475.

5. Wright, *The Beginnings of Unitarianism in America*, p. 3.

6. Alan Heimert and Perry Miller, eds., *The Great Awakening: Documents Illustrating the Crisis and Its Consequences* (Indianapolis and New York: Bobbs-Merrill, 1967), p. 231. Further quotations will be cited parenthetically.

7. William Ellery Channing, *The Works of William Ellery Channing, D.D.* (Boston: American Unitarian Association, 1875), p. 370. Hereafter cited as *Works*.

8. Alexander Pope, *The Complete Poetical Works of Alexander Pope*, ed. Henry W. Boynton, Cambridge Edition (Boston: Houghton Mifflin, 1903), p. 135.

9. Arthur C. McGiffert, *Protestant Thought before Kant* (1911; rpt. New York: Harper and Brothers, 1961), pp. 199, 207, 209. See also Perry Miller, *Nature's Nation* (Cambridge: The Belknap Press of Harvard University Press, 1967), pp. 121–33; and Conrad Wright, *The Liberal Christians: Essays on American Unitarian History* (Boston: Beacon Press, 1970), pp. 1–21.

10. Samuel Clarke, *The Works of Samuel Clarke, D.D.*, 4 vols. (1738; rpt. New York: Garland, 1978), II, 667.

11. Ebenezer Gay, *Natural Religion, as Distinguish'd from Revealed* (Boston: John Draper, 1759), p. 5. Further quotations will be cited parenthetically.

12. Earl Morse Wilbur, *A History of Unitarianism in Transylvania, England, and America* (Cambridge: Harvard University Press, 1952), p. 386.

13. Wright, *The Beginnings of Unitarianism in America*, p. 89.

14. Jonathan Mayhew, *Seven Sermons* (London: John Noon, 1750), reprinted in Jonathan Mayhew, *Sermons* (New York: Arno Press, 1969), p. 61. Further quotations will be cited parenthetically.

15. Charles Chauncy, *Five Dissertations on the Scripture Account of the Fall* (London, 1785), pp. 186–87, quoted in James W. Jones, *The Shattered Synthesis: New England Puritanism before the Great Awakening* (New Haven: Yale University Press, 1973), p. 180.

16. See Wright, *The Beginnings of Unitarianism in America*, pp. 187–93; and Griffin, *Old Brick*, pp. 176–77, for discussions of the book's background. The complete text is available in a recent reprint. Charles Chauncy, *The Mystery Hid from Ages and Generations, Made Manifest by the Gospel-Revelation; or, The Salvation of All Men* (1784; rpt. New York: Arno Press, 1969). Further quotations will be cited parenthetically.

17. Benjamin Franklin, *The Autobiography of Benjamin Franklin: A Genetic Text*, ed. J. A. Leo Lemay and P. M. Zall (Knoxville: University of Tennessee Press, 1981), p. 76. Editorial symbols and Franklin's deletions have been omitted.

18. Joseph Priestley, *Theological and Miscellaneous Works*, ed. John Towill Rutt (1831; rpt. New York: Kraus Reprint Co., 1972), I, part i, p. 212. Hereafter cited as *Works*. See also the discussion in A. Owen Aldridge, *Benjamin Franklin and Nature's God* (Durham, NC: Duke University Press, 1967), pp. 211–12.

19. Wilbur, *History*, p. 396. See also pp. 293–315; and Anne Holt's account of the destruction of Priestley's home in *A Life of Joseph Priestley* (London: Oxford University Press, 1931), pp. 145–78.

20. Wright, *The Beginnings of Unitarianism in America*, p. 161.

21. Priestley, *Works*, II, 21.

22. Priestley, *Works*, V, 8. Further quotations will be cited parenthetically.

23. Henry Wilder Foote, *The Religion of Thomas Jefferson* (Boston: Beacon Press, 1960), p. 69.

24. Ibid., p. 76. See also pp. 69–76; and Conrad Wright, *Individualism in Historical Perspective*, Unitarian Universalist Advance Study Paper No. 9, 1979, pp. 2–4.

25. See Wright, *Individualism in Historical Perspective*, pp. 2–9.

## CHAPTER 3

1. For two recent studies of Buckminster, see Lawrence Buell, "Joseph Stevens Buckminster: The Making of a New England Saint," *Canadian Review of American Studies*, 10 (Spring 1979), 1–29; and Lewis P. Simpson, *The Man of Letters in New England and the South* (Baton Rouge: Louisiana State University Press, 1973), pp. 3–31.

2. Buell, "Joseph Stevens Buckminster," pp. 4–5. On the development of sermon form among the Unitarians generally, see Lawrence Buell, *Literary Transcendentalism: Style and Vision in the American Renaissance* (Ithaca, NY: Cornell University Press, 1973).

3. Eliza Buckminster Lee, *Memoirs of Rev. Joseph Buckminster, D.D., and of His Son, Rev. Joseph Stevens Buckminster* (Boston: William Crosby and H. P. Nichols, 1849), p. 338. On Buckminster's preaching, see Samuel Kirkland Lathrop, *A History of the Church in Brattle Street, Boston* (Boston: William Crosby and H. P. Nichols, 1851), pp. 171–76.

4. Jerry Wayne Brown, *The Rise of Biblical Criticism in America, 1800–1870* (Middletown, CT: Wesleyan University Press, 1969).

5. Joseph Stevens Buckminster, "Notice of Griesbach's Edition of the New-Testament, Now Printing at Cambridge," *Monthly Anthology and Boston Review*, 5 (January 1808), 19.

6. Joseph Stevens Buckminster, "Abstract of Interesting Facts Relating to the New Testament," *Monthly Anthology and Boston Review*, 5 (October 1808), 544. The article continued in the November and December issues, pp. 580–85 and 633–40, respectively.

7. Ibid., p. 639.

8. See Wright, *The Beginnings of Unitarianism in America*, pp. 200–201.

9. Conrad Wright, "The Controversial Career of Jedidiah Morse," *Harvard Library Bulletin*, 31 (Winter 1983), 87.

10. For discussions of the controversy surrounding the Belsham book, see William C. Gannett, *Ezra Stiles Gannett: Unitarian Minister in Boston, 1824–1871* (Boston: Roberts Bros., 1875), pp. 48–55; Jack Mendelsohn, *Channing: The Reluctant Radical* (Boston: Little, Brown, 1971), pp. 140–46; and Wright, "The Controversial Career of Jedidiah Morse."

11. William Ellery Channing, *A Letter to the Rev. Samuel C. Thacher, on the Aspersions contained in a Late Number of the Panoplist, on the Ministers of Boston and the Vicinity*, 3rd ed. (Boston: Wells and Lilly, 1815), p. 6. Further quotations will be cited parenthetically. For an abridgement of the *Letter*, see William Henry Channing, *The Life of William Ellery Channing, D.D.*, Centenary Memorial ed. (Boston: American Unitarian Association, 1875), pp. 194–205.

12. On the variety and nature of the controversies in the pamphlet wars, see Wilbur, *History*, pp. 401–34.

13. On the background of "Unitarian Christianity," see Conrad Wright, *Three Prophets of Religious Liberalism: Channing-Emerson-Parker* (Boston: Beacon Press, 1961), pp. 5–19. On Channing's career see Mendelsohn, *Channing*, pp. 35–283, and Wright, "The Rediscovery of Channing," in Wright, *The Liberal Christians*, pp. 22–40.

14. Channing, *Works*, p. 368. Further quotations will be cited parenthetically.

15. Ralph Waldo Emerson, *The Collected Works of Ralph Waldo Emerson*, vol. 2, ed. Joseph Slater and Jean Ferguson Carr (Cambridge: The Belknap Press of Harvard University Press, 1979), p. 27. Hereafter cited as CW.

16. Conrad Wright, "The Election of Henry Ware: Two Contemporary Accounts," *Harvard Library Bulletin*, 17 (July 1969), 245–78.

17. Ibid., p. 251.

18. Brown, *Rise*, pp. 46–48.

19. On the founding of Harvard Divinity School, see Conrad Wright, "The Early Period (1811–40)," in *The Harvard Divinity School: Its Place in Harvard University and in American Culture*, ed. George H. Williams (Boston: Beacon Press, 1954), pp. 21–77.

20. Channing, *Works*, p. 279. Further quotations will be cited parenthetically.

21. Wilbur, *History*, p. 431.

22. Charles C. Forman, "Elected Now by Time," in *A Stream of Light*, ed. Conrad Wright (Boston: Unitarian Universalist Association, 1975), p. 31.

23. Channing, *Life*, p. 218.

24. Gannett, *Ezra Stiles Gannett*, pp. 102–3.

25. On the formation of the AUA see Ibid., pp. 97–104; George Willis Cooke, *Unitarianism in America* (Boston: American Unitarian Association, 1902), pp. 106–36; and Virgil E. Murdock, *The Institutional History of the American Unitarian Association*, Minns Lectures, 1975–76 (Boston, 1976). William Hutchison, *The Transcendentalist Ministers: Church Reform in the New England Renaissance* (New Haven: Yale University Press, 1959), pp. 1–21, is especially helpful on the problems of organization. Officers of the AUA are listed in Wright, ed., *A Stream of Light*, pp. 172–73.

## CHAPTER 4

1. Octavius Brooks Frothingham, *Boston Unitarianism, 1820–1850: A Study of the Life and Work of Nathaniel Langdon Frothingham* (New York: Putnam's, 1890), p. 38.

2. Andrews Norton, *A Statement of Reasons for Not Believing the Doctrine of Trinitarians, concerning the Nature of God and the Person of Christ* (1833; rpt. Boston: American Unitarian Association, 1890), p. 40. For biographical information on Norton, see William Newell, "Biographical Notice of Mr. Norton," in Norton, ibid., pp. ix–l; and Daniel Walker Howe, *The Unitarian Conscience: Harvard Moral Philosophy, 1805–1861* (Cambridge: Harvard University Press, 1970), pp. 15–16, 312–13.

3. Andrews Norton, *The Evidences of the Genuineness of the Gospels*, 2nd ed., 3 vols. (Boston: William Crosby and H. P. Nichols, 1848), III, 332. Further quotations will be cited parenthetically.

4. For the definitive discussion of Unitarian pietism, see Howe, *The Unitarian Conscience*, pp. 151–73. The major source of information on Ware is John Ware, *The Life of Henry Ware, Jr.*, 2 vols. in 1 (1846; rpt. Boston: American Unitarian Association, 1890).

5. Ware's demurrer, *The Personality of the Deity* (1838), has been reprinted with an introduction in Kenneth Walter Cameron, "Henry Ware's *Divinity School Address*— A Reply to Emerson's," *American Transcendental Quarterly*, 13 (Winter 1972), 84–91. For the best discussion of the Emerson-Ware controversy, see Hutchison, *Transcendentalist Ministers*, pp. 76–81.

6. Henry Ware, Jr., *On the Formation of the Christian Character*, in *The Works of Henry Ware, Jr., D.D.*, 4 vols. (Boston: James Munroe, 1846), IV, 283–391. Further quotations will be cited parenthetically.

7. Gannett, *Ezra Stiles Gannett*, p. 149. Further quotations will be cited parenthetically.

8. See Howe, *Unitarian Conscience*, 236–69; and Daniel T. McColgan, *Joseph Tuckerman: Pioneer in American Social Work* (Washington, DC: Catholic University of America Press, 1940).

9. Edward Everett Hale, ed., *Joseph Tuckerman on the Elevation of the Poor* (Boston: Roberts Bros., 1874), p. 39. Further quotations will be cited parenthetically.

10. Henry David Thoreau, *Walden*, ed. J. Lyndon Shanley (Princeton, NJ: Princeton University Press, 1971), 74. For details of Channing's position see David Robinson, "Channing and the Problem of Social Reform," *Kairos*, 16 (Autumn 1979).

11. Joseph Tuckerman, *Gleams of Truth; or, Scenes from Real Life*, rev. ed. (1835; Boston: James Munroe, 1852), p. 110.

## CHAPTER 5

1. On Murray's theology and his debt to Relly, see Russell E. Miller, *The Larger Hope: The First Century of the Universalist Church in America, 1770–1870* (Boston: Unitarian Universalist Association, 1979), pp. 40–41. Miller's study is the definitive work on American Universalism, and a second volume on later denominational development is underway. On Chauncy's publication of his universalist views and his attitude toward Murray, see Wright, *The Beginnings of Unitarianism in America*, pp. 187–90.

2. John Murray, *Records of the Life of John Murray* (1816), quoted in Ernest Cassara, *Universalism in America: A Documentary History* (Boston: Beacon Press, 1971), pp. 56–59.

3. Miller, *Larger Hope*, p. xxiii, termed Murray the "founder" of Universalism. For the following information on Murray, I have relied on the following: Miller, ibid., pp. 3–33; Paul Ivar Chestnut, "The Universalist Movement in America, 1770–1803" (Ph.D. diss., Duke University, 1974), pp. 3–21; Cassara, *Universalism in America*, pp. 10–14, 55–77; and George Huntston Williams, "American Universalism: A Bicentennial Historical Essay," *Journal of the Universalist Historical Society* (hereafter cited as JUHS), 9 (1971), 1–94 (entire issue). On the Baptists, see William McLoughlin, *New England Dissent, 1630–1883: The Baptists and the Separation of Church and State*, 2 vols. (Cambridge: Harvard University Press, 1971), II, 697–722; and Stephen A. Marini, *Radical Sects of Revolutionary New England* (Cambridge: Harvard University Press, 1982).

4. For an entertaining account of his debate with Hopkins, see Thomas Whittemore, *The Modern History of Universalism, from the Era of the Reformation to the Present Time* (Boston, 1830), pp. 322–25.

5. On Rich, see Miller, *Larger Hope*, p. 67; and Marini, *Radical Sects*, pp. 72–75. Marini included interesting detail on the nature of Rich's visionary experiences.

6. Edwin Martin Stone, *Biography of Rev. Elhanan Winchester* (Boston: H. B. Brewster, 1836), reprinted in *Reverend Elhanan Winchester: Biography and Letters* (New York: Arno, 1972), p. 30.

7. Ibid., p. 42. On Winchester, in addition to Chestnut and Miller, see Charles White McGehee, "Elhanan Winchester: A Decision for Universal Restoration," JUHS, 1 (1959), 43–58; and Marini, *Radical Sects*, pp. 69–71.

8. It is important to note George H. Williams's distinction between the "much enlarged framework of Calvinism" informing Murray's work and the perhaps unconscious "Origenism" of Winchester's (Williams, "American Universalism," pp. 6–11). For indications that the Calvinist milieu was also important to Winchester, see Williams, ibid., pp. 86–87.

9. Elhanan Winchester, *The Universal Restoration: Exhibited in Four Dialogues between a Minister and His Friend* (Philadelphia: Gihon, Fairchild, & Co., 1843), pp. 5–17. First edition published in 1788.

10. Stone, *Biography*, p. 61.

11. Ibid., p. 62.

12. Winchester, *Universal Restoration*, pp. 32, 40–41.

13. David A. Johnson, "George de Benneville and the Heritage of the Radical Reformation," *JUHS*, 8 (1969–70), 25–43.

14. Ernest Cassara, ed., "The Life and Trance of Dr. George de Benneville," *JUHS*, 2 (1960–61), 71–87. Further quotations will be cited parenthetically.

15. For biographical information on Rush, see David Freeman Hawke, *Benjamin Rush: Revolutionary Gadfly* (Indianapolis and New York: Bobbs-Merrill, 1971); and Donald J. D'Elia, "Benjamin Rush: Philosopher of the American Revolution," *Transactions of the American Philosophical Society*, 64 n.s. (September 1974), 1–113. Rush's life can also be studied in Benjamin Rush, *The Autobiography of Benjamin Rush*, ed. George W. Corner (Princeton, NJ: Princeton University Press, 1948); and idem, *Letters of Benjamin Rush*, ed. Lyman H. Butterfield, 2 vols. (Princeton, NJ: Princeton University Press, 1951).

16. Rush, *Letters*, I, 584.

17. Rush, *Autobiography*, pp. 163–64.

18. Rush, *Letters*, I, 419.

19. Quoted in Cassara, *Universalism in America*, p. 110; and Miller, *Larger Hope*, pp. 45–46.

20. Marini, *Radical Sects*, p. 108. My sources for the discussion of early Universalist organizational efforts are Cassara, *Universalism in America*, pp. 93–110; Miller, *Larger Hope*, pp. 34–97; and Marini, *Radical Sects*, pp. 106–9, 122–27.

21. Marini, *Radical Sects*, p. 107.

22. Miller, *Larger Hope*, p. 76.

23. Ibid., p. 77.

24. Walter Ferriss, quoted in Cassara, *Universalism in America*, pp. 107–8.

25. Nathaniel Stacy, *Memoirs* (1850), quoted in ibid., p. 109.

## CHAPTER 6

1. Hosea Ballou, *A Treatise on Atonement*, 14th ed. (Boston: Universalist Publishing House, 1902), introduction by John Coleman Adams, p. xxix. On the various editions of this work, see Miller, *Larger Hope*, pp. 863–65.

2. The definitive biography of Ballou, and my principal source of information on his career, is Ernest Cassara, *Hosea Ballou: The Challenge to Orthodoxy* (Boston: Universalist Historical Society and Beacon Press, 1961). On the earlier biographies of Ballou, see Cassara's bibliography, in ibid., pp. 177–78.

3. Cassara discussed these influences on Ballou in detail in ibid., pp. 22–31.

4. Ballou, *A Treatise on Atonement*, p. 2. Further quotations will be cited parenthetically.

5. Ferdinand Olivier Petitpierre, *Thoughts on the Divine Goodness* (Hartford: Elisha Babcock, 1794), preliminary discourse and p. 212. Further quotations will be cited parenthetically.

6. John White Chadwick, *William Ellery Channing: Minister of Religion* (Boston and New York: Houghton Mifflin, 1903), p. 111.

7. See the discussions of Miller, *Larger Hope*, pp. 111–26; and Cassara, *Hosea Ballou*, pp. 119–29. Earlier accounts can be found in Thomas Whittemore, *The Early Days of Thomas Whittemore* (Boston: James M. Usher, 1859), pp. 305–16; and Richard Eddy, *Universalism in America: A History*, 2 vols. (Boston: Universalist Publishing House, 1884–86), I, 260–342.

8. Eddy, *Universalism*, II, 262–63; and Miller, *Larger Hope*, p. 112.

9. The terms *restless* and *contentious* are those of Cassara, *Hosea Ballou*, p. 117; and Miller, *Larger Hope*, p. 115. Whittemore, *The Early Days of Thomas Whittemore*, pp. 307–8.

10. Miller, *Larger Hope*, p. 123.

11. Eddy, *Universalism*, p. 262.

12. Ibid., p. 265.

13. Chadwick, *William Ellery Channing*, pp. 110–11; Emerson, CW, II, 64, 56.

14. Hosea Ballou, *An Examination of the Doctrine of Future Retribution* (1834; rpt. Boston: James M. Usher, 1849), p. 35.

15. Hosea Ballou 2d, *The Ancient History of Universalism* (Boston: Marsh and Capen, 1829). Further quotations will be cited parenthetically. On Ballou's life, see Russell E. Miller, "Hosea Ballou 2d: Scholar and Educator," JUHS, 1 (1959), 59–79; and Hosea Starr Ballou, *Hosea Ballou, 2d, D.D., First President of Tufts College: His Origin, Life, and Letters* (Boston: E. P. Guild, 1896).

16. Miller, *Larger Hope*, p. 133; Thomas Baldwin Thayer, *Theology of Universalism* (1862; rpt. Boston: Tompkins and Co., 1863), p. iii. Further quotations will be cited parenthetically.

17. Thomas Whittemore, *The Plain Guide to Universalism*, 15th ed. (1840; rpt. Boston: James M. Usher, 1849), p. 7. Further quotations will be cited parenthetically.

18. William H. McGlauflin, *Faith with Power: A Life Story of Quillen Hamilton Shinn, D.D.* (Boston and Chicago: Universalist Publishing House, 1912), p. 66. Further quotations will be cited parenthetically.

## CHAPTER 7

1. Emerson, CW, I, 201. Further quotations will be cited parenthetically as CW.

2. Perry Miller, *The Transcendentalists: An Anthology* (Cambridge: Harvard University Press, 1950), p. 7. An excellent source on members of the Transcendentalist movement is Joel Myerson, *The New England Transcendentalists and the Dial* (Rutherford, NJ: Fairleigh Dickinson University Press, 1980).

3. Miller, *The Transcendentalists*, p. 8. For an assessment of the historiography of the Unitarian-Transcendentalist split, see David Robinson, "Unitarian Historiography and the American Renaissance," *ESQ: A Journal of the American Renaissance*, 23 (2nd Quarter 1977), 130–37. For a specific study of Emerson in this context, see Wright, *The Liberal Christians*, pp. 41–61; and David Robinson, *Apostle of Culture: Emerson as Preacher and Lecturer* (Philadelphia: University of Pennsylvania Press, 1982). Miller himself commented on the revisionist view of Unitarians some eleven years after completing his anthology. See Perry Miller, *Nature's Nation*, pp. 134–49.

4. William Hutchison, *The Transcendentalist Ministers*, pp. 56–57.

5. George Ripley, review of James Martineau, *The Rationale of Religious Enquiry*, *Christian Examiner*, 21 (November 1836), quoted in Miller, *The Transcendentalists*, p. 131. Further quotations will be cited parenthetically.

6. Ralph Waldo Emerson, *The Journals and Miscellaneous Notebooks of Ralph Waldo Emerson*, ed. William H. Gilman, et al., 16 vols. (Cambridge: Harvard University Press, 1960–82), V, 471. Hereafter cited as JMN. Further quotations will be cited parenthetically as JMN. See also Conrad Wright, *Three Prophets of Religious Liberalism*, for background on Emerson's and Parker's addresses.

7. Andrews Norton, "The New School in Literature and Religion," *The Boston Daily Advertiser*, August 27, 1838, quoted in Miller, *The Transcendentalists*, p. 195. Further quotations will be cited parenthetically.

8. On the Divinity School Address, see Wright, *The Liberal Christians*, pp. 41–61; Hutchison, *The Transcendentalist Ministers*, pp. 64–82; and Cameron, "Henry Ware's *Divinity School Address*—A Reply to Emerson's," pp. 84–91. The address and Emerson's relationship with Henry Ware, Jr., are discussed in more detail in Robinson, *Apostle of Culture*, pp. 40–44, 123–37.

9. Theodore Parker, *The Transient and Permanent in Christianity* (1841), quoted in Wright, *Three Prophets of Religious Liberalism*, p. 118. Further quotations will be cited parenthetically. On Parker's development, see Brown, *Rise*, pp. 153–70; and John White Chadwick, *Theodore Parker: Preacher and Reformer* (Boston and New York: Houghton Mifflin, 1901), pp. 22–47.

10. Wright, *Three Prophets of Religious Liberalism*, p. 39.

11. Miller, *Nature's Nation*, pp. 148–49.

12. Robert M. Hemstreet, *Identity and Ideology: Creeds and Creedlessness in Unitarianism and Universalism*, Unitarian Universalist Advance Study Paper No. 3, 1977, p. 11.

13. Hemstreet, *Identity*, pp. 12–13, 33; and Hutchison, *Transcendentalist Ministers*, pp. 128–36.

14. Chadwick, *Theodore Parker*, p. 235. On the interesting question of the politics of Transcendentalism, see Taylor Stoehr, *Nay-Saying in Concord: Emerson, Alcott, and Thoreau* (Hamden, CT: Archon Books, 1979); and Anne C. Rose, *Transcendentalism as a Social Movement, 1830–1850* (New Haven and London: Yale University Press, 1981).

15. Lydia Maria Child, *An Appeal in Favor of That Class of Americans Called Africans* (1833; rpt. New York: Arno, 1968); Octavius Brooks Frothingham, *Recollections and Impressions, 1822–1890* (New York: Putnam's, 1891), p. 47; Andrew Delbanco, *William Ellery Channing: An Essay on the Liberal Spirit in America* (Cambridge: Harvard University Press, 1981), pp. 116–53.

16. Wright, *The Liberal Christians*, pp. 62–80. See also Douglas C. Stange, *Patterns of Anti-Slavery among American Unitarians, 1831–1860* (Rutherford, NJ: Fairleigh Dickinson University Press, 1977).

17. Emerson, JMN, XI, 411–12; Chadwick, *Theodore Parker*, pp. 260–63; and Henry Steele Commager, *Theodore Parker* (Boston: Little, Brown, 1936), pp. 231–47.

18. On Brownson and Channing, see Miller, *The Transcendentalists*, pp. 429–49. For details on the Channing-Emerson relationship, see also David Robinson, "The Political Odyssey of William Henry Channing," *American Quarterly*, 34 (Summer 1982), 165–84.

19. George Ripley, Letter to Ralph Waldo Emerson of November 9, 1840, quoted in Miller, *The Transcendentalists*, p. 464.

20. Julia Ward Howe, *Reminiscences, 1819–1899* (1899; rpt. New York: Negro Universities Press, 1969), p. 166.

21. On Fuller, see the three collections of her writings, with excellent introductions: Perry Miller, *Margaret Fuller: American Romantic* (Ithaca, NY: Cornell University Press, 1963); Bell Gale Chevigny, *"The Woman and the Myth": Margaret Fuller's Life and Writings* (Old Westbury, NY: Feminist Press, 1976); and Margaret Fuller, *Essays on American Life and Letters*, ed. Joel Myerson (New Haven: College and University Press,

1978). On Peabody, see Miller, *The Transcendentalists*, pp. 140–42; and Louise Hall Tharp, *The Peabody Sisters of Salem* (Boston: Little, Brown, 1950).

## CHAPTER 8

1. Rush Welter, *The Mind of America, 1820–1860* (New York and London: Columbia University Press, 1975), pp. 331–91; and Sacvan Bercovitch, "The Rites of Assent: Rhetoric, Ritual, and the Ideology of American Consensus," in *The American Self*, ed. Sam B. Girgus (Albuquerque: University of New Mexico Press, 1980), pp. 5–42.

2. Henry W. Bellows, *Re-Statements of Christian Doctrine* (New York: D. Appleton, 1860), p. 11. For the definitive biography of Bellows, see Walter Donald Kring, *Henry Whitney Bellows* (Boston: Skinner House, 1979).

3. Bellows used the term churchman in *The Suspense of Faith* (New York: C. S. Francis, 1859), p. 4, and this is the emphasis that Kring, *Bellows*, rightly gave to his career. See also John White Chadwick, *Henry W. Bellows: His Life and Character* (New York: S. W. Green's Son, 1882); and Wright, *Liberal Christians*, pp. 81–109.

4. Kring, *Bellows*, p. 191.

5. Chadwick, *Bellows*, p. 11.

6. Ibid., p. 13; Harry M. Stokes, "Henry Whitney Bellows's Vision of the Christian Church," *Proceedings of the Unitarian Historical Society* (hereafter cited as PUHS), 15 (1965), 6–10; Wright, "Salute the Arriving Moment," in *A Stream of Light*, ed. Wright, p. 62; and Kring, *Bellows*, p. 191. Kring offered a detailed analysis of the address in ibid., pp. 191–96.

7. Bellows, *The Suspense of Faith*, p. 5. Further quotations will be cited parenthetically.

8. Kring, *Bellows*, p. 196. See also Stokes, "Bellows's Vision," pp. 11–14.

9. Walt Whitman, *Specimen Days* (New York: Signet, 1961), pp. 42–43; (first edition published in 1882); William Quentin Maxwell, *Lincoln's Fifth Wheel: The Political History of the United States Sanitary Commission* (New York: Longmans, Green, 1956), pp. 4–5.

10. For details, see Kring, *Bellows*, pp. 224–39; and *The United States Sanitary Commission: A Sketch of Its Purposes and Work* (Boston: Little, Brown, 1863).

11. On the National Conference, Wright, "Henry W. Bellows and the Organization of the National Conference," in Wright, *The Liberal Christians*, pp. 81–109, is the definitive treatment. See also Stow Persons, *Free Religion: An American Faith* (New Haven: Yale University Press, 1947), pp. 12–17; J. Wade Caruthers, *Octavius Brooks Frothingham: Gentle Radical* (University: University of Alabama Press, 1977), pp. 101–3; and Kring, *Bellows*, pp. 305–22.

12. Wright, *The Liberal Christians*, pp. 84, 87, 94.

13. Frothingham, *Recollections and Impressions, 1822–1890*, p. 117. See David B. Parke, *The Epic of Unitarianism* (Boston: Beacon Press, 1957), pp. 119–22, for portions of the debate over the preamble and portions of the constitution.

14. Kring, *Bellows*, p. 321.

15. Charles H. Lyttle, *Freedom Moves West: A History of the Western Unitarian Conference, 1852–1952* (Boston: Beacon Press, 1953), p. 57.

16. Ibid., p. 59.

17. On Meadville, see Cooke, *Unitarianism in America*, pp. 310–20.

18. Charlotte C. Eliot, *William Greenleaf Eliot: Minister, Educator, Philanthropist*

(Boston and New York: Houghton Mifflin, 1904), p. 42. Hereafter cited as Charlotte C. Eliot. Further quotations will be cited parenthetically as Charlotte C. Eliot. James Freeman Clarke, *Autobiography, Diary and Correspondence*, ed. Edward Everett Hale (Boston and New York: Houghton Mifflin, 1891), p. 336. Further quotations will be cited parenthetically as Clarke. See also Elizabeth McKinsey's discussion in *The Western Experiment: New England Transcendentalists in the Ohio Valley* (Cambridge: Harvard University Press, 1973), pp. 32–34.

19. On the *Western Messenger*, see Clarence L. F. Gohdes, *The Periodicals of American Transcendentalism* (Durham, NC: Duke University Press, 1931); and two recent dissertations: Judith A. Green, "Religion, Life, and Literature in the *Western Messenger*" (Ph.D. diss. University of Wisconsin—Madison, 1981); and Robert D. Habich, "The History and Achievement of the *Western Messenger*, 1835–1841" (Ph.D. diss., Pennsylvania State University, 1982). A revised version of Habich's study is forthcoming from the Fairleigh Dickinson University Press.

20. McKinsey, *Western Experiment*, p. 33.

21. Charlotte C. Eliot, p. 16; and Joseph Henry Allen, *Sequel to "Our Liberal Movement"* (Boston: Roberts Bros., 1897), p. 101.

22. Stewart H. Holbrook, *The Yankee Exodus: An Account of Migration from New England* (New York: Macmillan, 1950), p. viii. See also George Reeves Throop, "William Greenleaf Eliot," *PUHS*, 4 (1935), 33–43.

23. Henry Chamberlain Meserve, "The First Unitarian Society in San Francisco, 1850–1950," *PUHS*, 1 (1951), 24–44; Wallace W. Robbins, "Charles A. Farley—Messenger of Liberalism," *PUHS*, 6 (1938), 1–12.

24. Richard Frothingham, *A Tribute to Thomas Starr King* (Boston: Ticknor and Fields, 1865), p. 121. The remark is attributed to Thomas Gold Appleton in Williams, "American Universalism," p. 3. Further quotations from Frothingham, *Tribute*, will be cited parenthetically.

25. Arnold Crompton, *Unitarianism on the Pacific Coast: The First Sixty Years* (Boston: Beacon Press, 1957), pp. 25–27.

26. Although Crompton gives Bellows credit for the arrangement, which is true to an extent, Frothingham reported that Bellows actually endorsed the call from Cincinnati (Frothingham, *Tribute*, pp. 148–49).

27. William G. Eliot, Jr., "Thomas Starr King in Oregon, 1862," *Oregon Historical Quarterly*, 32 (June 1943), 112.

28. Earl Morse Wilbur, *Thomas Lamb Eliot, 1841–1936* (Portland, OR: privately published, 1937), p. 20. Further information on Eliot's career can be found in John F. Scheck, "Transplanting a Tradition: Thomas Lamb Eliot and the Unitarian Conscience in the Pacific Northwest, 1865–1905" (Ph.D. diss., University of Oregon, 1969). I would like to acknowledge support from the Oregon Committee for the Humanities for my research on Eliot.

29. These parallels of father and son are stressed in Scheck's study.

30. Thomas Lamb Eliot, letter of June 22, 1866, Thomas Lamb Eliot Papers, Reed College Library. Quoted by permission of Reed College.

31. Henry Wilder Foote, "Thomas Lamb Eliot," in *Heralds of a Liberal Faith*, ed. Samuel Atkins Eliot, 4 vols. (Boston: American Unitarian Association and Beacon Press, 1910–52), IV, 128.

32. Thomas Lamb Eliot, "Spiritual Sympathy," sermon of August 5, 1866, Thomas Lamb Eliot Papers, Reed College Library.

33. Ibid.

34. Ibid.

35. Wright, *A Stream of Light*, pp. 70–71.

36. Francis Greenwood Peabody, *Reminiscences of Present-Day Saints* (Boston and New York: Houghton Mifflin, 1927), pp. 54–55.

37. Joel Myerson, "Frederic Henry Hedge and the Failure of Transcendentalism," *Harvard Library Bulletin*, 23 (October 1975), pp. 396–410. See also Doreen Hunter, "Frederic Henry Hedge, What Say You?" *American Quarterly*, 32 (Summer 1980), 186–201.

38. Frederic Henry Hedge, *Reason in Religion* (Boston: Walker, Fuller, 1865), p. 56. Further quotations will be cited parenthetically. On Hedge's theology, see George H. Williams, *Rethinking the Unitarian Relationship with Protestantism: An Examination of the Thought of Frederic Henry Hedge (1805–1890)* (Boston: Beacon Press, 1949).

39. Frederic Henry Hedge, "Anti-Supernaturalism in the Pulpit," *Christian Examiner*, 77 (September 1864), p. 157.

40. Myerson, "Frederic Henry Hedge and the Failure of Transcendentalism," p. 407.

41. James Freeman Clarke, *Ten Great Religions: An Essay in Comparative Theology* (Boston and New York: Houghton Mifflin, 1886).

42. James Freeman Clarke, "Why I Am Not a Free Religionist," *North American Review*, 145 (October 1887), 380.

43. James Freeman Clarke, *Self-Culture: Physical, Intellectual, Moral, and Spiritual* (Boston: J. R. Osgood, 1880); and idem, *Vexed Questions in Theology* (Boston: George H. Ellis, 1886), pp. 9–18.

44. Clarke, *Vexed Questions in Theology*, pp. 10–16.

## CHAPTER 9

1. Cooke, *Unitarianism*, pp. 193, 201–2.

2. Wright, "Salute the Arriving Moment," p. 73.

3. Frothingham, *Recollections and Impressions*, p. 119.

4. William R. Hutchison, *The Modernist Impulse in American Protestantism* (Cambridge: Harvard University Press, 1976), p. 2.

5. Francis Ellingwood Abbot, "The Intuitional and Scientific Schools of Free Religion," *Index* 2 (April 15, 1871), 113.

6. John White Chadwick, *Old and New Unitarian Belief* (Boston: George H. Ellis, 1894), p. 237.

7. On Spencer's vogue in America, see Richard Hofstadter, *Social Darwinism in American Thought* (Boston: Beacon Press, 1955), pp. 31–50; and Ronald E. Martin, *American Literature and the Universe of Force* (Durham, NC: Duke University Press, 1981), pp. 32–58. On Emerson's relation to science, see Harry Hayden Clark, "Emerson and Science," *Philological Quarterly*, 10 (July 1931), 225–60; and Robinson, *Apostle of Culture*, pp. 74–85.

8. Sydney Ahlstrom, "Francis Ellingwood Abbot and the Free Religious Association," *PUHS*, 17 (1973–75), 1–21 (quotations, p. 3).

9. Thomas Paine, *The Age of Reason* (1794), in *American Literature: Tradition and Innovation*, ed. Harrison T. Meserole, Walter Sutton, and Brom Weber (Lexington, MA: D. C. Heath, 1974), I, 495. On details of the formation of the FRA, see Ahlstrom, "Abbot," pp. 1–21. See also Persons, *Free Religion*, pp. 42–53. On Bartol, see Wil-

liam R. Hutchison, "To Heaven in a Swing: The Transcendentalism of Cyrus Bartol," *Harvard Theological Review*, 56 (October 1963), 275–95.

10. Abbot, "The Intuitional and Scientific Schools of Free Religion." See also Persons, *Free Religion*, pp. 35–38.

11. Cyrus A. Bartol, *Radical Problems* (Boston: Roberts Bros., 1872), p. 112. Further quotations will be cited parenthetically as Bartol. On the Bartol-Bellows relationship, see Kring, *Bellows*, pp. 58–60.

12. As Hutchison pointed out, *Radical Problems* was the work of "an essentially unrepentant transcendentalist." Hutchison, *The Modernist Impulse*, p. 31.

13. Octavius Brooks Frothingham, *Theodore Parker: A Biography* (New York: Putnam's, 1880), p. 352.

14. Octavius Brooks Frothingham, *The Religion of Humanity* (1873; rpt. Hicksville, NY: Regina Press, 1975), p. 15. Further quotations will be cited parenthetically as Frothingham.

15. Ralph Waldo Emerson, *The Early Lectures of Ralph Waldo Emerson*, ed. Stephen E. Whicher and Robert E. Spiller, 3 vols. (Cambridge: The Belknap Press of Harvard University Press, 1964), II, 13–14.

16. Abbot, "The Intuitional and Scientific Schools of Free Religion," p. 114. Further quotations will be cited parenthetically.

17. Francis Ellingwood Abbot, "Philosophical Biology," *North American Review*, 107 (October 1868), 377–422. Further quotations will be cited parenthetically.

18. Francis Ellingwood Abbot, *Scientific Theism* (Boston: Little, Brown, 1885). Further quotations will be cited parenthetically as Abbot.

19. Emerson, CW, I, 201.

20. John White Chadwick, *The Faith of Reason* (Boston: Roberts Bros., 1879), p. 14. Further quotations will be cited parenthetically.

21. Cooke, *Unitarianism*, p. 170.

22. Ibid., pp. 169–71.

23. For discussions of the western issue in this chapter, I have relied upon Cooke, *Unitarianism*, pp. 225–30; Lyttle, *Freedom*, pp. 163–91; William H. Pease, "Doctrine and Fellowship: William Channing Gannett and the Unitarian Creedal Issue," *Church History*, 25 (1956), 210–38; and Wright, "Salute the Arriving Moment," pp. 84–91.

24. Lyttle, *Freedom*, p. 127. Biographical information on Jones is drawn principally from Lyttle, ibid., pp. 117–38; and Richard Jones, "Jenkin Lloyd Jones," in *Heralds of a Liberal Faith*, ed. Eliot, IV, 164–73.

25. Jones, "Jenkin Lloyd Jones," p. 169.

26. Pease, "Doctrine," p. 212.

27. Biographical information on Gannett is from Pease, "Doctrine," pp. 3–31; and Lewis S. Gannett, "William Channing Gannett," in *Heralds of a Liberal Faith*, ed. Eliot, IV, 142–46.

28. Frank S. C. Wicks, "Jasper Lewis Douthit," in *Heralds of a Liberal Faith*, ed. Eliot, IV, 120.

29. For information on Douthit I have relied on Lyttle, *Freedom*, pp. 134–43, and Wicks, "Jasper Lewis Douthit," pp. 120–21. On Sunderland, see Lyttle, *Freedom*, pp. 163–64; Pease, "Doctrine," pp. 215–18; and Spencer Lavan, *Unitarians in India: A Study of Encounter and Response* (Boston: Beacon Press, 1977).

30. Pease, "Doctrine," p. 213.

31. See Wright, "Salute the Arriving Moment," pp. 83–84.

32. Jabez T. Sunderland, *The Issue in the West* (n.p., [1886]), p. 10. Further quotations will be cited parenthetically.

33. Lyttle, *Freedom*, pp. 184–86.

34. Ibid., p. 190.

35. *Unity*, June 4, 1887, p. 200. I want to thank Alan Seaburg of the Andover-Harvard Theological Library for locating the text of the resolution.

36. Wright, "Salute the Arriving Moment," p. 89.

37. Cooke, *Unitarianism*, p. 229.

## CHAPTER 10

1. Williams, "American Universalism," pp. 1–8.

2. Ibid., p. 86.

3. George H. Williams has reminded us of the comment of Jenkin Lloyd Jones, who hoped to lead a merger of Unitarians, Universalists, and others into a larger and truly universal church: "it is a poor Universalism that prays for a universality on the other side of death which they distrust and avoid on this side." Quoted in ibid., p. 73. See Williams's discussion, ibid., pp. 71–85.

4. Ibid., p. 17.

5. Ibid., pp. 9–36.

6. Adin Ballou, *Autobiography of Adin Ballou*, ed. William S. Heywood (1896; rpt. Philadelphia: Porcupine Press, 1975), p. 46.

7. Ibid., p. 84.

8. On Ballou's theological development, see ibid., pp. 170–82.

9. Ibid., p. 322.

10. Adin Ballou, *History of the Hopedale Community* (1897; rpt. Philadelphia: Porcupine Press, 1972), p. 289. On the history of Hopedale, see Ballou, *Autobiography*, pp. 318–38; and idem, *History of Hopedale*. The commune failed when two principal stockholders withdrew their assets, and Ballou insisted that in fact this was not a financial failure, since the community was generating profits before the withdrawal. See idem, *History of Hopedale*, pp. 346–50.

11. On the history of Brook Farm, see Lindsay Swift, *Brook Farm: Its Members, Scholars, and Visitors* (1900; rpt. New York: Corinth, 1961); Miller, *The Transcendentalists*, pp. 464–65; and Edith Roelker Curtis, *A Season in Utopia: The Story of Brook Farm* (New York: Thomas Nelson and Sons, 1961). An important interpretation of the ideas behind the commune can be found in Richard Francis, "The Ideology of Brook Farm," in *Studies in the American Renaissance, 1977*, ed. Joel Myerson (Boston: Twayne, 1978), pp. 1–48.

12. Adin Ballou, *Christian Non-Resistance in All Its Important Bearings*, 2nd ed. (1910; rpt. New York: Da Capo Press, 1970), pp. xiii, 12. First edition published in 1846.

13. Ibid., p. 16.

14. Ibid., p. 16. For commentary, see Merle E. Curti, "Non-Resistance in New England," *New England Quarterly*, 2 (January 1929), 34–57; and Lewis Perry, "Adin Ballou's Hopedale Community and the Theology of Anti-Slavery," *Church History*, 39 (September 1970), 372–89.

15. Ballou, *Christian Non-Resistance*, p. 23.

16. Ibid.

17. Ibid., p. 174.

18. Ann Douglas, *The Feminization of American Culture* (New York: Knopf, 1977).

19. Constantia [Judith Sargent Murray], "On the Equality of the Sexes" (1790), in *Up from the Pedestal: Selected Writings in the History of American Feminism*, ed. Aileen S. Kraditor (Chicago: Quadrangle, 1968), p. 34. See also Nancy F. Cott, "Passionlessness: An Interpretation of Victorian Sexual Ideology, 1790–1850," in *A Heritage of Her Own*, ed. Nancy F. Cott and Elizabeth H. Pleck (New York: Simon and Schuster, 1979), p. 171; and Miller, *Larger Hope*, pp. 534–35.

20. Olympia Brown, *An Autobiography*, ed. Gwendolen B. Willis, in JUHS, 4 (1963), p. 26.

21. Miller, *The Larger Hope*, p. 546.

22. Nina Baym, *Women's Fiction: A Guide to Novels by and about Women in America, 1820–1870* (Ithaca, NY: Cornell University Press, 1978), p. 18; Nancy F. Cott, *The Bonds of Womanhood: "Woman's Sphere" in New England, 1780–1835* (New Haven: Yale University Press, 1977), p. 9.

23. Other important women are discussed in Catherine F. Hitchings, "Universalist and Unitarian Women Ministers," JUHS, 10 (1975).

24. Seth Curtis Beach, *Daughters of the Puritans* (1905; rpt. Freeport, NY: Books for Libraries Press, 1967), pp. 79–119; and Joel Myerson, "Lydia Maria Child," *The American Renaissance in New England*, ed. Myerson, vol. 1 of *Dictionary of Literary Biography* (Detroit: Gale Research, 1978), pp. 26–27. Quotation from James M. McPherson, Introduction to Child, *Appeal*.

25. Lydia Maria Child, *The Frugal Housewife* (London: T. Hegg and Son, 1835), pp. 140–41.

26. Lydia Maria Child, *Letters from New York*, 10th ed. (New York: G. S. Francis, 1849), pp. 246–50.

27. R. W. Emerson, W. H. Channing, and J. F. Clarke, *Memoirs of Margaret Fuller Ossoli* (Boston: Phillips, Sampson, 1852), I, 14–15. Further quotations will be cited parenthetically as *Memoirs*. For recent interpretations of Fuller's career, see Douglas, *Feminization*, pp. 313–48; Joel Myerson, "Sarah Margaret Fuller, Marchesa D'Ossoli," in *The American Renaissance in New England*, ed. Myerson, pp. 66–72; Bell Gale Chevigny, "Growing Out of New England: The Emergence of Margaret Fuller's Radicalism," *Women's Studies*, 5 (1978), 65–100; Margaret Vanderhaar Allen, *The Achievement of Margaret Fuller* (University Park, PA: Pennsylvania State University Press, 1979); Albert J. von Frank, "Life as Art in America: The Case of Margaret Fuller," *Studies in the American Renaissance, 1981*, ed. Joel Myerson (Boston: Twayne, 1981), 1–26; David Robinson, "Margaret Fuller and the Transcendental Ethos: *Woman in the Nineteenth Century*," PMLA, 97 (January 1982), 83–98.

28. Vivian G. Hopkins, "Margaret Fuller: Pioneer Women's Liberationist," *American Transcendental Quarterly*, 18 (Spring 1973), 33; Margaret Fuller, *Woman in the Nineteenth Century*, in *Margaret Fuller: Essays on American Life and Letters*, ed. Joel Myerson (New Haven: College and University Press, 1978), p. 204.

29. Douglas, *Feminization*, pp. 338–48.

30. Miller, *Larger Hope*, pp. 567–73.

31. Mary A. Livermore, *The Story of My Life* (Hartford: A. D. Worthington, 1899), p. 481. Further quotations will be cited parenthetically.

32. Miller, *Larger Hope*, p. 571. Williams, "American Universalism," p. 30, quoting Livermore.

33. Brown, *An Autobiography*, ed. Willis. Further quotations will be cited parenthetically. Brown previously was accorded the distinction of being the first woman to receive denominational ordination, but recent research by Charles Semowich revealed that Lydia Jenkins was ordained in 1860 by the Ontario Association of Universalists in Geneva, New York. For details, see the biography of Jenkins included in the biographical dictionary in this volume. Brown was ordained in 1863 in Malone, New York, by the St. Lawrence Association of Universalists. See Catherine F. Hitchings's discussion of Brown's ordination and career in "Universalist and Unitarian Women Ministers," pp. 30–34. As Russell E. Miller noted, the power of ordination was claimed by the New York State Convention in 1836 (Miller, *Larger Hope*, pp. 686–90). The lines of division between the New York State Convention and the several local associations in New York, such as the Ontario Association and the St. Lawrence Association, were not always clear. Brown considered herself to be the first woman ordained by full denominational authority (Brown, *An Autobiography*, ed. Willis, p. 30), although it appears that Jenkins's ordination by the Ontario Association had the same authority as Brown's, given the institutional structure of the Universalist denomination at that time. I know of no evidence that either Jenkins's or Brown's ordination was confirmed or denied by the New York State Convention. Also relevant to this issue is Hitchings's discussion of the ordination of Antoinette Brown Blackwell in 1853. See Hitchings, "Universalist and Unitarian Women Ministers," pp. 155–56.

34. Sydney E. Ahlstrom, *A Religious History of the American People* (New Haven: Yale University Press, 1972), pp. 787, 789. Henry F. May, *Protestant Churches and Industrial America* (New York: Harper and Brothers, 1949), pp. 91–111.

35. Jurgen Herbst, "Francis Greenwood Peabody: Harvard's Theologian of the Social Gospel," *Harvard Theological Review*, 54 (1961), pp. 45–69; see also Peabody, *Reminiscences of Present-Day Saints*, for autobiographical reflections.

36. Peabody, *Reminiscences*, p. 65.

37. Francis Greenwood Peabody, *Jesus Christ and the Social Question* (New York: Grosset and Dunlap, 1900). Further quotations will be cited parenthetically in the text. On the importance of the book, see David B. Parke, "Liberals and Liberalism since 1900," PUHS, 15 (1964), 12–25.

38. Carl Hermann Voss, *Rabbi and Minister: The Friendship of Stephen S. Wise and John Haynes Holmes* (Cleveland and New York: World, 1964), p. 96. See also Voss, ibid., pp. 84–88, 93–98; and John Haynes Holmes, *I Speak for Myself* (New York: Harper's, 1958), pp. 187–96.

39. John Haynes Holmes, *The Revolutionary Function of the Modern Church* (New York: Putnam's, 1912). Further quotations will be cited parenthetically.

40. Voss, *Rabbi*, p. 157. See also Voss, ibid., pp. 154–59.

41. John Haynes Holmes, *New Wars for Old* (New York: Dodd, Mead, 1917). Further quotations will be cited parenthetically.

42. Voss, *Rabbi*, p. 200. See also Voss, ibid., pp. 198–200; and John Haynes Holmes, *My Gandhi* (New York: Harper and Brothers, 1953), pp. 31, 9.

43. Holmes, *I Speak for Myself*, pp. 173, 178.

44. Alan Seaburg, "Clarence Russell Skinner: A Bibliography," JUHS, 5 (1964–65), 66.

45. Emerson Hugh Lalone, *And Thy Neighbor as Thyself: A Story of Universalist Social Action* (Boston: Universalist Publishing House, 1939), pp. 109–12.

46. James D. Hunt, Introduction to Clarence R. Skinner, *The Social Implications of*

*Universalism*, JUHS, 5 (1964–65), 86. Clarence R. Skinner, *A Religion for Greatness* (Boston: Murray Press, 1945), p. 11. Further quotations will be cited parenthetically.

47. Clarence R. Skinner, *Liberalism Faces the Future* (New York: Macmillan, 1937). Further quotations will be cited parenthetically.

## CHAPTER 11

1. David B. Parke, "A Wave at Crest," in *A Stream of Light*, ed. Wright, p. 111.

2. James Freeman Clarke, *Common-Sense in Religion* (Boston: Houghton Mifflin, 1890), p. 63.

3. Minot J. Savage, *Belief in God: An Examination of Some Fundamental Theistic Problems* (Boston: George H. Ellis, 1896), p. 81.

4. Lyttle, *Freedom*, pp. 243–45; and Mason Olds, *Religious Humanism in America: Dietrich, Reese, and Potter* (Washington, DC: University Press of America, 1978), pp. 30–52.

5. On Dietrich, see Lyttle, *Freedom*, p. 244; and Olds, *Religious Humanism*, pp. 43–61.

6. On Reese, see Lyttle, *Freedom*, p. 242; and Olds, *Religious Humanism*, pp. 210–30. On Potter, see Olds, *Religious Humanism*, pp. 159–70; and Charles F. Potter, *The Preacher and I: An Autobiography* (New York: Crown, 1951).

7. Curtis W. Reese, "Do You Believe What He Believes?" *Christian Register*, 99 (September 9, 1920), 883–84. Further quotations will be cited parenthetically. For analysis see Lyttle, *Freedom*, pp. 244–45; and Olds, *Religious Humanism*, pp. 36–37.

8. Lyttle, *Freedom*, pp. 249–51; and Olds, *Religious Humanism*, pp. 42–46.

9. William L. Sullivan, "God, No-God, Half-God," *Christian Register*, 100 (August 8, 1929), 775–76. Further quotations will be cited parenthetically.

10. The manifesto is reprinted in its entirety in Parke, *The Epic of Unitarianism*, pp. 139–42.

11. Curtis W. Reese, ed., *Humanist Sermons* (Chicago: Open Court, 1927). Further quotations will be cited parenthetically as Reese.

12. Curtis W. Reese, *The Meaning of Humanism* (Boston: Beacon Press, 1945), p. 20.

13. Francis Greenwood Peabody, "The Humanism of William Ellery Channing," *Christian Register*, 109 (May 15, 1930), 408.

14. Lyttle, *Freedom*, pp. 256–58.

15. Alfred P. Stiernotte, ed., *Frederick May Eliot: An Anthology* (Boston: Beacon Press, 1959), pp. 212–13. Further quotations will be cited parenthetically.

16. William Wallace Fenn, "Modern Liberalism," *American Journal of Theology* 17 (October 1913), p. 516. See also Hutchison, *The Modernist Impulse*, pp. 220–25.

17. Hutchison, *The Modernist Impulse*, p. 225.

18. James Luther Adams, *On Being Human—Religiously*, ed. Max L. Stackhouse (Boston: Unitarian Universalist Association, 1976), p. 34. Further quotations will be cited parenthetically. The original articles from the *Journal of Liberal Religion* are abridged in this volume.

19. Martin Green, *The Problem of Boston: Some Readings in Cultural History* (New York: W. W. Norton, 1976), p. 12.

20. Perry Miller, "Individualism and the New England Tradition," in *The Responsibility of Mind in a Civilization of Machines*, ed. John Crowell and Stanford J. Searl,

Jr. (Amherst: University of Massachusetts Press, 1979), pp. 26–44. Further quotations will be cited parenthetically.

21. "The Faith behind Freedom," *Christian Register*, 122 (June 1943), pp. 200–201.

22. Conrad Wright, *Individualism in Historical Perspective*, Unitarian Universalist Advance Study Paper No. 9, 1979, p. 6. Further quotations will be cited parenthetically.

## CHAPTER 12

1. Murdock, *The Institutional History of the American Unitarian Association*, p. 72.

2. Arthur C. McGiffert, Jr., *Pilot of a Liberal Faith: Samuel Atkins Eliot, 1862–1950* (Boston: Beacon Press, 1976), p. 68. Further quotations will be cited parenthetically.

3. Murdock, *The Institutional History of the American Unitarian Association*, p. 53.

4. Ibid., pp. 42–43.

5. McGiffert, *Pilot*, pp. 64–73.

6. Parke, "A Wave at Crest," p. 115.

7. McGiffert, *Pilot*, p. 68; and Parke, "A Wave at Crest," p. 115.

8. See Carol R. Morris, "It Was Noontime Here," in *A Stream of Light*, ed. Wright, pp. 125–28; and George H. Williams, "James Luther Adams and the Unitarian Denomination," *Andover-Newton Quarterly*, 17 n.s. (January 1977), 173–74.

9. Adams, *On Being Human*, p. 12.

10. Commission of Appraisal of the American Unitarian Association, *Unitarians Face a New Age* (Boston: American Unitarian Association, 1936), pp. 10–11. Further quotations will be cited parenthetically.

11. Ibid., pp. 14–49.

12. Carol R. Morris, "The Election of Frederick May Eliot to the Presidency of the A.U.A.," PUHS, 17, pt. 1 (1970–72), 1–45.

13. Stiernotte, *Frederick May Eliot: An Anthology*, p. 32. Further quotations will be cited parenthetically.

14. Morris, "It Was Noontime Here," p. 129.

15. Ibid., pp. 132–37.

16. Ibid., p. 142.

17. Hemstreet, *Identity and Ideology*, p. 18.

18. Stiernotte, *Frederick May Eliot: An Anthology*, pp. 68–69.

19. Laile E. Bartlett, *Bright Galaxy: Ten Years of Unitarian Fellowships* (Boston: Beacon Press, 1960), pp. 37–38.

20. Stiernotte, *Frederick May Eliot: An Anthology*, pp. 60–62.

21. Miller, *Larger Hope*, p. 794. I have benefited from Miller's extensive description of the historical precedents of the merger, which is the definitive account of those precedents (pp. 783–841).

22. Ballou, quoted in ibid., p. 803. See also ibid., p. 808.

23. George Huntston Williams, "The Attitudes of Liberals in New England Toward Non-Christian Religions, 1784–1885," *Crane Review*, 9 (Winter 1967), 59–89.

24. Miller, *Larger Hope*, pp. 807–8; Cooke, *Unitarianism*, pp. 193–94.

25. Lyttle, *Freedom*, p. 160.

26. Ibid., pp. 205–8.

27. Williams, "American Universalism," p. 82.

28. Cassara, *Universalism in America*, p. 269.

29. Brainerd F. Gibbons, "New Wine and Old Bottles!" *The Christian Leader*, 131 (November 1949), quoted in Cassara, *Universalism in America*, p. 272.

30. Williams, "American Universalism," pp. 72–82; Cassara, *Universalism in America*, pp. 39–40.

31. Skinner, "The Social Implications of Universalism," p. 104.

32. Ibid., p. 104.

33. Cassara, *Universalism in America*, p. 257.

34. Dana McLean Greeley, *25 Beacon Street and Other Recollections* (Boston: Beacon, 1971), pp. 79–80; Parke, "A Wave at Crest," pp. 121–22; Commission, *Unitarians Face a New Age*, pp. 16–19.

35. Greeley, *25 Beacon Street*, pp. 79–81; Morris, "It Was Noontime Here," pp. 150–55; and "Consolidation Plan Wins Resounding Indorsement for May Meetings Action," *Unitarian Register*, 139 (May 1960), 17. On Greeley's election, see Joseph Barth, "Contests for the Presidency: A.U.A., 1958–U.U.A., 1961," PUHS, 15 (1964), 26–65.

36. See Irving R. Murray, "A Case for Merger," *Unitarian Register*, 138 (March 1959), 6, 30; and Walter Donald Kring, "A Case Against Merger," *Unitarian Register*, 138 (March 1959), 7, 31.

37. On the Syracuse meeting, see "Plan for Unitarian-Universalist Consolidation approved at Syracuse, Then Sent to Plebiscite," *Unitarian Register*, 138 (December 1959), 19–24; and Morris, "It Was Noontime Here," pp. 151–55. On the process of ratification, see "Consolidation Plan Wins Resounding Indorsement for May Meetings Action," *Unitarian Register*, 139 (May 1960), 17; and "Consolidation Procedures Go into Operation within Twenty-Four Hours after Plan Voted," *Unitarian Register*, 139 (Midsummer 1960), 24–26.

38. Commissions on the Free Church in a Changing World, *The Free Church in a Changing World* (Boston: Unitarian Universalist Association, 1963). Further quotations will be cited parenthetically.

39. Robert B. Tapp, *Religion among the Unitarian Universalists: Converts in the Stepfather's House* (New York and London: Seminar Press, 1973), p. 205.

40. Ibid., pp. 205–6. Further quotations will be cited parenthetically.

41. Robert B. Tapp, "A Look at Unitarian Universalist Goals," *Christian Century*, 84 (April 19, 1967), 516.

42. James M. Hutchinson, *Growth and Decline: Trends and Speculations*, Unitarian Universalist Advance Study Paper No. 8, 1978, pp. 8–9.

43. David B. Parke, "The Gift of Blackness," *Unitarian Universalist World*, 15 (March 15, 1984), p. 6. For accounts of the black empowerment issue, see Unitarian Universalist Association Commission on Appraisal, *EmPOWERment: One Denomination's Quest for Racial Justice, 1967–82* (Boston: Unitarian Universalist Association, 1984), and Victor H. Carpenter, *The Black Empowerment Controversy and the Unitarian Universalist Association, 1967–70*, Minns Lectures 1983 (Boston, 1984); these lectures are excerpted in "Minns Lecturer Reviews Black Power Controversy of 60s," *Unitarian Universalist World*, 14 (April 15, 1983), p. 3. A symposium on the issue is published as "Religious Liberals Share Views on Black Empowerment: Review of the Controversy Evokes Powerful Emotions," *Unitarian Universalist World*, 15 (March 15, 1984), pp. 4–5, 8.

44. Donald S. Harrington, "A Foolhardy Strategy," *Unitarian Universalist World*,

15 (March 15, 1984), p. 4. Harrington's essay is part of the symposium cited in note 43.

45. Parke, "The Gift of Blackness," p. 6.

46. See Carpenter, *The Black Empowerment Controversy and the Unitarian Universalist Association*; Mark D. Morrison-Reed, *Black Pioneers in a White Denomination*, rev. ed. (Boston: Beacon, 1984); and Robert Hohler, "A Class-Bound Church," *Unitarian Universalist World*, 15 (March 15, 1984), p. 4. Hohler's essay is part of the symposium cited in note 43.

47. Hutchinson, *Growth*, p. 13. He also characterized the decline not as a result of members dropping out but as a result of the failure to attract new members (p. 12). This strengthens the argument against too facile a correlation of political activism and membership decline and suggests larger social and demographic factors as explanatory to the decline. On the problems of arriving at a consensus for social action, see John Ruskin Clark, "Criteria for Responsible Political Action by UU Churches and Fellowships and by the UUA," reprinted from the *Newsletter of the Unitarian Universalist Advance*, April 15, 1977.

48. Quoted in David B. Parke, "Beyond Sexist Language," *Unitarian Universalist World*, 14 (August 15, 1983), p. 6.

49. Valerie C. Saiving, "Androgynous Life: A Feminist Appropriation of Process Thought," in *Feminism and Process Thought: The Harvard Divinity School/Claremont Center for Process Studies Symposium Papers*, ed. Sheila Greeve Davaney (New York and Toronto: Edwin Mellen Press, 1981), pp. 11–31. Further quotations will be cited parenthetically.

50. Ronald E. Clark, "Where Are We Going?" Paper delivered at the Unitarian Universalist Advance Conference on Growth, October 25, 1978, in Tulsa, Oklahoma, and distributed through the Unitarian Universalist Advance.

51. Hemstreet, *Identity and Ideology*, p. 23.

52. Charles Hartshorne, *A Natural Theology for Our Time* (La Salle, IL: Open Court, 1967), p. 2. For a comparative historical study of Hartshorne and Wieman from which I have profited here, see John B. Cobb, Jr., *Process Theology as Political Theology* (Manchester, Eng.: Manchester University Press and Philadelphia: The Westminster Press, 1982), pp. 19–43.

53. Robert W. Bretall, ed., *The Empirical Theology of Henry Nelson Wieman* (New York: Macmillan, 1963), p. 4. Further quotations will be cited parenthetically.

54. Henry Nelson Wieman, "The Ultra-Human," *Christian Century*, 52 (July 24, 1935), 962.

55. See in particular Henry Nelson Wieman, *The Source of Human Good* (Carbondale: Southern Illinois University Press, 1946), pp. 54–83.

56. Charles Hartshorne, *Creative Synthesis and Philosophic Method* (La Salle, IL: Open Court, 1970), p. 1.

57. See Charles Hartshorne, *Reality as Social Process: Studies in Metaphysics and Religion* (Glencoe, IL: The Free Press; and Boston: Beacon Press, 1953).

58. Charles Hartshorne, *The Divine Relativity: A Social Conception of God* (New Haven: Yale University Press, 1948), p. 20. Further quotations will be cited parenthetically.

59. Hartshorne, *A Natural Theology for Our Time*, p. 12.

60. The differences are made clear in Wieman's review of Hartshorne's *Divine Relativity*, in *Philosophical Review*, 58 (1949), 78–82.

61. C. Conrad Wright, "In Search of a Usable Past," *Collegium Proceedings* (1979), p. 132. See also idem, "A Doctrine of the Church for Liberals," an address delivered before the Massachusetts Bay Unitarian Universalist Ministers annual retreat, March 22, 1983, published and distributed by the Unitarian Universalist Ministers Association.

62. Commissions, *The Free Church in a Changing World*, p. 2.

63. Adams, *On Being Human*, p. 61.

64. Commissions, *The Free Church in a Changing World*, p. 6.

65. Adams, *On Being Human*, p. 58. Further quotations will be cited parenthetically.

# Part Two

# A BIOGRAPHICAL DICTIONARY OF UNITARIAN AND UNIVERSALIST LEADERS

# ABBREVIATIONS FOR STANDARD REFERENCE SOURCES

AAUP

*Annals of the American Unitarian Pulpit*, ed. William B. Sprague (New York, 1865). Also published as volume 8 of *Annals of the American Pulpit*, ed. William B. Sprague, 9 vols. (New York, 1857–69).

CA

*Contemporary Authors: International Bio-Bibliographical Guide to Current Authors and Their Works*, ed. James M. Ethridge, 119 vols. to date (Detroit, 1962–83).

DAB

*Dictionary of American Biography*, ed. Allen Johnson and Dumas Malone, 20 vols. (New York, 1928–37).

DARB

*Dictionary of American Religious Biography*, by Henry Warner Bowden (Westport, CT, 1977).

DAS

*Directory of American Scholars*, 8th ed., 4 vols. (New York, 1982).

DLB

*Dictionary of Literary Biography*, vol. 1, *The American Renaissance in New England*, ed. Joel Myerson (Detroit, 1978).

Heralds

*Heralds of a Liberal Faith*, ed. Samuel A. Eliot, 4 vols. (Boston, 1910–52).

NAW

*Notable American Women*, ed. Edward T. James et al. (Cambridge, MA, 1971–80).

NCAB

*National Cyclopedia of American Biography*, 74 vols. to date (New York, NY, and Clifton, NJ, 1892–1982).

Who's Who in America

*Who's Who in America*, 42 eds. to date (Chicago, 1899–1983). Edition specified by year in the bibliography.

Who's Who of American Women

*Who's Who of American Women*, 13 eds. to date (Chicago, 1958–83). Edition specified by year in the bibliography.

Who Was Who in America

*Who Was Who in America*, 8 vols. to date (Chicago, 1963–81).

The following periodical abbreviations are also used:

| JUHS | *Journal of the Universalist Historical Society* |
| PUHS | *Proceedings of the Unitarian Historical Society* |
| PUUHS | *Proceedings of the Unitarian Universalist Historical Society* |

# A

---

**ABBOT, FRANCIS ELLINGWOOD** (6 November 1836, Boston, MA–23 October 1903, Beverly, MA). *Education*: A.B., Harvard, 1859; attended Harvard Divinity School, 1859–60; graduated from Meadville Theological School, 1863; Ph.D., Harvard, 1881. *Career*: Headmaster, girls' school, Meadville, PA, 1860–63; minister, Dover, NH, 1864–69; cofounder, Free Religious Association, 1867; minister, First Independent Society, Toledo, OH, 1869–73; editor, *Index*, 1870–80; headmaster, boys' school, New York, 1880–81; boys' school, Cambridge, MA, 1881–92; active retirement, 1892–1903.

Francis Ellingwood Abbot was one of the leaders of the dissent from moderate Unitarianism in the middle nineteenth century. He was active in the formation of the Free Religious Association and editor of the *Index*, the periodical that was the voice of the movement. Moreover, he was perhaps the most profound intellectual leader of the Free Religion movement, maintaining an active philosophical quest his entire lifetime.

Abbot saw the formation of the National Conference in 1865 as a threat to intellectual liberty. He later called its adoption of a "preamble-creed" that professed "allegiance to the Lord Jesus Christ . . . the most momentous [decision] in the whole history of Christianity," because it proved that even the most liberal church could not come to terms with "the modern spirit" ("Valedictory," p. 306). Abbot's uncompromising attitude in part sparked the Free Religious Association's (FRA's) rebellion and led to his own resignation of his Dover pastorate and his move to Toledo, where the Unitarian church proclaimed itself "Independent" to accommodate him. There he began his work for the *Index*, which he continued until 1880. The last phase of Abbot's career was devoted chiefly to writing. His *Scientific Theism* (1885) was an attempt to replace the old religious radicalism of the Transcendentalists, based upon idealist and intuitionist philosophy, with a realist and scientific variety. He saw evolutionary philosophy as the first opening of an insight into the universe as an evolving organism and thus saw the pursuits of science and religion as fundamentally the same. He anticipated, in some respects, the process philosophy of the twentieth century.

*Bibliography*

A. "Valedictory" (autobiographical), *Index*, June 24, 1880, pp. 306–8; *Scientific Theism* (Boston, 1885); *The Way Out of Agnosticism; or, The Philosophy of Free Religion* (Boston, 1890); *The Syllogistic Philosophy*, 2 vols. (Boston, 1906).

B. DAB 1, 11–12; DARB, 3–4; NCAB 24, 113; "Valedictory" (see above); Stow Persons, *Free Religion: An American Faith* (New Haven, 1947); Sydney E. Ahlstrom, "Francis Ellingwood Abbot and the Free Religious Association," PUHS, 17, pt. 2 (1973–75), 1–21.

**ABBOT, JOHN EMERY** (6 August 1793, Exeter, NH–6 October 1819, Exeter, NH). *Education*: B.A., Bowdoin College, 1810; theological study, Cambridge, MA, 1810–15. *Career*: Minister, North Church, Salem, MA, 1810–17.

John Emery Abbot exemplified through his preaching the intensely devotionalist piety that flourished in nineteenth-century Unitarianism as a complement to the public reputation of liberalism as a "rational" religion. After graduating from Bowdoin in 1810, he came to read divinity at Cambridge with William Ellery Channing* and insisted that his preparation for the ministry consist of a cultivation of the character and moral sensibility as well as of the intellect. He accepted a call to the North Church in Salem in 1815, where he made a reputation for movingly emotional preaching. But his health was frail, and he died of tuberculosis in 1819, having only begun to establish his ministry and influence. Like Joseph Stevens Buckminster,* with whom he has been compared, he was mourned greatly, and most liberals believed that in his early death they had lost a great potential leader.

*Bibliography*

A. *Extracts from Sermons by the Late Rev. John Emery Abbot, of Salem, Mass., with a Memoir of His Life*, by Henry Ware, Jr. (Boston, 1830).

B. AAUP, 466–72; Henry Ware, Jr., *Memoir* (see above); Daniel Walker Howe, *The Unitarian Conscience: Harvard Moral Philosophy, 1805–1861* (Cambridge, 1970).

**ADAMS, JAMES LUTHER** (12 November, 1901, Ritzville, WA). *Education*: B.A., University of Minnesota, 1924; S.T.B., Harvard Divinity School, 1927; A.M., Harvard, 1930; study in Europe, 1935–36; Ph.D., University of Chicago, 1945. *Career*: Unitarian minister, Second Church, Salem, MA, 1927–34; instructor in English, Boston University, 1929–32; editor, *Christian Register*, 1933–34; minister, First Unitarian Society, Wellesley Hills, MA, 1934–35; professor of psychology and philosophy of religion, Meadville Theological School, 1936–43; editor, *Journal of Liberal Religion*, 1939–44; professor of theology, Federated Theological Faculties, University of Chicago, 1943–46; professor of religious ethics, 1946–56; founder and member, Society for the Scientific Study of Religion, 1953–present; Edward Mallinckrodt, Jr., Professor of Divinity, Harvard Divinity School, 1957–68; Distinguished Professor of Social Ethics, Andover Newton Theological Seminary, 1968–72; active retirement, 1972–present.

In a pattern that has typified many of the leaders of liberal religion in the twentieth century, James Luther Adams was raised in a religiously conservative home and came to his liberalism only after a difficult spiritual struggle. His father was a "Baptist country preacher" whom Adams remembers as a man of uncompromising spiritual principle ("Taking Time Seriously," p. 1067). But fundamentalist evangelicalism could not satisfy Adams intellectually, and by his college years at Minnesota, he was in open rebellion against religion and a disciple of John H. Dietrich's* scientific Humanism. The Humanism of Dietrich, and later the literary Humanism of his Harvard teacher Irving Babbitt, freed him from fundamentalism but did not satisfy his spiritual appetite, and his spiritual quest has continued. Adams's debts to a long and varied line of thinkers—Babbitt, Karl Marx, Rudolf Otto, Alfred North Whitehead, Baron Friedrich von Hügel, Paul Tillich, to name a few—give some sense of the varied nature of his quest in his early years. But that it was more than an intellectual quest is suggested by his account of the profound spiritual impact that Bach's *St. Matthew's Passion* had upon him during his years in Divinity School (see "Taking Time Seriously" for autobiographical details). Nor was this a quest that would affect Adams alone. Coming to distrust the "atomistic individualism" of religious liberalism as he had found it in the 1920s, he rejected "unhistorical" religion and pressed his insistence on social engagement on the Unitarian denomination as a whole ("Taking Time Seriously," p. 1069). Adams was a leader in the move for the denominational Commission of Appraisal in the 1930s and was important in the general intellectual critique of liberalism in the 1930s. As a social ethicist, he has given centrality to the concept of the "voluntary association" as the vehicle by which ideas can take historical form and individual freedom can also be preserved. The primitive church was the first expression of the voluntary principle in Christianity, but those associations have multiplied since. For Adams, the *voluntary principle* is "the dimension in which the churches have been able with some concreteness to move in the direction of a theology of culture and to attempt to fulfill the mission of the Church in a new age" (*On Being Human*, p. 79). George H. Williams* ranked Adams with William Ellery Channing* and Henry W. Bellows* as the three great leaders in the history of Unitarianism. Indeed, Adams's spiritual odyssey incarnates much of the story of twentieth-century liberal religion.

*Bibliography*

A. "Taking Time Seriously," *Christian Century*, 56 (September 1939), 1067–70; *Paul Tillich's Philosophy of Culture, Science, and Religion* (New York, 1965); *On Being*

*Human—Religiously*, ed. Max L. Stackhouse (Boston, 1976); numerous other essays—see the bibliography in Wilcox, below.

B. DAS, 1982, vol. 4; *Who's Who in America* (1980–81), 1, 16; James D. Hunt, "Voluntary Associations as a Key to History," in *Voluntary Associations: A Study of Groups in Free Societies*, ed. D. B. Robertson (Richmond, VA, 1966); Max L. Stackhouse, "James Luther Adams: A Biographical and Intellectual Sketch," in *Voluntary Associations*; Walter G. Muelder, "James Luther Adams as Theological Ethicist," *Andover Newton Quarterly*, 17, (1977), 186–94; George H. Williams, "James Luther Adams and the Unitarian Denomination," *Andover Newton Quarterly*, 17 (1977), 173–83; John R. Wilcox, *Taking Time Seriously: James Luther Adams* (Washington, DC, 1978).

**ATWOOD, ISAAC MORGAN** (24 March 1838, Pembroke, NY–26 October 1917, Canton, NY). *Career*: Universalist minister, Churchville, NY; Clifton Springs, NY; Watertown, NY; Portland, ME; Bridgewater, MA; Chelsea, MA, c. 1859–c. 1879; editor, *Boston Universalist*, 1867–72; *New York Christian Leader*, 1873–74; minister, North Cambridge, MA, 1874–79; associate editor, *Universalist Leader*, 1874–1908; president, Canton Theological School (St. Lawrence University), 1879–98; general superintendent, Universalist church, 1898–1907; secretary, Universalist General Convention, 1906–12; professor of theology and philosophy, St. Lawrence University, and minister, Universalist church, Canton, NY, 1912–17.

A dirt-poor farm boy, Isaac M. Atwood aspired toward the wider cultivation that a college education would bring him, but he was thwarted by economic necessity from achieving that goal. At age eleven he was bound out to farm work to help support his family, and later in his teen years he worked as a mule driver, bartender, and stable cleaner. Meanwhile, he prepared himself for college, reading by candlelight, and injured his eyes in the process. By dint of this hard work, he qualified himself for Yale but had to decline the chance to go, in order to help his family. His life changed, however, when he took a teaching position in Corfu, New York, and came into the influence of the H. P. Porter family, prominent and cultivated Universalists. He converted from his Baptist faith to Universalism and began a long service then to the denomination as a minister, educator, and administrator. He served two decades as the head of the theological school at St. Lawrence and resigned that position to become the first general superintendent of the Universalist church. Atwood took the position at a point when a significant element in the denomination was hoping for a firmer organization. Atwood perceived his responsibility primarily as one that combined denominational extension with aid to existing churches and engaged in enormous travel and correspondence in pursuing those goals. As his son John M. Atwood* recalled, "My father carried in the band of his hat the business of the Universalist Church" (Cummins, p. 28). With Quillen H. Shinn,* Atwood is one of Universalism's most distinguished churchmen of the late nineteenth century.

*Bibliography*

A. *Latest Word of Universalism* (coauthor, Boston, 1878); *Walks about Zion* (Boston, 1882); *Revelation* (Boston, 1889).

B. NCAB 10, 202; Who Was Who in America 1, 36; Robert Cummins, "The General Superintendency of the Universalist Church of America," JUHS, 3 (1962), 14–29.

**ATWOOD, JOHN MURRAY** (25 September 1869, Brockton, MA–4 November 1951, Canton, NY). *Education*: B.A., St. Lawrence University, 1889; B.D., St. Lawrence University, 1893; M.A., St. Lawrence University, 1900. *Career*: Reporter, *Rocky Mountain News*, Denver, CO, 1889–90; Universalist minister, Clifton Springs, NY, 1893–95; Minneapolis, MN, 1895–98; Portland, ME, 1899–1905; instructor, theological school of St. Lawrence University, 1898–99; professor of sociology and ethics, 1905–13; Gaines Professor of Philosophy, St. Lawrence University, 1913–14; dean of the theological school and professor of theology, St. Lawrence University, 1914–51; president, Universalist General Convention, 1923–27.

John Murray Atwood had a long and memorable career as professor and dean of the theological school at St. Lawrence University. His father, Isaac Morgan Atwood,* had been a Universalist minister and denominational leader and had also served as president of the theological school of St. Lawrence. Thus John M. Atwood's roots were deep in both the life of the Universalist denomination and of St. Lawrence University. After a brief stint as a reporter in Denver, Atwood decided to enter the Universalist ministry and held several pastorates before becoming a professor of sociology and ethics at the theological school at St. Lawrence in 1905. In 1914 he became dean of the school. Clinton Lee Scott described him as a "master teacher," and he continued as a teacher throughout his career, maintaining an extraordinary rapport with his students (Scott, p. 243). The small faculty of the theological school demanded versatility in teaching, and the school's slim finances presented administrative problems, but Atwood met both of these challenges admirably, engrafting his identity on the school. He was also a prominent denominational leader and served as president of the Universalist General Convention. A heart condition forced him to give up administrative duties at the theological school in 1951, but he continued to teach until his death.

*Bibliography*

B. NCAB 41, 155–56; Clinton Lee Scott, *These Live Tomorrow: Twenty Unitarian Universalist Biographies* (Boston, 1964).

# B

BALLOU, ADIN (23 April 1803, Cumberland, RI–5 August 1890, Hopedale [Milford], MA). *Career*: Preached variously at Mendon, Bellingham, Medway, Boston, and Milford, MA; and New York, 1823–28; minister, Milford, MA, c. 1828–41; founder and member of Hopedale Community, 1841–68; pastor, Hopedale Parish Church (Unitarian), which merged with Hopedale Community, 1868–80.

Adin Ballou began preaching against Universalism in the early 1820s but found the arguments he was trying to refute too persuasive and converted to Universalism in 1823. He came to be one of the earliest exemplars of the social conscience of the movement, founding the utopian Hopedale Community in 1841. His was a pioneering attempt, like the later Unitarian experiment at Brook Farm, to pursue Christian truths through alternative modes of social and economic organization. Always practical in his theology, he had joined a brief rebellion and exodus of ministers with Restorationist views from Universalism in 1831. These men were critical of the "ultra-Universalist" position of Hosea Ballou* and his followers and feared that Ballou's doctrine of no future punishment (rather than limited future punishment) might invite moral laxity. Ballou later articulated a theory of political nonresistance to war and violence, based on the biblical injunction "Resist not evil." This form of pacifism was one of the earliest and most persuasive versions of that doctrine in the Unitarian Universalist tradition.

*Bibliography*

A. *Christian Non-Resistance* (Philadelphia, 1846); *Practical Christian Socialism* (Hopedale, MA, and New York, 1854); *Autobiography of Adin Ballou, 1803–1890*, ed. William S. Heywood (Lowell, MA, 1896); *History of Hopedale Community* (Lowell, MA, 1897).

B. DAB 1, 556–57; Heralds 2, 297–300; *Autobiography* (see above).

**BALLOU, HOSEA** (30 April 1771, Richmond, NH–7 June 1852, Boston, MA). *Career*: Universalist minister, Dana, MA, 1794–1803; Barnard, VT, 1803–9; Portsmouth, NH, 1809–15; Salem, MA, 1815–17; Second Universalist Society, Boston, 1817–52.

Although John Murray* can be said to be the founder of American Universalism, Hosea Ballou ranks as the single most important leader in the denomination's history. Through the force of his preaching, writing, and character he assumed the leadership of the denomination during most of the first half of the nineteenth century, a period at which Universalism can be said to have firmly established its denominational identity. Ballou's most important theological work, and arguably his most significant contribution to the denomination, was his *Treatise on Atonement* (1805). In that work Ballou fused several disparate influences—the free thinking of Ethan Allen, the rejection of endless punishment by Charles Chauncy,* and the quietist determinism of Ferdinand Olivier Petitpierre—into a volume that was a frontal attack on Calvinism and its doctrines of limited election to grace. Ballou's eventual position, which came to be known as "ultra-Universalism," was that the consequences of sin manifested themselves in this life only. This position was opposed by many "Restorationists," who assumed there would be a limited future punishment, and led to one of the deepest schisms in the history of the denomination.

Ballou assumed the pastorate of the Second Universalist Church in Boston in 1817, several years after the death of John Murray, who had pastored Boston's First Universalist Church. Ballou's move to Boston marked a change in the leadership of Universalism, and until his death he was by far the most influential Universalist minister. Ballou was a largely self-educated man of intellectual courage and originality. He announced publicly a version of doctrines that later thinkers such as Ralph Waldo Emerson,* in his essay "Compensation," would embrace. He was also an effective preacher, who based his sermons, like his theological writings, on close analyses of biblical passages. However progressive his theological conclusions, he continued to base them, like most Universalists, on the tradition of scripture analysis and interpretation. His motivating idea was that of God's benevolence, and he was utterly convinced that a loving God would not condemn humankind to eternal punishment. For Ballou, the consequences of sin were the spiritual, psychological, and physical harm to the sinner, not the punishment of an angry God. Both his ideas and his personality molded to the Universalist identity in the nineteenth century.

*Bibliography*

A. *Notes on the Parables of the New Testament* (Randolph, VT, 1804); *A Treatise on Atonement* (Randolph, VT, 1805); *A Series of Lecture Sermons* (Boston, 1819); *Select Sermons* (Boston, 1832); *An Examination of the Doctrine of Future Retributions* (Boston, 1834); *A Voice to Universalists* (Boston, 1849).

B. DAB 1, 557–59; DARB, 27–29; Maturin M. Ballou, *Biography of Rev. Hosea Ballou* (Boston, 1852); Thomas Whittemore, *Life of Rev. Hosea Ballou*, 4 vols. (Boston, 1854–55); Oscar F. Safford, *Hosea Ballou* (Boston, 1889); John C. Adams, *Hosea Ballou and the Gospel Renaissance of the Nineteenth Century* (Boston, 1903); Ernest Cassara, *Hosea Ballou: The Challenge to Orthodoxy* (Boston, 1961).

**BALLOU, HOSEA, 2d** (18 October 1796, Guilford, VT–27 May 1861, Medford, MA). *Career*: Minister, Stafford, CT, 1817–21; minister of New Universalist Church, Roxbury, MA, 1821–38; minister, Medford, MA, 1838–54; president, Tufts College, 1854–61.

Hosea Ballou, 2d, grandnephew of Hosea Ballou,* made a major contribution to the development of Universalism with his thorough scholarship and historiography, the most important product of which was his *Ancient History of Universalism* (1829). He was an able student, although he did not attend college, and worked as a schoolteacher before taking his first pastorate in 1817. His move to Roxbury, Massachusetts, in 1821 put him within the intellectually stimulating environment of Boston, and he ministered and kept school there until moving to Medford in 1838. During his years in Roxbury he researched and wrote his *Ancient History of Universalism*, which attempted to discover the attitudes of the early Christian church on the questions of eternal punishment and universal salvation. Ballou found much confirmation for the Universalism of his own day in the thought of Origen and argued that the doctrines of endless punishment were largely the product of Augustine's influence on early Christian thinking rather than an original tenet of the early church. This location of historical precedent was important in the establishment of an identity and tradition for the embattled early Universalists. Ballou was also an important Universalist journalist, taking a hand in editing and writing for several Universalist periodicals. His lifelong interest in education and scholarship culminated in his presidency of Tufts College.

*Bibliography*

A. *The Ancient History of Universalism* (Boston, 1829).

B. DAB 1, 559–60; Hosea Starr Ballou, *Hosea Ballou, 2d, D.D., First President of Tufts College: Origin, Life, and Letters* (Boston, 1896); Russell E. Miller, "Hosea Ballou, 2d: Scholar and Educator," JUHS, 1 (1959), 59–79; Russell E. Miller, *Light on the Hill: A History of Tufts College, 1852–1952* (Boston, 1966).

**BARTH, JOSEPH NICHOLAS** (3 May 1906, Salina, KS). *Education*: Attended Creighton University, 1924–26; Kansas Wesleyan University, 1928; Ph.B., University of Chicago, 1935; B.D., Meadville Theological School, 1935. *Career*: Unitarian minister, Channing Church, Newton, MA, 1935–38; First Unitarian Church of Miami, 1939–54; King's Chapel, Boston, 1956–66; director, Department of Ministry, Unitarian Universalist Association (UUA), 1966–71; director of church extension, UUA, 1968–71; retirement, 1971–present.

In the sermon "The God I Believe In," Joseph Barth articulated a theological position representative of many midtwentieth-century religious liberals. "And to what do I refer when I say I believe in 'God'? I mean that I need a word that will stand in speech, in a shorthand way, for all reality in which we live and move and have our being" (*The Art of Staying Sane*, p. 30). Barth's theological position tries to preserve the religious value of theological concepts and language but to avoid a supernatural view of the cosmos. Thus Barth said that "the God I believe in is a naturalistically conceived God," one who could be equated with "nature entire" (pp. 34–35). Barth's theological vision made room for both joy and tragedy, and those he saw as interdependent experiences. "Life is a miracle, and death is a fact," he wrote. He urged his readers "to use that miracle for all it is worth of loving, striving, understanding, studying and playing, trying, searching, and . . . [enjoying] the moments of creativity as they fleet by" (p. 189). But he also warned that "no person, I think, can enjoy more than he has suffered" (p. 190). Barth's optimism, in other words, was tempered by a full recognition of complexity and tragedy but deepened as a result. This well-articulated theology has made him an influential spokesman in contemporary liberal religion.

*Bibliography*

A. *The Art of Staying Sane* (Boston, 1948); *Toward a Doctrine of the Liberal Church*, Minns Lectures (Boston, 1956).

**BARTOL, CYRUS AUGUSTUS** (30 April 1813, Freeport, ME–16 December 1900, Boston, MA). *Education*: B.A., Bowdoin College, 1832; graduated from Harvard Divinity School, 1835. *Career*: Unitarian preacher, Cincinnati, 1835–36; minister, West Church, Boston, 1837–89.

During his long ministry at the West Church in Boston, Cyrus Bartol was a figure of some importance in the various phases of Unitarian theological development. He was a man of wide sympathies but of a fierce intellectual independence, a combination of characteristics that allowed him to be part of the Transcendentalist movement, yet one of its critics, and a leader of the radical movement toward Free Religion, yet a close friend of the radicals' most frequent target, Henry W. Bellows.* Bartol devoted himself to what he called a "religion of the spirit," an intuitive conception of religious experience that allied him in many ways with Transcendentalism. Yet he remained somewhat aloof from the movement for a complex variety of reasons, choosing his own way intellectually. During the early 1850s, he became more closely aligned with conservative and denominationally oriented Unitarianism, but he emerged from this phase to encourage the dissent of O. B. Frothingham* and other radicals against Bellows's National Conference. While helping to set the stage for the founding of the Free Religious Association by gathering the dissenters at his home after their defection from the 1866 Syracuse Conference, he refused to assume leadership when the organization was formed, maintaining his independence even from an organization dedicated to such independence. Bartol continued to expound a spiritual form of Free Religion in the 1870s and 1880s, and he must be classified with the group that Francis Ellingwood Abbot* termed the "intuitionist" school of Free Religion in opposition to the "scientific" school that Abbot represented. In the variety of his sympathies, and his uncompromising individual quest for a way to embody his religion of the spirit, Bartol is, as William Hutchison argued, a representative of the experience of Unitarianism in the mid-nineteenth century.

*Bibliography*

A. *Discourses on the Christian Spirit and Life* (Boston, 1850); *Discourses on the Christian Body and Form* (Boston, 1853); *Church and Congregation* (Boston, 1858); *The Word of the Spirit to the Church* (Boston, 1859); *Radical Problems* (Boston, 1872); *Principles and Portraits* (Boston, 1880).

B. DAB 2, 17; DLB 1, 10; Heralds 3, 17–22; Stow Persons, *Free Religion: An American Faith* (New Haven, 1947); William R. Hutchison, "To Heaven in a Swing: The Transcendentalism of Cyrus Bartol," *Harvard Theological Review*, 56 (October 1963), 275–95; William R. Hutchison, *The Modernist Impulse in American Protestantism* (Cambridge, and London, 1976); William G. Heath, Jr., "Cyrus Bartol's Transcendental Capitalism," in *Studies in the American Renaissance, 1979*, ed. Joel Myerson (Boston, 1979).

**BELLOWS, HENRY WHITNEY** (11 June 1814, Boston, MA–30 January 1882, New York, NY). *Education*: A.B., Harvard College, 1832; graduated from Harvard Divinity School, 1837. *Career*: Minister, Mobile, AL, 1837–38; First Congregational (Unitarian) Church, New York, 1838–82, named Church of All Souls, 1855; editor, *Christian Inquirer*, later the *Liberal Christian*, 1846–77(?); founder, United States Sanitary Commission, 1861; National Conference of Unitarian Churches, 1865; editor, *Christian Examiner*, 1865–69.

Henry W. Bellows stands as the leading Unitarian churchman of the nineteenth century. Through his efforts the National Conference of Unitarian Churches was founded in 1865, a step that ranks as the most important denominationwide organizational effort of the nineteenth century. After his education at Harvard College and the Divinity School, and a brief ministry in the South, Bellows began a highly successful and influential ministry in New York at the church that would come to be known as All Souls. Bellows had many talents: he was an eloquent preacher, possessed an astute theological mind, and had enormous physical and intellectual energy. But his greatest strength was his force of personality, which made him an effective builder of organizations. His involvement with the northern war effort in the 1860s resulted in the formation of the U.S. Sanitary Commission, and this organizational experience led Bellows to form the National Conference in 1865. It was a historic, although controversial act, because one faction of the denomination feared the centralization of power and the possibility of creedalism that Bellows's efforts represented to them. But Bellows thought that liberalism had to be organized further than it was under the American Unitarian Association, which was composed of individual Unitarians, not Unitarian churches as the National Conference was. Bellows thus assumed the leadership of the Broad Church group in the denomination, moderates and liberals whose chief common goal was the institutional strengthening of the liberal movement. The intellectual foundations of Bellows's organizational efforts can be discerned in his 1859 address "The Suspense of Faith," in which he noted the crisis that the decay of old forms of faith were causing and held out the hope of a revitalized and universal church of the future. Bellows conceived of this as a Christian church, but as Conrad Wright* noted, his desire for a Christian identity for the National Conference, which so alienated the radicals, was based largely on his sense of the necessary historical continuity of the Christian past with the present. In his sense of the need of an institutional grounding for liberalism, and in his successful efforts to secure that grounding, Bellows changed the course of American Unitarianism.

*Bibliography*

A. *The Suspense of Faith* (New York, 1859); *Re-Statements of Christian Doctrine in Twenty-Five Sermons* (New York and London, 1860); *The Old World in Its New Face*, 2 vols. (New York, 1868–69); Russell N. Bellows, ed., *Twenty-Four Sermons Preached in All Souls Church New York, 1865–1881* (New York, 1886).

B. DAB 2, 169; Heralds 3, 23–33; Conrad Wright, "Henry W. Bellows and the Organization of the National Conference," in *The Liberal Christians* (Boston, 1970); Walter Donald Kring, *Henry Whitney Bellows* (Boston, 1979).

**BLACKWELL, ANTOINETTE LOUISA BROWN** (20 May 1825, Henrietta, NY–5 November 1921, Elizabeth, NJ). *Education*: Completed the literary course, Oberlin College, 1847; completed the theological course, Oberlin College, 1850, but denied degree. *Career*: Lecturer and preacher, 1850–52; minister, Congregational Church, South Butler, NY, 1852–54; social worker, New York, 1855; homemaker, author, lecturer, principally in Newark and Somerville, NJ, and New York, 1856–1901; founder and pastor emeritus, All Souls Unitarian Church, Elizabeth, NJ, 1908–21.

Antoinette Brown Blackwell was one of the pioneers in the women's rights movement in nineteenth-century America. She began her struggles in the feminist cause by gaining entrance to Oberlin, completing a literary course in 1847 and a theological course in 1850. But she was denied her degree and license to preach because of her sex. She sought her own opportunities to preach and lecture, expounding women's rights, the abolition of slavery, and temperance. In 1852 she became the first regularly ordained American woman, although the ordination did not have full denominational support. In 1853 she raised controversy by attempting to exercise her right as a delegate to speak at the World's Temperance Convention in New York, but because of the prejudice against women in the pulpit, she was denied her request to speak. Unable to affirm the orthodox tenets of Congregationalism, she resigned her pastorate in 1854, becoming a Unitarian thereafter. Her marriage in 1856 to Samuel C. Blackwell was long and successful. She raised a large family and continued to stay active as an author, devoting much effort to the question of the relation of theology to modern science. One of her works, *The Sexes throughout Nature* (1875), was a feminist critique of the evolutionary theories of Darwin and Spencer, in which she argued that nature demonstrated the equality of sexes throughout the species. Late in her life she organized a Unitarian Church in Elizabeth, New Jersey, and continued to be a presence in the feminist movement, living to cast her vote, at age ninety-five, in the 1920 election. She stands as one of the most accomplished and fascinating of America's early feminists.

*Bibliography*

A. *The Sexes throughout Nature* (New York, 1875); *Philosophy of Individuality* (New York, 1892); *The Making of the Universe* (Boston, 1914); *The Social Side of Mind and Action* (New York, 1915).

B. DAB 2, 319–20; Heralds 4, 52–54; NAW 1, 158–61; Elinor Rice Hays, *Those Extraordinary Blackwells* (New York, 1967); Catherine F. Hitchings, "Universalist and Unitarian Women Ministers," JUHS, 10 (1975), 155–56; Elizabeth Cazden, *Antoinette Brown Blackwell: A Biography* (Old Westbury, NY, 1983).

**BOWEN, FRANCIS** (8 September 1811, Charlestown, MA–21 January 1890, Boston, MA). *Education*: A.B., Harvard, 1833. *Career*: Mathematics teacher, Phillips Exeter Academy, 1833–35; tutor in intellectual philosophy and political economy, Harvard, 1835–39; 1840–53; study and travel in Europe, 1839–40; editor, *North American Review*, 1843–54; Alford Professor of Natural Religion, Moral Philosophy, and Civil Polity, Harvard, 1853–89.

In 1837 Francis Bowen reviewed Ralph Waldo Emerson's* *Nature* for the *Christian Examiner*, the leading Unitarian publication of the day. Noting that Emerson's book was "representative" of a "new school" of philosophy that had been "dignified . . . with the title of Transcendentalism," Bowen criticized the work for its "vagueness," "mysticism," and general philosophical wrong-headedness. His description of its impact suggests the differing sensibilities that composed the two sides of the Transcendentalist controversy: "The reader feels as in a disturbed dream, in which shows of surpassing beauty are around him, and he is conversant with disembodied spirits, yet all the time he is harassed by an uneasy sort of consciousness, that the whole combination of phenomena is fantastic and unreal" (Miller, *The Transcendentalists*, p. 174). As this passage suggests, Bowen was a logician who liked to keep his feet firmly planted on empirical ground. His philosophical allegiance was with the Scottish commonsense philosophies, and he distrusted the Platonic idealism that he found in *Nature* and in other Transcendentalist writing. Bowen continued at Harvard as a spokesman for relatively conservative Christian Unitarian values. As editor of the *North American Review* and later the holder of the Alford professorship at Harvard, he continued to have great intellectual influence in the Boston community but often found himself using that influence for rear-guard conservative ends. He was a staunch critic of Darwin and evolutionary philosophy in general in the late 1850s and 1860s and an opponent of the educational reforms—the lecture and elective systems—that were introduced at Harvard in the late 1860s and 1870s. Bowen was nevertheless an able historian and in 1877 wrote a history of philosophy that led one recent scholar to note that "as a historian of modern philosophy he has had no superior at Harvard" (Kuklick, p. 28). Always outspoken and of a vigorous and independent mind, his critique of Transcendentalism was far more searching, although much less prominent, than that of Andrews Norton.*

*Bibliography*

A. *Critical Essays on a Few Subjects Connected with the History and Present Condition of Speculative Philosophy* (Boston, 1842); *Principles of Political Economy Applied to the Conditions, Resources, and Institutions of the American People* (Boston, 1856); *Modern Philosophy, from Descartes to Schopenhauer and Hartmann* (New York, 1877).

B. DAB 2, 503–4; DLB 1, 12; Perry Miller, *The Transcendentalists: An Anthology* (Cambridge, 1950); Daniel Walker Howe, *The Unitarian Conscience: Harvard Moral Philosophy, 1805–1861* (Cambridge, 1970); Bruce Kuklick, *The Rise of American Philosophy* (New Haven, 1977).

**BROWN, EGBERT ETHELRED** (11 July 1875, Falmouth, Jamaica–17 February 1956, New York, NY). *Education*: Attended Meadville Theological School, 1910–12. *Career*: Jamaican Civil Service, 1894–1907; Unitarian minister, Montego Bay, Jamaica, 1908–14; Kingston, Jamaica, 1914–20; Harlem Community Church, later named Harlem Unitarian Church, Harlem, New York, 1920–56.

Ethelred Brown was a notable black Unitarian preacher who battled to establish a Unitarian Church in Harlem for over three decades. "This man possessed a vision, and he never ceased following it," wrote Mark Morrison-Reed in his sensitive and revealing discussion of Brown (Morrison-Reed, p. 63). Yet the pursuit of that vision was difficult indeed, as one learns from both Morrison-Reed and from Brown's own memoir of his career. Brown characterized himself as both unusually inquisitive and truthful as a child, traits which led to difficulties with the orthodox religious belief. He was struck, one Easter, by the "strangeness of the Trinitarian arithmetic" in the Athanasian Creed, and that same day fell upon Channing's* "Unitarian Christianity." ("The Harlem Unitarian Church," p. 2). His reading of that and other literature made him "a Unitarian without a church" (p. 2). For a number of years he served as organist and choir leader in orthodox churches, remaining Unitarian in his beliefs. But in 1907 he was dismissed from the Jamaican Civil Service, and he took that event as a definite call to the ministry. Although he was welcomed by the African Methodist Church when he inquired about entering the ministry, he also wrote to Meadville Theological School. President Franklin Southworth's reply, as recounted by Brown, was frank and not encouraging: "as there was no Unitarian Church in America for colored people, and . . . as white Unitarians require a white minister he was unable to predict what my future would be at the conclusion of my training" (p. 3). This did not daunt Brown, who "wanted to be a minister only of that church in which I would be absolutely honest" (p. 3). So after two false starts, because of immigration and financial difficulties, he enrolled in a special two-year course at Meadville, and returned after his training to work toward the establishment of a Unitarian presence in Jamaica. Brown eventually admitted defeat in the Jamaica experiment and went to New York to found the Harlem Church. His struggles were not over. The church was "undertaken without experience and without careful survey of local conditions, and without knowledge of the difficulties of the situation" (p. 5). John Haynes Holmes* took an interest in it and gave Brown much help over the years, but Brown's relationship with the American Unitarian Association (AUA) was strained. As Morrison-Reed reported, Brown was not blameless in this relationship, but he never got steady support for his work until the administration of Frederick May Eliot* in the late 1930s. It was in 1937 that his church formally affiliated with the AUA, although Brown had considered himself a Unitarian minister throughout his career and fought to retain his fellowship in the late 1920s and early 1930s.

Brown's church did not have a building and met primarily at the American West Indian Association Lodge Rooms, and later at the YWCA and YMCA Chapel. There was significant experimentation with a public forum in the worship services, and while Brown noted success with the experiment, there was friction at times because of a highly charged political atmosphere in the church. "Political freedom," Morrison-Reed noted, "emerged as a central element in Brown's ministry, and as a significant aspect of the lives of a number of church members" (Morrison-Reed, p. 91). Brown was disappointed that the church never attained great size, and his task was made harder because of its very limited financial resources. Nevertheless, he remained an optimist about its future. His career, in both its successes and its struggles, is a particularly significant example to the Unitarian Universalist denomination.

*Bibliography*

A. "The Harlem Unitarian Church," typescript from the Unitarian Universalist Association Archives, Boston, MA.

B. "Ethelred Brown," *Christian Register* (April 1946); Mark D. Morrison-Reed, *Black Pioneers in a White Denomination* (rev. ed., Boston, 1984).

**BROWN, OLYMPIA** (5 January 1835, Prairie Ronde, MI–23 October 1926, Baltimore, MD). *Education*: Attended Mount Holyoke Female Seminary, 1854–55; B.A., Antioch College, 1860; graduated from the theological school, St. Lawrence University, 1863. *Career*: Itinerant Universalist preacher, VT, 1863–64; Universalist minister, Weymouth, MA, 1864–70; reformer on women's issues, 1866–1926; cofounder, New England Woman Suffrage Association, 1884–1912; president, Federal Suffrage Association. 1903–20.

Olympia Brown, a leader in the woman suffrage movement in the nineteenth century, was one of the first women ordained to the ministry by an American denomination (1863). While at Antioch she led a movement among women students to bring a woman lecturer to the college. That lecturer was Antoinette Brown (Blackwell),* one of the first prominent women in the American pulpit, who gave both inspiration and encouragement to Olympia Brown. Brown reported that during college she "had been gradually forming the determination to become a preacher" ("Autobiography," p. 26). She wanted to preach against the doctrines of endless punishment that, to her horror, had been prevalent at Mount Holyoke. "I knew nothing then of the difficulties I was to experience later," she said in reference to pursuing her career (p. 26). At seminary in St. Lawrence, her determination gradually wore down the initial opposition she felt, and she gradually began to find opportunities to preach after an initial engagement in which she simply went to a small New York town, announced her intention to preach, and gathered a choir. Her first congregation in Weymouth, Massachusetts, was progressive, supporting her in most of her work and leaving her with memories of it as "perhaps the most enjoyable part of my ministerial career" (p. 33). During the late 1860s, while she was pastor there, she began to become seriously involved in lecturing and organizing for woman suffrage, taking an important role in the founding of the New England Woman Suffrage Association. Brown's second pastorate, at Bridgeport, Connecticut, was not the pleasant experience her first had been. A small faction there opposed women in the pulpit and stirred up division in the congregation, and Brown finally resigned. She then moved to Racine, Wisconsin, another parish, like Bridgeport, "in a run-down and unfortunate condition" (p. 40). Her remarks on her difficulties in finding pastoral work are revealing: "The pulpits of all the prosperous churches were already occupied by men, and were looked forward to as the goal of all the young men coming into the ministry with whom I, at first the only woman in the denomination, had to compete. All I could do was to take some place that had been abandoned by others and make something of it, and this I was only too glad to do" (p. 41). Brown's church in Racine prospered, and in Wisconsin she assumed leadership of the woman suffrage movement. As her work continued, she saw that she "must give [herself] more to the suffrage work" and eventually resigned her ministry to devote herself fully to that cause (p. 62). She traveled extensively as a speaker and organizer, campaigning in Wisconsin and elsewhere and living to see the accomplishment of her goal in 1920.

*Bibliography*

A. *Acquaintances Old and New, among Reformers* (Milwaukee, WI, 1911); editor, *Democratic Ideals: A Memorial Sketch of Clara B. Colby* (n.p., 1917); "Olympia

Brown: An Autobiography,'' edited and completed by Gwendolen B. Willis, JUHS, 4 (1963).

B. DAB 3, 151; NAW 1, 256–58; "Autobiography" (see above); Catherine F. Hitchings, "Universalist and Unitarian Women Ministers," JUHS, 10 (1975).

**BROWNSON, ORESTES AUGUSTUS** (16 September 1803, Stockbridge, VT–17 April 1876, Detroit, MI). *Career:* Schoolteacher, Stillwater, NY, 1823–24; Detroit, MI, 1824; Elbridge, NY, 1824–26; converted to Universalism, 1824; ordained Universalist minister, Jaffrey, NH, 1826; Universalist preacher, NH, VT, and NY, 1826–30; editor, *Gospel Advocate and Impartial Investigator*, c. 1828–29; corresponding editor, *The Free Enquirer*, 1829–30; editor, *Genesee Republican and Herald of Reform*, 1829–30; political organizer for Working-men's party, 1829–30; converted to Unitarianism, 1831; editor, *The Philanthropist*, 1831–32; Unitarian minister, Walpole, NH, 1832–34; Canton, MA, 1834–36; editor, *The Boston Reformer* 1836–38; organizer and minister, Society for Christian Union and Progress, Boston, 1836–44; founder and editor, *Boston Quarterly Review*, 1838–42; staff, *United States Magazine and Democratic Review*, 1842–44; converted to Catholicism, 1844; founder and editor, *Brownson's Quarterly Review*, 1844–64; 1873–75; independent journalist and author, 1844–76.

Orestes Brownson's movement through various shades of religious belief and political outlook reflects in many ways the turbulent current of thought that converged for a while in the Transcendentalist movement. Brownson's "pilgrimage" began with his rejection of Presbyterian Calvinism and his adoption of one of the anti-Calvinist ideologies available to him, Universalism. As a Universalist Brownson espoused a political outlook more radical than was comfortable for many others of that denomination. He was influenced in the late 1820s by the ideas of Frances Wright and Robert Dale Owen and the reformist outlook of the Working-men's party, and this commitment to laboring class politics permanently colored his political outlook. But in the late 1820s he also underwent a period of religious crisis and was rescued from skepticism by reading William Ellery Channing's* *Likeness to God* (1828), which he called "the most remarkable sermon since the Sermon on the Mount" (*Works* 4, 46). This brought him into Unitarianism, and his pastorate at Walpole, New Hampshire, also brought him near the intellectual center of Unitarianism, Boston. Brownson's reputation as a spokesman for the working class grew, and he developed a close friendship with George Ripley,* taking part in the ferment of new views that came to be known as Transcendentalism. In 1836 Brownson established in Boston what he hoped would be a new version of the church, The Society for Christian Union and Progress, which was aimed at bringing progressive religion to the working class. Many of the Unitarian clergy hoped that Brownson's efforts would fill the needs of that class, which did not seem to be attracted to Boston Unitarianism as it stood.

Brownson launched the *Boston Quarterly Review* in 1838, an influential vehicle for Transcendentalist writing, and used that journal to publish his essay
"The Laboring Classes," one of the most challenging critiques of the self-culture doctrine of Channing. Brownson argued that political reform had to pre-
cede self-culture, that in fact the possibility of self-culture was dependent on a
general reform of property distribution. Brownson's hope by now rested in the
Democratic party, but the Whig victory of 1840 came as a crushing blow to
him, and in the early 1840s he entered another period of crisis. Politically he
became attracted to John Calhoun and the "states' rights" philosophy, and theologically he embraced a revivified Christology and eventually converted to Catholicism. Brownson's arrival at Catholicism completed his religious search, and
he continued as an active writer on political and religious affairs in the later
part of his life. His *American Republic* crystallized his later political thought.

*Bibliography*

A. *New Views of Christianity, Society, and the Church* (Boston, 1836); *Charles El-
   wood; or, The Infidel Converted* (Boston, 1840); "The Laboring Classes," *Boston
   Quarterly Review*, July, October 1840; *The Convert; or, Leaves from My Experience*
   (New York, 1857); *The American Republic: Its Constitution, Tendencies, and Destiny* (New York, 1866); *The Works of Orestes A. Brownson*, ed. Henry F. Brownson, 20 vols. (Detroit, 1882–87).

B. DAB 3, 178–79; DLB 1, 13–20; Henry F. Brownson, *Orestes A. Brownson's Early
   Life, from 1803–1844; Orestes A. Brownson's Middle Life, from 1845–1855; Orestes A. Brownson's Latter Life, from 1856–1876*, 3 vols. (Detroit, 1898–1900);
   Arthur M. Schlesinger, Jr., *Orestes A. Brownson: A Pilgrim's Progress* (Boston,
   1939); Leonard Gilhooley, *Contradiction and Dilemma: Orestes Brownson and the
   American Idea* (New York, 1972); Thomas R. Ryan, *Orestes A. Brownson: A Definitive Biography* (Huntington, IN, 1976); Leonard Gilhooley, ed., *No Divided Allegiance: Essays in Brownson's Thought* (New York, 1980); Anne C. Rose, *Transcendentalism as a Social Movement, 1830–1850* (New Haven, 1981).

**BUCKMINSTER, JOSEPH STEVENS** (26 May 1784, Portsmouth, NH–9
June 1812, Boston, MA). *Education*: A.B., A.M., Harvard College, 1800, 1803.
*Career*: Minister, Brattle Street Church, Boston, 1805–12.

Joseph Stevens Buckminster was an early leader in bringing the German higher
criticism of the Bible to America and was also the most eloquent of the early
liberal preachers in Boston. Son of the clergyman Joseph Buckminster, the
younger Buckminster entered Harvard at the age of thirteen and received an
A.B. in 1800. After a period of teaching and tutoring, he was called to Brattle
Street Church in Boston in 1804 and launched an almost legendary career of
eloquent preaching, biblical scholarship, and literary production. He in many
ways set the tone for the pattern of the minister as a man of letters, which prevailed in nineteenth-century Boston Unitarianism. In addition to preaching, he
contributed to the *Monthly Anthology and Boston Review*, one of the earliest

literary periodicals in America. Buckminster preached a distinctly liberal message of rational religion and character development, themes that his contemporary William Ellery Channing* would later develop. He also influenced the denomination heavily in his adoption of the attitude of rational investigation into the Bible, a stand that insisted that the scriptures be read in their historical context and be subjected to the same scrupulous scholarly investigation given other texts from antiquity. Buckminster suffered a tragic early death by epilepsy when his powers were only reaching their height, and his death was an enormous blow to Boston Unitarianism.

*Bibliography*

A. *The Works of Joseph Stevens Buckminster* 2 vols. (Boston, 1839).

B. AAUP, 384–406; DAB 3, 233–34; Heralds 2, 134–53; Eliza Buckminster Lee, *Memoirs of Rev. Joseph Buckminster, D.D., and of His Son, Rev. Joseph Stevens Buckminster* (Boston, 1849); Jerry Wayne Brown, *The Rise of Biblical Criticism in America, 1810–1870* (Middletown, CT, 1969); Daniel Walker Howe, *The Unitarian Conscience: Harvard Moral Philosophy, 1805–1861* (Cambridge, 1970); Lewis P. Simpson, *The Man of Letters in New England and the South* (Baton Rouge, LA, 1973); Lawrence Buell, "Joseph Stevens Buckminster: The Making of a New England Saint," *Canadian Review of American Studies*, 10 (Spring 1979), 1–29.

# C

CALL, LON RAY (6 October 1894, Advance, NC). *Education*: A.B., Wake Forest College, 1916; B.D., University of Chicago Divinity School, 1920. *Career*: Ordained Baptist minister, 1915; military chaplain, 1918–19; minister, Second Baptist Church, St. Louis, MO, 1920–23; entered Unitarian ministry, 1923; minister, First Unitarian Church, Louisville, KY, 1923–30; West Side Unitarian Church, New York, 1930–31; associate minister, Community Church, New York, 1931–33; minister, All Souls Unitarian Church, Braintree, MA, 1933–35; executive secretary, Western Unitarian Conference, and regional director for midwestern states, American Unitarian Association (AUA), 1935–41; minister-at-large, AUA, 1941–51; minister, South Nassau Unitarian Church, Freeport, NY, 1951–60; minister emeritus, since 1960, with a number of interim pastorates.

Lon Ray Call is one of the preeminent leaders in twentieth-century Unitarian extension work, having guided the fellowship program of the late 1940s from the theoretical stages of planning to its implementation under the direction of Munroe Husbands.* Call had been raised a Baptist, but he studied at the University of Chicago during the years when the conflict between fundamentalism and theological modernism was acute, and he was gradually won over to liberalism. Curtis Reese,* one of the leaders of the Humanist movement and himself a former Baptist, was instrumental in Call's entry into the Unitarian ministry. The origins of the Unitarian Fellowship movement lay in part in Call's recognition during his Louisville pastorate of how several small Kentucky churches "had been kept going by laymen for years on end without benefit of clergy" ("Fellowships," p. 6). He gained further experience in church organization as AUA minister-at-large, during which time he founded thirteen Unitarian churches. When the fellowship program was launched in 1948, it contributed to a significant growth in Unitarianism. Call saw the fellowship as a vehicle that called out the talents of its members and said that "the matching of great talent to the crying need for leadership has happily been a major result of the fellowship movement" (p. 10). In 1967 Call was given the Unitarian Universalist Award for Distinguished Service to Liberal Religion.

*Bibliography*

A. "Fellowships: Yesterday, Today and Tomorrow—with the Accent on Yesterday," in Department of Extension, Unitarian Universalist Association, *Take a Giant Step: Two Decades of Fellowships* (Boston, c. 1967).

B. "Lon Call Honored," *Unitarian Universalist World*, 13 (July 15, 1982), 2.

**CHADWICK, JOHN WHITE** (19 October 1840, Marblehead, MA–11 December 1904, Brooklyn, NY). *Education*: Studied at Bridgewater Normal School and Phillips Exeter Academy; graduated from Harvard Divinity School, 1864. *Career*: Minister, Second Unitarian Church, Brooklyn, NY, 1864–1904.

John White Chadwick was a prominent spokesman for the radical wing of late nineteenth-century American Unitarianism. While a student at Harvard Divinity School (1861–64), Chadwick became a convert to the theories of evolution associated with Charles Darwin and Herbert Spencer. Thereafter he spent much of his intellectual energy in demonstrating the religious implications of evolutionary science, arguing that Darwin's theories helped to confirm a view of nature and humanity as part of an evolving cosmos unified by a God who was revealed in that evolutionary process. Chadwick became minister of the Second Unitarian Church in Brooklyn in 1864 and remained there for his entire ministerial career. Very much a scholar-minister, he prepared carefully crafted sermons that his church began to print and circulate widely in 1875. In addition to preparing and delivering sermons, he was a book reviewer for the *Nation* and other periodicals, a poet, and an author of distinguished biographies of Theodore Parker* (1900) and William Ellery Channing* (1903). Although he devoted himself primarily to his preaching and other scholarly endeavors, Chadwick was a supporter of the noncreedal and antisupernaturalist impulses of the Free Religion movement in the denomination. His later biographical studies of Channing and Parker were signal contributions to Unitarian historiography.

*Bibliography*

A. *The Faith of Reason* (Boston, 1879); *Old and New Unitarian Belief* (Boston, 1894); *Theodore Parker: Preacher and Reformer* (Boston and New York, 1900); *William Ellery Channing: Minister of Religion* (Boston and New York, 1903).

B. DAB 3, 588–89; Heralds 4, 75–82; Stow Persons, *Free Religion: An American Faith* (New Haven, 1947).

**CHANNING, WILLIAM ELLERY** (7 April 1780, Newport, RI–2 October 1842, Bennington, VT). *Education*: A.B., Harvard College, 1798; theological study in Cambridge, MA, 1800–1802. *Career*: Tutor, Richmond, VA, 1798–1800; minister, Federal Street Church, Boston, 1803–42.

William Ellery Channing is the single most important figure in the history of American Unitarianism. He provided the movement with intellectual leadership of rare quality at the moment of its inception, when Unitarians were beginning to see themselves as more than simply the liberal wing of New England Congregationalism. After a period of tutoring in Virginia, marked by both a spiritual crisis and a break in his health, Channing returned to New England in 1800 and was called to the Federal Street Church in Boston in 1803, where he remained as minister until his death. Because of his frail health and the financial independence he gained through his marriage to Ruth Gibbs, Channing's role as a day-to-day pastor at the Federal Street Church was gradually taken over by his associate Ezra Stiles Gannett.*

Channing was thrust into the public eye when he replied to the attacks on Boston liberals by Jedidiah Morse and Jeremiah Evarts in 1815. From that moment he was generally acknowledged the leader of American Unitarianism. His 1819 sermon "Unitarian Christianity" stands as the defining statement of the movement, and in its wake the American Unitarian Association was formed in 1825. Channing went on to offer important critiques of Calvinism and to develop an affirmative philosophy of human development or self-culture that profoundly influenced nineteenth-century moral philosophy. Moreover, he wrote an important indictment of slavery. Although he never aligned himself with the radical abolitionists, he did put his enormous influence behind the antislavery movement and helped to give it philosophical grounding. Channing was revered later in the century by both the radical wing of Unitarianism and the more traditional element of the denomination, who called themselves the "Channing Unitarians." His eloquence in the pulpit, the defense of human dignity at the core of his theology, and his moral example all combined to make his impression on the denomination, and the century, a deep one.

*Bibliography*

A. *A Sermon Delivered at the Ordination of the Rev. Jared Sparks* (Unitarian Christianity) (Baltimore, 1819); *A Discourse on the Evidences of Revealed Religion*, Dudleian Lecture (Boston, 1821); *A Discourse Delivered at the Ordination of the Rev. Frederick A. Farley* (Likeness to God) (Boston, 1828); *Slavery* (Boston, 1835); *Self-Culture* (Boston, 1838); *Works*, 6 vols. (Boston, 1841–43).

B. AAUP, 360–84; DAB 4, 4–8; DARB, 94–95; DLB 1, 21–22; Heralds 2, 118–33; William Henry Channing, *Memoir of William Ellery Channing, with Extracts from His Correspondence and Manuscripts*, 3 vols. (Boston, 1848); John White Chadwick, *William Ellery Channing: Minister of Religion* (Boston, 1903); Madeleine Hooke Rice, *Federal Street Pastor* (New York, 1961); Conrad Wright, *The Liberal Christians* (Boston, 1970); Jack Mendelsohn, *Channing: The Reluctant Radical* (Boston, 1971); Andrew Delbanco, *William Ellery Channing: An Essay on the Liberal Spirit in America* (Cambridge, 1981); David Robinson, "The Legacy of Channing: Culture as a Religious Category in New England Thought," *Harvard Theological Review*, 74 (1981), 221–39.

**CHANNING, WILLIAM HENRY** (25 May 1810, Boston, MA–23 December 1884, London, England). *Education*: A.B., Harvard College, 1829; graduated from Harvard Divinity School, 1833. *Career*: Preaching in the Boston area and in Meadville, PA, 1833–34; travel in Europe, 1835–36; minister-at-large, New York, 1836–37; Unitarian minister, Cincinnati, OH, 1837–41; editor, *Western Messenger*, 1839–41; editor, *Present*, 1843–44; minister, New York, 1843–45; founder, Religious Union of Associationists, 1847–50; editor, *Spirit of the Age*, 1849; minister, Rochester, NY, 1850–52; Unitarian minister, Liverpool, England, 1854–61; Washington, DC, 1861–63; chaplain, U.S. House of Representatives, 1863–64; lived and preached in England, 1866–84.

William Henry Channing was a leader in pre–Civil War social-reform movements and is an exemplar of the social conscience of the Transcendentalist movement. His uncle William Ellery Channing* was a surrogate father to him after he lost his own father, and he graduated from Harvard College (1829) and Divinity School carrying the legacy of his famous uncle. He was attracted to the challenge of the ministry-at-large, as pioneered by Joseph Tuckerman* in Boston, and he moved to New York in 1836 to begin such a ministry to the urban poor there. But with little training and inadequate support, he ended his ministry there in 1837 and moved to a new challenge in the Midwest by accepting a pastorate in Cincinnati in 1839. There he collaborated with James Freeman Clarke* and others on the *Western Messenger*, an important early Transcendentalist and Unitarian periodical. But Channing underwent a spiritual crisis during his western ministry that eventuated in his return to New York, where he established himself as a reform preacher and founded the *Present*, a journal devoted to political ends. He established a close association with the Brook Farm commune and helped move that group toward embracing the ideas of Charles Fourier, until the commune began to collapse after the fire of 1846. In the late 1840s and 1850s his attentions were increasingly drawn to antislavery causes, which he pursued in the Rochester, New York, ministry. But in 1854 he took the pulpit of James Martineau in Liverpool, England. He seems to have found a satisfying place in England after his many moves, and although he returned to the United States during the Civil War, he did not remain but went back to England for the rest of his life. Channing's contribution to Transcendentalism was his attempt to change the individualist emphasis of the movement to one that focused instead on the progress of the human race as a whole.

*Bibliography*

A. *The Present* (periodical, New York) (editor, 1843–44); *Memoir of William Ellery Channing*, 3 vols. (Boston and London, 1848); *The Spirit of the Age* (periodical, New York) (editor, 1849–50).

B. DAB 4, 9–10; DLB 1, 24; Heralds 3, 59–66; O. B. Frothingham, *Memoir of William Henry Channing* (Boston and New York, 1886); Perry Miller, *The Transcendentalists: An Anthology* (Cambridge, MA, 1950); Elizabeth McKinsey, *The Western Experiment: New England Transcendentalists in the Ohio Valley* (Cambridge, 1973); Joel Myerson, *The New England Transcendentalists and the Dial* (Rutherford, NJ, 1980); David Robinson, "The Political Odyssey of William Henry Channing," *American Quarterly*, 34 (1982), 165–84.

**CHAPIN, AUGUSTA JANE** (16 July 1836, Lakeville, NY–30 June 1905, New York, NY). *Education*: Attended Olivet College, Olivet, MI, c. 1852; M.A., University of Michigan, 1884. *Career*: Itinerant preacher, MI, 1859–62; ordained, Lansing, MI, 1863; Universalist minister, Portland, MI, 1864–66; Mt. Pleasant, IA, 1866–69; Iowa City, IA, 1870–74; Pittsburgh, PA, 1875–76; Blue Island, IL, 1876–78; Aurora, IL, 1879; Decatur, MI, 1881–83; Hillsdale, MI, 1884–85; Oak Park, IL, 1886–92; Omaha, NE, 1894–96; Mt. Vernon, NY, 1897–1901; extension lecturer on literature and art, Lombard College, 1886–97; extension lecturer in English, University of Chicago, 1892–97.

Augusta Jane Chapin converted to Universalism while a student at Olivet College—she had earlier been denied admission to the University of Michigan because of her sex—and resolved to make a career of preaching her new faith. She began to do so in Michigan in 1859, facing the double difficulties of being a woman in the pulpit and preaching an unpopular doctrine that had as yet made little headway in that region. But she overcame those difficulties to become one of the earliest women ordained into the Universalist ministry, in 1863. Her career in the ministry consisted of a succession of pulpits primarily in the Midwest but also included many other activities. She eventually did gain admission to Michigan and received a master's degree in 1884. She involved herself in denominational affairs, becoming a prominent participant in Universalist Centennial in 1870. She was active in the Temperance movement, was a founding member of the Association for the Advancement of Women, and was a lecturer in literature for extension programs at Lombard College and the University of Chicago. In addition to engaging in this profusion of activity, she was also an independent lecturer. By her example of accomplishment, she helped to establish a female presence in Universalist leadership and to make that denomination well known for its hospitality to the women's movement.

*Bibliography*

B. NAW 1, 320–21; *Who Was Who in America* 1, 211; George Huntston Williams, "American Universalism: A Bicentennial Historical Essay," JUHS, 9 (1971); Catherine F. Hitchings, "Universalist and Unitarian Women Ministers," JUHS, 10 (1975), 43–44; Russell E. Miller, *The Larger Hope* (Boston, 1979).

**CHAPIN, EDWIN HUBBELL** (29 December 1814, Union Village, NY–26 December 1880, New York, NY). *Career*: Universalist minister, Richmond, VA, 1838–41; Charlestown, MA, 1841–47; associate minister, Second Universalist Church, Boston, 1847–48; minister, Fourth Universalist Church (Church of the Divine Paternity), New York City, 1848–80.

Edwin H. Chapin's oratorical eloquence was the stuff of legends in the nineteenth century. Starr King,* something of a phenomenon for eloquence himself, insisted when sharing a platform with Chapin that he be allowed to speak before Chapin and not after him. Henry Ward Beecher, perhaps Chapin's chief rival for oratorical brilliance, offered this tribute: "It was a trance to sit under him in his ripest and most inspired hours; it was a vision of beauty; the world seemed almost dark and cold for an hour afterward" (Ellis, p. 209). Chapin's biographer Sumner Ellis told of reporters at his speeches who "dropped their pencils in the midst of his stormy passages, and awoke at the close of a lecture, as from an opium dream," realizing that they had taken no notes for their story (pp. 210–11). It was this sort of oratorical power that allowed Chapin to build the Church of the Divine Paternity into one of New York's leading churches. There Chapin preached a broadly Christian version of Universalism, departing from his former colleague in Boston Hosea Ballou* on the question of future punishment. Chapin held that "the effects of sin, at least, are felt in another existence, and that, therefore, misery is produced to those upon whom they operate" (p. 257). But this misery was limited in duration. "Between endless and limited retribution in the future world there is an *infinite* difference," Chapin wrote, and he preached the eventual redemption of all humanity by a merciful God (pp. 258–59). Chapin extended the Universalist idea of the unity of all humanity into the social realm by preaching and lecturing on urban problems and the need for social and philanthropic measures to address them. In *Humanity in the City* he noted the jarring contrasts in urban social conditions and said that "they teach us our duty and our responsibility in lessening social inequality and need" (*Humanity in the City*, p. 23). He depicted the effects of poverty, especially on children, in moving and explicit terms, as a searing of "every fine chord of human nature" through "the darkness of the moral faculties and by the pressure of animal wants" (p. 189). For Chapin, this meant that Christianity was "not merely a theory of existence" but a "*working-power*" (p. 240). This pragmatic sense of religion combined well with his powerful oratory to make Chapin one of the more influential American preachers in the last half of the nineteenth century.

*Bibliography*

A. *Duties of Young Men* (Boston, 1840); *Discourses on Various Subjects* (Boston, 1841); *The Philosophy of Reform* (New York, 1843); *Duties of Young Women* (Boston, 1848); *Moral Aspects of City Life* (New York, 1853); *Humanity in the City* (New York and Boston, 1854); *Christianity the Perfection of True Manliness* (New York and Auburn, NY, 1856); *Lessons of Faith and Life* (New York, 1877).

B. DAB 4, 15; NCAB 6, 89; *Who Was Who in America, Historical Volume*, 101; Sumner Ellis, *Life of Edwin H. Chapin, D.D.* (Boston, 1882); Richard Eddy, *Universalism in America*, vol. 2 (Boston, 1886); Russell E. Miller, *The Larger Hope* (Boston, 1979).

**CHAUNCY, CHARLES** (1 January 1705, Boston, MA–10 February 1787, Boston, MA). *Education*: A.B., A.M., Harvard College, 1721, 1724. *Career*: Minister, First Church of Boston, 1727–87.

Charles Chauncy was a leader of the liberal or Arminian theological movement in New England, the historical progenitor of Unitarianism. After completing his undergraduate education at Harvard in 1721 and being awarded the master's degree in 1724, he was ordained at Boston's First Church in 1727, where he served as minister until his death. For the first forty-two years of that ministry, he served as the colleague of Thomas Foxcroft. He was thrust into prominence, and gained historical importance, in his opposition to the Great Awakening of the 1740s, for out of his opposition of that revival the liberal party in New England theology took shape. In his later years Chauncy became an ardent supporter of the move for national independence. After the war he extended his theological liberalism by publishing his argument for the universalist position that the punishments of hell were not eternal, and that all humanity would be eventually redeemed. He set this argument out in a work entitled *The Mystery Hid from Ages and Generations*, substantially completed in the 1750s and later circulated in manuscript among his friends but not published until 1784. It stands as one of the most interesting and important documents in the early history of American liberal theology.

*Bibliography*

A. *Enthusiasm Describ'd and Caution'd Against* (Boston, 1742); *A Letter from a Gentleman in Boston, to Mr. George Wishart, one of the Ministers of Edinburgh, concerning the State of Religion in New-England* (Edinburgh, 1742); *Seasonable Thoughts on the State of Religion in New England* (Boston, 1743); *The Benevolence of the Deity, Fairly and Impartially Considered* (Boston, 1784); *The Mystery Hid from Ages and Generations* (London, 1784); *Five Dissertations on the Scripture Account of the Fall and Its Consequences* (London, 1785).

B. AAUP, 8–13; DAB 4, 42–43; DARB, 98–99; Heralds 1, 20–34; Conrad Wright, *The Beginnings of Unitarianism in America* (Boston, 1955); James W. Jones, *The Shattered Synthesis: New England Puritanism before the Great Awakening* (New Haven, 1973); Edward M. Griffin, *Old Brick: Charles Chauncy of Boston, 1705–1787* (Minneapolis, 1980); Charles H. Lippy, *Seasonable Revolutionary: The Mind of Charles Chauncy* (Chicago, 1981).

**CHILD, LYDIA MARIA FRANCIS** (11 February 1802, Medford, MA–20 October 1880, Wayland, MA). *Career*: Author, Watertown, MA, 1820–28; schoolkeeper, Watertown, 1825–28; author, Boston, 1828–37; Northampton, MA, 1837–40; editor, *National Anti-Slavery Standard*, New York, 1841–43; author, New York, 1843–50; West Newton, MA, 1850–52; Wayland, MA, 1852–74; Wayland and Boston, 1874–80.

In 1824 Lydia Maria Francis published the novel *Hobomok*, a popular success that launched her lifelong career as an author. She was at the time residing with her brother Convers Francis,* the Unitarian minister in Watertown, Massachusetts, and from that position she met and befriended many Boston and Cambridge intellectuals and reformers. She married reform-minded David Child in 1828 and continued her writing, increasingly recognizing her female audience and offering them works of self-help and advice about "woman's sphere," such as *The Frugal Housewife* (1829) and *The Mother's Book* (1831). Her career became controversial when she wrote a strong antislavery tract, *An Appeal in Favor of That Class of Americans Called Africans* (1833), a work that achieved fame on its own and also influenced William Ellery Channing's* famous *Slavery* (1835). Meanwhile, the financial support of herself and her husband fell increasingly to her, as he failed in an attempt to raise sugar beets as an alternative to southern cane sugar. She edited the *National Anti-Slavery Standard* in the early 1840s as an extension of her antislavery work. Although she was moderate in comparison with many feminists, she advocated women's independence and self-reliance, touching on the questions of women's rights in her *Letters from New York* (1843–45). She also made an early entrance into the study of comparative religion with her *Progress of Religious Ideas through Successive Ages* (1855). As an author, an advocate of women's independence, a historian of religion, and a writer against slavery, Child had an influential and memorable career.

*Bibliography*

A. *Hobomok: A Tale of Early Times* (Boston, 1824); *The Frugal Housewife* (Boston, 1829); *The Mother's Book* (Boston and Baltimore, 1831); *An Appeal in Favor of That Class of Americans Called Africans* (Boston, 1833); *Letters from New-York* (New York and Boston, 1843); *Letters from New York: Second Series* (New York and Boston, 1845); *The Progress of Religious Ideas through Successive Ages* (New York and London, 1855); *The Freedmen's Book* (Boston, 1865); *Lydia Maria Child: Selected Letters, 1817–1880*, ed. Milton Meltzer and Paricia G. Holland (Amherst, MA, 1982).

B. DAB 4, 67–69; DLB 1, 26–37; NAW 1, 330–33; Seth Curtis Beach, *Daughters of the Puritans* (Boston, 1905); Helene G. Baer, *The Heart Is Like Heaven: The Life of Lydia Maria Child* (Philadelphia, 1964); Milton Meltzer, *Tongue of Flame: The Life of Lydia Maria Child* (New York, 1965); William S. Osborne, *Lydia Maria Child* (Boston, 1980).

**CLARKE, JAMES FREEMAN** (4 April 1810, Hanover, NH–8 June 1888, Boston, MA). *Education*: A.B., Harvard, 1829; graduated, Harvard Divinity School, 1833. *Career*: Unitarian minister, Louisville, KY, 1833–40; editor, *Western Messenger*, 1836–39; minister, Church of the Disciples, Boston, 1841–50; convalescence and ministry, Meadville, PA, 1850–53; minister, Church of the Disciples, Boston, 1854–88.

James Freeman Clarke was one of the most important churchmen in nineteenth-century Unitarianism and can be thought of as the most representative figure among the Unitarian clergy and leadership. His enunciation of the "Five

Points of the New Theology" stands as a classic summation of late nineteenth-century Unitarian values: "1. the Fatherhood of God; 2. the Brotherhood of man; 3. the Leadership of Jesus; 4. Salvation by Character, and 5. the Continuity of Human Development . . . or, the Progress of Mankind, onward and upward forever" (*Vexed Questions*, pp. 10–16). Clarke was educated at Harvard and the Harvard Divinity School and took a pastorate in Louisville in 1833, looking on the position as a great opportunity to spread the liberal message in the West. During his years at Harvard he had developed a love for German literature and shared that enthusiasm with Frederic Henry Hedge* and Margaret Fuller.* But in Louisville, Clarke found himself in comparative intellectual isolation and worked hard to combat it through correspondence but especially through his editorship of the *Western Messenger*. It was the earliest Transcendentalist periodical, in that it defended Ralph Waldo Emerson* and published his poetry, but it was also a vehicle for expounding more traditional Unitarian views. Clarke returned to Boston in 1841 to found the Church of the Disciples, a free church that Clarke formed with the hope of bringing together those with common practical goals rather than common theological opinions. This pragmatic strand in Clarke's thinking distanced him from Emersonian Transcendentalism and the later Free Religion movement, because Clarke felt strongly the necessity of church building and organized ethical activity. This aligned him with Hedge and Henry W. Bellows* as the leaders of the "Broad Church" movement in the denomination. Clarke's career in Boston was interrupted in 1850 by poor health, but after recuperating in Meadville at the home of his father-in-law, Harm Jan Huidekoper,* he returned to Boston and resumed his pastorate in 1854. Thereafter came the period of his greatest leadership in denominational affairs, in which he served as American Unitarian Association general secretary, editor of the *Unitarian*, and a leader in the formation of the National Conference. He was also a prolific author in those years, expounding what could be called a practical theology for daily life and writing a study in comparative religion, *Ten Great Religions* (1871–73). Few Unitarians of his day or after have made a larger contribution to Unitarianism.

*Bibliography*

A. *Orthodoxy: Its Truths and Errors* (Boston, 1886); *Steps of Belief* (Boston, 1870); *Ten Great Religions* 2 vols. (Boston, 1871–73); *Self-Culture: Physical, Intellectual, Moral, and Spiritual* (Boston, 1880); *Manual of Unitarian Belief* (Boston, 1884); *Vexed Questions in Theology* (Boston, 1886).

B. DAB 4, 153–54; DARB, 100–102; DLB 1, 27–28; Heralds 3, 67–75; Edward Everett Hale, ed., *James Freeman Clarke: Autobiography, Diary, and Correspondence* (Boston, 1891); John W. Thomas, *James Freeman Clarke: Apostle of German Culture in America* (Boston, 1949); Arthur S. Bolster, Jr., *James Freeman Clarke* (Boston, 1954).

**COBB, SYLVANUS** (17 July 1798, Norway, ME–31 October, 1866, Boston, MA). *Education*: Study with Rev. Sebastian Streeter, Portsmouth, NH, 1820–

21. *Career*: Universalist minister, Winthrop and Waterville, ME, 1821–28; Malden, MA, 1828–38; Waltham, MA, 1838–41; East Boston, MA, 1841–44, 1846–48; founder and editor, *Christian Freeman and Family Visiter*, 1839–62.

Sylvanus Cobb was an early exponent of Universalism in Maine and later an influential minister, theological journalist, legislator, and social reformer in the Boston area. In 1839 he founded the *Christian Freeman and Family Visiter*, a periodical that combined theological writing, religious education, and a clear antislavery perspective. This made him, in Russell Miller's words, "probably the best known and most influential" Universalist social reformer before the Civil War (*The Larger Hope*, p. 302). Cobb founded and guided his paper, as Miller told it, despite opposition from other Universalists like Thomas Whittemore,* who thought it unwise to mix controversial political issues with a denominational newspaper. His career thus exemplifies the identification of Universalism with political reform, which grew throughout the nineteenth century.

*Bibliography*

A. *The Christian Freeman and Family Visiter* (periodical) (editor, 1839–62); *A Compend of Christian Divinity* (Boston, 1846); *The New Testament of Our Lord and Savior Jesus Christ, with Explanatory Notes and Practical Observations* (Boston, 1864); *Autobiography of the First Forty-One Years of the Life of Sylvanus Cobb, D.D., to Which Is Added a Memoir, by His Eldest Son Sylvanus Cobb, Jr.* (Boston, 1867).

B. DAB 4, 245–46; *Autobiography* (see above); Russell E. Miller, *The Larger Hope* (Boston, 1979).

**COLLYER, ROBERT** (8 December 1823, Keighley, England–30 November 1912, New York, NY). *Career*: Apprentice and blacksmith, Ilkley, England, c. 1838–50; Methodist lay preacher, Ilkley, England, 1849–50; immigrated to America, 1850; blacksmith, laborer, and Methodist lay preacher, Shoemakertown, PA, 1850–59; Unitarian minister-at-large, 1859; Unity Church, Chicago, 1859–79; minister, Church of the Messiah, New York, 1879–1903; minister emeritus, 1903–12.

Robert Collyer, the "blacksmith-preacher," lived a life of remarkable variety in which he rose from a youth of child labor in the English cotton mills to the status of one of America's best-loved ministers and lyceum lecturers. His youth was one of grinding poverty in which he began to work fourteen-hour days at the age of eight. At age fourteen he was apprenticed to a blacksmith, following the trade of his father, and he continued that trade through his early manhood. The turning point in his life came in tragedy. His wife died in childbirth, and in his grief over her death, Collyer began to develop a religious sensibility. What began as testimonials to his faith in Methodist meetings led eventually to his becoming a lay preacher. After remarrying, Collyer immigrated to the United States, continuing to work as a blacksmith in a small town near Philadelphia and continuing his lay preaching. Another turning point came for him when he heard the Quaker antislavery crusader Lucretia Mott and was stirred to join the abolitionist cause. This brought him under the influence of Philadelphia Unitarian leader William Henry Furness,* who recognized Collyer's abilities, invited him to preach at his church, and recommended that he take a ministry to the poor that was open in Chicago. Collyer thus launched his ministry as a Unitarian, finding it a relief to give up the dogmatic burdens of Methodism. His natural eloquence made him an effective church builder in Chicago, and he became very well known as a preacher in the 1860s. In addition to being an eloquent preacher, Collyer was enormously successful on the lecture circuit. His lively and anecdotal style, his Yorkshire accent, and his past as a smithy all contributed to that popularity, but his message also found a responsive chord in audiences all over the country. One of his most popular lectures, "Clear Grit," dealt with the fortitude and purpose necessary for a life of fulfillment. "Clear Grit" included, as Collyer described it, a measure of self-denial ("the power to save yourself"), the willingness to help others ("the power to give yourself"), and the ability to act decisively for the right without worrying about the obstacles or consequences to your acts (*Clear Grit*, p. 9). He also counseled a life of contentment in simple tasks and the enjoyment of family and home, advice that was plainly intended to counter the restlessness of American life. The last phase of Collyer's career was a long and influential ministry at the Church of the Messiah in New York, where he was the senior colleague of both Minot J. Savage* and John Haynes Holmes.* American Unitarianism has had few leaders with as unique a combination of talents and experiences as Collyer.

*Bibliography*

A. *Nature and Life* (Boston, 1867); *The Simple Truth* (Boston and New York: 1878); *Father Taylor* (Boston, 1906); *Some Memories* (autobiography) (Boston, 1908); *Thoughts for Daily Living* (Boston, 1911); *Clear Grit: A Collection of Lectures, Addresses and Poems*, ed. John Haynes Holmes (Boston, 1913).

B. DAB 4, 310–11; Heralds 4, 94–103; John Haynes Holmes, *The Life and Letters of Robert Collyer, 1823–1912* (New York, 1917).

**CONE, ORELLO** (16 November 1835, Lincklaen, NY–23 June 1905, Canton, NY). *Education*: Attended the New Woodstock Academy and Cazenovia Seminary, NY, and St. Paul's College, Palmyra, MO. *Career*: Instructor, St. Paul's College, 1858–61; private study, 1861–64; minister, Universalist Church at Little Falls, NY, 1864–65; professor of biblical languages and literature, St. Lawrence University, 1865–80; president, Buchtel College, Akron, OH, 1880–96; study in Europe, 1897–98; minister, Unitarian Church, Lawrence, KS, 1898–99; Richardson Professor of Biblical Theology, St. Lawrence University, 1900–1906.

Orello Cone was the foremost biblical scholar to have been produced by the Universalist denomination and an important contributor as a faculty member to the efforts in theological education made at St. Lawrence University. Cone began his career in the Universalist ministry but soon found a much more suitable life's work when he joined the faculty at St. Lawrence University to teach biblical literature. When he took that position in 1865, he joined Ebenezer Fisher* as the only other member of the theological faculty. While teaching there, he was also a frequent contributor to the *Universalist Quarterly*, establishing his reputation as a scholar. In 1880 he took the presidency of the Universalists' struggling Buchtel College. There he began to publish the works that secured his reputation. *Gospel-Criticism and Historical Christianity* (1891) was an attempt to show how the "critical process" of objective and historical scholarship can be applied to the Gospels and dealt extensively with the problems of the formation of the biblical canon (p. vii). He followed this volume with *The Gospel and Its Earliest Interpretations* (1893), which traced the phases of interpretation of the teachings of Jesus in early Christianity. Cone argued that "the historical study of religion has been greatly impeded by . . . dogmatic interest" that attempted to freeze a particular interpretation into a final truth (p. 2). This he opposed in his work. Although he achieved much as a scholar, Cone's tenure at Buchtel was not wholly successful, in large part due to continuing financial crises there. He resigned in 1896, continuing his scholarly work with *Paul, the Man, the Missionary, and the Teacher* (1898). Cone was a disciple of German biblical scholarship and edited a collection of essays by the German theologian Otto Pfleiderer. He moved from Buchtel to a brief Unitarian pastorate in Lawrence, Kansas, and then returned to St. Lawrence University in 1900 to continue his teaching career.

*Bibliography*

A. *Essays, Doctrinal and Practical* (editor, Boston, 1889); *Gospel-Criticism and Historical Christianity* (New York and London, 1891); *The Gospel and Its Earliest Interpretations* (New York and London, 1893); *Paul, the Man, the Missionary, and the Teacher* (New York and London, 1898); Otto Pfleiderer, *Evolution and Theology and Other Essays*, ed. and trans. O. Cone (London, 1900); *The Epistles to the Hebrews, Colossians, Ephesians, and Philemon* . . . (New York and London, 1901); *Rich and Poor in the New Testament* (New York and London, 1902).

B. DAB 4, 341–43; NCAB 10, 203; *Who Was Who in America* 1, 249; Russell E. Miller, *The Larger Hope* (Boston, 1979).

**COOK, MARIA** (1779–21 December 1835, Geneva, NY). *Career*: Itinerant preacher, Sheshequin, PA, c. 1810; NY, 1811–12.

One wishes that there were more historical information about the life, personality, and message of Maria Cook, who in Russell Miller's words is "generally considered to have been the first woman to have preached in Universalist pulpits" (Miller, p. 546). Based on an 1850 account of her by Nathaniel Stacy, we know that in 1810, when she was about thirty, she held religious meetings for several weeks in Sheshequin, Pennsylvania, and then requested the opportunity to speak at the Universalist Western Association at Bainbridge, New York, in 1811. Her request caused an immense stir, because, as Stacy put it, "some of our brethren and friends were a little fastidious about allowing a woman to preach, supposing St. Paul forbade it" (Eddy, pp. 137–38). Others thought women's work in the pulpit had divine sanction. "But," Stacy continued, "as the phenomenon of a female preacher appearing among us was so *extraordinary*, and curiosity was on tiptoe among the mass of the congregation, to hear a woman preach, our opposing brethren finally withdrew their objections, and she very cheerfully obliged us with a discourse" (p. 138). Conflict, sensation, opposition—all of these burdens that women preachers faced are captured in this account of Cook's attempt to speak. Her address was successful enough, however, to result in her being awarded a letter of fellowship to preach by the association. Cook accepted the letter but destroyed it a few weeks later, feeling that it had not been offered to her in complete and unanimous sincerity. She continued to preach for a year or two after that, drawing large crowds and receiving larger-than-ordinary contributions. But she also met with "vituperations and uncharitable remarks" that led her to the defensive tactic of "long arguments in vindication of her right to preach; which would not infrequently constitute the whole burden of her discourse" (p. 139). As Stacy saw it, this made her sermons "rather stale and uninteresting," and her audiences dwindled (p. 139).

After this period of preaching in New York she continued to travel but preached less. She was later arrested and jailed on a trumped-up vagrancy charge in Cooperstown, New York, by "some malignant spirit, who wanted to spit his venom against Universalism in some form" (p. 140). Cook remained in jail for several weeks, continuing to preach to the prisoners and calmly frustrating the magistrates' attempts to get her "to pay any respect to their authority" (pp. 142–43). Cook eventually gave up preaching, convinced that God's work must be done instead "by organizing an apostolic society—a community of interest, of property" (p. 143). The details of her plans are not known, although she made "a number of efforts to get such a society established" (p. 143). She was probably influenced to an extent by the Shakers, having lived among them for several months in 1811–12. Stacy reported that she lived the last part of her life in retirement, "pretty much secluded from the world" (p. 144). Her courage, her hopes, her successes and failures, although not known in great detail, still provide an important historical paradigm for woman's role in the ministry.

*Bibliography*

B. Nathaniel Stacy, *Memoirs of the Life of Nathaniel Stacy, Preacher of the Gospel of Universal Grace* (Columbus, PA, 1850); Richard Eddy, *Universalism in America: A History*, 2 vols. (Boston, 1884–86) (Eddy reprinted Stacy's discussion of Cook); Russell E. Miller, *The Larger Hope* (Boston, 1979).

**CORNISH, LOUIS CRAIG** (18 April 1870, New Bedford, MA–7 January 1950, Orlando, FL). *Education*: Attended Harvard, 1889–91; 1892–93; A.B.,

Stanford, 1894; A.M., Harvard, 1899. *Career*: Secretary to William Lawrence, Episcopal bishop of MA, 1894–98; Unitarian minister, First Parish Church, Hingham, MA, 1900–1915; secretary-at-large, American Unitarian Association (AUA), 1915–25; administrative vice-president, AUA, 1925–27; president, AUA, 1927–37; president, International Association for Liberal Christianity and Religious Freedom, 1937–46.

With the resignation of Samuel Atkins Eliot* from the presidency of the AUA in 1927, leadership of the Unitarian denomination fell to Louis Craig Cornish, formerly a minister at Hingham and a member of the AUA administrative staff under Eliot. To follow a strong administrative leader such as Eliot would be no easy chore for anyone, but Cornish's role was made more difficult by his temperamentally cautious nature and by the disastrous effects of the Depression on Unitarian finances and morale. Cornish came into the presidency with a solid reputation for leadership in international religious affairs. In the early 1920s he had led an investigation of the persecution of religious minorities, including Unitarians, in Transylvania. His great ability and passion as AUA president lay in cultivating international relationships among liberal religions, and he traveled extensively in this cause. The sense of Unitarianism and Universalism as "world religions" had been growing in both denominations since the late nineteenth century, and Cornish attempted to realize these dreams in more substantial terms. But tragically, the international religious integration he sought was blunted by the rising tensions leading to World War II. On the domestic front Cornish presided over a denomination beset with financial woes and decreasing morale. "The history of the denomination in these years is strewn with missed opportunities," David Parke has written, and he offered evidence to suggest that both financial problems and failures in leadership account for this (Wright, pp. 114–24). Cornish's administration ended following the report of the Commission of Appraisal in 1936, and he continued his work for international religious cooperation in the decade after his retirement from the AUA presidency.

*Bibliography*

A. *Transylvania in 1922* (Boston, 1923); *The Religious Minorities in Transylvania* (Boston, 1925); *Work and Dreams and the Wide Horizon* (Boston, 1937); *The Phillipines Calling* (Philadelphia, 1942); *Transylvania: The Land Beyond the Forest* (Philadelphia, 1947).

B. NCAB 38, 240–41; *Who Was Who in America* 2, 129; Frances E.F. Cornish, *Louis Craig Cornish, Interpreter of Life* (Boston, c. 1953); Conrad Wright, ed., *A Stream of Light* (Boston, 1975).

**CRANCH, CHRISTOPHER PEARSE** (8 March 1832, Alexandria, VA–20 January 1892, Cambridge, MA). *Education*: B.A., Columbian College (now George Washington University), 1831; graduated, Harvard Divinity School, 1835. *Career*: Unitarian supply preacher, New England, 1835–36; Ohio Valley, 1836–39; New England and New York, 1839–42; author and painter, 1842–92.

Christopher Pearse Cranch is a good representative of the aesthetic, as opposed to the religious or literary, sensibility among the New England Transcendentalists. He studied at Harvard Divinity School during the early days of the Transcendentalist ferment and then began to preach in various Unitarian pulpits, moving to the Ohio Valley in 1836. There he lent a hand to James Freeman Clarke* in the production of the *Western Messenger*, an important early Unitarian and Transcendentalist periodical. In that journal Cranch praised Ralph Waldo Emerson's* "American Scholar" address and defended the religious motivation of the Transcendentalist movement. As a result of his Transcendental leanings, Cranch thought that many pulpits and professional opportunities were closed to him, because he was not on "the list of *safe* men" in the eyes of the American Unitarian Association. "I have the misfortune to have associated with Emerson, Ripley & those corrupters of youth," he noted wryly, "and have written for the *Dial*, and these are unpardonable offenses" (Myerson, "Transcendentalism," pp. 366–67). Cranch had begun to write poetry by this time and found encouragement from Emerson, who saw to the publication of some poems in the *Dial*. But Cranch was unhappy as a preacher and in the early 1840s took a new interest in painting. He became a good landscape artist and combined that with a continuing interest in poetry, translation, children's stories, and literary criticism. The Cranches spent several periods in Italy and France, where he painted and they became part of an American expatriate presence in Europe. Perhaps his most historically memorable work, however, was a series of mildly satirical caricatures of the "New Philosophy" of Transcendentalism that he drew in the 1830s and circulated among his friends. The drawings of Emerson as a "transparent eyeball" and a pumpkin, based on passages from Emerson's *Nature*, have become well known to students of American literature.

*Bibliography*

A. *Poems* (Philadelphia, 1844); *The Last of the Huggermuggers: A Giant Story* (Boston, 1856); *Kobboltozo: A Sequel to the Last of the Huggermuggers* (Boston, 1857); translator, *The Aeneid of Virgil* (Boston, 1872); *Satan: A Libretto* (Boston, 1874); *The Bird and the Bell, with Other Poems* (Boston, 1875); *Ariel and Caliban, with Other Poems* (Boston, 1887).

B. DAB 4, 501–2; DLB 1, 29–30; Leonora Cranch Scott, *The Life and Letters of Christopher Pearse Cranch* (Boston, 1917); F. DeWolfe Miller, *Christopher Pearse Cranch and His Caricatures of New England Transcendentalism* (Cambridge, 1951); Perry Miller, *The Transcendentalists: An Anthology* (Cambridge, 1951); Joel Myerson, "Transcendentalism and Unitarianism in 1840: A New Letter by C. P. Cranch," *CLA Journal*, 16 (1973), 366–68; David Robinson, "The Career and Reputation of Christopher Pearse Cranch: An Essay in Biography and Bibliography," in *Studies in the American Renaissance, 1978*, ed. Joel Myerson (Boston, 1978); Joel Myerson, *The New England Transcendentalists and the Dial* (Rutherford, NJ, 1980).

**CROTHERS, SAMUEL McCHORD** (7 June 1857, Oswego, IL–9 November 1927, Cambridge, MA). *Education*: Graduated from Wittenberg College, 1873; A.B., Princeton, 1874; graduated from Princeton Theological Seminary, 1877; attended Harvard Divinity School, 1882. *Career*: Presbyterian minister, Eureka and Gold Hill, NE, 1877–79; Santa Barbara, CA, 1879–81; converted to Unitarianism, 1881; Unitarian minister, Brattleboro, VT, 1882–86; St. Paul, MN, 1886–94; First Parish Church, Cambridge, MA, 1894–1927.

Of Scottish Presbyterian ancestry and trained at Princeton Theological Seminary, Samuel M. Crothers began a promising career in the Presbyterian ministry. But in 1881, during his pastorate in Santa Barbara, he came to admit that his liberal views had outgrown Presbyterian doctrine, and he became Unitarian. Several influential Unitarian pastorates followed for him, notably his long ministry in Cambridge. Crothers began to achieve national prominence, however, not as a preacher but as a lecturer and essayist. A temperamentally shy man, Crothers was able to fashion in his essays a mood of remarkable intimacy with his hearers, an authorial ideal that he had propounded in his best-known essay "The Gentle Reader." There Crothers wondered "What has become of the Gentle Reader?" (*The Gentle Reader*, p. 1). To Crothers, it seemed a great loss that the Gentle Reader was being supplanted by "the Intelligent Reading Public," and his defense of the dying art of reading for pleasure was characteristic of the combination of a bemused tone and a serious thrust in his essays (p. 1). Irony was his chief literary tactic, as his memorable enumeration of "The Honorable Points of Ignorance" demonstrates. Crothers amusingly took the side of the bewildered nonspecialist and recognized that "on this minute division of intellectual labor the exact sciences thrive, but conversation, poetry, art, and all that belongs to the humanities languish" (p. 164). The defense of ignorance thus became the defense of honest unpretentiousness: "To say 'I do not know' is not nearly as painful as it seems to those who have not tried it" (pp. 165–66). Crothers's essays were contributions to American literature, but his religious outlook was not unrelated to them. In a series of lectures in 1913, he defined "Ethics, Religion, Art, Science, Politics, Industry" as "phases of one great struggle for the liberation of humanity" (*Three Lords of Destiny*, p. 4). This struggle for the individual could be delineated in the successive spiritual steps of courage (the faith to do good), skill (the ability to do it), and love (the setting of objectives beyond our personal good). For Crothers, these "Three Lords of Destiny" constituted the earned liberty that was the core of the religious life.

*Bibliography*

A. *The Gentle Reader* (Boston and New York, 1903); *The Endless Life* (Boston and New York, 1905); *Among Friends* (Boston and New York, 1910); *Three Lords of Destiny* (Boston and New York, 1913); *The Dame School of Experience* (Boston and New York, 1920); *The Cheerful Giver* (Boston and New York, 1923).

B. DAB 4, 572–73; Heralds 4, 107–10; NCAB 22, 384–85.

**CUMMINS, ROBERT** (1897, Sydney, OH–3 April 1982, Brunswick, ME). *Education*: B.A., Miami University (Ohio); M.A., University of Cincinnati; Th.M., University of California. *Career*: Universalist minister, educator, Bangkok, Thailand; Milford, Newton, and Montgomery, OH; Cincinnati, OH, 1926–32; Throop Memorial Universalist Church, Pasadena, CA, 1932–38; general superintendent, Universalist Church of America, 1938–53.

Robert Cummins led the Universalist Church as its general superintendent during the difficult period around World War II. This period of leadership followed previous work as a teacher in Thailand and a Universalist minister in several American pastorates. Cummins had a major interest in the institutional development of Universalist religion and understood the sound business principles necessary to that task. Philip R. Giles* called him "the modern architect of organized Universalism" and noted that his broad sense of the meaning of Universalism was resisted by some but made him an inspirational leader to many (p. 207). In the middle 1940s Cummins led a failed effort to gain admission of the Universalist Church into the Federal Council of Churches. George H. Williams* called attention to this effort of Universalism to unite itself with other Protestant denominations as one of "three denominational options left for faltering Universalism" in the middle twentieth century (Williams, "Dimensions of Faith," p. 3). Cummins was head of the Universalist Church when the first movement toward merger with Unitarianism in the early 1950s began.

*Bibliography*

A. *Excluded: The Story of the Council of Churches and the Universalists* (Boston, 1964).

B. George H. Williams, "American Universalism: A Bicentennial Historical Essay," JUHS, 9 (1971); Williams, "Dimensions of Faith: The Universalist Way," *Unitarian Universalist World*, 13 (June 15, 1982), 1, 3; Philip R. Giles, "Robert Cummins," in *Unitarian Universalist Association Directory, 1983* (Boston, 1983), 207–8.

# D

---

**DAVIES, ARTHUR POWELL** (5 June 1902, Birkenhead, England–26 September 1957, Washington, DC). *Education*: B.D., Richmond College, University of London, 1925. *Career*: Minister, Becontree Methodist Central Hall, Ilford, England, 1925–28; Methodist Churches of Goodwin's Mills and Clark's Mills, ME, 1928–29; Pine Street Methodist Church, Portland, ME, 1929–32; converted to Unitarianism, 1932; minister, Community Church (Unitarian), Summit, NJ, 1933–44; All Souls Church (Unitarian), Washington, DC, 1944–57.

The Unitarian denomination underwent a remarkable resurgence in the post–World War II period, gaining in membership, influence, and vitality. One of the major contributors to this important phase of the denomination's history was A. Powell Davies. He was an eloquent preacher and a prolific author, and as minister in Washington, D.C., at All Souls Church, he exerted a leadership among Unitarians in national affairs. Davies was born near Liverpool and was raised a Methodist. At age seventeen he decided to train for the Methodist ministry, beginning as a lay preacher. His education was postponed because of World War I, and after the war he had some involvement with the trade union movement. But he entered the theological school of the University of London and, after graduating in 1925, took his first pastorate in Ilford, a London suburb. In 1928, because of a lifelong fascination with America, Davies moved to the United States, taking Methodist pulpits in Maine before converting to Unitarianism in 1932. Davies was attracted to the noncreedal tradition of the denomination. He made a large impact on Unitarianism through his work with Unitarian Advance, an organization dedicated to furthering the influence and numerical growth of the denomination. Davies's long interest in international affairs, about which he often preached, resulted in his *American Destiny* (1942), a book that gained him national prominence. William O. Douglas offered this succinct summary of Davies's argument: "America . . . must take the leadership in a world which has become a single, vast, reluctant community" (Douglas, p. 20). In 1944 Davies moved to an enormously successful pastorate of All Souls Church, preaching to overflow congregations and continuing his writing. There his political influence could be felt not only in his preaching but in his part in founding the Americans for Democratic Action, his work for civilian control of atomic energy, and his opposition to the witchhunting of the McCarthy era. His sudden death in 1957 cut short his career while his influence and stature were still great. He set the tone, in many ways, for that strand of liberal religion that has found its most effective outlet in national political affairs—a strand that has grown since Davies's death.

*Bibliography*

A. *American Destiny* (Boston, 1942); *The Faith of an Unrepentant Liberal* (Boston, 1946); *America's Real Religion* (Boston, 1949); *Man's Vast Future: A Definition of Democracy* (New York, 1951); *The Temptation to Be Good* (New York, 1952); *The Urge to Persecute* (Boston, 1953); *The Meaning of the Dead Sea Scrolls* (New York, 1956); *The First Christian: A Study of St. Paul and Christian Origins* (New York, 1957).

B. *Who Was Who in America* 3, 210; William O. Douglas, ed., *The Mind and Faith of A. Powell Davies* (Garden City, NY, 1959).

**DEAN, PAUL** (1789, Barnard, NY–10 October 1860, Framingham, MA). *Career*: Associate minister, First Universalist Church, Boston, 1813–15; minister, 1815–23; Bulfinch Street Church (Universalist, changing to Unitarian), 1823–40; editor, *Independent Messenger*, 1835–38; editor, *The Restorationist*, 1837–c. 1839; retirement, 1840–60.

In 1813 Paul Dean became the associate of the aged John Murray* of the First Universalist Church in Boston, and at Murray's death in 1815 he assumed the pastorate of this most influential of Universalist Churches. But Dean's apparent ascendancy to denominational leadership was thwarted by the call to Boston in 1817 of Hosea Ballou,* who as minister of the Second Universalist Church quickly became the denomination's leader. To complicate this professional rivalry, there was a deep theological disagreement between the two men. Dean dissented vigorously from Ballou's rejection of all future punishment and insisted on a limited but real suffering for sinners after death. This became the "Restorationist" position in what was to be the major schism in the early history of Universalism. Dean's position may in fact have been the opinion of a majority of Universalists, but he did not find complete sympathy from his congregation in his opposition to Ballou. In 1823 he withdrew from the First Universalist Church, taking part of the congregation with him, and became minister of another Universalist church at Bulfinch Street. He also formally withdrew from Universalist fellowship but rejoined the denomination in 1824. Dean's discontent had not ended, however. He was a leader in the move of several

Universalist clergy to establish a new denomination, the Restorationists. The movement splintered from Universalism in the late 1830s, finding in Adin Ballou* a spokesman and organizer, but by 1841 it had largely exhausted itself. Dean gradually faded from prominence among the Universalists and became Unitarian, but he was eased from his pulpit in 1840. By one report, Dean "retired broken in hopes, in spirit, in mind, and in health, from the Christian ministry" (quoted in Miller, p. 126). He did serve later for some period as minister of the Unitarian Church at Easton, Massachusetts. His efforts to point the denomination away from the leadership of Ballou and even to aid in forming a new sect were failures.

*Bibliography*

A. *A Course of Lectures in Defence of the Final Restoration* (Boston, 1832).

B. Francis S. Drake, *Dictionary of American Biography, Including Men of the Time* (Boston, 1879), p. 258; *Appleton's Cyclopedia of American Biography* (New York, 1900), 2, 115; A. A. Miner, "The Century of Universalism," in *Memorial History of Boston*, ed. Justin Winsor, 4 vols. (Boston, 1882), 3, 483–508; Richard Eddy, *Universalism in America: A History*, 2 vols. (Boston, 1884–86); Russell E. Miller, *The Larger Hope* (Boston, 1979).

**DE BENNEVILLE, GEORGE** (26 July 1703, London, England–March, 1793, Germantown, PA). *Career*: Itinerant preacher of Universalism, France, c. 1720–22; arrested, imprisoned, and almost executed, 1722; itinerant preacher of Universalism, Germany and Holland, c. 1722–41; physician and preacher, Germantown, PA, 1741–93.

In his youth George de Benneville was tortured by a vision of himself "burning as a firebrand in hell," convinced that his sins "were too many and too great to be forgiven" (*Life and Trance*, p. 75). Only a vision of Jesus directly interceding with the Father to save his soul was able to liberate him from his fear, and that vision gave him a sense not only of his own salvation but of the salvation of the whole world. De Benneville's conversion had made him a Universalist. These early experiences occurred in England, where de Benneville's French Huguenot parents had come to escape religious persecution. De Benneville himself took his message back to France, where he preached Universalism in defiance of the authorities and was arrested and condemned to death. A reprieve for him came after he had actually been brought to the guillotine. After further imprisonment he went to Germany and Holland, living and preaching with a pietist group for some two decades. In 1741 he went to America, settling among German pietists who held Universalist views near Philadelphia. There he served as both a physician and preacher. He has been accorded the historical distinction of being the first preacher of Universalism in America, and although he was not a founder of churches, he did influence Elhanan Winchester,* a leading early Universalist preacher. In particular, he arranged the publication of Paul Siegvolck's *Everlasting Gospel*, a book that was instrumental in converting

Winchester. De Benneville's intensely mystical pietism suggests the deep impact of experiential religion in the founding of the American Universalist movement.

*Bibliography*

A. *A True and Remarkable Account of the Life and Trance of Dr. George De Benneville* (1800), reedited by Ernest Cassara, JUHS, 2 (1960–61), 71–87.

B. David A. Johnson, "George de Benneville and the Heritage of the Radical Reformation," JUHS, 9 (1969–70), 25–43; Russell E. Miller, *The Larger Hope* (Boston, 1979).

**DIETRICH, JOHN HASSLER** (14 January 1878, Chambersburg, PA–22 July 1957, Berkeley, CA). *Education*: B.A., Franklin and Marshall College, 1900; M.A., Franklin and Marshall College, 1902; graduated from Eastern Theological Seminary (Reformed Church), Lancaster, PA, 1905. *Career*: Minister, St. Mark's Church, (Reformed), Pittsburgh, PA, 1905–11; entered the Unitarian ministry, 1911; minister, First Unitarian Society, Spokane, WA, 1911–16; First Unitarian Society, Minneapolis, MN, 1916–38; minister emeritus, 1938–57.

John H. Dietrich was one of the founders and major spokesmen for the Humanist movement in early twentieth-century Unitarianism. His intellectual and spiritual life began on conservative grounds, however, with his upbringing and early ministry in the Reformed Church. During his seminary training and first pastorate in Pittsburgh, Dietrich found it increasingly difficult to speak his mind on theological issues without encountering the creedal restraints of his church. After a long conflict with conservative elements that led eventually to his defrocking on charges of heresy, Dietrich entered the Unitarian ministry and began to articulate the Humanist message that became such an important aspect of the dialogue of modern liberalism. Word of his unusual preaching at his first Unitarian pulpit in Spokane reached Charles F. Potter,* then at Edmonton, Alberta, who was moving in the same direction as Dietrich. After Dietrich moved to Minneapolis, he met Curtis Reese* of Des Moines and found support for his convictions. During the 1920s and 1930s Dietrich made the pulpit of the First Unitarian Church in Minneapolis a major locus for the dissemination of Humanist thought. His *Humanist Pulpit* series distributed published versions of his sermons and made his ideas available to a wider audience. He saw a major part of his mission as the reinvigoration of intellectual preaching: when preaching "has fallen into almost unparalleled contempt, [I] have done all that I can to dignify, magnify, and glorify it" ("Ten Years in a Free Pulpit," p. 11). He must have had some success, for he continually filled his church to overcrowding to hear his lengthy discourses.

Dietrich claimed the distinction of being the first Unitarian minister to have preached Humanism regularly and "attempted something like a reconstruction of religion in harmony with it" (p. 6). His religion was naturalistic, heavily influenced by evolution and bounded by science. "If human life is to have meaning we must give it that meaning,'' he wrote in 1934, an indication of how far the radical impulse of liberal religion had traveled in the early twentieth century ("What I Believe," *Humanist Pulpit*, 7 [1934], p. 174).

*Bibliography*

A. *The Fathers of Evolution and Other Addresses* (Minneapolis, 1927); *The Significance of the Unitarian Movement* (Boston, 1927); *The Humanist Pulpit*, 7 vols. (Minneapolis, 1927–34); *Humanism* (Boston, 1934).

B. *Who Was Who in America* 6, 112–13; "Ten Years in a Free Pulpit" (autobiographical), in *Humanist Pulpit*, vol. 1 (Minneapolis, 1927); Carleton Winston, *This Circle of Earth: The Story of John H. Dietrich* (New York, 1942); Charles H. Lyttle, *Freedom Moves West* (Boston, 1952); Mason Olds, *Religious Humanism in America: Dietrich, Reese, and Potter* (Washington, DC, 1978).

**DOUTHIT, JASPER LEWIS** (10 October 1834, Shelbyville, IL–11 June 1927, Shelbyville, IL). *Education*: Studied at Wabash College; graduated from Meadville Theological School, 1867. *Career*. Circuit preacher and founder of several Unitarian churches, Shelbyville, IL, area, 1861–1927; editor, *Our Best Words*, 1880–c. 1919.

Jasper Douthit was a frontier circuit-riding preacher and church builder in Illinois in the late nineteenth century, a pattern of life and career usually found among the evangelical Protestant denominations. But Douthit was a Unitarian, attracted to the denomination in the early 1860s by its creedal freedom and the antislavery reputation of James Freeman Clarke* and Theodore Parker.* Douthit preached a relatively conservative and Christ-centered brand of Unitarianism, a stance that made him one of the key opponents of the theological radicalism of many other western *Unity* men like Jenkin Lloyd Jones* and William Channing Gannett.* Douthit began his career as an independent preacher, organizing a church near Shelbyville in 1861 and becoming ordained as a Unitarian in 1862. He later attended Meadville Theological School and returned to the Shelbyville area to continue his lifelong ministry. As the Western Unitarian Conference became increasingly modernist in its theological outlook under the leadership of Jones, Douthit increased his dissent, founding the periodical *Our Best Words* to compete with Jones's *Unity*. Douthit could not countenance the increasing distance that the *Unity* men put between Unitarianism and a Christianity centering upon Christ and the Father. For him, an "ethical basis" was not enough. Douthit's form of western, grass-roots, evangelical Unitarianism was rare in the denomination, and his voice was distinctive.

*Bibliography*

A. *Our Best Words* (periodical, Shelbyville, IL) (editor, 1880–c. 1919); *Jasper Douthit's Story: The Autobiography of a Pioneer* (Boston, 1909).

B. *Heralds* 4, 120–21; NCAB 14, 510; *Who Was Who in America* 4, 261; *Autobiography* (see above); Charles H. Lyttle, *Freedom Moves West* (Boston, 1952).

# E

**EDDY, RICHARD** (21 June 1828, Providence, RI–16 August 1906, Gloucester, MA). *Education*: Studied at Clinton Liberal Institute, Clinton, NY, c. 1848. *Career*: Universalist minister, Rome, NY; Buffalo, NY; Philadelphia, PA; and Canton, NY, c. 1848–61; military chaplain, 1861–63; librarian, Pennsylvania Historical Society, 1864–68; minister, Franklin, MA; Gloucester, MA; and Akron, OH, 1868–81; president, Universalist Historical Society, 1876–1906; minister, Gloucester, MA, 1881 until retirement; editor, *Universalist Quarterly*, 1886–91.

Russell E. Miller called Richard Eddy "the leading nineteenth-century historian of Universalism," and anyone who has consulted his still-useful two-volume *Universalism in America: A History* (1884–86) will certainly confirm Miller's judgment (Miller, p. 285). Eddy held a number of pastorates before the Civil War and then served as a chaplain in the Sixtieth New York Regiment. He worked as librarian of the Pennsylvania Historical Society after the war but returned to the ministry and to his historical work. In 1876 he was elected president of the Universalist Historical Society, a post he held until the end of his life. His history of Universalism brought a more orderly view to the history of the movement in its first century in America than had previously existed, and his work has only recently been superseded in the work of George Huntston Williams* and Russell E. Miller. Eddy also served as editor of the *Universalist Quarterly*, the most scholarly Universalist periodical. He was also active in the temperance reform movement and wrote a history of "intemperance in all ages" (*Alcohol in History*, 1887) as part of that cause.

*Bibliography*

A. *History of the Sixtieth Regiment New York State Volunteers* (Philadelphia, 1864); *Universalism in America: A History*, 2 vols. (Boston, 1884–86); *Alcohol in History:*

An Account of Intemperance in All Ages (New York, 1887); The Life of Thomas J. Sawyer . . . and of Caroline M. Sawyer (Boston and Chicago, 1900).

B. Appleton's Cyclopedia of American Biography (New York, 1900), 2, 300–301; Who Was Who in America 1, 357; Russell E. Miller, The Larger Hope (Boston, 1979).

**ELIOT, FREDERICK MAY** (15 September 1889, Boston, MA–17 February 1958, Boston, MA). Education: A.B., Harvard College, 1911; A.M., Harvard College, 1912; S.T.B., Harvard Divinity School, 1915. Career: Associate minister, First Parish in Cambridge, MA, 1915–17; minister, Unity Church, St. Paul, MN, 1917–38; president, American Unitarian Association, 1937–58.

Frederick May Eliot was the leading churchman of twentieth-century American Unitarianism. He was an active parish minister, religious thinker and denominational worker during his ministry at the Unity Church in St. Paul. But his real rise to prominence came when he headed the American Unitarian Association (AUA) Commission of Appraisal, which issued its historic report Unitarians Face a New Age in 1936. The report both identified the current weaknesses in the Unitarian denomination and made specific recommendations for reform, but perhaps its most significant outcome was to make Eliot's leadership qualities clear to the denomination. He assumed the AUA presidency thereafter and led a revival of both the body and spirit of the denomination. Although hospitable to the Humanist movement of the 1920s and 1930s, and even taken by many to be a Humanist, Eliot argued eloquently for a nondogmatic theism, based on an understanding of the word God as symbolic of the deepest human needs and strivings. He envisioned a growing, universal liberal church and worked toward the first step in that direction, a Unitarian and Universalist merger, which was accomplished after his death.

*Bibliography*

A. Fundamentals of the Unitarian Faith (St. Paul, MN, 1926); Toward Belief in God (St. Paul, MN, 1928); Frederick May Eliot: An Anthology, ed. Alfred P. Stiernotte (Boston, 1959).

B. Wallace W. Robbins, "Frederick May Eliot, (1889–1958)," in Frederick May Eliot: An Anthology, ed. Alfred P. Stiernotte; Carol R. Morris, "The Election of Frederick May Eliot to the Presidency of the A.U.A.," PUHS, 17, 1 (1970–72), 1–45; Conrad Wright, ed., A Stream of Light (Boston, 1975).

**ELIOT, SAMUEL ATKINS** (24 August 1862, Cambridge, MA–15 October 1950, Boston, MA). Education: A.B., Harvard, 1884; A.M. 1889. Career: Missionary minister, Seattle, WA, 1887–88; minister, Unity Church, Denver, CO, 1889–93; Church of the Saviour, Brooklyn, NY, 1893–98; secretary, American Unitarian Association (AUA), 1898–1900; president, AUA, 1900–27; minister, Arlington Street Church, Boston, 1927–35; minister emeritus, 1935–50.

When he was elected secretary of the AUA in 1898, Samuel A. Eliot began the work of reorganizing and solidifying it, an undertaking that would stand as his major life's work and his most important contribution to the denomination. With the later AUA president Frederick May Eliot,* Samuel Eliot stands as one of the most important administrative talents in twentieth-century Unitarian history. Eliot's Boston Unitarian roots were deep. One grandfather had been mayor of Boston and a leader in founding the AUA, and another had been minister of Boston's King's Chapel. His father, Charles William Eliot, served as president of Harvard University. Eliot decided against possible careers in law and business in early manhood, entering Harvard Divinity School in 1885 and later becoming missionary to Seattle. After extremely successful pastorates in Denver and Brooklyn, Eliot took the post of AUA secretary, which was then the chief administrative post of the organization. In his reorganization efforts, he turned the AUA presidency into the central administrative position and began to assert strong leadership after he assumed that role. He put the AUA on a sound financial footing with effective business practices and used AUA resources in a successful campaign of loans and grants to build new congregations nationwide. Bostonian by heritage, Eliot was national in his outlook for Unitarianism, in part because of his early western ministries and later extensive travel. All of these activities for denominational strength and expansion grew out of Eliot's conviction of the importance of the institutional embodiment of liberal values in the church. As he had begun his career as a pastor, he ended it as minister of the Arlington Street Church in Boston.

*Bibliography*

A. *Biographical History of Massacuhsetts* (editor, Boston, 1909); *Heralds of a Liberal Faith*, 3 vols. (editor, Boston, 1910); *A History of Cambridge, Massachusetts* (Cambridge, MA, 1913).

B. NCAB 12, 46–47; Henry Wilder Foote, " 'Always Young for Liberty!' " *Christian Register*, 130 (April 1951), 11–12; Conrad Wright, ed., *A Stream of Light*, (Boston, 1975). Virgil E. Murdock, *The Institutional History of the American Unitarian Association*, Minns Lectures, 1975–76 (Boston, 1975); Arthur Cushman McGiffert, Jr., *Pilot of a Liberal Faith: Samuel Atkins Eliot, 1862–1950* (Boston, 1976).

**ELIOT, THOMAS LAMB** (13 October 1841, St. Louis, MO–26 April 1936, Portland, OR). *Education*: B.A., Washington University, 1862; graduated from Harvard Divinity School, 1865. *Career*: Minister-at-large, St. Louis, MO, 1862–64; associate minister, Church of the Messiah (Unitarian), St. Louis, MO, 1865–66; minister, First Unitarian Society, Portland, OR, 1867–93; minister emeritus, 1893–1936; founder, Reed College, Portland, OR, 1911.

Thomas Lamb Eliot followed the example of his father, William Greenleaf Eliot,* in moving west as a Unitarian missionary pastor. His father had gone to Boston from St. Louis in 1834, and Thomas was born there, graduating from the newly formed Washington University in 1862. After study at the Harvard Divinity School and ministerial work with his father, he accepted a call to a newly formed Unitarian church in Portland, Oregon. Arriving in Portland in 1867, he continued there for the remainder of his life, building a strong church and making an enormous impact on the cultural and political development of the city. The strength of his ministry in Portland made his church the bedrock of Pacific Northwest Unitarianism and one of the principal centers of Unitarian activity on the West Coast. He also served on numerous public boards and projects in Portland, helping to found the Library Association and Art Association there. After his retirement from his ministry, he was the leader in founding Reed College in 1911.

*Bibliography*

B. Heralds 4, 125–30; Earl Morse Wilbur, *Thomas Lamb Eliot, 1841–1936* (Portland, OR, 1936); John Frederick Scheck, "Transplanting a Tradition: Thomas Lamb Eliot and the Unitarian Conscience in the Pacific Northwest, 1865–1905" (Ph.D. diss., University of Oregon, 1969).

**ELIOT, WILLIAM GREENLEAF** (5 August 1811, New Bedford, MA–23 January 1887, Pass Christian, MS). *Education*: B.A., Columbian College, 1830; graduated from Harvard Divinity School, 1834. *Career*: Minister, Church of the Messiah (Unitarian), St. Louis, MO, 1834–73; founder, Washington University, 1854; chancellor, Washington University, 1872–87.

William Greenleaf Eliot was one of the early exponents of New England Unitarianism in the Midwest, and his long ministry in St. Louis constitutes an important phase in the development of western Unitarianism. After completion of studies at Harvard Divinity School in 1834, he was ordained at William Ellery Channing's* Federal Street Church in Boston and soon left for what would be his lifetime post in St. Louis, declaring as he went that he intended to stay permanently in the Midwest. He was a powerful church administrator and community organizer and became an important public figure in Missouri. He was instrumental in aligning Missouri with the Union in the Civil War and founded the Western Sanitary Commission to aid the Union cause, following Henry W. Bellows's* example with the U.S. Sanitary Commission. He was a major spokesman for a conservative and Christologically oriented Unitarianism in the West, in opposition to the more radical religion that characterized the Western Unitarian Conference later in the century. He was primarily an educator in the latter part of his career, founding and guiding Washington University in St. Louis.

*Bibliography*

B. DAB 6, 82–83; Heralds 3, 90–98; Charlotte C. Eliot, *William Greenleaf Eliot, Minister, Educator, Philanthropist* (Boston and New York, 1904).

**EMERSON, RALPH WALDO** (25 May 1803, Boston, MA–27 April 1882, Concord, MA). *Education*: A.B., Harvard College, 1821; theological study,

Harvard Divinity School, 1825–26. *Career:* Minister, Second Church, Boston, 1829–32; independent lecturer and author, 1833–82.

Ralph Waldo Emerson was the leader of the Transcendentalist movement in New England and is arguably the most important American cultural figure of the nineteenth century. His father, William Emerson, was the minister of the First Church in Boston but died during Emerson's youth. Despite severe financial problems, young Emerson was able to attend Harvard College, and he graduated in 1821. After a period of schoolkeeping and theological study, he was called to be Henry Ware, Jr.,'s* assistant at Boston's Second Church in 1828, assuming the pastorate in 1830. He found preaching to his liking, but little else in the job appealed to him. After his wife's death, he resigned his pastorate, his congregation being unable to grant his request not to administer the Lord's Supper. After a tour of Europe, he launched a career as an independent lecturer in 1833, although he continued to preach in East Lexington, Massachusetts, for several years. His first book, *Nature* (1836), propounded an intuitional and idealistic system of religion based upon the monistic unity of God, nature, and the human soul. He continued to develop and enunciate this message in lectures, essays, and poems, which were met with enthusiasm by many of the young but skepticism by others. His Divinity School Address at Harvard (1838) criticized the historical Christianity of Andrews Norton* and other Unitarians and caused a storm of controversy, although Emerson was always unwilling to debate his opponents or extend the theological dispute. His reputation grew in both religious and literary circles, and in the 1840s and 1850s he seemed to complement his youthful message with much pragmatic wisdom, always keeping the moral life and the necessity for the continuing culture of the soul as fundamental premises. His thought continues to be influential in the twentieth century, and he is generally acknowledged to be one of the two or three most important American authors of the nineteenth century.

*Bibliography*

A. *Nature* (Boston, 1836); *An Address Delivered before the Senior Class in Divinity College, Cambridge* (Boston, 1838); *Essays* (Boston, 1841); *Essays: Second Series* (Boston, 1844); *Representative Men* (Boston, 1850); *The Conduct of Life* (Boston, 1860); *Complete Works*, ed. Edward W. Emerson, 12 vols. (Boston and New York, 1903–4); *Letters*, ed. Ralph L. Rusk, 6 vols. (New York, 1939); *Early Lectures*, ed. Stephen E. Whicher, Robert E. Spiller, and Wallace E. Williams, 3 vols. (Cambridge, 1959–72); *Journals and Miscellaneous Notebooks*, ed. William H. Gilman et al., 16 vols. (Cambridge, 1960–82).

B. DAB 6, 132–41; DARB, 145–50; DLB 1, 48–60; Ralph L. Rusk, *The Life of Ralph Waldo Emerson* (New York, 1949); Stephen E. Whicher, *Freedom and Fate: An Inner Life of Ralph Waldo Emerson* (Philadelphia, 1953); Joel Porte, *Representative Man: Ralph Waldo Emerson in His Time* (New York, 1979); Gay Wilson Allen, *Waldo Emerson* (New York, 1981); B. L. Packer, *Emerson's Fall: A New Interpretation of the Major Essays* (New York, 1982); David Robinson, *Apostle of Culture: Emerson as Preacher and Lecturer* (Philadelphia, 1982).

**EVERETT, CHARLES CARROLL** (19 June 1829, Brunswick, ME–16 October 1900, Cambridge, MA). *Education*: B.A., Bowdoin College, 1850; medical study, Bowdoin, 1850–51; study in Europe, 1851–52; graduated from Harvard Divinity School, 1859. *Career*: Librarian and instructor in modern languages, Bowdoin, 1853–57; Unitarian minister, Bangor, ME, 1859–69; Bussey Professor of Theology, Harvard Divinity School, 1869–1900; dean, Harvard Divinity School, 1878–1900.

Under the administration of Harvard president Charles W. Eliot, the Harvard Divinity School moved toward an identity as a nondenominational graduate school of religion, in accordance with the original aim of its founders that it pursue "serious, impartial, and unbiased investigation of Christian truth" with no required assent from students or instructors "to the peculiarities of any denomination of Christians" (Peabody, p. 120). Charles Carroll Everett, who served as professor and later dean of the school, was instrumental in guiding it through this period, setting a tone for thorough scholarship and hospitable tolerance for the insights of the religions of the world. After abandoning plans to enter medicine after his college work at Bowdoin, Everett taught at his alma mater and was chosen for a professorship until questions about his theological orthodoxy blocked his appointment. This set Everett on a course for the Unitarian ministry, which he began in Bangor, Maine. During his pastorate there, Everett wrote a study of Hegelian logic, *The Science of Thought*, which led to his appointment at Harvard. During his tenure at Harvard, he gained a wide reputation for theological acumen, literary judgment, and conversational wit, while continuing as a leading American exponent of German philosophy. His most important intellectual work during these years was devoted to a course of lectures on theology at the Divinity School that were posthumously edited from student notes. In these lectures Everett gave serious attention to the non-Christian religions. His interests in world religion were wide, but he remained a Christian and Unitarian, arguing that Christianity was the "absolute" religion because of the universality of its application, its intuitive nature, and its grounding in the person of Jesus (*Theism and the Christian Faith*, p. 334). His final definition of religion suggests the accommodation he had reached between the Christian revelation and the demands of comparative religion: "Religion . . . is the Feeling toward a Spiritual Presence manifesting itself in Truth, Goodness and Beauty, especially as illustrated in the life and teaching of Jesus and as experienced in every soul that is open to its influence" (p. 489; in all capital letters in the original).

*Bibliography*

A. *The Science of Thought: A System of Logic* (Boston, 1869); *Fichte's Science of Knowledge: A Critical Exposition* (Boston, 1884); *Poetry, Comedy, and Duty* (Boston and New York, 1888); *Immortality and Other Essays* (Boston, 1902); *The Psychological Elements of Religious Faith*, ed. Edward Everett Hale (New York and

London, 1902); *Theism and the Christian Faith*, ed. Edward Everett Hale (New York and London, 1909).

B. DAB 6, 221–22; Heralds 3, 105–8; Francis Greenwood Peabody, *Reminiscences of Present-Day Saints* (Boston and New York, 1927).

# F

FAHS, SOPHIA LYON (2 August 1876, Hangchow, China–17 April 1978, Hamilton, OH). *Education*: B.A., College of Wooster, 1897; M.A., Columbia University, 1904; B.D., Union Theological Seminary, 1926. *Career*: Traveling secretary for student volunteer movement, 1897–1902; instructor in religious education, Union Theological Seminary, 1926–44; church school staff, Riverside Church, New York, 1933–42; editor of curricular materials, American Unitarian Association, 1937–51; ordained to Unitarian ministry, February 8, 1959.

Sophia L. Fahs was the principal figure in the remaking of liberal religious education by the American Unitarian Association (AUA) in the 1930s. She was the daughter of Presbyterian missionaries in China and later was educated at the College of Wooster, graduating in 1897. She earned a master of arts degree at Columbia Teacher's College in 1904 and later a bachelor of divinity degree at Union Theological Seminary (1926). Her work at the Church School of the Riverside Church in New York (1933–42) helped mark her as one of the outstanding experimenters in liberal religious education. This helped bring her the appointment as curricular editor of the AUA in 1937, in the wake of the Commission of Appraisal Report of 1936, which noted that Unitarianism had lost its traditional leadership in the field of religious education. She restored that leadership by launching the important New Beacon Series in Religious Education, one of the factors that contributed to the general renaissance of Unitarianism under the direction of Frederick May Eliot.* Fahs's basic approach to education was to emphasize the often overlooked importance of early childhood education and to see in early childhood the opportunity "to sensitize the children to the opportunities their present experiences afford them for their own nurture" ("Growth Both Wide and Deep," *Unitarian Register*, 138 [May 1959], 10). Her emphasis on establishing a pattern of individual growth early in childhood was a culmination of the ethos of self-cultivation that had marked liberal religion since the early nineteenth century. In 1951 Fahs was given the Unitarians' Annual Award for Meritorious Service, and in 1959, at the age of eightytwo, Fahs was ordained into the Unitarian ministry.

*Bibliography*

A. *The New Beacon Series in Religious Education* (editor, Boston); *Today's Children and Yesterday's Heritage* (Boston, 1952); *Worshipping Together with Questioning Minds* (Boston, 1965).

B. *Who's Who of American Women* (1961–62), 2, 312; Robert L. H. Miller, "The Educational Philosophy of the New Beacon Series in Religious Education" (Th.D. diss., Boston University, 1957); David B. Parke, "The Historical and Religious Antecedents of the New Beacon Series in Religious Education" (Ph.D. diss., Boston University, 1965); Edith F. Hunter, *Sophia Lyon Fahs* (Boston, 1966); "Sophia Lyon Fahs," *Unitarian Universalist Association, 1979 Directory,* p. 164.

**FENN, WILLIAM WALLACE** (12 February 1862, Boston, MA–6 March 1932, Weston, VT). *Education*: A.B., Harvard College, 1884; A.M., 1887; S.T.B., Harvard Divinity School, 1887. *Career*: Minister, Unity Church, Pittsfield, MA, 1887–91; First Unitarian Society, Chicago, 1891–1900; Shaw Lecturer in Biblical Literature, Meadville Theological School, 1892–1901, 1905–7; Preacher to Harvard University, 1896–98, 1902–5; Bussey Professor of Systematic Theology, Harvard Divinity School, 1901–32; dean, Harvard Divinity School, 1906–22.

As a theologian and educator, William Wallace Fenn made an important contribution to the direction of liberal religion during the crucial period of transition from nineteenth-century liberalism to twentieth-century modernism. When he came to Chicago in 1891, he played a key role in moving the Western Unitarian Conference out of the control of Jenkin Lloyd Jones* and, eventually, in securing the healing of the split between the American Unitarian Association and the western radicals. His 1913 essay "Modern Liberalism" has since been recognized as a seminal work in preparing what would become a full-scale critique of liberal optimism in the twentieth century. In that essay Fenn insisted that liberals had to reassess whether their religion could "bear the weight of the tragedies of human experience" (p. 516). Despite prodigious learning, Fenn published relatively little, and as Daniel Evans noted, he "died with more unwritten knowledge, perhaps, especially of New England theology, than any man living" (DAB, p. 196). His teaching and leadership at Harvard Divinity School, where he served as dean, were important contributions to the education of the liberal ministry.

*Bibliography*

A. "Modern Liberalism," *American Journal of Theology,* 17 (October 1913); *Theism and Immortality* (Cambridge, 1921); *The Theological Method of Jesus* (Boston, 1938); *Theism: The Implication of Experience,* ed. Dan Huntington Fenn (Peterborough, NH, 1969).

B. DAB, Supplement 1, 296; Herald 4, 130–34; *Who Was Who in America* 1, 396; William Wallace Fenn, "The Western Issue" (autobiographical), PUHS 17, pt. 2 (1973–75), 92–94; William R. Hutchison, *The Modernist Impulse in American Protestantism* (Cambridge, 1976).

**FISHER, EBENEZER** (6 February 1815, Charlotte, ME–21 February 1879, Canton, NY). *Career*: Supply preacher, Milltown, ME, Universalist society, 1839; elected to Maine legislature, 1840; ordained as Universalist minister, 1841; minister, Addison Point, ME, 1841–47; Salem, MA, 1847–53; South Dedham, MA, 1853–58; principal of the theological school, St. Lawrence University, 1858–79.

When in 1858 the Universalists established their first theological school as part of St. Lawrence University, Ebenezer Fisher was chosen to be its head, a position he held, through many trials, until his death in 1879. Fisher was raised on the Maine frontier in a situation of limited economic resources and educational opportunity. After periods of work in a furniture establishment and as a schoolkeeper in his early manhood, he began to preach in 1839 and took a pastorate at Addison Point, Maine, in 1841. This followed service in the Massachusetts legislature in 1840. Fisher actively contributed to the denominational publications *Universalist Quarterly* and the *Trumpet*, and they helped augment his reputation as he proceeded through pastorates in Salem and South Dedham, Massachusetts. He accepted the responsibility of the theological school at St. Lawrence but was to find that the school was poorly supported financially and teetered on the brink of extinction in its early years. Fisher was, for long periods, not only the head but the only faculty member, and he struggled to gain additional endowment funds to support another teacher, student aid, and the like. Many students came to Fisher lacking not only in financial resources but in past training. One of his great talents was his ability to bring these ill-prepared but usually highly motivated students forward to active and productive ministries. Fisher's work at St. Lawrence exemplifies the spirit of sacrifice and the hardship that often accompanied the early efforts to establish Universalist educational institutions.

*Bibliography*

A. *The Christian Doctrine of Salvation: A Discussion between Rev. E. Fisher, D.D., and Rev. J. H. Walden on the Proposition "All Men Will Be Finally Saved"* (Boston, 1869).

B. DAB 6, 406; NCAB 10, 201–2; *Who Was Who in America, Historical Volume, 1607–1896*, 181; George H. Emerson, *Memoir of Ebenezer Fisher, D.D.* (Boston, 1880); William H. McGlauflin, *Faith with Power: A Life Story of Quillen Hamilton Shinn, D.D.* (Boston and Chicago, 1912); Russell E. Miller, *The Larger Hope* (Boston, 1979).

**FRANCIS, CONVERS** (9 November 1795, West Cambridge, MA–7 April 1863, Cambridge, MA). *Education*: A.B., Harvard, 1815; attended Harvard

Divinity School, 1815–18. *Career*: Unitarian minister, Watertown, MA, 1819–42; Parkman Professor of Pulpit Eloquence, Harvard, 1842–63.

As minister of the Unitarian church in Watertown, Massachusetts, for more than two decades, Convers Francis gained the trust of both the moderate Unitarians and the younger Transcendentalists who began to go beyond the Unitarian theological synthesis in the later 1830s. Joel Myerson aptly compared Francis to Frederic Henry Hedge,* because like Hedge, he shared many of the radical theological notions of Transcendentalism but remained committed to the institution of the church. His sister Lydia Maria Child* attributed to him much of her intellectual development. Francis also befriended Theodore Parker* early in his career, lending him books and encouraging him in his theological growth, and he was a warm supporter of Ralph Waldo Emerson.* "Was ever a mind cast in a finer mould, than E.'s? He seems to have already anticipated the purity of the spiritual state," he remarked in an 1837 journal entry (Myerson, p. 23). Because of this intellectual sympathy with Emerson and others, Francis was included in the Transcendental Club and looked to as one of the purveyors of the "new views" in the late 1830s. In 1842 Francis succeeded Henry Ware, Jr.,* as Harvard's Parkman Professor of Pulpit Eloquence, an appointment hailed by the Transcendentalists as a promise of progress at Harvard. But Francis disappointed Parker when he refused to exchange pulpits with him during the controversy over Parker's advocacy of absolute religion. Francis's action has been viewed by Perry Miller as a falling away from unpopular ideas under social pressure, but to Francis, Parker was unnecessarily disruptive in his pursuit of his views. Francis remained at Harvard until his death and maintained his admiration for Emerson throughout his life.

*Bibliography*

A. *An Historical Sketch of Watertown* (Cambridge, 1830); *Christianity as a Purely Internal Principle* (Boston, 1836); *Life of John Eliot* (Boston, 1836).

B. DAB 6, 577; DLB 1, 64–65; John Weiss, *Discourse Occasioned by the Death of Convers Francis* (Cambridge, 1863); William Newell, "Memoir of the Rev. Convers Francis," *Proceedings of the Massachusetts Historical Society*, 8 (1865), 233–53; Perry Miller, *The Transcendentalists: An Anthology* (Cambridge, 1950); Joel Myerson, "Convers Francis and Emerson," *American Literature*, 50 (1978), 17–36.

**FREEMAN, JAMES** (22 April 1759, Charlestown, MA–14 November 1835, Newton, MA). *Education*: A.B., Harvard, 1777. *Career*: Reader, King's Chapel, Boston, 1782–87; minister, 1787–1826; retirement, 1826–35.

The American Revolution left the Episcopal churches in America in a difficult position of being cut off from their ecclesiastical leaders in England and having to reformulate church government in the new republic. King's Chapel in Boston, the first Episcopal church in New England, found itself under particular difficulties as the war came. Its congregation was divided between loyalists and supporters of the Revolution, and its minister, a loyalist, was forced to flee Boston in 1776. As the church began to rebuild itself after the war, James Freeman was appointed "reader" in 1782 in the absence of available Episcopal clergy. Freeman's background was in New England congregationalism, and he wrote to his father after his appointment to assure him that "I have imbibed no High Church notions" (AAUP, p. 164). But Freeman was also beginning to have difficulty with the doctrine of the Trinity, which was a prominent part of the Episcopal creed. Freeman recognized that he could probably "obtain the settlement [at King's Chapel] for life," but his growing liberalism brought him to the brink of resigning in the early 1780s (p. 164). Freeman's friends, however, persuaded him to lay out the doctrinal basis of his objections to the Trinity in a series of sermons, and after hearing his exposition, the congregation agreed in 1785 to amend the liturgy as Freeman suggested, eliminating most references to the doctrine of the Trinity. This was a major transformation in the church, but the changes were not made with the explicit intention of withdrawing from the Episcopal denomination. A further problem arose, however, concerning Freeman's ordination. He sought Episcopal ordination on the sole basis of his "declaration of faith in the Holy Scriptures" but was told that "for a man to subscribe to the Scriptures, was nothing, . . . for it could never be determined from that what his creed was" (p. 166). His frank disavowal of the Trinity thus prevented his ordination, and the result was that Freeman was ordained by the church itself in 1787. F. W. P. Greenwood memorably characterized the transformation of the church: "Thus the first Episcopal church in New England became the first Unitarian Church in the New World" (p. 165). Freeman's open avowal of the Unitarian name, at a time when those of similar views in New England were referred to as "liberals" or "Arminians," gave him the distinction of being "the first avowed Preacher of Unitarianism in the United States" (p. 162). But Freeman had closer relations than other New Englanders with the English Unitarian movement and had been particularly influenced by William Hazlitt, an English Unitarian and associate of Joseph Priestley* who had moved to Boston in 1784. Hazlitt's Socinian Christology was shared to a large extent by Freeman, and that set him apart from the Boston liberals who held an Arian Christology and wanted to maintain their distance from the Unitarianism of Joseph Priestley. Thus although Freeman was a pioneer of Unitarianism in Boston, his views were outside the mainstream liberalism of Charles Chauncy,* Joseph Stevens Buckminster,* and William Ellery Channing,* the founders of American Unitarianism.

*Bibliography*

A. *Sermons on Particular Occasions* (Boston, 1812); *Eighteen Sermons and a Charge* (Cambridge, 1829).

B. AAUP, 162–76; DAB 7, 10–11; Heralds 2, 1–19; F. W. P. Greenwood, *A History of King's Chapel* (Boston, 1833); Henry Wilder Foote, *Annals of King's Chapel from the Puritan Age of New England to the Present Day*, 2 vols. (Boston, 1882); Henry

Wilder Foote, "The Historical Background of the Present King's Chapel," JUHS 8, pt. 2 (1950); Conrad Wright, *The Beginnings of Unitarianism in America* (Boston, 1955).

**FRITCHMAN, STEPHEN HOLE** (12 May 1902, Cleveland, OH–31 May 1981, Los Angeles, CA). *Education*: B.A., Ohio Wesleyan University, 1924; B.D., Union Theological Seminary, 1929; M.A., New York University, 1929; graduate study, Harvard, 1930–32. *Career*: Religious news editor, New York *Herald-Tribune*, 1925–27; associate professor of English, School of Religious Education, Boston University, 1929–32; minister, Unitarian Church, Petersham, MA, 1930–32; Unitarian Church, Bangor, ME, 1932–38; youth director, American Unitarian Association, 1938–47; editor, *Christian Register*, 1942–47; minister, First Unitarian Church, Los Angeles, 1947–69; retirement, 1969–81.

Stephen Fritchman embodied the concern for social change that has been an important current of twentieth-century liberal religion. "He called himself a heretic and called the Unitarian Universalist church a radical organization," Carl Seaburg noted (Seaburg, "Stephen Hole Fritchman"). Fritchman's sense of the responsibility for political engagement in liberal religion made him a controversial figure, and the most difficult of those controversies was his disagreement with Frederick May Eliot* and the American Unitarian Association (AUA) Board of Directors over the political stance and editorial procedures of the *Christian Register*. As editor of the magazine in the 1940s, he moved it from a denominational periodical to a more broadly political one. But he was caught in part in the political hysteria of the times and accused of taking the journal too far in a left-wing direction. Eliot supported Fritchman in his editorship despite protests against him, until Fritchman demanded full editorial freedom from the AUA, refusing specifically to tone down the language in one of his editorials. Fritchman saw the issue as one of free speech; Eliot saw it as one of administrative control of a denominational publication. Fritchman lost his editorship as a result, in a painful decision for Eliot. This incident, however, was only a prelude to Fritchman's long service in his Los Angeles parish. As Seaburg reminded us, "he was an excellent minister with a strong sense of churchliness." (Seaburg, "Stephen Hole Fritchman"). In 1976 Fritchman was named recipient of the Unitarian Universalist Association (UUA) Award for Distinguished Service to the Cause of Liberal Religion.

*Bibliography*

A. *Men of Liberty* (Boston, 1944); *Heretic: A Partisan Autobiography* (Boston, 1977).

B. Lawrence G. Brooks, "Frederick May Eliot as I Knew Him," PUHS, 13 (1960), 87–100; Conrad Wright, ed., *A Stream of Light* (Boston, 1975); Carl Seaburg, "Stephen Hole Fritchman," *Unitarian Universalist Association Directory, 1981/82* (Boston, 1981).

**FROTHINGHAM, OCTAVIUS BROOKS** (28 November 1822, Boston, MA–
27 November 1895, Boston, MA). *Education*: A.B., Harvard College, 1843;
graduated from Harvard Divinity School, 1846. *Career*: Minister, North Church,
Salem, MA, 1847–55; Jersey City, NJ, 1854–59; Third Unitarian Society, later
the Independent Liberal Church, New York, 1859–79; independent writer and
scholar, 1879–95.

O. B. Frothingham was a leader of the radical wing of late nineteenth-century Unitarianism and a founder of the Free Religious Association. He was raised
in the heart of Boston Unitarianism. His father, Nathaniel Langdon Frothingham, was a Boston Unitarian minister, and the younger Frothingham completed studies at Harvard College and Divinity School, where he was taught a
conservative version of Unitarianism. But his own intellectual inclinations were
toward the Transcendentalist theology and reformist politics of Theodore Parker,* and he came to know Parker well during his ministry in Salem. In 1854
he set the radical course of his career by preaching an antislavery sermon strongly
critical of the church's complicity with that institution, especially in the case of
the return of escaped slave Anthony Burns to bondage, a man whom Parker
had defended. After the war he emerged as a leader of the radical faction, critical of Henry W. Bellows's* organization of the National Conference. He was
instrumental in the formation and continuance of the Free Religious Association
and led his own congregation in New York to the status of an "Independent
Liberal Church." His *Religion of Humanity* (1873) was a central statement of
modernist thinking in theology, and he also made important contributions to the
early historiography of the Transcendentalist movement, notably in his *Transcendentalism in New England* (1876).

*Bibliography*

A. *The Religion of Humanity* (New York, 1873); *Life of Theodore Parker* (New York,
    1874); *Transcendentalism in New England* (New York, 1876); *Recollections and
    Impressions, 1822–1891* (autobiographical) (New York, 1891).

B. DAB 7, 44; Heralds 3, 120–27; *Recollections and Impressions* (see above); Stow
    Persons, *Free Religion: An American Faith* (New Haven, 1947); William R. Hutch-
    ison, *The Modernist Impulse in American Protestantism* (Cambridge, 1976); J. Wade
    Caruthers, *Octavius Brooks Frothingham: Gentle Radical* (University, AL, 1977).

**FULLER (OSSOLI), SARAH MARGARET** (23 May 1810, Cambridgeport,
MA–19 July 1850, near Fire Island, NY). *Career*: Teacher, Temple School,
Boston, 1836–37; Greene Street School, Providence, RI, 1837–38; leader,
Conversations for Women, Boston, 1939–44; editor, *Dial*, 1840–42; writer, New
York *Tribune*, 1844–50; travel and writing in Italy, 1847–50.

Margaret Fuller was the preeminent feminist thinker of her day, taking the
principles of Transcendentalism and broadening them into a thorough case for
women's rights. Her father gave her a rigorous education in her youth—too
rigorous, Fuller later thought. Although she did not have access to the formal

education of her male contemporaries, she stayed ahead of them through her wide reading, sharing with her friends James Freeman Clarke* and Frederic Henry Hedge* a love for German culture, which was sweeping through New England. Her later essay on Goethe was a landmark in the American reception of this author. She formed a close friendship with Ralph Waldo Emerson,* which was crucial for the intellectual development of both of them. Her conversations for women held in Boston from 1839 to 1844, forums on culture, politics, and feminism that Fuller organized and conducted, were important steps toward her articulation of a feminist position. Her major feminist statement was published in 1843 in the *Dial*, a journal that she founded with Emerson and served as first editor. After taking a position with the New York *Tribune* in 1844, she expanded her *Dial* article into the book *Woman in the Nineteenth Century* (1845). In 1847 she arrived in Italy, going as foreign correspondent for the *Tribune*, and became involved in the Italian revolution. She married a supporter of that revolution, Giovanni Angelo, Marchese d'Ossoli. Returning to America with her husband and child in 1850, she died in a shipwreck off Fire Island, New York. Fuller's reputation has undergone a major revival in the 1960s and 1970s, as she is coming to be understood as a pioneering feminist, an important literary critic, and a central figure in the Transcendentalist movement.

*Bibliography*

A. "Goethe," *Dial*, 2 (1841); *Summer on the Lakes, in 1843* (Boston, 1843); *Woman in the Nineteenth Century* (New York, 1845); *Papers on Literature and Art* (New York, 1846); *The Letters of Margaret Fuller*, ed. Robert N. Hudspeth, 2 vols. to date (Ithaca, NY, 1983– ).

B. DAB 7, 63–66; DLB 1, 66–72; NAW 1, 678–82; Ralph Waldo Emerson, William H. Channing, and James Freeman Clarke, *Memoirs of Margaret Fuller Ossoli*, 2 vols. (Boston, 1852); Mason Wade, *Margaret Fuller: Whetstone of Genius* (New York, 1940); Madeleine B. Stern, *The Life of Margaret Fuller* (New York, 1942); Joseph Jay Deiss, *The Roman Years of Margaret Fuller* (New York, 1969); Bell Gale Chevigny, "Growing Out of New England: The Emergence of Margaret Fuller's Radicalism," *Women's Studies*, 5 (1978); David Robinson, "Margaret Fuller and the Transcendental Ethos: *Woman in the Nineteenth Century*," *PMLA*, 97 (1982).

**FURNESS, WILLIAM HENRY** (20 April 1802, Boston, MA–30 January 1896, Philadelphia, PA). *Education*: A.B., Harvard, 1820; graduated from Harvard Divinity School, 1823. *Career*: Minister, Unitarian Church, Philadelphia, 1825–75; minister emeritus, 1875–96.

In 1825 William Henry Furness accepted an invitation to take the pastorate of the Unitarian church in Philadelphia, a church that had been founded by Joseph Priestley* in 1796 but that had continued without a minister for twenty-nine years. Furness remained active minister of the church for fifty years and was minister emeritus until his death. His long pastorate there helped to extend and solidify the Unitarian presence outside Boston, but Furness also became important for his scholarly and speculative work in biblical criticism. In 1836, as the Transcendentalist controversy was just beginning, Furness published his *Remarks on the Four Gospels*, a work that rejected the use of the biblical miracles as a basis for Christian faith. This established Furness's sympathy with the Transcendentalists on the miracles question, and placed him in opposition to his former teacher Andrews Norton.* Furness did not contest the fact that the miracles occurred, but he did argue that they were in fact natural events, and that religious faith did not require confirmation of supernatural events. Furness did not call the miracles "Monsters," as Ralph Waldo Emerson* did in the Divinity School address, but his position in many ways prefigures Emerson's assertion there that "man's life was a miracle, and all that man doth" (Emerson, *Collected Works* [Cambridge, MA, 1971], vol. 1, p. 81). Even so, Furness remained something of a moderate during the controversy, partly because of his noninflammatory style and procedure. Moreover, Furness continued in his devotion to biblical studies, unlike many of the other Transcendentalists. He followed his work on the Gospels with a series of works on the life of Jesus, whom he portrayed in human and historical terms. In this he was influenced by German biblical scholarship, and he also took an interest in German philosophy, as his Hegelian-influenced *Christianity a Spirit* (1859) suggests. Furness's long work in Philadelphia isolated him from most of his Unitarian colleagues in New England, and as a result his opportunities for pulpit exchanges were rare. He reported that he stopped counting his sermons after he reached fifteen hundred. He remained active until the end of his life, and it fell to him to preach the funeral sermon of his lifelong friend Emerson in 1882.

*Bibliography*

A. *Remarks on the Four Gospels* (Philadelphia, 1836); *Jesus and His Biographers* (Philadelphia, 1838); *A History of Jesus* (Boston, 1850); *Discourses* (Philadelphia and Boston, 1855); *Thoughts on the Life and Character of Jesus of Nazareth* (Boston, 1859); *The Veil Partly Lifted and Jesus Becoming Visible* (Boston, 1864).

B. DAB 7, 80; DLB 1, 73; Heralds 3, 133–38; Perry Miller, *The Transcendentalists: An Anthology* (Cambridge, MA, 1950); William Hutchison, *The Transcendentalist Ministers: Church Reform in the New England Renaissance* (New Haven, 1959); Elizabeth Geffen, *Philadelphia Unitarianism: 1796–1861* (Philadelphia, 1961); R. Joseph Hoffman, "William Henry Furness: The Transcendentalist Defense of the Gospels," *New England Quarterly*, 66 (1983), 238–60.

# G

**GANNETT, EZRA STILES** (14 May 1801, Cambridge, MA–26 August 1871, near Boston, MA). *Education*: A.B., Harvard, 1820; graduated from Harvard Divinity School, 1823. *Career*: Assistant minister and then minister, Federal Street Church, Boston, 1824–71; secretary, American Unitarian Association (AUA), 1825–31; coeditor, *Christian Examiner*, 1847–51; president, AUA, 1844–49.

In 1824 Ezra Stiles Gannett, then a young graduate of the Harvard Divinity School, was called to be colleague of William Ellery Channing* at Boston's Federal Street Church. Gannett was a man who, it was hoped, could relieve the frail Channing from day-to-day pastoral tasks of the church. Gannett was indeed an ideal colleague for Channing, for as his son William Channing Gannett* later described him, he was "by nature an organizer, not a seeker, of material" (Gannett, p. 141). Gannett devoted his enormous energies to the pastoral role at Federal Street, but his practical and organizational abilities also led him to play an important part in organizing religious structures beyond his church. He was a key member of a group of young liberal ministers who formed the AUA in 1825, a step that Gannett took without the support of Channing, who did not feel that sectarian organization was the best course for the emerging liberal party. Gannett became the first secretary of the AUA, the real position of administrative leadership at that time, and later also served as president. He played a similar role in the formation of the Benevolent Fraternity of Churches, an organization formed to support efforts of the ministry-at-large to the urban poor. Gannett was preeminently a worker and organizer, but he was also an active preacher whose theological views were moderate for his day. In 1835 he summarized the five key points of his preaching as follows: "Filial reverence for God, brotherly love for man, a grateful faith in Christ, receiving him as the revelation of divine and the model of human character; the reality of the spiritual world and regeneration, consisting in such a change of the temper and way of life as may be wrought by one's own will and effort'' (pp. 84–85). These views placed him in a camp opposed to the Transcendentalists, and he explicitly rejected Theodore Parker's* intuitionist views and defended the right of ministers who thought Parker was in error not to exchange pulpits with him. Yet he maintained, as some did not, Parker's identity as a Christian. Gannett's chief contribution to Unitarianism was his organizational and administrative work in its early years, when the liberal party was emerging as a denomination.

*Bibliography*

A. William Channing Gannett, *Ezra Stiles Gannett: Unitarian Minister in Boston, 1824–1871* (Boston, 1875); contains extensive selections from Gannett's sermons and writing.

B. DAB 7, 122–23; Heralds 3, 138–46; William Channing Gannett, *Ezra Stiles Gannett: Unitarian Minister in Boston, 1824–1871* (see above).

**GANNETT, WILLIAM CHANNING** (13 March 1840, Boston, MA–15 December 1923, Rochester, NY). *Education*: A.B., Harvard College, 1860; A.M., Harvard, 1863; study in Europe, 1865–66; graduated from Harvard Divinity School, 1868. *Career*: Work for New England Freedmen's Society, 1861–65; Unitarian minister, Milwaukee, WI, 1868–70; East Lexington, MA, 1871–72; Unity Church, St. Paul, MN, 1877–83; minister-at-large, Western Unitarian Conference, 1883–87; minister, Hinsdale, IL, 1887–89; Rochester, NY, 1889–1908, emeritus, 1908–23.

The son of one of the leading Boston Unitarian ministers, Ezra Stiles Gannett,* William Channing Gannett followed his father into the Unitarian ministry but parted ways from him intellectually in his own career. He was an early supporter of a noncreedal and antisupernaturalist religion and supported the activities of the Free Religious Association. His social concern and abolitionist stance was demonstrated early in his work for freed slaves under the auspices of the New England Freedmen's Association. After completing Divinity studies he took a pastorate in Milwaukee but returned to Boston in 1871 and prepared a memorial biography of his father published in 1875. When he returned to the West, he became a close associate of Jenkin Lloyd Jones,* took a hand in editing *Unity*, and became one of the staunchest defenders of western radicalism. He had a poetic gift and was a collaborator on *Unity Hymns and Chorals* (1880). But he influenced the denomination most strongly by writing the statement of *The Things Most Commonly Believed To-day among Us* (1887), which provided the basis for western and, eventually, national unity among Unitarians. Not written as a creed, it was nevertheless a lyrical and persuasive description of the mind of liberal religion at the end of the nineteenth century.

*Bibliography*

A. *Ezra Stiles Gannett: Unitarian Minister in Boston, 1824–71* (Boston, 1875); coeditor, *Unity Hymns and Chorals* (Chicago, 1880); *The Things Most Commonly Believed To-day among Us* (Chicago, 1887); originally published in *Unity*, June 4, 1887.

B. DAB 7, 124–25; Heralds 4, 142–47; *Who Was Who in America* 1, 438; Charles H. Lyttle, *Freedom Moves West* (Boston, 1952); William H. Pease, "Doctrine and Fellowship: William Channing Gannett and the Unitarian Creedal Issue," *Church History*, 25 (1966), 210–38.

**GAY, EBENEZER** (15 August 1696, Dedham, MA–18 March 1787, Hingham, MA). *Education*: A.B., Harvard College, 1714. *Career*: Minister, Hingham, MA, 1717–87.

Ebenezer Gay was an important early exponent of Arminianism, the eighteenth-century form of religious liberalism in America. He graduated from Harvard in 1714 and thereafter began ↑ ministry at the church in Hingham, Massachusetts, in 1717, where he remained until his death in 1787—a ministry of nearly seventy years. Gay was a close associate of Charles Chauncy* and an opposer of the Great Awakening, but he was less inclined to engage in theological controversy than Chauncy. He advanced liberal ideas not by attacks on the old Calvinism, but simply by omitting any references in his preaching to key Calvinist doctrines such as election to grace and original sin. Gay was an important exponent of "supernatural rationalism," a theology that insisted that the revealed religion of the Bible and the natural religion of rational speculation and scientific observation were in no sense incompatible. His Dudleian Lecture at Harvard in 1759, *National Religion, as Distinguish'd from Revealed*, set out the arguments for a religion derived from human reason and the evidences of nature. This religion was also commensurate with human moral capacity. Gay, with other eighteenth-century liberals such as Chauncy and Jonathan Mayhew,* helped lay the ground work for the liberalism of William Ellery Channing* and his associates in the nineteenth century.

*Bibliography*

A. *Natural Religion, as Distinguish'd from Revealed*, Dudleian Lecture (Boston, 1759).
B. AAUP, 1–7; DAB 7, 194–95; Heralds 1, 1–19; Conrad Wright, *The Beginnings of Unitarianism in America* (Boston, 1955); James W. Jones, *The Shattered Synthesis: New England Puritanism before the Great Awakening* (New Haven, 1973); Robert J. Wilson III, *The Benevolent Deity: Ebenezer Gay and the Rise of Rational Religion in New England, 1697–1787* (Philadelphia, 1984).

**GILES, PHILIP RANDALL** (23 January 1917, Haverhill, MA). *Education*: A.B., S.T.B., Tufts University, 1942. *Career*: Minister, First Universalist Church, Southbridge, MA, 1938–42; Universalist Community Church, South Woodstock, VT, summers 1938–41; military service, 1942–45; minister, White Memorial Universalist Church, Concord, NH, 1946–49; director, Unified Appeal, Universalist Church of America (UCA), Boston, 1949–51; military service, 1951–53; assistant to the general superintendent, UCA, 1953; director, Departments of Extension and Ministry, UCA, 1954–56; general superintendent, UCA, 1957–61; vice-president for field relations, Unitarian Universalist Association (UUA), 1961–63; executive secretary, Priestley District, UUA,

Baltimore, 1963–70; vice-president for development, UUA, Boston, 1970–74; minister, Unitarian Universalist Church, Muncie, IN, 1974–78; First Universalist Church, Denver, CO, 1978–82; minister, Unitarian Church, Corpus Christi, TX, 1982–83; Universalist Parish, Provincetown, MA, 1982, 1983–84.

The impulse toward a merger of the Universalists and the Unitarians had origins in the nineteenth century, but its final completion came only after a long and delicate process in which the advantages of unity were weighed against the cost to each denomination in unique identity. Philip R. Giles came to administrative leadership of the Universalist Church of America in the period just before the completion of merger. He brought both administrative experience and work in the Universalist parish ministry with him to that job and had the distinction of guiding his denomination through the merger process. Having served as the last general superintendent of the UCA, Giles continued both administrative and ministerial service to the new Unitarian Universalist Association after 1961.

*Bibliography*

B. David B. Parke, "Universalist and Unitarian Chiefs: Pre-Merger History," *Unitarian Universalist World*, 14 (December 15, 1983), 4–5.

**GORDON, ELEANOR ELIZABETH** (10 October 1852, Hamilton, IL–6 January 1942, Keokuk, IA). *Education*: Attended University of Iowa, 1873–74; Cornell University, 1889. *Career*: Assistant minister, Unitarian Church, Sioux City, IA, 1885–89; minister, 1889–96; coeditor, *Old and New*, 1891–1908; minister, Iowa City, IA, 1896–1900; Burlington, IA, 1900–1902; Fargo, ND, 1902–4; associate minister, Des Moines, IA, 1904–6; field secretary, State Unitarian Conference of Iowa, 1907–10; minister, Orlando, FL, 1912–18; retirement, 1918–42.

Eleanor E. Gordon was a close friend and associate of Mary Safford,* the leader of the "Iowa Band" or "Iowa Sisterhood," an important group of midwestern women ministers in Iowa around the turn of the century. Like Safford, Gordon held a twin commitment to liberal religious values and to the cause of fuller women's rights. This engaged her in the doubly difficult struggle of establishing and maintaining Unitarianism in a region where more conservative Protestantism had stronger roots and of maintaining women's rights to full political and professional opportunities. Much of Gordon's ministerial work was of the missionary variety—organizing churches and maintaining newly formed ones. Gordon was a strong supporter of increased educational opportunities for women and increased professional roles for women. In the 1930s she deplored the "distinct trend in both the professional and industrial worlds . . . against woman's place in both" (quoted in Hitchings, p. 74). Her personal example did much to establish the place of women in the liberal ministry.

*Bibliography*

B. Heralds 4, 57; Charles H. Lyttle, *Freedom Moves West* (Boston, 1952); Catherine F. Hitchings, "Universalist and Unitarian Women Ministers," JUHS, 10 (1975).

**GREELEY, DANA McLEAN** (5 July 1908, Lexington, MA). *Education*: S.B., Harvard, 1931; S.T.B., Harvard Divinity School, 1933. *Career*: Unitarian minister, Lincoln, MA, 1932–34; Concord, NH, 1934–35; Arlington Street church, Boston, 1935–58; secretary, American Unitarian Association (AUA), 1945–53; president, Unitarian Service Committee, 1953–58; president, AUA, 1958–61; president, Unitarian Universalist Association, 1961–69; minister, First Parish in Concord, MA, 1970–present.

In 1961 Dana M. Greeley became the first president of the newly formed Unitarian Universalist Association (UUA), the result of the merger of the American Unitarian Association with the Universalist Church of America. This historically important opportunity of service came to Greeley after long service to the Unitarian denomination, including a ministry of more than two decades at Boston's Arlington Street Church. During that ministry, the church, itself historically important, took into affiliation two other historically significant Boston churches—the Second Universalist Church, which had been the church of Hosea Ballou,* and the Church of the Disciples, founded by James Freeman Clarke.* In going to the church, Greeley recalled, he felt himself committed to spend the rest of his life there, and that might have come to pass had he not become a candidate for AUA president in 1958. He was not the candidate of the AUA Board of Directors but was nominated by petition. Greeley brought to the office a strong social commitment. He was an early admirer of Theodore Parker,* and John Haynes Holmes* preached the sermon at his installation at the Arlington Street Church. He had also headed the Unitarian Service Committee before his election. Greeley was destined to be the last AUA president and played an important role in helping guide the Unitarian denomination through the merger with Universalism, thus realizing a process begun by his predecessor Frederick May Eliot.* Reluctant in some ways to see the end of the AUA, Greeley nevertheless saw the merger as a necessary step in the progress of liberal religion. The arguments by some Unitarians against the merger did not persuade him: "But spiritually it seemed to me we had no alternative but to go forward with the merger," he wrote. "We couldn't call ourselves liberals—either of us—and simultaneously reject the proposals for union" (*25 Beacon Street*, p. 83). Thus the merger of the two leading denominations of liberalism was accomplished, and a new phase of the organizational history of liberalism was begun. After his service as head of the UUA, Greeley returned to the parish ministry in Concord, Massachusetts.

*Bibliography*

A. *Toward a Larger Living: Sermons on Personal Religion* (Boston, 1944); *A Message to Atheists* (Boston, 1948); *25 Beacon Street and Other Recollections* (Boston, 1971).

B. *Current Biography* (1964), 163–65; *Who's Who in America* (1980–81), 1333; Joseph Barth, "Contests for the Presidency: A.U.A., 1958–U.U.A., 1961," PUHS, 15 (1964), 26–65; Conrad Wright, ed., *A Stream of Light* (Boston, 1975).

# H

**HALE, EDWARD EVERETT** (3 April 1822, Boston, MA–10 June 1909, Boston, MA). *Education*: A.B., Harvard College, 1839; private theological study, 1839–41. *Career*: Teacher, Boston Latin School, 1839–41; minister, Church of the Unity, Worcester, MA, 1846–56; South Church, Boston, MA, 1856–99; active retirement, 1899–1903; chaplain, United States Senate, 1903–9.

Edward Everett Hale was an influential Boston Unitarian minister and man of letters who took a role as one of the leaders of the "Broad Church" group of nineteenth-century Unitarians. This group, which included Henry W. Bellows* and James Freeman Clarke,* attempted to put the denomination on a more solid organizational basis through the formation of the National Conference of Unitarian Churches in 1865. Hale's role in attempting to organize the denomination nationally was one of many roles of public prominence that he played in his long ministry in Boston. He was of deep New England roots, related to the patriot Nathan Hale and the prominent Boston political figure Edward Everett. Hale prepared himself for the ministry through supervised private study rather than formal Divinity training and later insisted that this was an advantage to him. His early ministries in Worcester and Boston were strong but undistinguished, but the coming of the Civil War thrust him into national prominence as a patriotic leader and voice of public conscience. Before the war, he said, "I was only known in Boston as an energetic minister of an active church; then the war came along and brought me into public life, and I have never got back into simple parish life again" (Peabody, p. 102). One of the effects of his entry into public life was his work for the National Conference, mentioned above. Another effect was the launching of his literary fame, based on his patriotic story "The Man without a Country" (1863). The success of that story was followed by continuing literary efforts that gained a large popular following. "Lend-a-Hand" Clubs were begun as a result of his story "Ten Times One Is Ten"

(1870), whose motto summarized his message of optimism, progress, and philanthropy: "Look up and not down, look out and not in, look forward and not back, and lend a hand" (p. 95). Hale was an effective orator with a commanding voice and presence, but his larger influence was in the wide audience for his fiction. "He could preach best in story-telling," his younger friend Francis Greenwood Peabody* later said of him (p. 103). If Hale had a weakness it was a tendency to overcommitment, and Peabody reported that his astonishing range of pastoral, literary, and public endeavors led one critic to call him "Edward Everything Hale" (p. 111).

But he became a one-man institution in late nineteenth-century Boston because of his personal generosity and his popular message of optimistic progress, which captured many of the assumptions of nineteenth-century American liberalism. Perhaps in appropriate recognition of this, Hale came out of retirement to accept an appointment as chaplain of the U.S. Senate in 1903. Of this experience, Van Wyck Brooks reported one anecdote of interest. When asked "Do you pray for the Senators, Dr. Hale?" he replied, "No, I look at the Senators and pray for the country" (Brooks, p. 418). Even the humor of the remark reveals the public spirit of Hale.

*Bibliography*

A. *If, Yes, and Perhaps* (Boston, 1868); *Ten Times One Is Ten: The Possible Reformation* (Boston, 1871); *Crusoe in New York and Other Tales* (Boston, 1880); *A New England Boyhood* (autobiographical) (New York, 1893); *Ten Times One Is Ten and Other Stories* (Boston, 1899); *Memories of a Hundred Years* (partly autobiographical), 2 vols. (New York, 1902).

B. DAB 8, 99–100; Heralds 4, 150–54; *A New England Boyhood* and *Memories of a Hundred Years* (see above); Edward E. Hale, Jr., *The Life and Letters of Edward Everett Hale*, 2 vols. (Boston, 1917); Francis Greenwood Peabody, *Reminiscences of Present-Day Saints* (Boston and New York, 1927); Van Wyck Brooks, *New England: Indian Summer, 1865–1915* (New York, 1940); Jean Holloway, *Edward Everett Hale: A Biography* (Austin, TX, 1956); John R. Adams, *Edward Everett Hale* (Boston, 1977).

**HALL, FRANK OLIVER** (19 March 1860, New Haven, CT–18 October 1941, New York, NY). *Education*: B.D., Tufts Divinity School, 1884. *Career*: Universalist minister, Fitchburg, Lowell, and Cambridge, MA, 1884–1902; Church of the Divine Paternity, New York, 1902–37.

Frank O. Hall was a leading spokesman for Universalism in the early part of the twentieth century. During his long pastorate in New York he was recognized as an effective orator and civic leader. He had a long commitment to pacifism and was active in the Church Peace Union, an organization funded by Andrew Carnegie whose purpose was to explore avenues toward international peace through the leadership of the churches. Hall articulated forcefully the key tenet of Universalism, attacking the "hideous and sickening conception of God which makes him the creator of a little heaven for a select few and a big hell for the vast majority of the human race'' (*Soul and Body*, pp. 129–30). Hall's God was not only benevolent and equalitarian but in some descriptions seemed notably in line with modern speculative naturalism: ''God is the name we give to the creative energy.'' For Hall, this God of Creation continued to operate in the world, and humanity could share the joy of creation by participating with God ''in the process of making something worthy and beautiful'' (pp. 149–50). This call to moral service was characteristic of Hall's message of work toward self-development and social improvement. ''The object of life is development,'' he wrote, and the purpose of the universe ''is the production of the highest possible type of manhood and womanhood'' (*Common People*, p. 92). This self-development required self-sacrifice and a measure of self-giving, and in that necessity lay the mandate for the idea of service that Hall preached.

*Bibliography*

A. *Common People* (Boston, 1901); *Soul and Body: A Book of Sermons* (Boston, 1909).

B. *Current Biography* (1941), 361; *Who Was Who in America* 1, 505; *New York Times*, October 19, 1941, p. 44; Charles S. Macfarland, *Pioneers of Peace through Religion* (New York and London, 1946).

**HANAFORD, PHEBE ANN COFFIN** (6 May 1829, Nantucket, MA–2 June 1921, Rochester, NY). *Career*: Homemaker and author, Newton, Nantucket, Beverly, and Reading, MA, 1849–68; editor, *Ladies' Repository*, 1866–68; Universalist minister, Hingham, MA, 1868–70; First Universalist Church, New Haven, CT, 1870–74; Jersey City, NJ, 1874–84; Second Universalist Church, New Haven, CT, 1884–85; Portsmouth Church, Newport, RI, 1885–91; active retirement, New York, 1891–1921.

Phebe Hanaford was ordained into the Universalist ministry in 1868, becoming one of the earliest ordained Universalist women and the first woman regularly ordained in Massachusetts. But that distinction came after she had already led an active life as a homemaker and had entered the public sphere as an author and editor. She wrote fiction, poetry, children's books, and popular biographies, including a life of Abraham Lincoln. Her religious background was Quaker, and in that tradition she had the example of women in the ministry. She had later adopted the Baptist faith of her husband, but in the middle 1860s she converted to Universalism and began her career in the ministry, having been encouraged to do so by Olympia Brown.* At her ordination Brown emphasized that Hanaford, as one of the earliest women ministers, would be ''representative,'' and serve as an example to other women who might have professional ambitions (Hitchings, p. 79). Hanaford combined her preaching and pastoral work with increasing activity in the women's movement, becoming associated with the American Woman Suffrage Association and the Association for the Advancement of Women. One of her last projects as an author was a compilation of biographies of American women, published as *Women of the Century* in 1877. After her retirement from the ministry in 1891, she continued an active life until her death at age ninety-two.

*Bibliography*

A. *Lucretia the Quakeress* (Boston, 1853); *Abraham Lincoln: His Life and Public Services* (Boston, 1865); *Field, Gunboat, Hospital, and Prison* (Boston, 1866); *The Life of George Peabody* (Boston, 1870); *From Shore to Shore and Other Poems* (Boston and San Francisco, 1871); *Women of the Century* (Boston, 1877), revised as *Daughters of America; or, Women of the Century* (Augusta, ME, 1882).

B. DAB 8, 216–17; NAW 2, 126–27; *Daughters of America* (see above); Catherine F. Hitchings, "Universalist and Unitarian Women Ministers," JUHS, 10 (1975), 78–81; Russell E. Miller, *The Larger Hope* (Boston, 1979).

**HARTSHORNE, CHARLES** (5 June 1897, Kittanning, PA). *Education*: A.B., Harvard, 1921; A.M., 1922; Ph.D., 1923; study at the Universities of Freiburg and Marburg, 1923–25. *Career*: Instructor in philosophy and then research fellow, Harvard, 1925–28; instructor to professor of philosophy, University of Chicago, 1928–55; professor of philosophy, Emory University, 1955–62; Ashbel Smith Professor of Philosophy, University of Texas, 1962–76; professor emeritus, 1976–present.

"Can the idea of deity be so formulated to preserve, perhaps even increase, its religious value, while yet avoiding the contradictions which seem inseparable from the idea as customarily defined?" (*The Divine Relativity*, p. 1). With this question Charles Hartshorne opened his influential work on the philosophy of religion, *The Divine Relativity*. Although the question was basic to that book, it can also be said that it is perhaps the fundamental question behind most of Hartshorne's life work in philosophy. Hartshorne has come to be the most influential student of Alfred North Whitehead in our day and a leader of the school of process philosophy. He has also been an important force in the rising philosophical stature of Charles Sanders Peirce, serving as coeditor of the mammoth Peirce papers. For Hartshorne, the rational viability of the concept of God depends upon its being divorced from classical notions that argue that God's perfection precludes change and that God's absoluteness precludes a full social relationship with the creation. Hartshorne argued instead that God's perfection, although excluding "rivalry or superiority on the part of other individuals," does not preclude "self-superiority" or the process by which God increases in value. God is perfect, therefore, as "the selfsurpassing surpasser of all" (p. 20). Moreover, God's "sociability," or relatedness to the universe, is in fact a measure of perfection, not a limit to it. As a result, Hartshorne wrote, God is not the "transcendental snob, or the transcendental tyrant" but "the unsurpassably interacting, loving, presiding genius and companion of all existence" (*A Natural Theology for Our Time*, p. 137). Hartshorne's idea of God flows from two basic premises of process philosophy as most systematically elaborated by Whitehead: a conception of the universe in terms of becoming rather than being and an insistence on the social nature of every aspect of reality. As Hartshorne rendered his idea of God, it is one of religious value as well as philosophical consistency. Hartshorne's theological system stands as one of the most articulate and accessible approaches to the concept of God for religious liberals, and his influence beyond academic philosophy seems to be growing.

*Bibliography*

A. *Beyond Humanism: Essays in the New Philosophy of Nature* (Chicago, 1937); *The Divine Relativity: A Social Conception of God* (New Haven, 1948); *Reality as Social Process* (New York, 1953); *The Logic of Perfection and Other Essays in Neoclassical Metaphysics* (La Salle, IL, 1962); *A Natural Theology for Our Time* (La Salle, IL, 1967); *Insights and Oversights of the Great Thinkers* (Albany, NY, 1983); *Omnipotence and Other Theological Mistakes* (Albany, NY, 1984).

B. CA 9R, 367–68; DAS 4, 222; *Who's Who in America* (1981–82), 1467; Ralph E. James, *The Concrete God: A New Beginning for Theology—The Thought of Charles Hartshorne* (Indianapolis, IN, 1967); Eugene H. Peters, *Hartshorne and Neoclassical Metaphysics* (Lincoln, NB, 1970); Lewis S. Ford, ed., *Two Process Philosophers: Hartshorne's Encounter with Whitehead* (Tallahassee, FL, 1973); John B. Cobb, *Process Theology as Political Theology* (Philadelphia, 1982); Interview in *Unitarian Universalist World*, 13 (November 15, 1982), 1, 6–7.

**HEDGE, FREDERIC HENRY** (12 December 1805, Cambridge, MA–21 August 1890, Cambridge, MA). *Education*: A.B., Harvard College, 1825; graduated, Harvard Divinity School, 1828. *Career*: Minister, West Cambridge, MA, 1829–35; Bangor, ME, 1835–50; Providence, RI, 1850–56; First Unitarian Church, Brookline, MA, 1857–72; editor, *Christian Examiner*, 1857–61; professor of ecclesiastical history, Harvard Divinity School, 1857–76; professor of German literature, Harvard College, 1872–84.

Frederic Henry Hedge was one of the earliest New Englanders to take an interest in German literature and philosophy, and one of the principal supporters of the "new views" that came to be known in the 1830s as Transcendentalism. He was also an early exponent of intuition as a source of religious knowledge, a defining tenet of the Transcendentalist group. In fact, the Transcendental Club, which met periodically in the middle 1830s in the Boston area, was referred to as "Hedge's Club," because it gathered when Hedge came to Boston from Maine, where he held a pastorate. Hedge parted ways with Ralph Waldo Emerson* and certain other Transcendentalists, however, on the issue of the importance of the church in religious life. Although Emerson saw most institutions, including the church, as at best necessary evils, Hedge argued that the church and other institutions provided a necessary historical continuity that did not supersede religious intuition but supplemented it in importance. Hedge's insistence on the importance of history is exemplified in his career as a professor of ecclesiastical history at Harvard. His insistence that the church could be a balancing factor to private conscience also allied him with Henry W. Bellows,* James Freeman Clarke,* and the "Broad Church" group, who opposed the radicals of the Free Religious Association. Hedge was a man who provided much intellectual leadership for the early phases of Transcendentalism but for both intellectual and temperamental reasons found that it could not sustain him.

*Bibliography*

A. "Coleridge's Literary Character," *Christian Examiner,* 14 (March 1833); *Prose Writers of Germany* (editor, Philadelphia, 1848); "Anti-Supernaturalism in the Pulpit," *Christian Examiner,* 77 (1864); *Reason in Religion* (Boston, 1865); *Ways of the Spirit and Other Essays* (Boston, 1877); *Martin Luther and Other Essays* (Boston, 1888); *Sermons* (Boston, 1891).

B. DAB 8, 498–99; DARB, 198–99; DLB 1, 102–3; Heralds 3, 158–67; Orie W. Long, *Frederic Henry Hedge: A Cosmopolitan Scholar* (Portland, ME, 1940); Ronald V. Wells, *Three Christian Transcendentalists* (New York, 1943); George H. Williams, *Rethinking the Unitarian Relationship with Protestantism: An Examination of the Thought of Frederic Henry Hedge (1805–1890)* (Boston, 1949); Joel Myerson, "Frederic Henry Hedge and the Failure of Transcendentalism," *Harvard Library Bulletin,* 23 (1975); Joel Myerson, *The New England Transcendentalists and the Dial* (Rutherford, NJ, 1980); Charles Grady, "About Hedge—Bibliographically Speaking," *Unitarian Universalist Christian* 36 (1981), p. 75.


**HELVIE, CLARA COOK** (24 January 1876, Chaumont, NY–22 July 1969, Taunton, MA). *Education*: Graduated from Canton's Business College, Buffalo, NY; attended Emerson College of Oratory, Boston, 1901; graduated from Meadville Theological Seminary, 1917; postgraduate study, Meadville. *Career*: Various secretarial positions, c. 1901–17; ordained Unitarian minister, 1917; minister, Wheeling, WV, 1917–21; Moline, IN, 1921–26; Westboro, MA, 1927; Middleboro, MA, 1930–36; Milford, NH, 1938–42; retirement, 1942–69.

Clara Cook Helvie performed an invaluable service to the Unitarian and Universalist denominations in compiling two historical manuscripts on women in the ministries of both denominations. In 1928 she compiled the manuscript "Unitarian Women Ministers," and in 1950 she completed a similar manuscript on Universalist women. These works were based on correspondence with numerous women in the ministry and research in denominational publications and archives. The works, now deposited in the Unitarian Universalist Association (UUA) Archives and Harvard Divinity School, were never published but have provided information for later researchers, including Catherine F. Hitchings's valuable compilation of biographies of Unitarian and Universalist women ministers (1975). Helvie's interest in the history of women in the liberal ministry was awakened by her own hardships in pursuing a ministerial career and her sense of wasted opportunities for both women and the liberal movement. She prepared for the Unitarian ministry after being widowed in 1916, and, as Hitchings noted, when she sought ordination, she met discouragement, finding that more than a decade had elapsed between her ordination in 1917 and the last woman to be ordained before her. After almost twenty years in the ministry, she found herself unemployed for a period because of the financial constrictions of the Depression, which were particularly damaging to the careers of women. Helvie's work was a reminder to the denomination of a responsibility it was failing to meet early in the century.

*Bibliography*

A. "Unitarian Women Ministers," unpublished manuscript, Unitarian Universalist Association Archives, Boston, MA; "Necrology of Women Serving in the Universalist Ministry," unpublished manuscript, Unitarian Universalist Association Archives, Boston, MA.

B. Catherine F. Hitchings, "Universalist and Unitarian Women Ministers," JUHS, 10 (1975); Conrad Wright, ed., *A Stream of Light* (Boston, 1975).

**HIGGINSON, THOMAS WENTWORTH** (23 December 1823, Cambridge, MA–9 May 1911, Cambridge, MA). *Education*: A.B., Harvard College, 1841; graduated, Harvard Divinity School, 1847. *Career*: Unitarian minister, First Religious Society, Newburyport, MA, 1847–49; independent lecturer and abolitionist political activist, 1849–52; minister, Free Church, Worcester, MA, 1852–57; abolitionist political activist, 1857–62; U.S. military commander, First South Carolina Volunteers (freedmen), 1862–64; independent author and lecturer, 1864–1911.

Few men had more talents, or expressed these talents in more avenues during a lifetime, than Thomas Wentworth Higginson. Indeed, the range of his talents was a problem for Higginson, who could not at first find a career that would satisfy his various inclinations. After finishing Harvard he spent three years in private study and indecision, developing both poetic ambitions and a zeal for political reform through his involvement with the abolitionist movement. Intellectually, he was strongly influenced by Transcendentalism and was politically and theologically a "radical." Higginson eventually saw the Unitarian ministry as the best way to pursue his interests, entering Harvard Divinity School in 1844 and taking a pulpit in Newburyport in 1847, becoming meanwhile more firmly a disciple of Transcendentalism and Garrisonian abolitionism. His outspoken abolitionism at Newburyport alienated many in his congregation, and he found it necessary to resign, but his intense political activism continued. He led a raid on the Court House in Boston to try to free fugitive slave Anthony Burns, and was wounded in the attempt; later he aided the Free Soil fight in Kansas and became a supporter of John Brown. His political activities culminated in his military appointment as commander of a regiment of freed blacks. In 1863 Higginson was wounded in battle in South Carolina and discharged in 1864. For the rest of his life, Higginson wrote on a variety of topics and in a variety of forms, becoming an influential literary critic and popular lecturer. His account of his war experiences, *Army Life in a Black Regiment*, has been hailed by several modern critics as an overlooked masterpiece. He was a frequent contributor to influential periodicals such as the *Atlantic Monthly*, the *Nation*, and *Harper's Bazaar*, becoming an arbiter of literary taste and mentor to many aspiring young writers. Moreover, he became a spokesman for the rights of women, feeling that this was "the next great question" facing the country after the liberation of the slaves. Principally a reformer, his talents spilled over into a profusion of activities that marked him as one of the leading exponents of liberal values in the middle nineteenth century.

*Bibliography*

A. *Out-door Papers* (Boston, 1863); *Army Life in a Black Regiment* (autobiographical) (Boston, 1870); *Common Sense about Women* (Boston, 1882); *Cheerful Yesterdays* (autobiographical) (Boston, 1898); *The Writings of Thomas Wentworth Higginson*, 7 vols. (Boston, 1900); *Letters and Journals of Thomas Wentworth Higginson, 1846–1906*, ed. Mary Thacher Higginson (Boston, 1921).

B. DAB 9, 16–18; autobiographical volumes (see above); Mary Thacher Higginson, *Thomas Wentworth Higginson: The Story of His Life* (Boston, 1914); Anna Mary Wells, *Dear Preceptor: The Life and Times of Thomas Wentworth Higginson* (Boston, 1903); Tilden G. Edelstein, *Strange Enthusiasm: A Life of Thomas Wentworth Higginson* (New Haven, 1968); Richard B. Sewall, *The Life of Emily Dickinson*, 2 vols. (New York, 1974); James W. Tuttleton, *Thomas Wentworth Higginson* (Boston, 1978).

**HOLMES, JOHN HAYNES** (29 November 1879, Philadelphia, PA–3 April 1964, New York, NY). *Education*: A.B., Harvard, 1902; S.T.B., Harvard Divinity School, 1904. *Career*: Unitarian minister, Danvers, MA, 1902–4; Third Religious Society, Dorchester, MA, 1904–7; associate minister to minister, Church of the Messiah, New York, 1907–19; Community Church, formerly the Church of the Messiah, 1919–49; retirement, 1949–64.

While a student at Harvard Divinity School, John Haynes Holmes came under the influence of Harvard's pioneer social ethicist Francis Greenwood Peabody.* Peabody's insistence on the necessity of religion's facing the "social question" made a deep impact on Holmes, and he went on to a career of leadership among liberals in the social application of liberal theology. Peabody's social gospel combined with the strong influences of evolutionary philosohers Herbert Spencer and John Fiske to give Holmes a message of a new "revolutionary" function for the modern church. Holmes argued that a "new conception . . . of the kind of work which the church ought to accomplish" was more important than a new theology, and called for a " 'modernism' in the world of action as well as in the world of thought" (*The Revolutionary Function*, pp. 7, 11). His concept of this modernist action can best be understood by noting his staunch pacifism during World War I, his preaching of a form of economic socialism from his pulpit at New York's Church of the Messiah, and his involvement with liberal reformist institutions such as the National Association for the Advancement of Colored People and the American Civil Liberties Union.

Holmes grew increasingly dissatisfied with the denominational outlook of Unitarianism, although he reverenced the past examples of William Ellery Channing* and Theodore Parker.* In 1919 he led the Church of the Messiah to become the Community Church. He hoped to use the church as a proving ground for nonsectarian religion, a religion whose independence from traditional denominational ties could make it part of a larger structure transcending cultural, ethnic, and racial barriers. Holmes was among the first Americans to recognize the significance of Mohandas Gandhi and his nonviolent movement for Indian independence and became Gandhi's chief American disciple and publicist. He retired from his long New York pastorate in 1949 and continued writing and other activities during his retirement.

*Bibliography*

A. *The Revolutionary Function of the Modern Church* (New York, 1912); *New Wars for Old* (New York, 1916); *The Sensible Man's View of Religion* (New York, 1932); *Rethinking Religion* (New York, 1938); *My Gandhi* (New York, 1953); *I Speak for Myself* (autobiography) (New York, 1959).

B. DARB, 212–13; NCAB 15, 273–74; John Haynes Holmes, *I Speak for Myself* (see above); Carl Hermann Voss, *Rabbi and Minister: The Friendship of Stephen S. Wise and John Haynes Holmes* (Cleveland and New York, 1964).

**HOWE, JULIA WARD** (27 May 1819, New York, NY–17 October 1916, Newport, RI). *Career:* Author, lecturer, homemaker, Boston, 1845–1910; founder, New England Woman's Club, 1868, and president through most of 1871–1910; founder, New England Woman Suffrage Association, 1868; American Woman Suffrage Association, 1869; president, Massachusetts Woman Suffrage Association, 1870–78, 1891–93; founder and editor, *Woman's Journal*, 1870–90; founder, Association for the Advancement of Women, 1873; director, General Federation of Women's Clubs, 1893–98.

If Julia Ward Howe's "Battle Hymn of the Republic" made her a household name in midnineteenth-century America, it was only one small act in a life that touched almost every aspect of American cultural development. After her mother's death Julia Ward was reared by a well-meaning but strict father, who feared his daughter's "temperament and imagination oversensitive to impressions from without" and attempted to "guard [her] from exciting influences" (*Reminiscences*, p. 53). As a result, she developed in her youth the capacity for long study. "If I may sum up in one term the leading bent of my life, I will simply call myself a student," she later said (p. 205). In 1843 she married Samuel Gridley Howe, a brilliant doctor and medical innovator who took special interest in education for the blind, improving conditions for the insane, and general educational reform. He was a pioneer in advocating the teaching of language to deaf mutes. Julia Ward Howe respected her husband, but the two of them, both strong willed, clashed over the propriety of public roles for women. "During the first two-thirds of my life I looked to the masculine ideal of character as the only true one," she recalled, and her discovery of the free development of woman's character was to her "like the addition of a new continent to the map of the world" (pp. 372–73). When the Howes moved to Boston in the 1840s, her process of development began under the strong influence of Theodore Parker.* Through Parker she gained sympathy for the antislavery cause and associated much with Boston's reformers and abolitionist leaders in the 1840s and 1850s. She later became a parishioner of James Freeman Clarke* and preached often at his Church of the Disciples. At his suggestion, she tried to write "some good words for that stirring tune" "John Brown's Body" (pp. 274–75). The result was her scrawling the draft of the "Battle Hymn" after waking in "the gray of the morning twilight" (p. 275). Published in the *Atlantic*, the hymn made its way to the encampments and to the nation's heart. After the war Howe became an active advocate of woman's culture and woman's suffrage. Public work and recognition had been opened to women by the necessities of the war, she said, and nothing could halt this progress now that it had taken hold. She was especially active in the New England Woman's Club, a model of the type of organization that provided important avenues for women's growth and activities in the late nineteenth and early twentieth centuries. She was also active in Boston's Radical Club, a group of reformers and intellectuals who in some senses came to replace the Transcendental Club as a vehicle for new thought and exchange. Author, lecturer, organizer, and reformer—she played all of these roles. "What is the ideal aim of life?" she was once asked. Her response summarizes her ideals: "To learn, to teach, to serve, to enjoy!" (Richards, vol. II, p. 414).

*Bibliography*

A. *Words for the Hour* (Boston, 1857); *Sex and Education* (editor, Boston, 1874); *Modern Society* (Boston, 1881); *Reminiscences, 1819–1899* (autobiographical) (Boston and New York, 1899); *At Sunset* (Boston and New York, 1910); *The Walk with God*, ed. Laura E. Richards (New York, 1919).

B. DAB 9, 291–93; NAW 2, 225–29; Florence Howe Hall, *Julia Ward Howe and the Woman Suffrage Movement* (Boston, 1913); Laura E. Richards and Maud Howe Elliott, assisted by Florence Howe Hall, *Julia Ward Howe, 1819–1910*, 2 vols. (Boston, 1915); Louise Hall Tharp, *Three Saints and a Sinner* (Boston, 1956); Deborah Pickman Clifford, *Mine Eyes Have Seen the Glory: A Biography of Julia Ward Howe* (Boston, 1979).

**HUIDEKOPER, HARM JAN** (3 April 1776, Hoogeveen, The Netherlands–22 May 1854, Meadville, PA). *Education*: Attended an academy in Crefeld, Germany, c. 1793–95. *Career*: Immigrated to the United States, 1796; employed by the Holland Land Co., Trenton, NY, c. 1796–1802, and in Philadelphia, PA, 1802–4; land agent and land owner, Meadville, PA, 1804–54.

The life of Harm Jan Huidekoper illustrates the impact of a forceful personality on a frontier area. As a land agent and land holder at Meadville, Pennsylvania, Huidekoper took a direct hand in the development and settling of a wilderness. His economic importance to his community was matched by his religious influence there as well, for Huidekoper became a convinced Unitarian after a personal study of the Bible and led in the establishment of a Unitarian church at Meadville. His influence took on a national scope when his interest in religious education led him to bring many young ministers to Meadville and to found the Meadville Theological School as a place where Unitarian ministers could be trained in the West.

Huidekoper was raised in The Netherlands and found little opportunity for effective education until an older brother sent him to Crefeld, Germany, where he thought that important aspects of his intellectual life were opened. He went to the United States in 1796 and gained employment with the Holland Land Company, settling in Meadville in 1804. There he worked as an agent for the company, negotiating contract sales of farm land to settlers, and eventually becoming a land holder himself. His religious training was in the Dutch Reformed Church, but when his children began to reach the age of religious instruction, Huidekoper began a personal study of the Bible to determine his own views. The result was his espousal of Unitarianism, a belief that he professed so effectively in Meadville that a Unitarian church was established. Huidekoper brought to Meadville a number of bright young Divinity School graduates, as tutors to his children and preachers, establishing a unique western outpost for liberal religion. In the 1830s Huidekoper assisted James Freeman Clarke,* who married one of his daughters, both materially and by writing for the *Western Messenger*, the important early Unitarian and Transcendentalist publication. Huidekoper himself was an opponent of Transcendentalism, suspicious of its theological modernism and its identification with radical politics. In 1844 he took a lead in the establishment of Meadville Theological School, an institution that was badly needed to bolster Unitarianism's western presence. This stands as perhaps his most important contribution to the movement, although throughout his life he was an important presence to the denomination.

*Bibliography*

B.  DAB 9, 359–60; obituary by James Freeman Clarke, *Christian Examiner*, 52 (September 1854); Earl Morse Wilbur, *An Historical Sketch of the Independent Congregational Church at Meadville, Pennsylvania* (Meadville, PA, 1902); Francis A. Christie, *The Makers of Meadville Theological School, 1844–94* (Boston, 1927); Charles H. Lyttle, *Freedom Moves West* (Boston, 1952).

**HUSBANDS, MUNROE** (11 September 1909, Spokane, WA–4 January 1984, Needham, MA). *Education*: Graduated from University of Utah, 1931; graduated from Leland Powers School of Radio and Theatre, 1934. *Career*: Head of Speech Department, McCune School of Music and Art, 1934–42; military service, 1942–45; associate director of public relations, Blue Cross of Massachusetts, 1946–47; director of fellowships and associate director of extension,

American Unitarian Association and Unitarian Universalist Association, 1948–67; active retirement, 1967–84.

After World War II Unitarianism experienced an enormous surge of growth, due at least in part to a concerted denominational effort to encourage the formation of Unitarian fellowships. They were conceived as lay-led religious societies, not merely churches without ministers. In 1967 Lon Ray Call* emphasized that "the man who is primarily responsible for having made the fellowship movement . . . the success that it is, is Munroe Husbands" (Unitarian Universalist Association, p. 8). As the director of fellowships for the American Unitarian Association (AUA), Husbands traveled extensively to organize and nurture these new religious societies and was active in helping to prepare materials necessary for their functioning. Husbands noted that many to whom the fellowships appealed had "developed an antipathy toward the entire religious vocabulary: worship, God, prayer, invocation, benediction." But part of the fellowship experience addressed that mentality: "Slowly the individual divests himself of his negativism, talks out the resentment accumulated over the years, and begins formulating a positive philosophy of religion" ("Fellowship Can Accomplish Anything It Will," pp. 11–12). Thus the Unitarian fellowship was not only a unique experiment in religious organization, it might in many cases provide a unique form of religious experience to its members. Husbands also saw value in the fellowship's ability to bring out the "latent talents" of its members and encourage a strong degree of participation in the religious community. These things are important factors in a religious tradition that, since William Ellery Channing,* has stressed self-culture as a focus of the religious life. In 1974 Husbands was awarded the Unitarian Universalist Association (UUA) Annual Award for Distinguished Service to the Cause of Liberal Religion.

*Bibliography*

A. "Fellowship Can Accomplish Anything It Will," *Christian Register* (April 1957), 11–12.

B. Laile E. Bartlett, *Bright Galaxy: Ten Years of Unitarian Fellowships* (Boston, 1960); Unitarian Universalist Association, Department of Extension, *Take a Giant Step: Two Decades of the Fellowships* (Boston, 1967); Conrad Wright, ed., *A Stream of Light* (Boston, 1975).

# J

**JENKINS, LYDIA ANN MOULTON** (1824 or 25, Auburn, NY–7 May 1874, Binghamton, NY). *Career*: Speaker for women's rights, NY, c. 1850–74; Universalist preacher, NY and New England, c. 1857–60; cominister, Universalist society in Clinton, NY, 1860–62; minister, Farmer (now Interlaken) Universalist Society, 1862; itinerant Universalist preacher, 1862–66; physician, Binghamton, NY, 1866–74.

Lydia Jenkins was an early speaker and advocate for women's rights and one of the first women to preach as a Universalist. Russell E. Miller noted that she was "the first woman to be regularly fellowshipped as a Universalist preacher" (Miller, *The Larger Hope*, p. 547). Her preaching example, according to Miller, helped to change the attitude of the influential Thomas Whittemore* about women in the pulpit. Recent research by Charles Semowich indicates that Jenkins was ordained by the Ontario Association of Universalists in Geneva, New York, in 1860, an event that would stand in his words as "the first ordination of a woman by a denominational body in the United States" (Semowich, p. 10). That distinction had previously been accorded to Olympia Brown.* (For more details on this issue, see Chapter 10, note 33.) Although there is not an abundance of information on Jenkins, Semowich's research has shown that she was apparently brought up with Calvinist beliefs, moving beyond them toward Universalism in early womanhood. In the 1846–50 period she married Edmund Samuel Jenkins, and the two became a husband-wife ministerial team in New York State in the late 1850s. She wrote and spoke on women's rights issues in the 1850s and also began to preach as a Universalist, being granted a letter of fellowship from the Ontario Association in 1858. In May 1860 she and her husband became ministers of the Universalist Church in Clinton, New York. Semowich cited a report of the *Christian Ambassador* for June 23, 1860, noting that she and her husband were ordained. (For further discussion of the ordination issue, see Chapter 10.) This fact has probably been overlooked, as Semo-wich noted, because "the records of the Ontario Association are not extant for 1860 and . . . the newspaper that published the minutes exists in only two copies" (Semowich, p. 10). He also noted contemporary comment that the fear of controversy surrounding such an act may have caused it to remain unpubli-cized. The fact that Jenkins was part of a husband-wife team also probably less-ened the controversial aspect of her ordination. After several years of preach-ing, Jenkins prepared for medical practice in the early 1860s and settled with her husband in Binghamton, New York, to operate a medical facility. As an early activist in the women's movement, and a pioneer woman preacher, Jen-kins deserves a larger place in history than she has previously had.

*Bibliography*

A. "Women-Civil Rights," *The Lily* (February 1850).

B. E. R. Hanson, *Our Women Workers* (Chicago, 1881); Russell E. Miller, *The Larger Hope* (Boston, 1979); Charles Semowich, "Lydia Ann Jenkins: Women's Rights Activist, Physician, and First Recognized Woman Minister in the United States," unpublished typescript, 1983. I am grateful to Mr. Semowich for the use of his re-search in preparing this biography.

**JOHNSON, SAMUEL** (10 October 1822, Salem, MA–19 February 1882, North Andover, MA). *Education*: A.B., Harvard, 1842; graduated from Harvard Di-vinity School, 1846. *Career*: Candidate preaching in Unitarian churches in eastern Massachusetts, 1846–52; preacher, Central Unitarian Society, Lynn, MA, 1852–53; minister, Independent Church (formerly Central Unitarian Society), Lynn, MA, 1853–70; author, 1870–82.

Influenced by both the heritage of Transcendentalism and the ferment of Free Religion in the Unitarian denomination, Samuel Johnson preached and lived a radical brand of individualism. His career illustrates how difficult it was for religious radicalism to coexist with denominational and organizational struc-tures in the late nineteenth century. Johnson's difficulties with denominational restraints began early in his career when he preached in the Boston area as a candidate for Unitarian pulpits after graduating from Harvard Divinity School. Johnson was a committed antislavery man at this time and found that his polit-ical involvements impeded finding a pulpit. After preaching in Dorchester, Massachusetts, he was requested "not to introduce any political subject" into his next sermon. "I am accustomed to preach upon such subjects as I deem it my duty," he replied, "and in the performance of that I will not be interfered with" (*Lectures, Essays, and Sermons*, p. 34). Such unyielding principle and individuality marked Johnson's entire career, and when he finally settled as pastor to a Unitarian congregation in Lynn, Massachusetts, he persuaded the church to disassociate itself from the Unitarian denomination and become completely independent. Johnson carried his principle of individuality so far that he refused to join even so loose and nondogmatic a group as the Free Religious Association. He wrote to O. B. Frothingham* explaining this refusal, saying that "I do not put much trust in any arrangements or combinations, only in the spirit which dictates them" (Frothingham, p. 209). Perhaps more revealing of Johnson's individualism was the debate he carried on with James Freeman Clarke* in the late 1860s while the National Conference was being organized. In the exchange Johnson championed the position of pure individualism against Clarke's sense of the need for organization and unity within the Unitarian body. Johnson based his religious convictions on a Transcendental faith in an intuitive spiritual revelation, much in the tradition of Ralph Waldo Emerson.* He argued that God was "not an object, but an experience." That experience is exemplified in "the love we feel, the truth we pursue, the honor we cherish, [and] the moral beauty we revere," all of which "flow" from eternal principles (p. 211). With such a basis for religious truth, Johnson looked beyond the Judeo-Christian tradition to the religions of the world for confirmation. He was a pioneer in the study of Oriental religions, devoting most of his later years to the preparation of three volumes on comparative religion. Johnson's historical reputation rests largely on this work, the most extensive attempt to connect the universal religion toward which Free Religion was tending to the essence of all the world's religions. He also was an accomplished hymnist, and in collaboration with his close friend Samuel Longfellow,* he produced the widely used *Hymns of the Spirit.*

*Bibliography*

A.  *Hymns of the Spirit* (coeditor, Boston, 1864); *Oriental Religions and Their Relation to Universal Religion: India* (Boston, 1872); *Oriental Religions and Their Relation to Universal Religion: China* (Boston, 1877); *Lectures, Essays, and Sermons, with a Memoir by Samuel Longfellow* (Boston, 1883); *Oriental Religions and Their Relation to Universal Religion: Persia* (Boston, 1885); *Selected Writings of Samuel Johnson*, ed. Roger C. Mueller (Delmar, NY, 1977).

B.  DAB 10, 119–20; DLB 1, 115; Heralds 3, 185–90; O. B. Frothingham, *Recollections and Impressions, 1822–1890* (New York, 1891); Roger C. Mueller, "Samuel Johnson, American Transcendentalist: A Short Biography," *Essex Institute Historical Collections*, 115 (1979), entire issue; Carl T. Jackson, *The Oriental Religions and American Thought: Nineteenth-Century Explorations* (Westport, CT, 1981).

**JONES, JENKIN LLOYD** (14 November 1843, Cardiganshire, South Wales–12 September 1918, Chicago, IL). *Education*: Graduated from Meadville Theological School, 1870. *Career*: Military service, 1862–65; Unitarian minister, Winnetka, IL, 1870–71; All Souls Church, Janesville, WI, 1871–80; secretary, Western Unitarian Conference, 1875–84; founder, *Unity*, 1878; organizer and minister, All Souls Church, Chicago, 1882–1905; secretary, World's Parliament of Religions, 1892–93; director, Abraham Lincoln Centre, Chicago, 1905–18.

Jenkin Lloyd Jones was the leader of the *Unity* men, the radically modernist element in Midwest Unitarianism of the later nineteenth century. Jones had a forceful personality and was a tireless worker; he combined these traits to lead the Western Unitarian Conference on a largely independent path from Boston Unitarianism. He stressed an absolutely creedless "ethical basis" as the common element in the churches he wanted to bring together, a theological position that left Christology, and some believed even *theology*, in the background. He was also a pioneer in religious education, embodying his liberal views in Sunday-school work. Jones's boyhood was on a Wisconsin farm, and after service in the Civil War, he had to struggle hard to work his way through Meadville Theological School. As pastor at Janesville, Wisconsin, he developed his involvement with the Western Unitarian Conference (WUC), becoming its secretary in 1875 and a full-time missionary secretary in 1880. From that position he led western Unitarianism in a radical direction, founding the periodical *Unity* to help foster his efforts. Although Jones was the most powerful western figure in the denomination, he encountered friction from the American Unitarian Association (AUA) because of his independent course and friction within the WUC because of his theological radicalism. In 1882 Jones reorganized the Fourth Unitarian Society in Chicago as All Souls Church, and a decade later he played a central role in the World's Parliament of Religions, which brought together a number of world religious leaders. The conference seemed a step toward Jones's dream of a universal church for humankind. He ended his career as director of the Abraham Lincoln Centre in Chicago, where he continued to be a voice of reform. In his last years, he spoke as a pacifist in opposition to World War I.

*Bibliography*

A. *The Faith That Makes Faithful* (coauthor, Chicago, 1887); *Jess: Bits of Wayside Gospel* (New York and London, 1899); *A Search for an Infidel* (New York and London, 1901); *Love and Loyalty* (Chicago, 1907); *An Artillery Man's Diary* (Madison, WI, 1914); *Love for the Battle-Torn Peoples* (Chicago, 1916).

B. DAB 10, 179–80; Heralds 4, 164–73; *Who Was Who in America* 1, 648; Charles H. Lyttle, *Freedom Moves West* (Boston, 1952); Clinton Lee Scott, *These Live Tomorrow: Twenty Unitarian Universalist Biographies* (Boston, 1964); Thomas Graham, "Jenkin Lloyd Jones and the World's Columbian Exposition of 1893," *Collegium Proceedings*, 1 (1979), 61–81; Thomas Graham, "The Making of a Secretary: Jenkin Lloyd Jones at Thirty-One," PUUHS, 19, part 2 (1982–83), 36–55.

**JORDAN, JOSEPH FLETCHER** (1863, Gates County, NC–1 May 1929, Suffolk, VA). *Career:* Principal, Suffolk Normal Training School, 1904–29.

Although he became a presiding elder in the Methodist Church, Joseph Jordan was troubled by doctrine of "hell and endless punishment." He was converted to Universalism after hearing the preaching of Quillen H. Shinn,* and the *Universalist Year Book* describes his conversion in these terms: "Then came Dr. Shinn and Dr. Shinn's 'beautiful gospel.' He felt that necessity to proclaim this transforming message was laid upon him, and he entered the Universalist Church" (p. 124). After some preparation at St. Lawrence, Jordan went to Suffolk, Virginia, where he helped Thomas Wise in the educational and religious work begun there under the leadership of Joseph Jordan* (of no kin). In 1904 Jordan took charge of the work, remaining there as principal of the Suffolk Normal Training School until his death. The school grew significantly under his leadership and continued as the Jordan House. The *Universalist Year Book* noted the universal respect that Jordan commanded and his "strong, unique personality" (p. 124). He was one of the most important early black Universalist leaders.

*Bibliography*

B.  William H. McGlauflin, D.D., *Faith with Power: A Life Story of Quillen Hamilton Shinn, D.D.* (Boston and Chicago, 1912); *Universalist Year Book, 1930* (Boston, 1930), p. 124; Mark D. Morrison-Reed, *Black Pioneers in a White Denomination* (rev. ed., Boston, 1984).

**JORDAN, JOSEPH H.** (1842–3 June 1901, Norfolk, VA). *Career:* Ordained Universalist minister, 1889; leader, Universalist missionary church and school for Negroes, Norfolk, VA, 1894–1901.

Joseph Jordan was the first black to be ordained in the Universalist ministry, receiving ordination under the Rev. Edwin C. Sweetser of Philadelphia in 1889. Jordan's desire was to begin a missionary work in his home city, Norfolk, Virginia. In this undertaking he received the support of Sweetser and Quillen H. Shinn.* In 1893 he delivered an address to the Universalist General Convention in Washington, D.C., to ask support "for a mission to the negroes in the South" (McGlauflin, p. 87). The support was granted, and in 1894 a building was erected in Norfolk that was used for worship services and as a school and industrial center. Jordan's work grew, and in 1898, with his assistant Thomas Wise, another such project was begun in Suffolk, Virginia. Jordan died in 1901, but Joseph Fletcher Jordan,* of no kin, continued work begun in Suffolk as principal of the Suffolk Normal Training School.

*Bibliography*

B.  William H. McGlauflin, D.D., *Faith with Power: A Life Story of Quillen Hamilton Shinn, D.D.* (Boston and Chicago, 1912); Mark D. Morrison-Reed, *Black Pioneers in a White Denomination* (rev. ed., Boston, 1984).

# K

---

**KING, THOMAS STARR** (17 December 1824, New York, NY–4 March 1864, San Francisco, CA). *Career*: Various employment including office work and school principalship, with private study, 1839–46; minister, Universalist Church, Charlestown, MA, 1846–48; Hollis Street Unitarian Church, 1848–60; Unitarian Church, San Francisco, 1860–64; public lecturer, 1847–64.

Thomas Starr King was the most notable missionary of Unitarianism to the West Coast, and it was in his honor that the Starr King School for Religious Leadership in Berkeley is named. He was the son of the Universalist minister Thomas Farrington King, whose death in 1839 interrupted his son's education. King was forced into a variety of jobs to support his family after his father's death, but he continued a program of assiduous independent study to qualify himself for the ministry. Called to his father's old church in Charlestown in 1846, King was an energetic pastor and a magnetic public speaker. He then began to combine his preaching with public lecturing in the Boston area. His various skills caught the attention of the struggling Hollis Street Unitarian Church, which called him in 1848. King accepted the call and the change of denominations but maintained close ties to Universalism throughout his life. Despite his success in Boston, King decided to move west, accepting an invitation from the Unitarian Church in San Francisco in 1860, there launching the most historically important phase of his career. Although his pastoral work there was important, he also quickly established a reputation as a lecturer. This reputation increased when he began a lecture campaign to increase support for the Union cause in California. As the Civil War broke out, it was a state whose loyalties were much in doubt, and King helped to secure it for the North, continuing his war effort with a fund-raising drive for the Sanitary Commission. These speaking tours made King a prominent public figure in California, and even a career in politics seemed possible if he had wanted it. But his career was cut short with his death to diphtheria and pneumonia in 1864 at age thirty-nine. Despite his brief career, his impact on West Coast Unitarianism was immeasurable, and his life has been termed by Arnold Crompton one of "legend" (Crompton, *Unitarianism*, p. 22).

*Bibliography*

A. *The White Hills: Their Legends, Landscape, and Poetry* (Boston, 1859); *Patriotism and Other Papers*, ed. Richard Frothingham (Boston, 1864); *Christianity and Humanity*, ed. Edwin P. Whipple (Boston, 1877).

B. DAB 10, 403–5; Heralds 3, 191–201; Richard Frothingham, *A Tribute to Thomas Starr King, Patriot and Preacher* (Boston, 1921); Arnold Crompton, *Apostle of Liberty: Starr King in California* (Boston, 1950); Arnold Crompton, *Unitarianism on the Pacific Coast: The First Sixty Years* (Boston, 1957).

**KNEELAND, ABNER** (7 April 1774, Gardner, MA–27 August 1844, Salubria, IA). *Career*: Universalist minister, Langdon, NH, 1805–12; Charlestown, MA, 1812–13; private business, Charlestown, MA, 1813–17; Universalist minister, Whitestown, NY, 1817–18; Lombard Street Universalist Church, Philadelphia, PA, 1818–25; editor, *Christian Messenger*, 1819–21; *Philadelphia Universalist Magazine and Christian Messenger*, 1821–23; *Gazetteer*, 1824; minister, Prince Street Universalist Society, 1825–27; Second Universalist Society, 1827–29; editor, *Olive Branch and Christian Inquirer*, 1827–c. 1829; resigned from Universalist church, 1829; founder, First Society of Free Enquirers, Boston, c. 1829; founder, *Boston Investigator*, 1831; tried for blasphemy, with three appeals, Boston, 1834–38; jailed for sixty days, 1838; residence in Salubria, IA, 1839–44.

Abner Kneeland's religious pilgrimage took him from Baptist origins into the Universalist pulpit and from there to a controversial career as an advocate of free thinking in Boston in the 1830s. In fact, Kneeland so outraged the orthodox with his public advocacy of what they believed was atheism that he was tried and convicted for blasphemy and served a term of sixty days in jail in 1838. Kneeland's long quest began with his conversion to Universalism in 1803. After more than a decade of preaching, he became bothered by doubts about the divine origin of the Bible. He discussed these difficulties, and temporarily overcame them, in a correspondence with Hosea Ballou,* published in 1816. In pastorates in Philadelphia and New York (1818–29) he continued as a Universalist and edited several religious periodicals. But in 1829, in part under the influence of radicals Robert D. Owen and Frances Wright, Kneeland publicly rejected the evidences of Christianity and left the Universalist denomination. He moved to Boston, founded the First Society of Free Enquirers, and began an extensive campaign to spread free thinking. In 1831 he began to edit the *Boston Investigator*. "It was the *Investigator*," Henry Steele Commager wrote, "that got Kneeland into trouble" (Commager, p. 31). One of his articles in 1833 affirmed, among other things, that "Universalists believe in a god which

I do not,'' calling their God "nothing more than a chimera of their own imagination" (p. 32). This was taken to be a violation of the 1782 Act Against Blasphemy, and Kneeland was tried and convicted. He appealed, and after three more trials, as the case grew increasingly uncomfortable to the Boston establishment, his appeal was denied and he served the sentence. Kneeland was a problem for the Boston religious establishment for several reasons. His journey from Universalism to presumed atheism confirmed the warnings of many opponents of liberal religion that liberalism led to atheism. His being silenced for expressing his opinion certainly violated principles of free speech, causing some religious liberals to oppose the conviction while others supported it. William Ellery Channing* drew up a petition, which was unsuccessful, for Kneeland's release, and the trial seemed to expose the confluence of the Boston religious and political establishments. After his release from jail, Kneeland traveled to Iowa, where he had plans to establish a community of free thinkers. Although the community did not prosper, Kneeland lived there until his death in 1844.

*Bibliography*

A. *A Series of Lectures on the Doctrine of Universal Benevolence* (Philadelphia, 1818); *A Review of the Evidences of Christianity* (New York, 1829); *A Review of the Trial, Conviction, and Final Imprisonment . . . of Abner Kneeland for the Alleged Crime of Blasphemy* (autobiographical) (Boston, 1838).
B. DAB 10, 457–58; NCAB 24, 186–87; Henry Steele Commager, "The Blasphemy of Abner Kneeland," *New England Quarterly*, 8 (1935), 29–41; Roderick S. French, "Liberation from Man and God in Boston: Abner Kneeland's Free-Thought Campaign, 1830–39," *American Quarterly*, 32 (1980), 202–21; Anne C. Rose, *Transcendentalism as a Social Movement, 1830–1850* (New Haven, 1981).

**KUEBLER, ERNEST WILLIAM** (29 October 1929, Kansas City, MO). *Education*: Attended Kansas City Jr. College, 1921–23; Ph.B., Boston University, 1926; B.R.E., Boston University, 1929; A.M. and graduate study, Yale University, 1930–32. *Career*: General secretary, Dauphine Co., PA, Sabbath School Association, 1927–29; executive secretary, Harrisburg, PA, Council of Religious Education, 1929–30; director, Bridgeport, CT, Weekday Religious Education System, 1930–32; director of religious education, Central Congregational Church, Newtonville, MA, 1932–35; secretary, Department of Religious Education, American Unitarian Association (AUA), 1935–37; director, AUA Division of Religious Education, 1937–49; executive vice-president, AUA, 1949–54; administrative director, Division of Education, Council of Liberal Churches, 1954–61; president, International Association for Religious Freedom, 1958–61; director, Education Department, Unitarian Universalist Association (UUA), 1961–62; project director, Hugh Moore Fund, New York, 1962–64; executive director, St. Lawrence Unitarian Universalist District, 1964–67; minister-at-large, New York State Convention of Universalists, 1969–76; general editor, Beacon Books in Religious Education, 1937–62.

Ernest Kuebler has been one of the most important forces in religious education in twentieth-century liberal religion. Working with Frederick May Eliot* and Sophia L. Fahs,* Kuebler helped to fashion a major overhaul in Unitarian religious education in the 1930s. This program was not only an important part of the general revivification of Unitarianism in the late 1930s, but it helped to sustain the growth of the denomination in the late 1940s and 1950s, a period of major denominational expansion. Kuebler's reformation of the religious education curriculum moved Unitarian religious education "from a Bible centered to a child centered approach" ("Our Search for Roots," p. 2). In 1938 Kuebler was ordained to the "educational ministry," a service that symbolized his sense of the centrality of education to religious experience and maturity. Kuebler also lent his administrative talents to the Council of Liberal Churches, an organizational forerunner of the Unitarian and Universalist merger. At the death of Frederick Eliot in 1958, Kuebler was nominated for president by the AUA Board of Directors, but he lost a close election to Dana M. Greeley.* Kuebler's administrative work continued in New York State in the 1960s, and in 1980 he was given the Award for Distinguished Service to the Cause of Liberal Religion.

*Bibliography*

B. *Who's Who in America* (1978–79), 1851; Joseph Barth, "Contests for the Presidency: A.U.A., 1958–U.U.A., 1961," PUHS, 15 (1964), 26–65; "Our Search for Roots—An Interview with Dr. Ernest Kuebler," *St. Lawrence Unitarian Universalist District Newsletter*, no. 7 (February–March, 1976–77), 1–2; "Distinguished Service Citation," *Unitarian Universalist World*, August 15, 1980, p. 7.

# L

LIVERMORE, MARY ASHTON RICE (19 December 1820, Boston, MA–23 May 1905, Melrose, MA). *Career*: Teacher of Languages, Martha Whiting's Female Seminary, Charlestown, MA, 1836–38; private tutor, VA, 1839–42; school headmistress, Duxbury, MA, 1842–45; author and homemaker, 1846–61; associate editor, *New Covenant*, 1858–69; leader, Chicago Sanitary Commission, 1861–65; convened woman suffrage meeting, Chicago, 1868; editor, *Agitator*, 1869; editor, *Woman's Journal*, 1869–72; lyceum lecturer, 1870–95; first president, Association for the Advancement of Women, 1873; president, American Woman Suffrage Association, 1875–78; president, Massachusetts Woman's Christian Temperance Union, 1875–95.

As a girl Mary Rice was deeply troubled by the strict Calvinist doctrines taught her in her devout Baptist home. She recalled waking her parents often at night insisting upon "their rising to pray for the salvation of (her) younger sisters," already admitting that "I expect to be lost" (*The Story of My Life*, p. 62). She conceived God as "only a judge, who tried human beings, condemned or acquitted them, and sent them to reward or punishment." She thus directed her prayers to "Our Jesus who art in heaven" (p. 60). She was finally liberated from this religious torture when she took the faith of her husband, Daniel Livermore, a Universalist minister. The marriage was a long and happy partnership. Mary Livermore spent her early years as a homemaker and author as Daniel moved through several pastorates. When he founded the Universalist periodical *New Covenant* in Chicago, she helped him edit it. During the Civil War she became deeply involved in work for the Sanitary Commission, and this changed her political outlook. "During the war, and as a result of my own observations, I became aware that a large portion of the nation's work was badly done, or not done at all, because woman was not recognized as a factor in the political world" (p. 469). This awakened political consciousness led Livermore to a position of leadership in the Woman's Suffrage movement and eventually to her public prominence as a lecturer. She began touring as part of the lyceum movement in 1870 and became the "Queen of the Platform" (NAW, p. 412). "Neither school, college, nor university could have given me the education I have received in the lecture field," she wrote, but she was also engaged in a process of educating the public, having chosen the subject of women for her first course of lectures (*The Story of My Life*, p. 490). "What Shall We Do with Our Daughters?" was one of her most popular and widely repeated lectures. Livermore was also a leading spokesman for the Temperance movement and characterized the Women's Temperance Movement of the 1870s as "the anguished protest of hopeless and life-sick women against the drunkenness of the time, which threatened to fill the land with beggary and crime" (p. 578). Livermore's great power as a platform speaker gave her crusading views prominence, and she was one of the great popularizers of the reform movements of the nineteenth century.

*Bibliography*

A. *Pen-Pictures; or, Sketches from Domestic Life* (Chicago, 1862); *What Shall We Do with Our Daughters? Superfluous Women, and Other Lectures* (Boston, 1883); *My Story of the War* (Hartford, CT, 1887); *A Woman of the Century* (coeditor, Buffalo, 1893); *The Story of My Life* (Hartford, CT, 1897).

B. DAB 11, 306–7; NAW 2, 410–13; Charles A. Howe, "Daniel and Mary Livermore: The Biography of a Marriage," PUUHS 19, part 2 (1982–83), 14–35.

**LONGFELLOW, SAMUEL** (18 June 1819, Portland, ME–3 October 1892, Portland, ME). *Education*: A.B., Harvard, 1839; graduated from Harvard Divinity School, 1846. *Career*: Unitarian minister, Fall River, MA, 1848–51; traveled in Europe, 1851–52; minister, Second Unitarian Church, Brooklyn, NY, 1853–60; various preaching, writing, and traveling, 1860–73; Unitarian minister, Germantown, PA, 1878–82; active retirement, 1882–92.

Samuel Longfellow, brother of the poet Henry Wadsworth Longfellow, made his place in American Unitarian history as a hymnist, collaborating with Samuel Johnson* on the well-known collection *Hymns of the Spirit*. Longfellow attended Harvard College and Divinity School when the Transcendentalist ferment there was strong among the students. He was influenced by Theodore Parker* and formed there his lifelong friendship with Johnson. But in contrast to many of the Transcendentalists, Longfellow was interested in the act of corporate worship as well as individual devotion. This accounts for much of his concern with church music and the worship service. As students, he and Johnson compiled *A Book of Hymns for Public and Private Devotion*, which preceded the better-known *Hymns of the Spirit* by almost two decades. O. B. Frothingham* characterized the hymns of the two men as reflections of their complementary personalities: "Johnson's were the more intellectual, Longfellow's the most tender; Johnson's the more aspiring, Longfellow's the more de-

vout; Johnson's the more heroic and passionate, Longfellow's the more mystical and reflective" (Frothingham, p. 348). In addition to preparing his hymnody,
Longfellow was an active essayist and sermon writer and a biographer of his
brother. In Frances A. Christie's words, he was "a gentle and serene spirit, a
man of social charm, [who] gave and received abundant love" (DAB, p. 348).

*Bibliography*

A. *A Book of Hymns for Public and Private Devotion* (coeditor, Cambridge, 1846);
   *Thalatta: A Book for the Seaside* (Boston, 1853); *Hymns of the Spirit* (coeditor, Boston, 1864); *Life of Henry Wadsworth Longfellow* 2 vols. (Boston, 1886); *Hymns and
   Verses* (Boston, 1894); *Samuel Longfellow: Essays and Sermons*, ed. Joseph May
   (Boston, 1894).

B. DAB 11, 387–88; DLB 1, 125; Heralds 3, 216–23; O. B. Frothingham, *Transcendentalism in New England* (New York, 1876); *Samuel Longfellow: Memoir and Letters*, ed. Joseph May (New York, 1894).

# M

MAYHEW, JONATHAN (8 October 1720, Martha's Vineyard, MA–9 July 1766, Boston, MA). *Education*: A.B., Harvard College, 1744. *Career*: Minister, West Church, Boston, MA, 1747–66.

Jonathan Mayhew, an important eighteenth-century liberal, was called by Conrad Wright* one of "the two great leaders [with Charles Chauncy*] of the first generation of New England Arminians" (Wright, p. 63). A graduate of Harvard in 1744, he was called to Boston's West Church in 1747, a prosperous church known for its hospitality to liberal views. Mayhew was perhaps more public in his Arminianism than Chauncy and suffered a certain ostracism from many of his Boston colleagues who wanted to protect the Calvinist orthodoxy. In his preaching Mayhew distinguished himself as a strong opponent of creeds in any form, and his stand for intellectual liberty was an early instance of a long series of important affirmations of this principle in American Unitarian history. He also led the New England Arminians in their attack on the doctrines of original sin, laying the groundwork for an affirmation of human nature that would eventually develop in the thought of William Ellery Channing* and others into the doctrine of spiritual character development that was a hallmark of nineteenth-century Unitarianism. In politics Mayhew was an ardent supporter of the building colonial cause, although he died before the American Revolution broke out. "He nobly claimed that which he esteemed equally the right of others,—the liberty of thinking for himself," wrote Chauncy in his funeral sermon for Mayhew (AAUP, p. 26). His independence of mind, more than any other quality, secured his place in the history of American liberalism.

*Bibliography*

A. *Seven Sermons* (Boston, 1749): *Sermons upon the Following Subjects . . .* (Boston, 1755).

B.  AAUP, 22–29; DAB 12, 454–55; DARB, 300–301; Heralds 1, 34–48; Alden Bradford, *Memoir of the Life and Writings of Rev. Jonathan Mayhew, D.D.* (Boston, 1838); Conrad Wright, *The Beginnings of Unitarianism in America* (Boston, 1955); Charles W. Akers, *Called unto Liberty: A Life of Johathan Mayhew* (Cambridge, 1964).

**MEAD, SIDNEY EARL** (2 August 1904, Champlin, MN). *Education*: B.A., University of Redlands, 1934; studied at Yale Divinity School, 1934–36; M.A., University of Chicago Divinity School, 1938; Ph.D., University of Chicago Divinity School, 1941. *Career*: Instructor to professor, Federated Theological Faculty, University of Chicago, 1943–60; president, Meadville Theological School, 1956–60; professor of American church history, Southern California School of Theology, 1960–64; professor of religion in American history, University of Iowa, 1964–72; active retirement, 1972–present.

Sidney Mead's interest in the history of religion in America, and particularly in the distinguishing peculiarities of American religious development, has relevance for the developing sense of the place of Unitarianism in the American tradition. Mead distinguished himself as an American church historian through his emphasis on the sectarian diversity of the American religious experience. Moreover, he noted the rationalist basis for that diversity, flowing from Thomas Jefferson, Benjamin Franklin, and the Enlightenment school, a tradition committed to religious freedom and pragmatic morality. Ironically, Mead noted, it was this rationalism that liberated the more pietistic and antirationalist sects characteristic of revivalist Protestantism, even though they repudiated the rationalism of the Enlightenment. This rationalist heritage is of great importance to Unitarianism. As Mead noted in an address on Unitarian history, "when the overwhelming bulk of American Protestantism turned 'right' in a flight from Reason [during the early 1800s], Unitarianism turned 'left' in defense of Reason" ("An Address to Unitarians," p. 16). If this helps to explain the relatively small size of the Unitarian denomination, Mead also enumerated two other periods—the period from 1815 to 1840 and the two decades after the Civil War—when Unitarianism had a chance to become a large and popular religious movement. In both of these cases, internal and external forces prevented this most American of American religions from assuming greater national prominence. For Mead, this unfulfilled potential gave American Unitarianism "some of the character of a Greek tragedy" in which men held "expectations that the situation and their own characters made impossible of fulfillment" (p. 18). Mead recently characterized the "typical Unitarian" as "one for whom the standard religious formulas have failed, who lives therefore on the verge of a belief vacuum." For him, the liberal must look to "a shared quest with kindred souls" as the basis of the religious life ("Dimensions of Faith," p. 2). In the quest itself, if not in a realization of final truth, a fulfillment can be gained.

*Bibliography*

A. *Nathaniel William Taylor, 1786–1858: A Connecticut Liberal* (Chicago, 1942); "An Address to Unitarians," PUHS, 12 (1958), 12–22; *The Lively Experiment: The Shaping of Christianity in America* (New York, 1963); *The Nation with the Soul of a Church* (New York, 1976); *The Old Religion in the Brave New World* (Berkeley and Los Angeles, 1977); *History and Identity* (Missoula, MT, 1979); "Dimensions of Faith: The Unitarian Way," *Unitarian Universalist World*, 13 (May 15, 1982), 1–2.

B. CA P–1, 440; DAS 1, 509.

**MINER, ALONZO AMES** (17 August 1814, Lempster, NH–14 June 1895, Boston, MA). *Career*: Teacher, Chester, VT, 1834–35; academy head, Unity, NY, 1835–39; ordained Universalist minister, 1839; minister, Methuen, MA, 1839–42; Lowell, MA, 1842–48; associate pastor, Second Universalist Church, Boston, 1848–91; president, Tufts College, 1862–74.

After a period of schoolkeeping in his early manhood, Alonzo A. Miner dedicated himself to the Universalist ministry. His ordination in 1839 began a long and distinguished career in the service of American Universalism. After two pastorates in Massachusetts he was called to be the associate of Hosea Ballou* in Boston. There he made his mark in denominational affairs, became an active builder in the field of education, and took public stands as an opponent of slavery and a crusader for the temperance movement. Miner was best known as a temperance crusader, serving as head of the Massachusetts Temperance Alliance for a number of years and acting as a public watchdog in the battle to control the liquor traffic. Miner also reached public prominence as president of Tufts College (1862–74), accepting the presidency of the college on top of his ministerial duties. He took it over at one of the weakest points in its history, when the school was in debt and without sufficient dependable income. Miner's efforts saved the college, and when he resigned in 1874, he left it in a much more secure financial position as well as in a much improved academic state. Because of his work as an educator, and his leadership in the temperance cause, Miner stood as one of Boston's most prominent representatives of Universalism in the late nineteenth century.

*Bibliography*

A. *Bible Exercises; or, The Sunday School, 1st Class* (Boston, 1854); *Argument on the Right and Duty of Prohibition* (Boston, 1867); *The Old Forts Taken: Five Lectures on Endless Punishment and Future Life* (Boston, 1878).

B. DAB 13, 21–22; NCAB 1, 315; John G. Adams, *Fifty Notable Years* (Boston, 1882); George H. Emerson, *Life of Alonzo Ames Miner, S.T.D., LL.D.* (Boston, 1896); Russell E. Miller, *Light on the Hill: A History of Tufts College, 1852–1952* (Boston, 1966); Russell E. Miller, *The Larger Hope* (Boston, 1979).

**MURRAY, JOHN** (10 December 1741, Alton, England–3 September 1815, Boston, MA). *Career*: Itinerant Universalist preacher, 1770–74; preacher,

Gloucester, MA, and frequently traveling evangelist, 1774–93; chaplain in American Revolutionary army, 1775; preacher, Boston, 1793–1815.

The Universalist movement in America began when John Murray's boat from England ran aground in 1770 at Cranberry Inlet, New Jersey. There he met Thomas Potter, who had been waiting for God to send a preacher to him with a distinctive message. Murray, he believed, was that man, and Murray came to agree with him. Murray's background in England tells much about his own reasons for coming to Universalism and much about the emotional and intellectual basis of the entire movement as well. He was brought up a strict Calvinist and suffered much psychological torment from his fear that he was foreordained to damnation. The influence of John Wesley relieved that fear in some respects, but once the pattern of his progress away from the harsher elements of Calvinism had begun, it would not stop short of the total rejection of everlasting punishment. The key to Murray's development was his reading of James Relly's *Union* (1759) and his subsequent listening to his preaching. Relly argued that all humanity actually achieved union with Christ in his death and therefore had already paid the price for sin. Murray's espousal of this doctrine cost him friends and social standing, and his ostracism was accompanied by several other tragedies. He lost his child and his wife and was beset by economic difficulties, serving time in debtor's prison. His ultimate answer to his problems was the trip to America, which began his career as a preacher.

After landing in New Jersey, Murray began preaching extensively in the colonies, going in 1774 to Gloucester, Massachusetts, where he enjoyed the patronage of Winthrop Sargent, a prominent ship captain who had read and taken an interest in Relly. With Sargent's help, a Universalist church was formed in Gloucester in 1779, with Murray as its pastor. Murray's pastorate in Gloucester was marked by struggle against the prevailing orthodox religious opinion and numerous legal struggles to achieve the right to form a dissenting church. But his message grew, and in 1793 he moved to Boston, where he stayed as minister until his death. In 1788 he married Judith Sargent Stevens [Murray]*, the widowed daughter of Winthrop Sargent, whose literary career complemented Murray's religious work. Murray's pastorates were punctuated by extensive preaching elsewhere, as he worked to spread the Universalist message in the new nation.

*Bibliography*

A. *Letters and Sketches of Sermons*, 3 vols. (Boston, 1812–13); *Records of the Life of the Rev. John Murray . . . Written by Himself . . . to Which Is Added a Brief Continuation . . .* [by Mrs. Judith Sargent Murray] (Boston, 1816).

B. DAB 13, 360–62; *Records of the Life of the Rev. John Murray* (see above); Richard Eddy, *Universalism in America*, vol. 1 (Boston, 1884); Clarence R. Skinner and Alfred S. Cole, *Hell's Ramparts Fell: The Life of John Murray* (Boston, 1941); Russell E. Miller, *The Larger Hope* (Boston, 1979).

**MURRAY, JUDITH SARGENT STEVENS** (1 May 1751, Gloucester, MA– 6 July 1820, Natchez, MS). *Career*: Author of poetry, essays, and plays; resided in Gloucester, MA, 1751–93; Boston, 1793–1816; Natchez, MS, 1816– 20.

Judith Sargent Murray was one of America's earliest woman authors, attracting both contemporary notice and a place in literary history for her work as an essayist. She is also important to the history of Universalism because of her marriage to John Murray,* the founder of Universalism in America. Judith Sargent was a daughter of the prominent Gloucester sea captain Winthrop Sargent. She came into contact with John Murray when her father, who had been interested in the writings of James Relly, whose doctrine Murray preached, invited him to Gloucester. Judith Sargent had earlier married John Stevens, but after his death she married Murray and took an active part in his ministerial endeavors. During the illness at the close of his life she helped him edit his *Letters and Sketches of Sermons* (1812–13) and after his death completed the autobiography he had begun earlier. But her own literary reputation had been established before this work. She published poetry and wrote two plays, *The Medium* and *The Traveller Returned*, which were produced in Boston in 1795 and 1796. But her most important work was a series of essays published in 1792–94 as "The Gleaner." In 1798 a collection of her essays, plays, and poems was published. Murray was an early advocate of a fuller education and development of women and a defender of the equality of the sexes, and as such, hers is a pioneering voice in American cultural history.

*Bibliography*

A. *The Gleaner* (Boston, 1798).

B. DAB 13, 364–65; NAW 2, 603–5; Vena B. Field, *Constantia: A Study of the Life and Works of Judith Sargent Murray, 1751–1820* (Orono, ME, 1931); Aileen S. Kraditor, ed., *Up from the Pedestal: Selected Writings in the History of American Feminism* (Chicago, 1968); Russell E. Miller, *The Larger Hope* (Boston, 1979).

# N

---

**NORTON, ANDREWS** (31 December 1786, Hingham, MA–18 September 1853, Newport, RI). *Education*: A.B., Harvard College, 1804; A.M., Harvard College, 1809. *Career*: Lecturer and librarian, Harvard College, 1813–19; Dexter Professor of Sacred Literature, Harvard College, 1819–30; independent scholar, 1830–53.

Andrews Norton was a man destined to play two distinctly different roles in Unitarian history during his career as a biblical scholar and Harvard professor. In his early career he was among the young liberals like Joseph Stevens Buckminster* who sought to sweep away Calvinist orthodoxy through a rational interpretation of the Bible, and he authored an important polemical tract against Trinitarianism. But in his later career he became an agent of conservative reaction against Transcendentalism, remembered chiefly for his attacks on George Ripley* and Ralph Waldo Emerson.* His attack on Emerson's Divinity School Address, which he thought was heretical, was the nub of the Transcendentalist controversy. Norton's appointment as Dexter Professor of Sacred Literature in 1819 was an important step in his rise to scholarly prominence among Unitarians. From that position he worked toward the completion of what became his life's work, *The Evidences of the Genuineness of the Gospels* (1837–44), characterized by Perry Miller as "the perfect summation of Unitarian scholarship" (p. 205). When Ripley and Emerson, with their doctrine of religious intuition, rejected not only the miracles but the need for any empirical justification for religious ideas, they threw Norton's entire program out the window. His reaction to Transcendentalism was thus connected with his own quest for religious certitude. For Norton, the self and its intuitions were untrustworthy bases for a religious faith, and he saw in Transcendentalism the danger of self taking precedence over things of deeper importance.

*Bibliography*

A. *A Statement of Reasons for Not Believing the Doctrines of Trinitarians Respecting the Nature of God and the Person of Christ* (Boston, 1819); *A Discourse on the Latest Form of Infidelity* (Cambridge, MA, 1839); *The Evidences of the Genuineness of the Gospels*, 3 vols. (Boston, 1837–44).

B. AAUP, 430–35; DAB 13, 568–69; DARB, 334–35; Heralds 2, 193–98; William Newell, "Andrews Norton," *Christian Examiner*, 55 (November 1953), 425–52; Perry Miller, *The Transcendentalists: An Anthology* (Cambridge, 1950); William Hutchison, *The Transcendentalist Ministers: Church Reform in the New England Renaissance* (New Haven, 1959); Daniel Walker Howe, *The Unitarian Conscience: Harvard Moral Philosophy, 1805–1861* (Cambridge, 1970).

# P

---

**PARK, CHARLES EDWARDS** (14 March 1873, Mahabaleshwar, India–23 September 1962, Boston, MA). *Education*: A.B., Yale, 1896; attended University of Chicago Divinity School, 1896–99. *Career*: Minister, Second and New North Churches (Unitarian), Hingham, MA, 1900–1906; First Unitarian Church, Boston, 1906–46; minister emeritus, 1946–62.

When he retired from a pastorate of forty years at the First Unitarian Church in Boston, *Time* magazine called Charles E. Park "the Grand Old Man of U.S. liberal pulpits" ("The Man Who Stayed to Preach," p. 56). Park earned this prominence among Unitarians through his long and steady career in Boston, characterized by what Palfrey Perkins* called his devotion to "the ministry of the spoken word" (*Creative Faith*, p. ix). It was as a preacher that Park exerted his major influence on twentieth-century Unitarianism. Park came to the First Church in 1906 on an interim basis but won a permanent post. In contrast to many of the currents of modernism and Humanism among Unitarians, Park preached a Christian message based on the religion of Jesus, preaching that the central quest of Christianity was to "know Christ in his human character, as a man among men" (p. 6). This was not a supernatural view, because Park attributed to Paul, not Jesus, many of the supernatural elements of the Christian tradition. But he did view Jesus as a teacher whose mysticism was "the key to his whole personality" (*Christianity*, p. 6). This meant that the "core of our Christianity today is what was in the heart of Jesus," an intimacy with God (p. 48). From this core of religion arose the soul's imperative "[to attach] itself to other souls so as to form a community" (p. 100). For Park, the living out of this sense of God that had marked the life of Jesus was "the world's best hope," and it was the central message of his influential pulpit career (p. 121).

*Bibliography*

A. *The Inner Victory: Two Hundred Little Sermons* (Cambridge, 1946); *Christianity: How It Came to Us: What It Is: What It Might Be* (Boston, 1948); *Creative Faith* (Boston, 1951).

B. *Who Was Who in America* 4, 731; "The Man Who Stayed to Preach," *Time*, 78 (July 29, 1946), 56–57; "UCF to Honor Dr. Park," *Unitarian Universalist Register Leader*, 144 (January 1963), 25.

**PARKER, THEODORE** (24 August 1810, Lexington, MA–10 May 1860, Florence, Italy). *Education*: Nonresident student, Harvard College, 1830–31; graduated from Harvard Divinity School, 1836. *Career*: Minister, West Roxbury, MA, 1837–46; minister, Twenty-Eighth Congregational Society, Boston, 1846–59.

As a leader of the Transcendentalist movement and a committed churchman and reformer, Theodore Parker is one of the most important figures in nineteenth-century Unitarian history. Reared on a farm near Lexington, Massachusetts, Parker enrolled at Harvard in 1830, but financial difficulties forced him to take teaching positions until he was finally able to complete studies at Harvard Divinity School (1834–36). He became pastor at West Roxbury in 1837 and began to make his presence felt as a scholar and writer. In the middle and late 1830s he attended meetings of the Transcendental Club, formed a friendship with Ralph Waldo Emerson,* and after the *Dial* was begun in 1840, he contributed to it. Parker took the side of Emerson and George Ripley* against Andrews Norton* in the Transcendentalist controversy and then further enflamed that controversy with his famous sermon *A Discourse on the Transient and Permanent in Christianity* (1841). Because Parker argued there that most of the traditional supports of Christian belief such as the biblical miracles, the inspiration of the scriptures, and the divinity of Jesus were transient rather than permanent and necessary parts of religion, he was seen by many Unitarians as too radical. After the sermon Parker suffered ostracism from his fellow Unitarian ministers and assumed the role of rebel that he carried until death. In 1845 Parker began to preach regularly in Boston, forming the Twenty-Eighth Congregational Society there. From his Boston pulpit he increasingly involved himself in reform and antislavery causes, coming to be known as the leading reform preacher in Unitarian circles. The direction of his career was from theological to political radicalism. Parker's life was cut short by tuberculosis, but he left an enduring impact on liberal religion, with "Parkerism" coming to be the shorthand phrase for modernist and reformist stances within Unitarianism.

*Bibliography*

A. *A Discourse on the Transient and Permanent in Christianity* (Boston, 1841); *A Discourse of Matters Pertaining to Religion* (Boston, 1842); *Speeches, Addresses, and Occasional Sermons*, 2 vols. (Boston and New York, 1852); *Works*, 15 vols. (Boston, 1907–11).

B. DAB 14, 238–41; DARB, 352–53; DLB 1, 143–50; Heralds 3, 278–87; John Weiss, *Life and Correspondence of Theodore Parker*, 2 vols. (New York, 1864); John White Chadwick, *Theodore Parker: Preacher and Reformer* (Boston and New York, 1900); Henry Steele Commager, *Theodore Parker* (Boston, 1936); William Hutchison, *The Transcendentalist Ministers: Church Reform in the New England Renaissance* (New Haven, 1959); Perry Miller, *Nature's Nation* (Cambridge, 1967).

**PATTON, KENNETH LEO** (25 August 1911, Three Oaks, MI). *Education*: B.A., Eureka College, 1937; M.A., University of Chicago, 1939; B.D., University of Chicago, 1940. *Career*: Unitarian minister, Madison, WI, 1942–48; minister, Charles Street Meeting House (Universalist), Boston, MA, 1949–c. 1964; minister, Ridgewood Unitarian Universalist Society, Ridgewood, NJ, beginning 1964.

Kenneth L. Patton has been prominent in efforts to revitalize the concept and form of worship in the liberal tradition through recourse to the symbolic resources of world religion. In his pastorate at Madison he helped plan the multifunctional worship and parish building designed by Frank Lloyd Wright. When the Massachusetts Universalist Convention recognized the need of a Universalist church in Boston, it initiated the Charles Street Meeting House project to establish an experimental parish in the city. Patton became the pastor of the newly formed church. The major intellectual thrust of the experiment was to make "the basic ideals and concepts of Universalism grow to meet the necessities of a later time" by creating a "religion for one world" (*A Religion for One World*, p. 22, 4). The experiment drew heavily upon Patton's commitment to the use of art and symbolism for religious ends. Patton, himself a poet and hymnist, insisted that "religion cannot operate without symbols" and tried to bring to bear religious symbols from every world tradition, East and West, on the formation of a world religion (p. 56). The circle was used as a basic symbol, and the church interior arranged circularly to reflect this. Other symbols such as a bookcase of world scriptures, a mural of the Great Nebula in Andromeda, and a sculpture symbolizing the atom were also used. The church also continued the experiments in revising hymnals that Patton himself had begun, and he later participated in a denominationwide commission on revising the hymnals. Patton's work at the Charles Street Meeting House Project was a notable contribution to the effort to see Universalism as a movement of a unified world religion, and his work on the worship service captured the experimental mood of many religious liberals.

*Bibliography*

A. *The Visitor, and Hello, Man* (Boston, 1947); *Man's Hidden Search: An Inquiry in Naturalistic Mysticism* (Boston, 1954); *Readings for the Celebration of Life* (editor, Boston, 1957); *A Religion for One World* (Boston, 1964); *This World, My Home* (Boston, 1966); *Services and Songs for the Celebration of Life* (Boston, 1967); *The Sense of Life* (Ridgewood, NJ, 1974); *Strange Harvest: Collected Lyrics and Son-*

*nets, 1935–1975* (Ridgewood, NJ, 1976); *A Religion of Realities* (Ridgewood, NJ, 1977).

B. CA 17–20R, 569–70; *A Religion for One World* (see above); Ernest Cassara, *Universalism in America: A Documentary History* (Boston, 1971).

**PEABODY, ELIZABETH PALMER** (16 May 1804, Billerica, MA–3 January 1894, Jamaica Plain, MA). *Career:* Schoolteacher, Lancaster, PA, 1820; Boston, 1822–23; Hallowell and Gardiner, ME, 1823–25; Brookline, MA, with Mary Peabody (Mann), 1825–32; private tutoring and writing, 1832–34; teacher, Temple School, Boston, 1834–36; private study and writing, Salem, MA, 1836–40; founder, West Street Book Shop, Boston, 1840–50; moved to West Newton, MA, and taught in Boston and Perth Amboy, NJ, 1850–59; organized first kindergarten in Boston, 1860; kindergarten work, writing, and reform activities, 1860–94.

Elizabeth Palmer Peabody's life was so rich and various in its activities that it is hard to summarize briefly. But the activity for which she will probably be longest remembered was her work in educational theory and practice, especially that of childhood education. In this field she was very influential. Peabody's pioneering work in education was the practical application of her theories of personal development and self-culture, which she formulated in close connection with William Ellery Channing,* the progressive leader of Unitarianism, and Ralph Waldo Emerson* and Bronson Alcott, Transcendentalists who extended Channing's concern for self-culture. She met Channing in 1826, while she operated a school in Boston with her sister Mary. Peabody came to know Channing well and served him for some time as a copyist for his sermons, later writing a book of reminiscences of him (1880). She assisted Bronson Alcott in his experimental Temple School and in some ways made the formation of the school possible. Her *Record of a School* (1835) was written to make Alcott's views known. After he was branded a dangerous radical, and his school closed, Peabody's teaching career temporarily ended. She lived in Salem with her family in the late 1830s and moved back to Boston in 1840 to open a bookstore that became the gathering place for Transcendentalists and other reformers. Margaret Fuller's* conversations for women were held there in the early 1840s. She published one distinguished issue of the journal *Aesthetic Papers* (1849), contributed to the *Dial*, and was a conduit of personalities and ideas among Transcendentalists in the 1830s and 1840s. She later became a proponent of Friedrich Froebel's Kindergarten movement, and devoted much of her energy to publicizing its principles. With Fuller, she was one of the most prominent women among the Transcendentalists, and although her involvements in art, reform, and education were many, the controlling idea of her career, from Temple School to the Kindergarten movement, was the possibility of the nurture and full development of a child's, or any individual's inherent capacity for good, based on what her mentor Channing called a "likeness to God."

*Bibliography*

A. *Record of a School, Exemplifying the Principles of Spiritual Culture* (Boston, New York, and Philadelphia, 1835); "Language," *Aesthetic Papers* (1849), 214–23; *Moral Culture of Infancy and Kindergarten Guide* (coauthor, Boston, 1863); *Reminiscences of Rev. Wm. Ellery Channing* (Boston, 1880); *Last Evening with Allston and Other Papers* (Boston, 1886).

B. DAB 14, 335–36; DLB 1, 152–56; NAW 3, 31–34; Josephine E. Roberts, "Elizabeth Peabody and the Temple School," *New England Quarterly*, 15 (September 1942), 497–508; Louise Hall Tharp, *The Peabody Sisters of Salem* (Boston, 1950); Joel Myerson, *The New England Transcendentalists and the Dial* (Rutherford, NJ, 1980); Anne C. Rose, *Transcendentalism as a Social Movement* (New Haven, 1981).

**PEABODY, FRANCIS GREENWOOD** (4 December 1847, Boston, MA–28 December 1936, Cambridge, MA). *Education*: A.B., Harvard College, 1869; A.M., S.T.B., Harvard Divinity School, 1872; studied at University of Halle, Germany, 1872–73. *Career*: Teacher, Antioch College, 1873–74; minister, First Parish, Cambridge, MA, 1874–79; lecturer in ethics and homiletics (1880–81), Parkman Professor of Theology (1881–86), and Plummer Professor of Christian Morals (1886–1913), Harvard Divinity School; active retirement, 1913–36.

Francis Greenwood Peabody is the Unitarian thinker most closely associated with the social gospel movement in early twentieth-century Protestantism. David B. Parke characterized Peabody's *Jesus Christ and the Social Question* (1900) as "a pioneer statement of Christian social principles" (Parke, p. 1). Indeed, the book did much to move liberal thinking away from a concentration on individualism and personal development toward a sense of the ethical imperative in social life. Peabody's development of these views required a process of distancing from the nineteenth-century Boston Unitarianism of his youth. He was the son of Ephraim Peabody, minister of King's Chapel in Boston. His father's death in 1856 left his mother in difficult circumstances, but with help from friends and relations Peabody was educated at Harvard College and Divinity School. This part of his education he recalled with wry disdain: "I cannot remember attaining in seven years of Harvard classrooms anything that could be fairly described as an idea" (*Reminiscences of Present-Day Saints*, p. 66). There followed two decisive breaks in his life. The first was his study in Germany under Friedrich A. G. Tholuck, where he found the ideas he had been missing, and the second was his turn away from pastoral work to teaching because of his poor health. At Harvard Divinity School he began to develop the focus on social ethics that made him a pioneer in that field and resulted in his *Jesus Christ and the Social Question*. Peabody's chief argument was that modern economic conditions were threatening the foundations of the old social order, including family, property, and the state. This made political and economic questions into ethical ones and demanded a new spirit of service and self-sacrifice in the marketplace. A liberal rather than a radical, Peabody did not advocate a change in existing structures of society, except insofar as changed personal behavior might alter them. Peabody was influential as an author, but perhaps had greater impact through his teaching at Harvard. There he made "the social question" an integral part of the education of ministers, helping to foster the political consciousness that has become generally a part of the liberal ethical outlook.

*Bibliography*

A. *Jesus Christ and the Social Question* (New York, 1900); *Jesus Christ and the Christian Character* (New York, 1905); *The Approach to the Social Question* (New York, 1909); *The Christian Life in the Modern World* (New York, 1914); *The Apostle Paul and the Modern World* (New York, 1923); *The Church of the Spirit* (New York, 1925); *Reminiscences of Present-Day Saints* (partly autobiographical) (Boston and New York, 1927).

B. DAB 22, 518–19; DARB, 359–60; Jurgen Herbst, "Francis Greenwood Peabody: Harvard's Theologian of the Social Gospel," *Harvard Theological Review*, 54 (1961), 45–69; David B. Parke, "Liberals and Liberalism Since 1900," PUHS, 15, pt. 1 (1964), 1–25.

**PERKINS, PALFREY** (14 June 1883, Salem, MA–12 March 1976, Boston, MA). *Education*: A.B., Harvard, 1905; S.T.B., Harvard Divinity School, 1909. *Career*: Unitarian minister, First Parish, Brighton, MA, 1909–16; Weston, MA, 1916–26; First Unitarian Church, Buffalo, NY, 1926–33; King's Chapel, Boston, 1933–53; retirement, 1953–76.

Palfrey Perkins was an influential twentieth-century Unitarian minister whose career was marked by his active involvement in a number of educational, cultural, and public service activities. He was an active supporter of the Harvard Divinity School, a member of the Board of Preachers at Harvard University, and a chairman of the Board of Trustees of Wellesley College. He was also a prominent supporter of the Boston Symphony Orchestra. He was active in the formation of the Unitarian Service Committee, and in 1967 the Unitarian Universalist Service Committee named its international headquarters in Boston "The Palfrey Perkins House" in recognition of his service. The committee declared that it was its purpose in that dedication "to keep before succeeding generations the inspiration of his life, the strength of his convictions and the gentle wisdom of his ministry" ("Rev. Perkins").

*Bibliography*

B. "Rev. Perkins, Was King's Chapel Minister," *Boston Globe*, March 13, 1966; *Who Was Who in America* 7, 450.

**POTTER, CHARLES FRANCIS** (28 October 1885, Marlboro, MA–4 October 1962, New York, NY). *Education*: Attended Brown University, 1904–5; B.A., Bucknell University, 1907; M.A., Bucknell University, 1916; B.D., Newton Theological Institution, 1913; S.T.M., Newton Theological Institution, 1917. *Career*: Minister, Central Avenue Baptist Church, Dover, NH, 1908–10;

Baptist Church, Mattapan, MA, 1910–14; converted to Unitarianism, 1914; minister, First Unitarian Church, Edmonton, Alberta, 1914–16; Second Parish, Marlboro, MA, 1916–18; Wellesley Hills, MA, 1918–19; West Side Unitarian Church, New York, 1919–25; professor of comparative religion, Antioch College, 1925–26; head, Bureau of Lectures, National Association of Book Publishers, 1927; minister, Church of the Divine Paternity (Universalist), New York, 1927–29; founder and leader, First Humanist Society, New York, 1929; founder, Euthanasia Society of America, 1938.

Charles F. Potter was one of the leading spokesmen of the Humanist movement in liberal religion in the early decades of the twentieth century. He was also a tireless popularizer of the movement and publicist for the liberal cause generally. He began his ministerial career in the Baptist denomination, but while preaching at Mattapan, Massachusetts, his church leaders questioned his theological views. As a result he declared himself a Unitarian in 1914. As Potter told it, he conferred with the American Unitarian Association (AUA) national secretary Lewis G. Wilson about his views. Wilson asked him to preach a sermon about Jesus and, after hearing it, declared him a Unitarian. While preaching at his first Unitarian post in Edmonton, Alberta, Canada, he heard of the unusual views of John H. Dietrich,* then at Spokane, and realized that his version of theology was part of a larger movement. Potter came into national prominence by engaging in a series of debates in 1923–24 with the Baptist fundamentalist leader John R. Straton over the issues of biblical fundamentalism. Soon thereafter he served as a defense team expert in the famous Scopes trial on evolution, as the theological war between liberalism and fundamentalism expanded in the 1920s. In 1929 he founded the First Humanist Society of New York, obtaining help from John Haynes Holmes* in the work of establishing the society. This was one of the few "Humanist" churches, although a number of the Unitarian churches were led by Humanist ministers. The society gained much publicity through Potter's enunciation of ten "points of difference" between Humanism and older religions. In the first of these points, Potter rejected the doctrine that "the chief end of man is to glorify God" and declared instead that man should strive "to improve himself, both as an individual and as a race" (*The Preacher and I*, p. 367). As this change indicates, Potter preached an ethically centered religion of growth and rejected supernaturalism in religion. As an organizer, public leader, and promoter, he was central to the Humanist movement.

*Bibliography*

A. *The Story of Religion as Told in the Lives of Its Leaders* (Garden City, NY, 1929); *Humanism: A New Religion* (New York, 1930); *The Lost Years of Jesus Revealed* (Greenwich, CT, 1948); *Creative Personality: The Next Step in Evolution* (New York, 1950); *The Preacher and I: An Autobiography* (New York, 1951).

B. NCAB 52, 415–16; *New York Times*, October 5, 1962, p. 33; *Who Was Who in America* 4, 660; *The Preacher and I: An Autobiography* (see above); Mason Olds, *Religious Humanism in America: Dietrich, Reese, and Potter* (Washington, DC, 1978).

**POTTER, WILLIAM JAMES** (1 February 1829, North Dartmouth, MA–21 December 1893, Boston, MA). *Education*: Attended State Normal School, Bridgewater, MA; A.B., Harvard, 1854; attended Harvard Divinity School, 1856–57; study in Germany, 1857–58. *Career*: Minister, First Congregational (Unitarian) Society of New Bedford, MA, 1859–92; secretary, Free Religious Association, 1867–82; president, Free Religious Association, 1882–92; editor, *Index*, 1880–86.

The idea of the Free Religious Association can be traced to William J. Potter's desire to form a "spiritual anti-slavery society" in the wake of the dispute over the formation and principles of the National Conference in 1866 (Persons, p. 42). Potter's use of the metaphor of slavery to describe his sense of oppression at the hands of Henry W. Bellows* and the Unitarian leadership reveals the depth of his opposition to any attempt to formalize creedal statements. It also suggests the fervor with which he and other radicals were trying to move beyond the confining notion of Christianity to a more universal religion. Potter's position was enunciated in an 1871 address to the alumni of Harvard Divinity School, "The New Protestantism." For Potter, the radical movement was in essence the latest expression of the core of the Protestant tradition, the resistance to theological authority. He linked Free Religion to the heritage of the Protestant Reformation, noting that the Reformation's most fundamental affirmation was "*the independence of the individual soul*" ("The New Protestantism," p. 109). In the course of history, that drive to independence has swept away all vestiges of theological authority except one: "The general confession of allegiance to Jesus or his Gospel," which was embraced by the National Conference. For Potter, "this indefinite confession of allegiance to Jesus as the religious leader of the human race is the last refuge of the principle of authority in Protestant Christianity." Most importantly, it was "plainly impossible," as he thought, "to stay in this refuge and at the same time keep terms with reason" (pp. 116–117). For Potter, then, as for many in the Free Religion movement, reason demanded a creedless religious organization, open not only to the Christian tradition but to the influence of other world religions and of science. Potter exemplified these convictions in several ways during his long pastorate in New Bedford, although from all accounts he was a reserved and studious man, devoted principally to his reading and preaching. He persuaded his congregation to allow him not to administer the Lord's Supper, feeling unable conscientiously to administer the sacrament. He refused to label himself "Christian," and after an exchange of letters with American Unitarian Association (AUA) assistant secretary George W. Fox, he was dropped from the AUA yearbook in 1873. This turn of events added to the tensions between radicals and Unitarian moderates in the 1870s and 1880s. Most importantly, Potter was the mainstay of the Free Religious Association as both its secretary and later president. Stow Persons, the historian of the Free Religion movement, termed Potter the "moving spirit" of the organization, the man who "literally held the

Association together'' until his death (Persons, p. 83). The organization did little in the way of concrete activities, but it served as a rallying point for those alienated from traditional Protestantism, but who still wished to identify themselves as religious seekers.

*Bibliography*

A. "The New Protestantism: Its Relation to the Old," *Radical*, 9 (1871), 105–28; *Twenty Five Sermons of Twenty Five Years* (Boston, 1885); *The Free Religious Association: Its Twenty-Five Years and Their Meaning* (Boston, 1892); *Lectures and Sermons, with a Biographical Sketch*, edited by Francis Ellingwood Abbot (Boston, 1895).

B. DAB 15, 135; Heralds 3, 303–8; NCAB 13, 59; Stow Persons, *Free Religion: An American Faith* (New Haven, 1947); Conrad Wright, ed., *A Stream of Light* (Boston, 1975).

**PRIESTLEY, JOSEPH** (13 March 1733, Fieldhead, England–6 February 1804, Northumberland, PA). *Education*: Graduated from Daventry Academy, 1755. *Career*: Minister, Needham Market, 1755–58; minister and schoolmaster, Nantwich, 1758–61; tutor, Warrington Academy, 1761–67; minister, Mill Hill Chapel, Leeds, 1767–72; librarian and literary companion to Lord Shelburne, 1772–80; minister, Birmingham, 1780–91; minister, Hackney, 1791–94; retirement, with preaching and lecturing, in Northumberland, PA, 1794–1804.

Joseph Priestley was an important influence on the early stages of Unitarianism in America, but his career had greater impact in England, where he was a founder of the Unitarian movement. He was a precocious youth, able to read Latin, Greek, and Hebrew at age fourteen. Although his family intended for him to complete his education at one of the dissenting English academies with Calvinist views, Priestley protested, especially when he found that he "must subscribe [his] assent to ten printed articles of the strictest Calvinistic faith, and repeat it every six months" (*Theological and Miscellaneous Works*, I, 21). By now he had become Arminian in his theology and found more congenial atmosphere in the more liberal academy at Daventry. Despite a problem with stammering, which caused him great difficulty in public speaking, he decided on a career in the ministry. His speech defect and his increasingly liberal views on theology were burdens to his ministerial career, but Priestley compensated for them in his intellectual work. As his theology developed from the Calvinism of his family through Arminianism, Priestley eventually concluded that much accepted Christian dogma was in fact a "corruption" of the original Christian truth. This was the thesis of his best-known theological work, *An History of the Corruptions of Christianity*. In that work Priestley hoped to clear away theological error to exhibit the version of Unitarianism that he thought would eventually predominate as the Christian faith.

Priestley's theological career was paralleled by an interest in experimental chemistry, and he won greater fame as a scientist than as a theologian. With the encouragement of Benjamin Franklin, whom he met in London in 1764,

Priestley wrote *The History and Present State of Electricity*, which secured his scientific reputation and resulted in his election to the Royal Society. In later work on the nature of the atmosphere, he discovered the element oxygen. Because of his scientific work, Priestley's theology got a wider hearing, but he remained a controversial figure. He was publicly scorned for his campaign for full tolerance for all religious dissent and equality for all religious sects. To many, this seemed a disloyal attack on the Church of England. This, in combination with Priestley's known sympathy for the French Revolution, made him a target for conservative abuse. In 1791 his home and laboratory in Birmingham were burned, and Priestley and his family narrowly escaped harm. This began the end of Priestley's life in England. In 1794 he went to America, finding there a warm reception. He settled in Northumberland, Pennsylvania, where his sons lived. Priestley held worship services there and also gave lectures in Philadelphia, which led to the establishment of the first Unitarian Church in that city and the first church so named in America, in 1796. Although in New England Arminian views had by this time gained a strong hold, the split of the Standing-Order churches that resulted in the Unitarian denomination would not occur for some two decades. Although those churches were the denominational base of Unitarianism, Priestley's version of Enlightenment Unitarianism remains another significant part of the American liberal heritage.

*Bibliography*

A. *The History and Present State of Electricity* (London, 1767); *The Institutes of Natural and Revealed Religion*, 3 vols. (London, 1772–74); *An History of the Corruptions of Christianity*, 2 vols. (London, 1782); *Unitarianism Explained and Defended* (Philadelphia, 1796); *Memoirs*, 2 vols. (London, 1805–7); *The Theological and Miscellaneous Works*, ed. John Towill Rutt, 25 vols. (London, 1806–32; rpt. New York, 1972).

B. AAUP, 298–308; DAB 15, 223–26; DARB, 369–70; Anne D. Holt, *A Life of Joseph Priestley* (London, 1931); Earl Morse Wilbur, *A History of Unitarianism: In Transylvania, England, and America* (Cambridge, 1952); Clinton Lee Scott, *These Live Tomorrow* (Boston, 1964); Frederick W. Gibbs, *Joseph Priestley* (London, 1965).

# R

**REESE, CURTIS WILLIFORD** (3 September 1887, Madison County, NC–5 June 1961, Chicago, IL). *Education*: Preparatory education, Mar's Hill College, NC, 1908; Th.G., Southern Baptist Theological Seminary, Louisville, KY, 1910; Ph.B., Ewing College, Ewing, IL, 1911. *Career*: Baptist preacher, Bellwood, AL, 1908; Gratz, KY, and Pleasant Home, KY, 1908–10; state evangelist, Illinois State Baptist Association, 1910–11; minister, First Baptist Church, Tiffin, OH, 1911–13; converted to Unitarianism, 1913; minister, First Unitarian Church, Alton, IL, 1913–15; First Unitarian Church, Des Moines, IA, 1915–19; secretary, Western Unitarian Conference, 1919–30; editor, *Unity*, 1925–33; president, Lombard College, Galesburg, IL, 1928–29; dean, Abraham Lincoln Centre, Chicago, 1930–57.

Raised a Southern Baptist and educated at the Southern Baptist Theological Seminary, Curtis Reese grew beyond his fundamentalist heritage to become a leader of the Humanist movement in Unitarianism and the successor to western radical leader Jenkin Lloyd Jones* as dean of the Abraham Lincoln Centre in Chicago. Reese's transition from fundamentalism to Humanism was not easy. It began in his seminary study where his introduction to the higher criticism of the Bible began to eat away his belief in biblical inerrancy. Reese carried with him, however, a strand of populist radicalism from his upbringing, and as a result he was attracted to the social gospel teachings of Francis Greenwood Peabody.* After his conversion to Unitarianism in 1913, he pursued his newly formulated Humanist religion and his social concerns in two midwestern pastorates. He then moved to Chicago as Western Unitarian Conference secretary. Reese did not refer to his concept of religion as "Humanism" at first but as "Democratic" religion, as opposed to the old "Autocratic" religion of Christianity. The choice of wording is important, because the political analogy at its basis—humans as "subject" and the traditional God as "autocrat"—suggests the social thrust of Humanism as Reese propounded it. William L. Sullivan,* the theist leader, would later deride the back-slapping, democratic God of the Humanists, with Reese in mind, but the image of liberation from autocratic tyranny explains much of the fervent energy and sense of newness that the Humanist movement sparked in the 1920s. As leader of the Abraham Lincoln Centre in Chicago that Jones had founded, Reese was able to pursue the pragmatic, social aspect of Humanism as he understood it. He also gave his views more permanent form in his service to Meadville Theological School, working for the school's relocation in Chicago. Reese defined religion as "the integration of personality around commitment to ideals" and added that "the religious is the quality of behavior that enhances personality" (*The Meaning of Humanism*, p. 19). This functional, action-oriented view of religion was one of the most significant strands of the Humanist movement.

*Bibliography*

A. *Humanism* (Chicago, 1926); *Humanist Sermons* (editor, Chicago, 1927); *Humanist Religion* (New York, 1931); *The Meaning of Humanism* (Boston, 1945).

B. *Who Was Who in America* 4, 783; Charles H. Lyttle, *Freedom Moves West* (Boston, 1952); Mason Olds, *Religious Humanism in America: Dietrich, Reese, and Potter* (Washington, DC, 1978).

**RICE, WILLIAM BROOKS** (1905, Boston, MA–22 February 1970, Peterboro, NH). *Education*: A.B., S.T.B., Tufts School of Religion, 1938. *Career*: Unitarian minister, Dover, MA, 1934–45; Unitarian Society of Wellesley Hills, MA, 1945–70.

William B. Rice played an important role in modern religious liberalism as the chairman of the Joint Merger Commission, the body through which the groundwork was laid for the merger of the American Unitarian Association (AUA) and the Universalist Church of America in 1961. In a very active ministerial career, Rice served on the AUA Board of Directors and as chairman of the Department of the Ministry and the Ministerial Fellowship Committee. He was active in the General Commission of Army and Navy Chaplains and also was Protestant chaplain of the Suffolk County Jail in Boston. During his years in Wellesley, he had particularly large impact on the community as a founder of the Wellesley Human Relations Service, which promoted the idea of preventive community mental health. Rice's dedicated work for the Merger Commission gained him much respect in liberal religious circles, and after the completion of the merger, he became a candidate for the first presidency of the newly formed Unitarian Universalist Association. He lost a very narrow election to Dana M. Greeley.* Rice's strong advocacy of merger was based on his sense that in 1961 "a man would be hard put to spell out any clear difference between Unitarians as a whole and Universalists as a whole." Such differences as there were in liberal religion existed in both denominations but resulted in "creative tensions in both groups." Thus he called for both groups to "do all in our power to enter as equals into a new experience'' at the beginning of the period of merger (''The Spirit That Moves Us,'' p. 29).

*Bibliography*

A. ''The Spirit That Moves Us,'' *Unitarian Register and Universalist Leader*, 140 (May 1961), 29.

B. Joseph Barth, ''Contests for the Presidency: A.U.A., 1958–U.U.A., 1961,'' PUHS, 15 (1964), 26–65. For biographical details, I am grateful to John H. Nichols and the Unitarian Universalist Association.

**RICH, CALEB** (12 August 1750, Sutton, MA–1821, New Haven, VT). *Career*: Conversion experience, c. 1771; formed Universalist society, Warwick, MA, 1773; itinerant preacher, Warwick, Oxford, and Sutton, MA, c. 1773–77; ordained Universalist preacher, Warwick, MA, and Richmond and Jaffrey, NH, 1780; preached in New Haven, VT, 1803–21.

Although the known details of the life of Caleb Rich are few, there is enough information to accord him a place as an important founding voice in the New England Universalist movement. Stephen Marini recently called him ''the most important native New England Universalist leader'' (Marini, p. 72). In fact, although John Murray's* Gloucester Church is considered the first officially recognized Universalist Church, the church that Caleb Rich founded in Warwick, Massachusetts, in 1773, predates Murray's church, although it had no official legal recognition.

The story of the formation of Rich's church sheds some light on the revivalistic and ''enthusiastic'' roots of Universalism. At age twenty-one (1771) Rich had an intense conversion experience and became a member of a Baptist church in Warwick. But he was troubled about his religious motives, believing that a fear of hell was a selfish, and therefore tainted, motive for religious experience and moral action. His rebellion against the use of hell as a motive for conversion grew and was supplemented by visionary religious experiences confirming in him the doctrines of universal salvation. This led to his exclusion and that of his associates from the Baptist congregation and led him to form the Universalist society in Warwick. He also founded similar groups in Richmond and Jaffrey, New Hampshire, and in 1780 was ordained minister of these three churches. Rich apparently came to his Universalism independently of John Murray and differed from him in some respects. This suggests the spontaneous nature of the growth of Universalism, largely the result of the general chafing against the Calvinism of the established churches. One early account of Rich's beliefs, by William S. Balch, relates the story of a trip he made to Boston to visit John Murray. After some cordial discussion, Murray discovered some disagreements between himself and Rich and ''spoke decidedly against any innovation upon his views'' (Balch, p. 252). Rich, who had arrived at his views independently, and from deep experience, did not yield to Murray's arguments and ''returned from Boston with less reverence for human, and more for divine wisdom'' (p.

252). As Balch noted, the denomination at midnineteenth century held views closer to those of Rich than Murray. Among Rich's converts to Universalism, as Marini told us, was the denominational leader Hosea Ballou.*

*Bibliography*

A.  "A Narrative of Elder Caleb Rich," *Candid Examiner*, 2 (April 30–June 18, 1827) (autobiographical).

B.  "A Narrative of Elder Caleb Rich" (see above); Thomas Whittemore, *The Modern History of Universalism* (Boston, 1830); William S. Balch, "Reflections on the Life and Character of Elder Rich," *Universalist Union*, 4 (June 15, 1839), 252–53; Richard Eddy, *Universalism in America: A History*, 2 vols. (Boston, 1884–86); Russell E. Miller, *The Larger Hope* (Boston, 1979); Stephen A. Marini, *Radical Sects of Revolutionary New England* (Cambridge, 1982).

**RIPLEY, GEORGE** (3 October 1802, Greenfield, MA–4 July 1880, New York, NY). *Education*: A.B., Harvard College, 1823; graduate of Harvard Divinity School, 1826. *Career*: Minister, Purchase Street Church, Boston, 1826–41; founder of Brook Farm Community, 1841–47; staff, New York *Tribune*, and freelance writer, 1849–80.

George Ripley first made a name for himself in Unitarian circles for his series of essays in the *Christian Examiner*, in which he rejected the necessity of the biblical miracles as an underpinning for Christianity and defended Ralph Waldo Emerson's* Transcendentalism against the attacks of Andrews Norton.* He is best remembered for leading the communal experiment at Brook Farm in an attempt to translate Transcendental ideals into social reality. After a brilliant student career at Harvard College and Divinity School, Ripley was called to the newly formed Purchase Street Church in Boston in 1826, where he began to make a name for himself as a thorough scholar. Attracted to the new theology emanating from Germany, he found in Johann Gottfried von Herder, Friedrich Schleiremacher, and the English theologian James Martineau confirmation for an intuitive view of religious truth. This position, in conflict with the historicism of Norton, placed Ripley in the camp of Emerson and Theodore Parker,* and he became perhaps the leading controversialist for the Transcendentalists. After resigning his pastorate he headed the communal Brook Farm, where he shared with others an increasing attraction for the utopian views of Charles Fourier. After a disastrous fire at the farm in 1846, the commune could no longer continue, and Ripley moved to New York, dispirited and debt-ridden. But he was able to put together a career as a journalist, critic, and editor, maintaining a connection with the New York *Tribune* throughout the final phase of his life. With Parker and Frederic Henry Hedge,* he was among the most learned of the Transcendentalists, and he represents, with Parker and William Henry Channing,* that side of the movement that manifested itself primarily in the cause of political reform.

*Bibliography*

A. *Discourses on the Philosophy of Religion Addressed to Doubters Who Wish to Believe* (Boston, 1836); Review of James Martineau, *The Rationale of Religious Inquiry, Christian Examiner*, 21 (1836), 225–54.

B. DAB 15, 623–25; DLB 1, 158–59; Heralds 3, 330–35; O. B. Frothingham, *George Ripley* (Boston and New York, 1882); Perry Miller, *The Transcendentalists: An Anthology* (Cambridge, MA, 1950); William R. Hutchison, *The Transcendentalist Ministers: Church Reform in the New England Renaissance* (New Haven, 1959); Charles Crowe, *George Ripley: Transcendentalist and Utopian Socialist* (Athens, GA, 1967); Joel Myerson, *The New England Transcendentalists and the Dial* (Rutherford, NJ, 1980).

**RUSH, BENJAMIN** (24 December 1745, near Philadelphia, PA–19 April 1813, Philadelphia, PA). *Education*: A.B., College of New Jersey (Princeton), 1760; medical study with John Redman, Philadelphia, 1761–66; M.D., University of Edinburgh, 1768; medical training, St. Thomas's Hospital, London, 1768–69. *Career*: Medical practice, Philadelphia, 1769–1813; various appointments as professor of medicine, University of Pennsylvania, 1769–1813; medical service, Revolutionary Army, 1777–78; staff, Pennsylvania Hospital, 1783–1813; treasurer, United States Mint, 1797–1813.

As one of the leading physicians in America during his lifetime, Benjamin Rush's advocacy of the doctrine of universal salvation gave much impetus to that belief in eighteenth- and early-nineteenth-century Philadelphia. Rush's primary importance is in the history of medicine. He was an early advocate of hygiene and temperance but also a vehement advocate of bleeding as a cure for almost all diseases. His studies of the yellow-fever epidemic in Philadelphia in 1793 gained him much recognition, but his controversial cure of bleeding was shown to have a deleterious effect on the victims. To his credit, Rush developed relatively advanced theories for the treatment of mental disorder later in his career. Rush was very much a product of the Enlightenment, part of the intellectual milieu associated with Benjamin Franklin and others. He was one of the earliest American opponents of slavery, writing a tract against it in 1773. His Universalist views, which were much influenced by Elhanan Winchester,* were the product of the combination of his Enlightenment rationalism and a real belief in religious experience.

*Bibliography*

A. *Sermons to Gentlemen upon Temperance and Exercise* (London, 1772); *An Address to the Inhabitants of the British Settlements in America upon Slave-Keeping* (Philadelphia, 1773); *Essays: Literary, Moral, and Philosophical* (Philadelphia, 1798); *Medical Inquiries and Observations upon the Diseases of the Mind* (Philadelphia, 1812); *Medical Inquiries and Observations*, 4 vols. in 2 (Philadelphia, 1815); *The*

*Autobiography of Benjamin Rush*, ed. George W. Corner (Princeton, NJ, 1948); *Letters*, ed. L. H. Butterfield, 2 vols. (Princeton, NJ, 1951).

B. DAB 16, 227–31; Nathan G. Goodman, *Benjamin Rush: Physician and Citizen, 1746–1813* (Philadelphia, 1934); Carl Ringer, *Revolutionary Doctor: Benjamin Rush, 1746–1813* (New York, 1966); David Freeman Hawke, *Benjamin Rush: Revolutionary Gadfly* (Indianapolis, 1971).

# S

---

**SAFFORD, MARY AUGUSTA** (23 December 1851, Quincy, IL–25 October 1927, Orlando, FL). *Education*: Graduated from Iowa State University, c. 1878. *Career*: Founder and minister, Unitarian Church, Hamilton, IL, 1878; minister, Humboldt and Algona, IL, 1880–85; Sioux City, IA, 1885–89; Des Moines, IA, 1889–1910; retired to Florida and organized the Unitarian Church, Orlando, FL, 1910–27.

Mary Safford was an important woman in the nineteenth-century Unitarian ministry. She was a leader of what came to be known as the "Iowa Sisterhood" or the "Iowa Band." This group of women ministers actively promoted the cause of liberal religion in the Midwest in the late nineteenth century and insisted on the contribution to be made to that cause by women in the ministry. Safford was a builder of churches, taking a leading role in the early development of most of the churches that she served as minister, and also was a teacher and example to two other women who entered the ministry under her service: Eleanor E. Gordon* and Marie Jenney Howe. Active in denominational affairs, she served as a member of the Board of Directors of the American Unitarian Association and a director of the Women's Unitarian Conference, as well as secretary of the Iowa Unitarian Association. Both as a leader in the professional development of women and a liberal missionary in the Midwest, she had a distinguished career.

*Bibliography*

B. NCAB 14, 475; Heralds 4, 55–56; Charles H. Lyttle, *Freedom Moves West* (Boston, 1952); Catherine F. Hitchings, "Universalist and Unitarian Women Ministers," JUHS, 10 (1975).

**SAVAGE, MINOT JUDSON** (10 June 1841, Norridgewock, ME–22 May 1918, Boston, MA). *Education*: Graduated from Bangor Theological Seminary,

1864. *Career*: Congregational missionary, San Mateo and Grass Valley, CA, 1864–67; Congregational minister, Framingham, MA, 1867–69; minister, First Congregational Church, Hannibal, MO, 1869–72; converted to Unitarianism, 1872; minister, Third Unitarian Church, Chicago, IL, 1873–74; Church of the Unity, Boston, 1874–96; Church of the Messiah, New York, 1896–1906; retirement, 1906–18.

Minot J. Savage, who became one of the most popular and influential Unitarian preachers in the late nineteenth century, began his career in the Congregational Church and, only after a long process of growth toward liberalism, converted to Unitarianism. His early religious experience in Maine was marked by revivalism of the hell-fire variety, and at age thirteen, with fears of hell helping to impel him, he joined the church and eventually entered into seminary training. It was not until his ministry in Hannibal, Missouri, that his doubts about orthodox doctrines weighed heavily enough on him to cause his resignation. After a brief Unitarian pastorate in Chicago, he moved to Boston where his preaching began to attract large audiences. A major part of Savage's intellectual wrestling in the 1870s concerned the implications of Darwinian evolution for Christian faith. His *Religion of Evolution* was one of the earliest attempts to extract religiously satisfying and optimistic conclusions from evolutionary theory, and his message found an enormously responsive audience. He was a great pulpit orator, and he spoke without notes or text, which increased the impact he made on his hearers. These sermons, taken down by reporters, were then printed with little revision and circulated in the "Unity Pulpit" and later "Messiah Pulpit" series. They also formed the basis of his many books. Savage was a defender of theism on grounds of reason and human experience. He located his sense of God in the fact that "man is a moral being, . . . dreams of something that transcends him forever and makes his life an eternal pursuit" (*The Signs of the Times*, p. 82). Despite his enormous popularity in Boston, Savage moved to New York to become the colleague of Robert Collyer* at the Church of the Messiah. The friendship of these men had begun during Savage's ministry in Chicago. In New York he again established his drawing power from the pulpit, and his sermons and writings continued to have a large circulation. In this later period he also began to take an interest in spiritualism and questions of the nature of life after death. Poor health forced him to retire from his pulpit in 1906, but by that time his reputation as one of the great preachers of the era was secure.

*Bibliography*

A. *The Religion of Evolution* (Boston, 1876); *The Morals of Evolution* (Boston, 1880); *Belief in God* (Boston, 1881); *My Creed* (Boston, 1887); *The Signs of the Times* (Boston, 1889); *Life beyond Death* (New York and London, 1899).

B. DAB 16, 389–90; Heralds 4, 206–10; *My Creed* (see above).

**SAWYER, THOMAS JEFFERSON** (9 January 1804, Reading, VT–24 July 1899, Medford, MA). *Education*: B.A., Middlebury College, 1829; M.A., Middlebury College, 1833. *Career*: Minister, Orchard Street Universalist Church, New York, 1830–45; founder and coeditor, *Christian Messenger*, later *Universalist Union*, 1831–45; cofounder, secretary, and librarian, Universalist Historical Society, 1834–99; principal, Clinton Liberal Institute, 1845–52; minister, Orchard Street Church, New York, 1852–61; resident, near Clinton, NY, 1861–63; editor, *Christian Ambassador*, 1863–65; resident, Woodbridge, NJ, 1865–69; Packard Professor of Theology, Tufts Divinity School, 1869–82; dean, Tufts Divinity School, 1882–90; professor emeritus, Tufts, 1890–1909.

Thomas J. Sawyer ranks among the greatest of the pioneer educators of nineteenth-century Universalism. After completing his undergraduate degree at Middlebury despite financial hardships, he entered the Universalist ministry in New York City, going there at a time when, as Harris E. Starr reported, "organized Universalism had almost ceased to exist" (DAB, p. 398). Sawyer's ministry was a success, for he established a Universalist presence there and founded the periodical *The Christian Messenger*. During his pastorate he conceived and helped to found the Universalist Historical Society in 1834, for which he served as secretary and librarian until 1899. His first opportunity for direct involvement in education came in 1845, when he took over the operation of the Clinton Liberal Institute, a Universalist secondary school in Clinton, New York. Sawyer returned to the ministry in New York in 1852, and after brief periods of retirement in the 1860s, he accepted a professorship at Tufts in 1869. He had been a leader in the move to form a Universalist college at an 1847 Educational Convention at his former Orchard Street Church but refused an offer to be its first president. When a bequest from Silvanus Packard made the Divinity School and professorship in theology possible, Sawyer accepted the post, holding it until his retirement in 1890.

*Bibliography*

A. *Letters to the Rev. Stephen Remington in Review of His Lectures on Universalism* (New York, 1839); *Memoir of Rev. Stephen R. Smith* (Boston, 1852); *A Discussion of the Doctrine of Universal Salvation . . . Affirmative. Rev. T. J. Sawyer, D.D. Negative. Rev. Isaac Wescott* (New York, 1854); *Endless Punishment: In the Very Words of Its Advocates* (Boston, 1880).

B. DAB 16, 397–98; *Who Was Who in America* 1, 1083; Richard Eddy, *Universalism in America*, 2 vols. (Boston, 1884–86); Richard Eddy, *The Life of Thomas J. Sawyer . . . and of Caroline M. Sawyer* (Boston, 1900); Russell E. Miller, *The Larger Hope* (Boston, 1979).

**SHINN, QUILLEN HAMILTON** (1 January 1845, Bingamon, WV–6 September 1907, Cambridge, MA). *Education*: Graduated from the theological school, St. Lawrence University, 1870. *Career*: Universalist minister, Gaysville, VT, 1870–72; independent missionary preacher, WV, 1872–73; Universalist minister, Tyngsboro and Dunstable, MA, 1873–74; Second Universalist Church, Lynn, MA, 1874–77; Foxboro and Mansfield, MA, 1877–81; Plymouth, NH, 1881–c. 1884; Rochester, NH, c. 1884; Deering and Westbrook, ME, c. 1884–89; Rutland, VT, 1889; Omaha, NE, 1889–91; independent Universalist missionary, 1891–95; general missionary, Universalist General Convention, 1895–1900; southern missionary, Universalist General Convention, 1900–1907.

Universalism was a rare and exotic faith in the mountains of West Virginia, where Quillen H. Shinn grew up in the middle of the nineteenth century. Shinn and his family had become Universalist converts through reading George W. Quinby's pamphlet "The Salvation of Christ," but it was not until he was in his early twenties that Shinn was able to attend a Universalist service in Kent, Ohio. By that time he had had a range of experience that would equip him for his later strenuous life as a Universalist missionary. He had been raised in farm work, and at the outbreak of the war he fought for the Union and spent time in a Confederate prisoner of war camp. He kept school for a time after the war, but with some encouragement he decidced to enter the Universalist ministry. In 1867 he went to St. Lawrence University to study with Ebenezer Fisher* and began to show there the inspirational and organizational gifts that made him the greatest builder of Universalist churches of his time. The numerous pastorates he held after completing his theological training were some indication of the pattern of itinerant missionary work at which he excelled. In 1891 he took upon himself the role of independent Universalist missionary, raising his own financial support as he went until designated general missionary by the Universalist Convention in 1895. Shinn was remarkable in his ability to sow the seeds of Universalist congregations. He traveled twenty-five thousand to thirty thousand miles a year and preached in every state, reporting that by 1895 he had started "about fifty" churches and the same number of Sunday schools (McGlauflin, p. 64). He would typically come to a town where there were few or no Universalists, hire a hall, leaflet the town, and begin to preach, encouraging each of his hearers to bring others the next day. He tried to leave the town with some organization—a church, youth group, Sunday school, or Ladies' Aid Society. Although some of these groups were short-lived, others were not, and Shinn's efforts helped to spread Universalism beyond its New England roots. He preached an evangelical version of Universalism, grounded thoroughly in the Bible, which he could quote at great length from memory. He distrusted modernism in theology, insisting above all on a practical faith, relevant to the needs and hopes of ordinary folk. Shinn was well known for his annual summer meetings in New Hampshire, which began in 1882 and grew out of the tradition of Universalist grove meetings and evangelical brush-arbor revivals. Shinn loved his difficult and strenuous work, and it could indeed be said that he took the whole nation for his parish.

*Bibliography*

A.  William H. McGlauflin, *Faith with Power: A Life Story of Quillen Hamilton Shinn, D.D.* (Boston and Chicago, 1912) (contains excerpts of Shinn's writings).

B.  See McGlauflin above. Shinn's career will also be treated in the second volume of Russell E. Miller's history of Universalism, forthcoming.

**SKINNER, CLARENCE RUSSELL** (23 March 1881, Brooklyn, NY–26 August 1949, Cambridge, MA). *Education*: B.A., St. Lawrence University, 1904; M.A., St. Lawrence University, 1910. *Career*: Assistant minister, Church of the Divine Paternity, New York, 1904–6; minister, Universalist Church, Mt. Vernon, NY, 1906–11; secretary, Universalist Service Commission, 1910–19; minister, Grace Universalist Church, Lowell, MA, 1911–14; professor of applied Christianity, Crane Theological School, 1914–33; cofounder, The Community Church, Boston, 1920, and leader until 1936; dean, Crane Theological School, 1933–45; retirement, 1945–49.

Certainly the most important twentieth-century Universalist leader, Clarence Skinner was a central force in moving the denomination toward a more political and "this-worldly" understanding of the term Universalist. His work to foster the social engagement of the denomination began with his secretaryship of the Universalist Service Commission in 1910; through its auspices, Skinner wrote a progressive "Declaration of Social Principles," which was adopted by the denomination in 1917. In 1914 he began his long career at Tufts University's Crane Theological School, teaching applied Christianity and eventually becoming dean in 1933. But he was not only an educator; in 1920 with the aid of John Haynes Holmes,* who had led his New York Church in experimental directions, Skinner founded the Community Church in Boston. There he hoped to join others in "building a new kind of church adapted to the new age . . . a demonstration center that will prove what can be done by a radical reconstruction" (*A Free Pulpit in Action*, p. 1). Skinner served as "leader" rather than pastor or minister to the church, and its pulpit attracted a wide range of speakers. It pioneered in the now much-used open forum following the Sunday addresses and also maintained an active Social Justice Committee. Skinner's own writings attempted to define a liberalism that would be adequate to modern social conditions. His *Liberalism Faces the Future* (1937) offered a critique of the excessive past reliance of liberals on pure individualism, and his *Religion for Greatness* (1945) called for a Universalism that was not only religious but economic, racial, political, social, and scientific. It called for an enlightened, peaceful, and progressive world order based on democratic principles. Such a utopian sense of the possibilities of the liberal faith has helped to focus Universalist energies on the process of achieving a universal social salvation on earth.

*Bibliography*

A. *The Social Implications of Universalism* (Boston, 1915); *A Free Pulpit in Action* (editor, New York, 1931); *Liberalism Faces the Future* (New York, 1937); *Human Nature and the Nature of Evil* (Boston, 1939); *Hell's Ramparts Fell* (coauthor, Boston, 1941); *A Religion for Greatness* (Boston, 1945); *Worship and the Well-Ordered Life* (Boston, 1955).

B. *Who Was Who in America* 2, 490; Emerson Hugh Lalone, *And Thy Neighbor as Thyself: A Story of Universalist Social Action* (Boston, 1939); Alfred S. Cole, *Clarence Skinner: Prophet of Twentieth Century Universalism* (Boston, 1956); Charles A. Gaines, "Clarence R. Skinner: The Dark Years," JUHS, 3 (1962), 1–13; Clinton Lee Scott, *These Live Tomorrow: Twenty Unitarian Universalist Biographies* (Boston, 1964); James D. Hunt, Introduction to the reprint of *The Social Implications of Universalism* JUHS, 5 (1964–65), 79–88; Alan Seaburg, "The Writings of Dean Skinner," JUHS, 5 (1964–65), 65–77.

**SOULE, CAROLINE AUGUSTA WHITE** (3 September 1824, Albany, NY– 6 December 1903, Glasgow, Scotland). *Career*: Principal of the female department, Clinton Liberal Institute, Clinton, NY, 1842–43; homemaker, Albany, NY; Boston and Gloucester, MA; Hartford and Granby, CT, 1843–51; author, Granby, CT, 1852–54; Boonsboro, IA, 1854–64; editorial staff, *Ladies' Repository*, 1856–65; resident, Albany, NY, 1864–67; New York, 1867–78; founder and editor, *Guiding Star*, 1867–78; travel to England and Scotland, 1875; Universalist missionary, Scotland, 1878–79; minister, St. Paul's Universalist Church, Glasgow, Scotland, 1879–82; 1886–92; work for Woman's Centenary Association (Universalist), New York, 1882–86; retirement, Glasgow, 1892–1903.

Caroline Augusta Soule's intellectual gifts were recognized early in her life when she headed the female department of the Universalist secondary school, the Clinton Liberal Institute. There she met and married Henry B. Soule, who began a career as a Universalist minister, taking several pastorates in New England. Caroline Soule was widowed in 1852, with little financial support and five children in her care. She began to earn income by writing and teaching and was forced eventually by her financial difficulties to move to a log cabin in Boonsboro, Iowa. After moving to Albany and then New York City in the 1860s, she wrote and published *Guiding Star*, a Sunday-school publication, and became involved in work for the women's movement. She was an organizer of the Woman's Centenary Association, a Universalist women's organization that worked in fund-raising projects. A visit to Scotland in 1875 for health reasons led her to form associations with Scottish Universalists, and she returned to Scotland in 1878 as a Universalist missionary, becoming ordained in 1880 as minister of St. Paul's Universalist Church in Glasgow. This work in Scotland made her the first foreign missionary of the Universalist Church of America. Her health was always frail, and her many activities were accomplished despite poor health, financial difficulties, and family responsibilities. These brief facts give some indication of the range of challenges in her life and the strength of her response to them.

*Bibliography*

A. *Memoir of Rev. H. B. Soule* (New York and Auburn, NY, 1852); *Home Life; or, A Peep across the Threshold* (Boston, 1854); *The Pet of the Settlement: A Story of Prairie-Land* (Boston, 1860); *Wine or Water: A Tale of New England* (Boston, 1862).

B. *Appleton's Cyclopaedia of American Biography* (New York, 1900), 5, 610; NAW 3, 325–27; Alan Seaburg, "Missionary to Scotland: Caroline A. Soule," *Transactions of the Unitarian Historical Society* (London), 14 (1967), 28–41; Catherine F. Hitchings, "Universalist and Unitarian Women Ministers," JUHS, 10 (1975); Russell E. Miller, *The Larger Hope* (Boston, 1979).

**STEBBINS, HORATIO** (8 August 1821, Wilbraham (now Hampden), MA–8 April 1902, Cambridge, MA). *Education*: A.B., Harvard, 1848; graduated from Harvard Divinity School, 1851. *Career*: Unitarian minister, First Parish, Fitchburg, MA, 1851–54; First Parish, Portland, ME, 1855–64; First Unitarian Society, San Francisco, 1864–99, minister emeritus, 1899–1902.

To Starr King* goes the credit for establishing a Unitarian presence on the West Coast. To Horatio Stebbins and Thomas Lamb Eliot* goes the credit for maintaining that presence through their steady leadership of the two most stable West Coast churches, at San Francisco and Portland, Oregon. Stebbins was a hardworking Massachusetts farm boy who struggled to earn his education. He paid part of his expenses at Harvard one year, for instance, by growing a crop of potatoes on a lot on Oxford Street that had been lent him by the faculty. This sort of steadiness of purpose and unashamed hard work stood him well in the parish, and he appeared to be settled for life in Portland, Maine, at a venerable and distinguished church, when the call came to him from the West Coast. The immediate conveyor of that call was Henry Whitney Bellows,* who had temporarily taken over Starr King's church in San Francisco after King's untimely death in 1864. Bellows felt a personal obligation not to let King's work languish, as he knew it would without excellent leadership. But always dedicated to the growth of his denomination, he also saw what King had seen—the rare chance for growth in the West. If liberal religion did not establish itself at this key moment in the West—only five years before the completion of the transcontinental railroad—that religion would come to maturity with no solid point of entry for the liberals. So Bellows hand picked Stebbins for the San Francisco Church, and it was in one sense an unenviable position. Who could follow such a great orator? Stebbins was "strong, forcible, and impressive" in the pulpit but not a man of eloquence on King's terms (Heralds, p. 351). He wrote of the audience of "plucky-looking, come-if-you-dare, magnanimous, tender-hearted people" who faced him at first, but he went to work with them, clearing the debt on the church built by King, and never accumulating more debt (Crompton, p. 49). The rest of his life was devoted to the San Francisco

Church and the cause of Unitarianism on the Coast. One anecdote from Stebbins's Portland ministry suggests his character. Criticized at the outbreak of the Civil War for what some of his congregation thought was a too-blatant expression of patriotism and politics in the pulpit, Stebbins replied: "I have great respect for the people, and it gives me pain to come in collision with their convictions; but there is one man whose respect I must have, and his name is Stebbins" (Heralds, p. 350).

*Bibliography*

A. *Prayers* (San Francisco, 1903).

B. DAB 17, 549–50; Heralds 3, 349–52; Arnold Crompton, *Unitarianism on the Pacific Coast* (Boston, 1957).

**SULLIVAN, WILLIAM LAURENCE** (15 November 1872, East Braintree, MA–5 October 1935, Germantown, PA). *Education*: Bachelor of Philosophy, St. John's Ecclesiastical Seminary, Brighton, MA, 1896; S.T.B., Catholic University of America, 1899; licentiate in sacred theology, Catholic University of America, 1900. *Career*: Admitted to Missionary Society of St. Paul the Apostle, 1899; Paulist mission preacher, 1899–1901; ordained to Catholic priesthood, 1899; served at St. Thomas's Church, Washington, DC, 1900–1907; professor of theology, St. Thomas College, Washington, DC, 1902–6; pastor, Paulist Church, Austin, TX, c. 1907–9; writing and tutoring, Kansas City, MO, and Cleveland, OH, 1909–10; became a Unitarian, 1911; teacher, Ethical Culture School, New York, 1911–12; minister, All Souls Unitarian Church, Schenectady, NY, 1912–c. 1913; associate minister, All Souls Unitarian Church, New York, 1913–15; minister, 1915–22; mission preacher, Unitarian Laymen's League, 1922–24; minister, Church of the Messiah, St. Louis, MO, 1924–28; Germantown, PA, Unitarian Church, 1929–35.

William Laurence Sullivan was one of the chief advocates of Christian theism in twentieth-century Unitarianism. But the development of his final identity as a Unitarian minister was a difficult and painful process. Sullivan was from his early years a devout Roman Catholic and was ordained to the Catholic priesthood in 1899, serving as a Paulist mission preacher and then a professor of theology. His unwavering commitment to his faith and his religious vocation was broken by the 1907 encyclical of Pope Pius X condemning modernism. Even though Sullivan described Catholicism as "deeply rooted in the home soil of my nature," he could not with complete honesty continue in the church under the conditions laid down by the papal encyclical (*Under Orders*, p. 135). In his autobiography he called his anguished struggle over this issue a conflict between "heart's love" for the settled faith and the challenge of the active mind, and he stressed his rejection of the doctrine of papal infallibility as a major factor in his growing doubts about the church (p. 135). In his intellectual search he was influenced by the writings of the English Unitarian leader James Martineau. In 1911 he became a Unitarian and entered the Unitarian ministry in 1912.

Sullivan's later career was distinguished. He was one of the most effective pulpit orators in the denomination and held notable pastorates at New York City and Germantown, Pennsylvania. His identity within the denomination was based upon his unyielding theism and his scornful rejection of the Humanist movement. As Sullivan saw them, the Humanists were atheists or agnostics who were unwilling to accept that designation, styling themselves Humanist to preserve their respectability in a church that historically had been Christian. Sullivan led an unsuccessful fight to secure a theistic affirmation at a meeting of the National Conference in 1921. His theological creed began much in the tradition of William Ellery Channing* and Ralph Waldo Emerson* with an affirmation of the moral nature of the personality: "I am a moral personality under orders" (p. 159). This moral imperative was a "*via sacra*" that led to the theistic faith that he espoused (p. 160).

*Bibliography*

A. *Letters to His Holiness Pope Pius X* (Chicago, 1910); *The Priest: A Tale of Modernism in New England* (Boston, 1911); *From the Gospel to the Creeds: Studies in the Early History of the Christian Church* (Boston, 1919); "God, No-God, Half-God," *Christian Register*, 100 (August 8, 1921), 775–76; *Epigrams and Criticisms in Miniature* (Philadelphia and London, 1936); *Under Orders: The Autobiography of William Laurence Sullivan* (New York, 1944).

B. Biographical sketch in *Epigrams and Criticisms in Miniature* (see above); *Under Orders* (autobiography) (see above).

**SUNDERLAND, JABEZ THOMAS** (11 February 1842, Yorkshire, England– 13 August 1936, Ann Arbor, MI). *Education*: B.A., University of Chicago, 1867; M.A., University of Chicago, 1869; B.D., Baptist Union Theological Seminary, 1870. *Career*: Baptist minister, Milwaukee, 1871–72; converted to Unitarianism, 1872; minister, Northfield, MA, 1872–75; Chicago, IL, 1876–78; Ann Arbor, MI, 1878–98; editor, *Unitarian Monthly*, 1886–95; travel in India, 1895–96; minister, Oakland, CA, 1898–99; London, England, 1900–1901; Toronto, Canada, 1901–5; Hartford, CT, 1906–11; Ottawa, Canada, 1912–13; American Unitarian Association Billings Lecturer in the Orient, 1913–14; minister, Poughkeepsie, NY, 1914–28; active retirement, 1928–36.

Jabez T. Sunderland had a long and distinguished career in the Unitarian ministry. His presence made an impact on Unitarian history in two ways. First, he was a leading participant in the theological controversy in the Western Unitarian Conference (WUC) in the 1880s known as the "Western Issue." Second, he worked hard to educate Unitarians and others about the injustice of the colonization of India. Sunderland came into the Unitarian denomination from the Baptist ministry in 1872. Although he considered himself a disciple of

Theodore Parker,* he found himself playing a conservative role in the Western Unitarian Conference after taking the church in Ann Arbor in 1878. He opposed Jenkin Lloyd Jones* and the "*Unity* men" in their insistence that no theistic affirmation be required of member churches in the conference and forced controversy over that issue with his 1886 pamphlet *The Issue in the West.* Sunderland thought that some affirmation of a belief in God was necessary to ground the identity of the denomination, but was generally unable to wrest control of the WUC from Jones.

A decade after the western issue had boiled up, Sunderland traveled to India, where he became deeply concerned about colonial conditions. He returned to America and wrote much on the issue, becoming as Spencer Lavan noted, "the earliest public American supporter of the Indian nationalist movement" (Lavan, "Unitarianism and Acculturation," p. 74). Much of the rest of his career was devoted to strengthening the ties between American Unitarianism and India, in furthering the internationalization of liberal religion, and in promoting the cause of Indian self-rule. His writing on India culminated in his *India in Bondage,* a controversial work that was suppressed in India, bringing Sunderland much attention in the American press. Sunderland's sense of the importance of the Indian nationalist movement, advanced for its time, is especially significant to religious liberalism given the large impact that the teachings of Gandhi would have on that tradition in the twentieth century.

*Bibliography*

A. *The Issue in the West* (n.p., 1886); *The Bible: Its Origin, Growth, and Character* (New York and London, 1893); *The Spark in the Clod: A Study in Evolution* (Boston, 1902); *Because Men Are Not Stones* (Boston, 1923); *India in Bondage* (Calcutta, 1928).

B. Heralds 4, 219–20; *Who Was Who in America* 1, 1206; John Haynes Holmes, "Jabez T. Sunderland, 1892–1936," *Christian Register,* September 3, 1936, pp. 516–17; Charles H. Lyttle, *Freedom Moves West* (Boston, 1952); Spencer Lavan, "Unitarianism and Acculturation: Jabez T. Sunderland in India (1895–96)," PUHS, 17, pt. 2 (1973–75); Spencer Lavan, *Unitarians and India: A Study of Encounter and Response* (Boston, 1977).

# T

THAYER, THOMAS BALDWIN (10 September 1812, Boston, MA–12 February 1886, Roxbury, MA). *Education*: Private tutoring, Cambridge, MA, 1828–31. *Career*: Schoolkeeper and Universalist supply preacher, 1831–33; minister, First Universalist Society, Lowell, MA, 1833–45; editor, *The Star of Bethlehem*, 1841–42; Universalist minister, Brooklyn, NY, 1845–51; First Universalist Society, Lowell, MA, 1851–59; Shawmut Avenue Universalist Church, Boston, 1859–67; editor, *Universalist Quarterly*, 1864–86.

Russell E. Miller called Thomas B. Thayer's *Theology of Universalism* "the most thorough and systematic treatment of Universalist theology before the Civil War" (Miller, p. 133). Indeed, Thayer was at pains to show in that work that "Universalism is not a confused collection of doctrinal fragments, without continuity or relation of parts; but a system of divinity" (*Theology of Universalism*, p. iii). It is the word system that is important, for that meant a unified and logically coherent theory of religion for Thayer, in which the discovery of one element of truth led inexorably to a comprehensive body of truths. Thayer found that single truth in the question of evil and began his discussion there with the confidence that a thorough understanding of evil would make possible a thorough understanding of Universalism. For Thayer, evil was a means and not an end—a means ordained by God for the purposes of educating humanity. It was "a school wherein we are to be taught and trained for a higher sphere of life and action, both in the present and in the future" (p. 20). Most important, evil made possible the appearance of Jesus, who demonstrated the perfection of human nature. This exemplary nature of Jesus led to other conclusions about conversion. It was, for Thayer, "not a change of nature, miraculously and instantly wrought by the Holy Spirit" but "a change of heart, purpose, character, and life" (p. 166). In other words, humanity did not need to be changed in its nature but in its direction, and the educative powers of evil and the example of

Jesus could make that change. This potential perfection assured universal salvation, for God had ordained the perfect means to the realization of that potential, either in this life or the one to come. Thayer's theology was a version of the "fortunate fall," adapted to meet the needs of a theology of self-culture and spiritual development.

Thayer's theological contributions were one side of a busy career, which included over two decades of editing the *Universalist Quarterly*, a journal to which he was also a frequent contributor. This was the most scholarly of the Universalist journals of the nineteenth century. In his early pastorate at Lowell, Massachusetts, he found his congregation filled with young women employed at the Lowell Mills. With Abel Thomas, another Universalist pastor in Lowell, Thayer gave his support to "Improvement Circles" among the young women and helped to edit and publish some of the their work in *Star of Bethlehem*, a denominational periodical he coedited. Eventually, Thomas expanded the idea and went on to aid in publishing the *Lowell Offering*, a significant early outlet for women's writing. Thayer stands as one of the intellectual leaders of midnineteenth-century Universalism.

*Bibliography*

A. *The Bible Class Assistant; or, Scriptural Guide for Sunday Schools* (Boston, 1840); *The Origin and History of the Doctrine of Endless Punishment* (Boston, 1855); *Theology of Universalism* (Boston, 1862).

B. DAB 18, 411; John G. Adams, *Fifty Notable Years* (Boston, 1882); Richard Eddy, *Universalism in America: A History*, 2 vols. (Boston, 1884–86); Russell E. Miller, *The Larger Hope* (Boston, 1979).

**TUCKERMAN, JOSEPH** (18 January 1778, Boston, MA–20 April 1840, Havana, Cuba). *Education*: A.B., Harvard College, 1798; studied theology with Thomas Thacher, Dedham, MA, 1798–1801. *Career*: Minister, North Chelsea (now Revere), MA, 1801–26; minister-at-large, Boston, 1826–36.

Joseph Tuckerman pioneered the innovative ministry-at-large in Boston, an effort to take liberal religion to the new class of urban poor spawned by the rapidly urbanizing society of the early nineteenth century. Of a wealthy background, Tuckerman graduated from Harvard in 1798 and became minister in Chelsea, Massachusetts, in 1801, serving well there as a parish minister, but with no particular distinction as an innovator, until 1825. Under the leadership of William Ellery Channing* and Henry Ware, Jr.,* Unitarians in the early 1820s began to take measures to address the growing problem of poverty in Boston. Tuckerman was called to be the first full-time minister-at-large in Boston and entered upon the difficult task not only of addressing the needs of the poor but of educating the sometimes obtuse Unitarian clergy and laity about the nature of urban poverty. Tuckerman relied heavily upon visitation in this ministry, pioneering a form of urban social work in America. His efforts not only helped to sensitize Boston liberals to the problems of poverty but made some progress in finding ways to address that question. Moreover, Tuckerman's thinking about social reform laid the groundwork for later social work agencies. He unified Boston efforts in social work by founding the Benevolent Societies of Boston in 1834, a council of social agencies. Tuckerman's work was an important phase in the development of a social consciousness in the liberal religious tradition.

*Bibliography*

A. *Principles and Results of the Ministry-at-Large* (Boston, 1838).

B. AAUP, 345–56; DAB 19, 46; DARB, 476–77; Heralds 2, 103–17; Daniel T. McColgan, *Joseph Tuckerman: Pioneer in American Social Work* (Washington, DC, 1940); Daniel Walker Howe, *The Unitarian Conscience: Harvard Moral Philosophy, 1805–1861* (Cambridge, 1970); David Robinson, "Channing and the Problem of Social Reform," *Kairos,* 16 (Autumn 1979), p. 7.

# W

WALKER, JAMES (16 August 1794, Woburn, MA–23 December 1874, Cambridge, MA). *Education*: A.B., Harvard, 1814; graduated, Harvard Divinity School, 1817. *Career*: Unitarian minister, Harvard Church, Charlestown, MA, 1818–39; editor, *Christian Examiner*, 1831–39; Alford Professor of Natural Religion, Moral Philosophy, and Civil Polity, Harvard, 1839–53; president, Harvard, 1853–60; retirement, 1860–74.

James Walker was one of the early defenders of the liberal theology in the nineteenth century and took an active role in the formation of the American Unitarian Association in 1825. During a pastorate of more than two decades in Charlestown, Massachusetts, he established a reputation for scholarship and philosophical acumen and remained devoted to his parish in spite of several opportunities to move elsewhere. He was finally persuaded to take the Alford Chair at Harvard, and he remained at Harvard as professor and later as president of the University until his retirement. Walker was an adherent of the Scottish Common-Sense philosophy of Thomas Reid and Dugald Stewart, and he prepared editions of the works of both of them. Although this philosophical outlook suggests that Walker was part of the conservative Unitarian establishment against which the Transcendentalists rebelled, the case is more complicated. Perry Miller noted that it was Walker's tolerance of mind that allowed several of the Transcendentalists to publish their works in the *Christian Examiner*, the influential Unitarian journal that he edited. Moreover, Walker conceived and expounded his commonsense notions in a way that made them very nearly compatible with the intuitionist doctrine of the Transcendentalists. In one important sermon published in 1834, Walker in fact made religious intuition part of the commonsense system. He argued on grounds similar to those offered by Reid and Stewart that "our conviction of the existence of the sensible world does not rest on a logical deduction from the facts of sensation, or on sensation and consciousness. It rests on the constitution of our nature" (Walker, *The Philosophy of Man's Spiritual Nature*, quoted in Miller, p. 83). Having established human character as the foundation of our sense of external reality, he then extended the argument into religion. For Walker, an individual "believes in the existence and reality of the spiritual world, just as he believes in his own existence and reality, and just as he believes in the existence and reality of the outward universe,—simply and solely because he is so constituted that with his impressions or perceptions he cannot help it" (p. 84). Coming as it did in the middle 1830s, just as Transcendentalism was about to flower in Ralph Waldo Emerson's\* *Nature* (1836), Walker's views were taken as an encouraging sign by the younger generation. Daniel Walker Howe suggested that Walker's "early fire seems to have died down as he became comfortably situated in the Yard," and Walker expressed regret at never having completed a major theological work (Howe, p. 314). But he was a constant contributor to the *Christian Examiner*, an influential preacher, and a highly regarded public figure.

*Bibliography*

A. *The Philosophy of Man's Spiritual Nature in Regard to the Foundation of Faith* (Boston, 1834); *Sermons Preached in the Chapel of Harvard College* (Boston, 1861); *Reason, Faith, and Duty* (Boston, 1877).

B. DAB 19, 346–47; Heralds 2, 218–22; "James Walker," *Proceedings of the American Academy of Arts and Sciences*, 10 (1875), 485–95; Perry Miller, *The Transcendentalists: An Anthology* (Cambridge, 1950); Daniel Walker Howe, *The Unitarian Conscience: Harvard Moral Philosophy, 1805–1861* (Cambridge, 1970).

**WARE, HENRY** (1 April 1764, Sherborn, MA–12 July 1845, Cambridge, MA). *Education*: A.B., Harvard College, 1785. *Career*: Minister of First Parish, Hingham, MA, 1787–1805; Hollis Professor of Divinity, Harvard College, 1805–40.

Henry Ware's election as Hollis Professor of Divinity in 1805 was one of the earliest public manifestations of the growing split between Calvinists and liberals in New England, and the opposition voiced to his election by the Calvinists constituted the first phase of the Unitarian controversy. Ware was reared on a farm near Sherborn, Massachusetts, and entered Harvard in 1781, graduating with the highest honors in 1785. After a period of teaching and studying theology, he accepted a call to the First Parish in Hingham, Massachusetts, in 1787, following the long and distinguished pastorate of Ebenezer Gay.\* In 1805 he was elected to the Hollis professorship at Harvard, where he took an important role in developing course work in ministerial training that led to the establishment of the Harvard Divinity School. From 1820 to 1822 he engaged in an exchange of pamphlets with the Calvinist Leonard Woods. His son Henry Ware, Jr.,\* took a leading role among the next generation of liberals, helping to form the American Unitarian Association in 1825. The elder Ware resigned his professorship in 1840, in ill health, and died in 1845.

*Bibliography*

A. *Letters Addressed to Trinitarians and Calvinists, Occasioned by Dr. Woods' Letters to Unitarians* (Cambridge, 1820); *Answer to Dr. Woods' Reply, in a Second Series of Letters Addressed to Trinitarians and Calvinists* (Cambridge, 1822); *An Inquiry into the Foundations, Evidences, and Truths of Religion* (Cambridge, 1842).

B. AAUP, 199–203; DAB 19, 447–48; Heralds 2, 40–49; Conrad Wright, "The Election of Henry Ware: Two Contemporary Accounts Edited with Commentary," *Harvard Library Bulletin*, 17 (July 1969), 245–78; Daniel Walker Howe, *The Unitarian Conscience: Harvard Moral Philosophy, 1805–1861* (Cambridge, 1970).

**WARE, HENRY, JR.** (21 April 1794, Hingham, MA–22 September 1843, Framingham, MA). *Education*: A.B., Harvard College, 1812. *Career*: Minister, Second Church, Boston, MA, 1817–30; Professor of Pulpit Eloquence and the Pastoral Care, Harvard Divinity School, 1830–42.

Henry Ware, Jr., was an important figure in the Unitarian movement of the early nineteenth century and one of the leaders in the founding of the American Unitarian Association. His father had been a leader in the liberal movement, and his election in 1805 as the Hollis Professor of Divinity at Harvard occasioned one of the earliest instances of the Unitarian-Calvinist controversy in New England. The younger Ware completed Harvard in 1812 and was installed as minister of Boston's Second Church in 1817, a church with a proud history but one that was struggling in terms of membership and finance when Ware took over. He was a remarkably effective minister, combining gifts of personal warmth in his visitations with pulpit eloquence. He was an early experimenter in extemporaneous preaching, and his innovative energies resulted in his being appointed to the newly created post of Professor of Pulpit Eloquence and the Pastoral Care at Harvard in 1830. He left the church in the hands of his young colleague, Ralph Waldo Emerson.* It was hoped that this academic appointment would prevent the further deterioration of Ware's frail health, but he seemed to work all the harder in this post and was plagued by periodic bouts of illness. Ware wrote sermons, theology, poetry, and fiction during his career, but his most important work was the devotional manual *On the Formation of the Christian Character* (1831). In it Ware argued that the aim of religion is the cultivation of the ability to give "*your heart a permanent bias toward God*," an aim that must be pursued by a rigorous spiritual discipline (*Works*, IV, p. 311). The work was an important signpost of the pietist strand in liberal religion, a strand that was significant despite the fact that the public reputation of the denomination was that of a rational religion. Although a friend, and in some senses a guide to Emerson, Ware criticized Emerson's Divinity School address for its lack of an affirmation of a personal God and published his defense of that version of theism in *The Personality of the Deity* (1838). After suffering from increasingly deteriorating health in his last years, Ware died in 1843.

*Bibliography*

A. *On the Formation of the Christian Character* (Cambridge and Boston, 1831); *The Personality of the Deity* (Boston, 1838); *Works*, 4 vols. (Boston and London, 1846–47).

B. AAUP, 472–84; DAB 19, 448–49; Heralds 2, 223–38; John Ware, *Memoir of the Life of Henry Ware, Jr.*, 2 vols. (Boston, 1846); Daniel Walker Howe, *The Unitarian Conscience: Harvard Moral Philosophy, 1805–1861* (Cambridge, MA, 1970); David Robinson, *Apostle of Culture: Emerson as Preacher and Lecturer* (Philadelphia, 1982).

**WEISS, JOHN** (28 June 1818, Boston, MA–9 March 1879, Boston, MA). *Education*: A.B., Harvard, 1837; graduated from Harvard Divinity School, 1843; attended University of Heidelberg, Germany, 1842–43. *Career*: Unitarian minister, Watertown, MA, 1843–45, 1846–47; First Congregational Society, New Bedford, MA, 1847–59; Watertown, 1862–69; founding member, Free Religious Association, 1867; variously an independent lecturer and author, 1843–79.

When he addressed the graduating class of the Harvard Divinity School in 1869, John Weiss made clear to them his sense of contemporary religion's failure to respond to the challenge of science. Noting that many people of that day were "oppressed because the facts have gathered faster than the explanations," he argued that religion answered new problems with old formulas. "At the very moment when religion's opportunity first occurs to make the finite prove the infinite which she presumes, she continues the old prescription of church-extension, Bible-worship, claims of miracles, and conventional parish life" ("The Task of Religion," p. 187). Weiss's indictment of contemporary religion and his corresponding faith that science demonstrates "the divine method and purpose by means of all animate and inanimate things" suggest the major thrust of his thought (p. 184). This outlook made him one of the radicals of his day. His friend O. B. Frothingham,* with whom he worked to found the Free Religious Association, described his "overflow of nervous vitality, an excess of spiritual life that could not find vents enough for discharge" (Frothingham, p. 190). Frothingham's sketch of Weiss goes on to make clear why his ministerial career was finally a splendid and dazzling failure. He preached abstractly difficult sermons, punctuated with a startling "brusqueness" and a wit whose "sting" overbalanced "the laugh it raised" (p. 205). In short, he was "too far removed from the common ground of sympathy" (p. 207). Minot J. Savage* recalled an example of Weiss's sharp sarcasm from one of his addresses: "Time was that when the brain was out a man would die, but now they make a Unitarian minister out of him" (Heralds, p. 378). For Savage, there was more wit here than bitterness, but it is not hard to see how such a manner alienated some. To others, though, he was a charming and fascinating companion, the greatest conversationalist of the radical movement. The sharp edges of his personality and his uncompromising intellectuality made it difficult for Weiss to remain happy in the pulpit. He would not abandon the Unitarian denomination in forming the Free Religious Association, as some wanted to do, but he did aspire to a career as an independent lecturer, in the mold of Ralph Waldo Emerson.* This he never satisfactorily achieved. Nevertheless, Weiss made a great impact on his contemporaries, staunchly defending science as a mode of speculative advance congenial with religion. Frothingham called him "eminently religious," but his faith was "purely natural, scientific, . . . unorthodox to the last degree" (Frothingham, p. 192). Like many other post–Civil War radicals, Weiss looked to Theodore Parker* as a leader, and his biography of Parker (1863), still of value, is a monument to the man who Weiss believed had "conscience and humanity enough to feed a generation" (*Life and Correspondence of Theodore Parker*, p. viii).

*Bibliography*

A. *The Aesthetic Letters, Essays, and Philosophical Letters of Schiller, Translated with an Introduction* (Boston, 1845); *Life and Correspondence of Theodore Parker*, 2 vols. (London, 1863); "The Task of Religion," *Radical*, 6 (1869), 177–90; *American Religion* (Boston, 1871); *Wit, Humor, and Shakespeare: Twelve Essays* (Boston, 1876); *Goethe's West-Easterly Divan, Translated with Introduction and Notes* (Boston, 1877); *The Immortal Life* (Boston, 1880).

B. DAB 19, 615–16; DLB 1, 188; Heralds 3, 376–80; Cyrus A. Bartol, *Principles and Portraits* (Boston, 1880); O. B. Frothingham, *Recollections and Impressions, 1822–1890* (New York, 1891); Stow Persons, *Free Religion: An American Faith* (New Haven, 1947).

**WENDTE, CHARLES WILLIAM** (11 June 1844, Boston, MA–9 September 1931, Berkeley, CA). *Education*: Attended Meadville Theological School, 1866–67; graduated from Harvard Divinity School, 1869. *Career*: Minister, Fourth Unitarian Church, Chicago, 1869–75; First Unitarian Church, Cincinnati, 1876–82; Channing Memorial Church, Newport, RI, 1882–85; Unitarian missionary supervisor, West Coast, 1886–1901; minister, First Unitarian Church, Oakland, CA, 1886; supply minister, Unity Church, Los Angeles, 1898; general secretary, International Council of Liberal Religious Thinkers and Workers, 1900–1920; secretary of foreign relations, American Unitarian Association, 1905–15; minister, First Parish, Brighton, MA, 1905–8; secretary, National Federation of Religious Liberals, 1908–20; president, Free Religious Association, 1910–14.

Charles William Wendte was an important force in the establishment of Unitarianism on the West Coast and was a leader in Unitarian efforts to establish cooperation with religious liberals throughout the world. Wendte's parents came to the United States from Germany in 1842, and his father died in 1847. His mother supported the family through giving German lessons, and Theodore

Parker* was among her pupils. That early contact with Parker, as well as the sermons he heard when Parker preached at the Music Hall in Boston, were formative influences. When he went to California in the 1860s, he met there a second major influence, Starr King.* After a period of custom-house and banking work, he decided to enter the ministry. He was an effective minister, with successful pastorates in the Midwest and East Coast, but his nature was restless, and he was happier as a missionary and organizer than as a settled minister. The post of West Coast missionary supervisor for the American Unitarian Association gave outlet to those abilities first. He did much missionary preaching, tried to help new churches find ministerial leadership, and led in the move to establish the Pacific Unitarian School for the Ministry, now the Starr King School for Religious Leadership. In the first decade of the twentieth century he became the principal force behind a series of international religious congresses that brought American Unitarians together with European and Asian religious liberals. Wendte's hopes that these meetings would eventually develop into a real international religious movement were crushed by World War I. He spent the last years of his life in California, where he was involved with the Pacific Unitarian School. He was a versatile man who in addition to undertaking enormous administrative responsibilities wrote theology, poems, hymns, and biography and played and composed music. In Samuel A. Eliot's* summation, "He combined German diligence, California optimism and New England idealism" (Heralds, p. 248).

*Bibliography*

A. *Freedom and Fellowship in Religion* (editor, Boston, 1906); *The Unity of the Spirit* (editor, Boston, 1909); *Thomas Starr King: Patriot and Preacher* (Boston, 1921); *The Wider Fellowship*, 2 vols. (autobiography) (Boston, 1927); *The Transfiguration of Life by a Modernist Faith* (Boston, 1930).

B. DAB 19, 651–52; Heralds 4, 244–48; *The Wider Fellowship* (see above); Arnold Crompton, *Unitarianism on the Pacific Coast* (Boston, 1957).

**WHITTEMORE, THOMAS** (1 January 1800, Boston, MA–21 March 1861, Cambridge, MA). *Education*: Private theological study with Hosea Ballou, 1821. *Career*: Preached in Roxbury, MA, 1820; minister, Milford, MA, 1821; Cambridgeport, MA, 1822–28; editor, *Trumpet and Universalist Magazine*, 1828–61; Massachusetts legislator, 1831–36; bank director, later president, Cambridge, 1840; president, Vermont and Massachusetts Railroad, 1849.

Thomas Whittemore was the most prominent publicist and popularizer of Universalism in the early nineteenth century. His theological career began when he met Hosea Ballou,* who encouraged him to pursue his studies, suggested that he enter the ministry, and guided him in his theological preparation. Whittemore became the most prominent of Ballou's disciples and remained intensely loyal to him all of his life, defending his theological views and later preparing his biography. Whittemore's career included a wide variety of activities, but he is perhaps most notable for editing the *Trumpet and Universalist Magazine*, of which he assumed sole control in 1828, making it into a widely circulated and even profitable enterprise. It was the chief Universalist periodical in the pre–Civil War era and one of the most widely circulated of any Boston religious periodicals. Whittemore was a staunch defender of Universalist religious freedom, fighting against the Massachusetts tradition of tax support for the Standing Order churches, but he was politically cautious on other issues such as the question of slavery. In theology he defended Ballou's ultra-Universalism against the Restorationists. Perhaps his most significant theological contribution was his *Plain Guide to Universalism* (1838), a popular account of Universalist religion intended as a tool for evangelism and a support and guide to those newly converted to that faith. He also did much other theological, historical, and biographical writing. As if these activities did not constitute a busy enough life in themselves, he also served in the legislature and became something of an expert in business management, rescuing a Cambridge bank and the Vermont and Massachusetts Railroad from financial straits. He did not have the intellectual acumen of his mentor Ballou, and never claimed to have, but his extraordinary energy and organizational skills made an important contribution to Universalism at a key period of its development.

*Bibliography*

A. *The Modern History of Universalism* (Boston, 1830); *Notes and Illustrations of the Parables of the New Testament* (Boston, 1832); *A Plain Guide to Universalism* (Boston, 1838); *Life of Rev. Hosea Ballou*, 4 vols. (Boston, 1854–55); *The Early Days of Thomas Whittemore* (Boston, 1859).

B. DAB 20, 172–73; *The Early Days of Thomas Whittemore* (see above); John G. Adams, *Memoir of Thomas Whittemore* (Boston, 1878); Russell E. Miller, *The Larger Hope* (Boston, 1979).

**WIEMAN, HENRY NELSON** (19 August 1884, Rich Hill, MO–19 June 1975, Grinnell, IA). *Education*: B.A., Park College, 1906; B.D., San Francisco Seminary, 1910; studied at Jena and Heidelberg, 1910–11; Ph.D., Harvard, 1917. *Career*: Presbyterian minister, Davis, CA, 1911–15; professor of philosophy and religion, University of Chicago Divinity School, 1927–47; active retirement, 1947–75.

"My intellectual life has been focused on a single problem," Henry Nelson Wieman wrote in 1963 (*The Empirical Theology of Henry Nelson Wieman*, p. 3). "What operates in human life with such character and power that it will transform man as he cannot transform himself, saving him from evil and leading him to the best that human life can ever reach, provided he meet the required conditions?" (p. 3). This central question as Wieman articulated it was the basis of a religious investigation that has had a large and growing influence on religious liberalism. For Wieman, "faith" was one of the "required conditions" for the transformation of life, an act of "giving oneself" to that transforming power (p. 3). This surge of transforming creativity constituted for Wieman the essence of religious experience. In all of his work Wieman attempted to bring this experience out of the realm of speculative philosophy and metaphysics and into the realm of empiricism. He argued that "religious inquiry is misdirected when some presence pervading the cosmos is sought to solve the religious problem," but he did use the term God to designate the power that can create human transformation (p. 4). Thus he set his thinking in opposition to rationalist speculation and argued that religious truth, or God's revelation, had to be pursued in events, in human experience. In his recently edited *Creative Freedom*, Wieman pointed to human interchange and communication as central facets of the religious experience and saw in their promotion a role for the future of religious liberalism.

*Bibliography*

A. *Religious Experience and Scientific Method* (New York, 1926); *The Source of Human Good* (Chicago, 1926); *The Wrestle of Religion with Truth* (New York, 1927); *Man's Ultimate Commitment* (Carbondale, IL, 1958); *The Empirical Theology of Henry Nelson Wieman*, ed. Robert W. Bretall (New York, 1963); *Creative Freedom: Vocation of Liberal Religion*, ed. Creighton Peden and Larry E. Axel (New York, 1982).

B. DARB, 509–10; *New York Times*, June 21, 1975, p. 30; John B. Cobb, *Process Theology as Political Theology* (Philadelphia, 1982); essays by Brian S. Kopke, Larry E. Axel, and Marvin Shaw, *Kairos*, 30 (Fall 1983), 3–4 (supplement to *Unitarian Universalist World*, 14 [December 15, 1983]).

**WILBUR, EARL MORSE** (26 April 1866, Jericho, VT–8 January 1956, Berkeley, CA). *Education*: B.A., University of Vermont, 1886; A.M., S.T.B., Harvard University, 1890; postgraduate study, University of Berlin and Oxford University, 1898–99. *Career*: Assistant minister, First Unitarian Society, Portland, OR, 1890–93; minister, 1893–98; Independent Congregational (Unitarian) Church, Meadville, PA, 1899–1904; organizer, dean, and professor of practical theology, Pacific Unitarian (later Starr King) School for the Ministry, 1904–11; president and professor, 1911–31; research in Europe as Guggenheim Fellow and fellow of the Hibbert Trust, 1931–34; research and writing, 1934–56.

Earl Morse Wilbur was the most prominent modern student of the history of Unitarianism in Europe. His ground-breaking scholarly research has provided much of the information we have on the historical development of Socinian and Unitarian theology. Indeed, Wilbur's work in many respects made Americans aware of the rich history of Unitarian ideas in Eastern Europe. Wilbur began his ministerial career as the assistant to Thomas Lamb Eliot* in Portland, Oregon, where his deep connection with the Unitarian movement on the West Coast was formed. He took a leading role in the formation of the Pacific Unitarian School for the Ministry, now known as the Starr King School for Religious Leadership, and served as both professor and president of that institution. It was his work for Unitarian education that led to his research into Unitarian history. He planned a series of lectures at the school on the rise of Unitarian doctrines but discovered that there was no source for such lectures. A preliminary history of the movement, *Our Unitarian History* (1925), was prepared at the behest of the American Unitarian Association Department of Religious Education, but Wilbur recognized that a vast amount of research in European archives was needed to write a definitive history. He undertook this research in European trips of 1925–26 and 1931–34, when he discovered much little-known material on the Socinian tradition in Europe. This research required his use of some eight languages. He also attempted to visit personally every place of historical importance to Unitarianism. The result of his work was the two-volume *History of Unitarianism* (1945; 1952), the most important history of Unitarianism, which is definitive on the European Unitarian movement. As with every important scholarly endeavor, Wilbur's work opened many new questions and avenues of research and had a formative influence on much of the later and ongoing research in Unitarian history.

*Bibliography*

A. *History of the First Unitarian Church of Portland, Oregon* (Portland, OR, 1893); *History of the Independent Congregational Church of Meadville, Pennsylvania* (Meadville, PA, 1902); *Our Unitarian Heritage* (Boston, 1925); *Thomas Lamb Eliot* (Portland, OR, 1937); *A History of Unitarianism: Socinianism and Its Antecedents* (Cambridge, MA, 1945); *A History of Unitarianism: In Transylvania, England, and America to 1900* (Cambridge, MA, 1952).

B. NCAB 42, 92–93; "How the History Came to Be Written," PUHS, 9, pt. 1 (1951), 5–23.

**WILLIAMS, GEORGE HUNTSTON** (7 April 1914, Huntsburg, OH). *Education*: Studied at University of Munich, 1934–35; A.B., St. Lawrence University, 1936; B.D., Meadville Theological School, 1939; study at the University of Strasbourg, 1939–40; University of California, 1942–43; Th.D., Union Theological Seminary, 1946. *Career*: Assistant minister, Church of the Christian Union, Rockford, IL, 1940–41; faculty member, Starr King School and Pacific School of Religion, 1941–47; lecturer to Hollis Professor of Divinity, Harvard Divinity School, 1947–present.

George Huntston Williams is a church historian who has done notable work both on the history of the Protestant Reformation and on American Unitarianism and Universalism. His firm sense of the Protestant tradition is grounded in his work on the early Anabaptist, spiritualist, and evangelical rationalist movements in sixteenth-century Europe that comprised *The Radical Reformation*. Although not in the mainstream of the Protestant reform led by Luther, these movements were, and have remained, vital elements in the development of later Protestantism. Williams concluded in 1962 that these traditions may have continuing relevance for Christianity in an era of change. Williams has also devoted much attention to the Unitarian Universalist tradition. In a 1949 work on Frederic Henry Hedge,* Williams noted that a "spiritual ambivalence of Unitarianism constitutes one of the most remarkable features of our body" (*Rethinking the Unitarian Relationship with Protestantism*, p. 12). For Williams that ambivalence is summed up in the simultaneous existence of a "broad-*churchly* tradition" and a dissenting sectarianism (p. 11). "Unitarianism will do well to preserve both the broad conserving churchmanship of the former and the latter's intense spirit of prophetic dissent" (p. 12). In later work on Universalism, Williams also stressed the connections of the American Universalist movement to the larger traditions of Christian history and argued that the Universalist faith in "the goodness of the ultimate Force behind the creation of both nature and our human condition" can be an important element in the "merged denomination" by providing hope "for us of a generation rocked by ecological crises and more fearful of a cosmic catastrophe than hopeful of a benign millenium" ("American Universalism," pp. 88–89). The burden of Williams's work on the history of Unitarian Universalism has been to connect that movement to the worldwide history of the Christian church, a perspective that Williams believes is essential for the continuing spiritual vitality of the denomination.

*Bibliography*

A. *Rethinking the Unitarian Relationship with Protestantism: An Examination of the Thought of Frederic Henry Hedge (1805–1890)* (Boston, 1949); *The Norman Anonymous of 1100 A.D.* (Cambridge, 1951); *The Harvard Divinity School: Its Place in Harvard University and in American Culture* (editor, Boston, 1959); *Spiritual and Anabaptist Writers* (editor, Philadelphia, 1957); *The Radical Reformation* (Philadelphia, 1962); *Wilderness and Paradise in Christian Thought* (New York, 1962); "American Universalism: A Bicentennial Historical Essay," JUHS, 9 (1971), entire issue; "The Polish Brethren," 2 vols., PUHS, 18 (1976–77), editor and translator; *The Mind of John Paul II* (New York, 1981); "Dimensions of Faith: The Universalist Way," *Unitarian Universalist World*, 13 (June 15, 1982), 1, 3.

B. CA 1R, 1005; DAS 1, 829.


**WINCHESTER, ELHANAN** (30 September 1751, Brookline, MA–18 April 1797, Hartford, CT). *Career*: Baptist minister, Rehoboth, MA, 1771; itinerant minister, Massachusetts, 1772–74; minister, Welch Neck, SC, 1774–80; Philadelphia, 1780–81; Universalist minister, Philadelphia, 1781–87; itinerant preacher, England, 1787–94; itinerant preacher, United States, 1794–96; preacher, Hartford, CT, 1796–97.

Elhanan Winchester's gradual evolution toward Universalism began when he was spiritually moved by the later currents of the Great Awakening during his youth in Massachusetts. His father was a deacon in the Congregational church, but the younger Winchester became a Baptist in 1770 and began preaching in Baptist pulpits soon after, his theology changing from Arminianism to strict

Calvinism. In 1778, however, his Calvinism began to weaken, largely under the influence of "Paul Siegvolck's" (Georg-Klein Nicolai's) treatise *The Everlasting Gospel*. He continued as a Baptist, attracting large audiences for his sermons in Philadelphia, but when he began in 1781 openly to proclaim the "universal salvation," he was ousted from his church, taking a large portion of the congregation with him to form a Universalist society in Philadelphia. Although he had limited education, Winchester was an excellent linguist and had a remarkable memory for biblical passages that added much to the impact of his eloquent preaching. He specified Siegvolck's argument that there could not be "two endless contrary things," good and evil, or God and Satan, as being decisive in his move to Universalism. Because God was all-powerful, Winchester reasoned, and because he was benevolent, the eventual restoration of all souls was assured. Thus "the power of God" would "preserve and keep those who commit themselves to him" and also "destroy that covenant with death . . . whereby sinners are held in subjection to Satan" (*The Universal Restoration*, p. 15). In 1787 Winchester took his Universalist ideas to England, where he preached for several years and published a number of theological works. After his return to America, an asthmatic condition worsened, and his eventual death prematurely ended a remarkable preaching career. Indeed, he might well have come to rival John Murray* as the leader of his denomination had his death not come so soon.

*Bibliography*

A. *The Fate of Moses Unveiled by the Gospel* (Philadelphia, 1787); *The Universal Restoration, Exhibited in Four Dialogues* (London, 1788; rpt. with a "Memoir of the Author," Philadelphia, 1843); *A Course of Lectures on the Prophecies That Remain to Be Fulfilled*, 4 vols. (London, 1789–90); *The Restitution of All Things . . . Defended* (London, 1790); *The Three Woe Trumpets* (London, 1793); *Ten Letters Addressed to Mr. Paine* (New York, 1795).

B. DAB 20, 377–78; DARB, 518–20; William Vidler, *A Sketch of the Life of Elhanan Winchester* (London, 1797); Edwin M. Stone, *Biography of Rev. Elhanan Winchester* (Boston, 1836); "Memoir" (see *The Universal Restoration* above); Russell E. Miller, *The Larger Hope* (Boston, 1979).

**WOOLLEY, CELIA PARKER** (14 June 1848, Toledo, OH–9 March 1918, Chicago, IL). *Education*: Coldwater, MI, Female Seminary. *Career*: Editorial staff, *Unity*, 1884–1918; president, Chicago Woman's Club, 1888–90; Unitarian minister, Geneva, IL, 1893–96 (ordained 1894); Independent Liberal Church, Chicago, IL, 1896–98; organizer, Frederick Douglass Center, Chicago Settlement, 1904–18.

Celia Parker Woolley had a varied career as a journalist, civic leader, minister, and social worker in the Chicago area in the late nineteenth and early twentieth centuries. Moving to Chicago with her husband in 1876, she became involved in numerous women's groups and literary organizations and wrote a number of books. She also developed a close relationship with Jenkin Lloyd Jones* as a member of his All Souls Church and worked with his periodical *Unity* from the middle 1880s on. Her interest in Unitarianism finally led her to ordination in 1894 and pastorates at Geneva, Illinois, and the Independent Liberal Church in North Chicago. Increasingly drawn to issues of racial justice, she founded the Frederick Douglass Center in South Chicago, where she moved with her husband in 1904, staying until her death. Her hope was to establish a center for community organization that would both draw help to Chicago's black population and provide it the means of self-help. She was important both for her work in social reform and her presence as a woman in the ministry.

*Bibliography*

A. *Love and Theology* (republished as *Rachel Armstrong* [Boston, 1887]); *A Girl Graduate* (Boston and New York, 1889); *Roger Hunt* (Boston and New York, 1892); *The Western Slope* (Evanston, IL, 1893).

B. DAB 20, 515; Heralds 4, 58–59; *Who Was Who in America* 1, 1381; Catherine F. Hitchings, "Universalist and Unitarian Women Ministers," JUHS, 10 (1975).

**WRIGHT, CHARLES CONRAD** (9 February 1917, Cambridge, MA). *Education*: A.B., Harvard, 1937; A.M., Harvard, 1942; Ph.D., Harvard, 1947. *Career*: Instructor to assistant professor and lecturer in the humanities, Massachusetts Institute of Technology, 1946–54; lecturer in church history, Harvard Divinity School, 1954–69; registrar, Harvard Divinity School, 1955–67; professor of American church history, Harvard Divinity School, 1969–present.

Conrad Wright stands as the leading historian of American Unitarianism and has led a movement in the reinterpretation of Unitarian history that has influenced both American historians and literary scholars. His work has stressed the indigenous origins of the American Unitarian movement, locating them in the Arminian theology of eighteenth-century New England. The New England liberals of the period 1735–1805 were called Arminians, Wright has said, "not because they were directly influenced by Jacobus Arminius (1560–1609), the Dutch Remonstrant, but because their reaction to Calvinism was similar to his" (*The Beginnings of Unitarianism in America*, p. 6). Thus it was in the reaction to the Puritan Calvinism of the New England churches that liberal Christianity took shape. As Wright demonstrated, the major strands in that development were the rejection of the doctrine of original sin, a "supernatural rationalism" that stressed the need for both human reason and biblical revelation, and an Arian Christology that rejected the doctrine of the Trinity in orthodox Calvinism. Wright followed his influential study of American Unitarian origins with studies of the nineteenth century in which he stressed the importance of the often overlooked Henry W. Bellows* to Unitarian history. A builder and organizer, Bellows has often been slighted by those interested purely in the intellectual history of liberalism, but Wright argued that Bellows "was the leading spirit of organized or denominational Unitarianism" (*A Stream of Light*, p. 66). This emphasis on the organizational history of the movement has had further implications in later work of Wright in which he has emerged not only as a denominational historian but a prophetic voice. In one 1979 essay, "Individualism in Historical Perspective," Wright criticized the tradition of pure individualism in liberal religion as represented by Thomas Jefferson and Ralph Waldo Emerson* for its apparent rejection of the notion that "there is anything in human nature that needs religious community" (p. 5). Extending this thesis, Wright called in another address for a refurbished doctrine of the church. "We have come in this latter day to a truncated and impoverished understanding of congregationalism. We need to revitalize a sense of community" ("A Doctrine of the Church for Liberals," p. 16). This revitalization is dependent in part on a renewed sense of covenant as the bond of religious community and the basis of the church. Wright's work demonstrates the continuing source of vitality that history, the collective memory of a people, can lend to the liberal religious movement.

*Bibliography*

A. *The Beginnings of Unitarianism in America* (Boston, 1955); *Three Prophets of Religious Liberalism* (editor, Boston, 1961); *The Liberal Christians: Essays on American Unitarian History* (Boston, 1970); *A Stream of Light: A Sesquicentennial History of American Unitarianism* (coauthor and editor, Boston, 1975); "Individualism in Historical Perspective," Unitarian Universalist Advance Study Paper No. 9, 1979; "A Doctrine of the Church for Liberals" (Boston, 1983).

B. CA 21R, 956; DAS 1, 844; David Robinson, "Unitarian Historiography and the American Renaissance," *ESQ: A Journal of the American Renaissance*, 23 (1977), 130–37.

# APPENDIX: CHRONOLOGY

| | |
|---|---|
| 1742 | Charles Chauncy* writes his attack on the Great Awakening, *Enthusiasm Described and Caution'd Against*. |
| 1759 | Ebenezer Gay* delivers the Dudleian Lecture at Harvard, *Natural Religion, as Distinguish'd from Revealed*. |
| 1770 | John Murray* arrives in America. |
| 1782 | James Freeman* is appointed reader at King's Chapel, Boston. |
| 1784 | Charles Chauncy publishes his treatise on universal salvation, *The Mystery Hid from Ages and Generations*. |
| 1794 | Joseph Priestley* arrives in America. |
| 1803 | The Universalists adopt the Winchester Profession of Faith. |
| 1805 | Henry Ware* is elected Hollis Professor of Divinity at Harvard. |
| 1805 | Hosea Ballou* publishes *A Treatise on Atonement*. |
| 1805 | Joseph Stevens Buckminster* is ordained as pastor of the Brattle Street Church, Boston. |
| 1815 | William Ellery Channing* publishes *A Letter to the Rev. Samuel C. Thacher* replying to Calvinist attacks on the Boston liberals. |
| 1819 | William Ellery Channing delivers "Unitarian Christianity" in Baltimore. |
| 1820 | A legal decision allows the parish in Dedham, Massachusetts, to retain church property after a split with the church. |
| 1825 | The American Unitarian Association is formed. |
| 1826 | Divinity Hall at Harvard is completed. |
| 1829 | Hosea Ballou 2d* publishes *The Ancient History of Universalism*. |
| 1831 | Henry Ware, Jr.,* publishes *On the Formation of the Christian Character*. |
| 1838 | Ralph Waldo Emerson* delivers the Divinity School Address at Harvard. |
| 1841 | Theodore Parker* delivers *A Discourse on the Transient and the Permanent in Christianity*. |
| 1844 | Meadville Theological School is founded. |

| | |
|---|---|
| 1852 | The Western Unitarian Conference is formed. |
| 1859 | Henry Whitney Bellows* delivers *The Suspense of Faith*. |
| 1860 | Thomas Starr King* goes to San Francisco. |
| 1865 | The Universalist General Convention is formed. |
| 1865 | First meeting of the National Conference of Unitarian Churches. |
| 1865 | Frederic Henry Hedge* publishes *Reason in Religion*. |
| 1866 | Second meeting of the National Conference at Syracuse, New York, is marked by dissent from the radicals. |
| 1867 | The Free Religious Association is founded. |
| 1870 | Centennial Conference of American Universalism. |
| 1873 | Octavius Brooks Frothingham* publishes *The Religion of Humanity*. |
| 1886 | Jabez T. Sunderland* publishes *The Issue in the West*. |
| 1886 | James Freeman Clarke* publishes "The Five Points of Calvinism and the Five Points of the New Theology" in his *Vexed Questions in Theology*. |
| 1887 | William Channing Gannett's* "The Things Most Commonly Believed To-Day Among Us" is adopted by the Western Unitarian Conference. |
| 1894 | Meeting of the National Conference at Saratoga leads to broad agreement between the radicals and the moderates. |
| 1898 | Isaac M. Atwood* becomes the first general superintendent of the Universalist General Convention. |
| 1898 | Samuel A. Eliot* becomes secretary of the American Unitarian Association. |
| 1900 | In a reorganization, Samuel A. Eliot becomes president and chief executive officer of the American Unitarian Association. |
| 1906 | The Pacific Unitarian School for the Ministry is incorporated (now The Starr King School for Religious Leadership). |
| 1917 | The Universalist General Convention adopts a Declaration of Social Principles written by Clarence R. Skinner.* |
| 1921 | John H. Dietrich* and William L. Sullivan* debate Humanism at the National Conference. |
| 1933 | *A Humanist Manifesto* is published. |
| 1936 | The American Unitarian Association publishes a self-appraisal, *Unitarians Face a New Age*. |
| 1937 | Frederick May Eliot* assumes the presidency of the American Unitarian Association. |
| 1937 | Clarence R. Skinner publishes *Liberalism Faces the Future*. |
| 1948 | The American Unitarian Association begins an office of fellowships under the leadership of Lon Ray Call* and Munroe Husbands.* |
| 1953 | The Council of Liberal Churches is formed by the Unitarians and Universalists to combine some administrative functions of the two groups. |
| 1961 | The American Unitarian Association and the Universalist Church of America merge to form the Unitarian Universalist Association. |

# BIBLIOGRAPHIC ESSAY

The following essay is intended as a guide to further research in American Unitarian and Universalist history and is by no means an exhaustive bibliography of those sources.

## GENERAL HISTORIES AND BIOGRAPHICAL COLLECTIONS

The standard history of American Unitarianism is the collaborative history *A Stream of Light: A Sesquicentennial History of American Unitarianism*, ed. Conrad Wright* (Boston: Unitarian Universalist Association, 1975). This volume treats American Unitarianism in detail and augments that part of the second volume of Earl Morse Wilbur's* *History of Unitarianism*, 2 vols. (Cambridge: Harvard University Press, 1945, 1952), which deals with the United States. For an excellent brief overview, see William Wallace Fenn,* "The Revolt against the Standing Order," in *The Religious History of New England: King's Chapel Lectures* (Cambridge: Harvard University Press, 1917). An excellent guide to Unitarian historiography, which focuses on the relationship of Unitarianism and Transcendentalism, is Conrad Wright, "Unitarianism and Transcendentalism," in *The Transcendentalists: A Review of Research and Criticism*, ed. Joel Myerson (New York: Modern Language Association, 1984), pp. 45–55. This volume should be consulted for bibliographical information on individual members of the Transcendentalist movement, and for Transcendentalism and its milieu in general. Students of Unitarian history will find John C. Godbey, *A Bibliography of Unitarian Universalist History* (Chicago: Meadville Lombard Theological School, 1982), a useful tool. Earlier studies still of value are Joseph Henry Allen, *Our Liberal Movement in Theology* (Boston: Roberts Bros., 1892); *Sequel to "Our Liberal Movement"* (Boston: Roberts Bros., 1897); and George Willis Cooke, *Unitarianism in America* (Boston: American Unitarian Association, 1902).

A widely used and valuable documentary history is David B. Parke's *Epic of Unitarianism* (Boston: Beacon Press, 1957). Virgil E. Murdock's *Institutional History of the American Unitarian Association*, Minns Lectures, 1975–76 (Boston: American Unitarian Association, 1976) provides a useful overview of the American Unitarian Association (AUA) as a functioning organization from its inception to merger with Universalism. Although some of the essays that comprise this volume will be mentioned later individually, Conrad Wright's *Liberal Christians: Essays on American Unitarian History* (Boston: Beacon Press, 1970) contains some of the best interpretive historical writing on Unitarianism now available. Also valuable for its interpretive depth is Sidney E. Mead's* "Address to Unitarians," *Proceedings of the Unitarian Historical Society*, 12 (1958), 12–22 (hereafter PUHS). A good review of the issue of creeds in Unitarianism and Universalism is Robert M. Hemstreet, "Identity and Ideology: Creeds and Creedlessness in Unitarianism and Universalism," Unitarian Universalist Advance Study Paper No. 3, 1977. For a good survey of the black presence in the Unitarian and Universalist traditions, which focuses on the careers of Ethelred Brown* and Lewis A. McGee, see Mark D. Morrison-Reed, *Black Pioneers in a White Denomination* (Boston: Skinner House, 1980; rev. ed., Boston: Beacon, 1984).

The Unitarian tradition is rich in biographical material, and there are several useful collections of biographies. William Ware's *American Unitarian Biography*, 2 vols. (Boston and Cambridge: James Munroe, 1850), compiles a collection of biographical sketches and memoirs of early Unitarian leaders, as does William B. Sprague's *Annals of the American Unitarian Pulpit* (New York: Robert Carter and Brothers, 1865), later incorporated into the series *Annals of the American Pulpit*. The most comprehensive collection is Samuel A. Eliot,* ed., *Heralds of a Liberal Faith*, 4 vols. (Boston: American Unitarian Association, 1910–52). Recently, Catherine F. Hitchings compiled the valuable collection "Universalist and Unitarian Women Ministers," *Journal of the Universalist Historical Society*, 10 (1975) (hereafter JUHS).

Thomas Whittemore's* *Modern History of Universalism* (Boston: Published by the Author, 1830) is the first substantial attempt to write a history of American Universalism. Richard Eddy's* *Universalism in America: A History*, 2 vols. (Boston: Universalist Publishing House, 1884–86), superseded Whittemore. Eddy's book is an able work, still of value. An important early attempt to set Universalism in a general Christian context is Hosea Ballou 2d,* *The Ancient History of Universalism* (Boston: Marsh and Capen, 1829). Ernest Cassara's *Universalism in America: A Documentary History* (Boston: Beacon Press, 1971) collects, arranges, and introduces important source documents on the history of Universalism. Russell E. Miller's *Larger Hope: The First Century of the Universalist Church in America, 1770–1870* (Boston: Unitarian Universalist Association, 1979) supplanted Eddy as the standard history. It is a volume rich in detailed information. At this writing, Miller is preparing a second volume concerning the modern history of Universalism. Valuable biographical sketches of early Universalists are included in John G. Adams, *Fifty Notable Years: Views of the Ministry of Christian Universalism during the Last Half-Century* (Boston: Universalist Publishing House, 1882); and E. R. Hanson, *Our Woman Workers: Biographical Sketches of Women Eminent in the Universalist Church* (Boston: Star and Covenant Office, 1882). A good interpretive essay on Universalism is John Coleman Adams, "The Universalists," in *The Religious History of New England: King's Chapel Lectures* (Cambridge: Harvard University Press, 1917). But the most valuable interpretive essay on Universalism is George Huntston Williams's* "American Universalism: A Bicentennial Historical Essay," JUHS, 9 (1971), entire issue. For a solid overview of the historiography of Universalism as of 1972, see Alan Seaburg, "Recent Scholarship in American Universalism: A Bibliographical Essay," *Church History*, 41 (1972), 513–23. Seaburg noted the tendency of church historians "to ignore American Universalism" but noted increased interest in the field since the middle 1950s.

## UNITARIAN AND UNIVERSALIST ORIGINS

Conrad Wright's *Beginnings of Unitarianism in America* (Boston: Starr King Press, 1955) is the definitive account of the rise of the liberal theological movement, Arminianism, in eighteenth-century New England. Wright's study constitutes the history of Unitarianism before it was known as such. Wright's essay "Rational Religion in Eighteenth-Century America," in *The Liberal Christians*, is a good exposition of the system of "supernatural rationalism" that dominated New England theology in the eighteenth and early nineteenth centuries. Further detail can be gained through recent biographies of leaders of that movement. On Jonathan Mayhew,* see Charles W. Akers, *Called unto Liberty: A Life of Jonathan Mayhew* (Cambridge: Harvard University Press, 1964). On Charles Chauncy,* see Edward M. Griffin, *Old Brick: Charles Chauncy of Boston, 1705–1787* (Minneapolis: University of Minnesota Press, 1980); and Charles Lippy, *Seasonable Revolutionary: The Mind of Charles Chauncy* (Chicago: Nelson-Hall, 1981). On Ebenezer Gay,* see Robert J. Wilson III, *The Benevolent Deity: Ebenezer Gay and the Rise of Rational Religion in New England, 1696–1787* (Philadelphia: University of Pennsylvania Press, 1983). Mayhew, Chauncy and Gay are also treated in James W. Jones, *The Shattered Synthesis: New England Puritanism before the Great Awakening* (New Haven: Yale University Press, 1973). Students of eighteenth-century Unitarian thought will also find interest in *Jefferson's Extracts from the Gospels: "The Philosophy of Jesus" and "The Life and Morals of Jesus,"* ed. Dickinson W. Adams and Ruth W. Lester, introduction by Eugene R. Sheridan, in *The Papers of Thomas Jefferson*, Second Series (Princeton: Princeton University Press, 1983).

Stephen Marini's *Radical Sects of Revolutionary New England* (Cambridge: Harvard University Press, 1982) is an important interpretation of the rise of Universalism in the late eighteenth century. Marini viewed the Universalists with the Freewill Baptists and Shakers as emerging native sects challenging the New England Calvinist tradition. Aside from information in Eddy, Miller, and Marini, noted above, Universalist origins can best be studied in the biographies of John Murray* and Hosea Ballou,* the most prominent early leaders of the movements. Murray is treated in Clarence R. Skinner* and Alfred S. Cole, *Hell's Ramparts Fell: The Life of John Murray* (Boston: Universalist Publishing House, 1941). On Ballou, who has had a number of biographers, see Thomas Whittemore, *Life of Rev. Hosea Ballou*, 4 vols. (Boston: James M. Usher, 1854–55); and more recently, Ernest Cassara, *Hosea Ballou: The Challenge to Orthodoxy* (Boston: Universalist Historical Society, 1961). Cassara's *Hosea Ballou* is the definitive modern biography. Ballou's *Treatise on Atonement* (Randolph, VT: Sereno Wright, 1805) is the best exposition of his theological position.

## UNITARIAN DENOMINATIONAL CONSCIOUSNESS, 1805–36

Two essays by Conrad Wright are particularly helpful in understanding the emergence of Unitarianism from Arminian liberalism in the first decades of the nineteenth century. In "The Election of Henry Ware: Two Contemporary Accounts, Edited with Commentary," *Harvard Library Bulletin*, 17 (1969), 245–78, Wright offered an account of the specifics of Ware's election to the chair of Hollis Professor of Divinity at Harvard, the event that drove a wedge between the liberals and orthodox in Massachusetts congregationalism. In "The Controversial Career of Jedidiah Morse," *Harvard Library Bulletin*, 31 (1983), 64–87, Wright detailed the life of the man who, in an ironic sense, founded the Unitarian sect through his attacks on liberal theology. It was in answering Morse's attacks that the liberals found a cohesive program for denominational action.

The best overview of the intellectual milieu of pre-Civil War Unitarianism is Daniel Walker Howe's *Unitarian Conscience: Harvard Moral Philosophy, 1805–1861* (Cambridge: Harvard University Press, 1970). In his study, Howe stressed the coalescence of liberal thinking in Boston and Harvard College around the issues of moral philosophy. He also discussed the emotional and pietistic element in early Unitarianism, a factor often lost sight of in the conception of Unitarianism as rational religion. Students of this period can also benefit from Ann Douglas's *Feminization of American Culture* (New York: Knopf, 1977), a study that argues for the connections between liberal theology, in which Unitarianism is a leading element, and the development of a popular woman's literature before the war. Two nineteenth-century biographies, studies of more conservative Unitarian fathers by their radical sons, are of value. William Channing Gannett's* *Ezra Stiles Gannett: Unitarian Minister in Boston, 1824–1871* (Boston: Roberts Bros., 1875) chronicles the life of AUA leader Gannett in the context of the formation and development of the Unitarian movement. Similar in its intention and scope is Octavius Brooks Frothingham's* *Boston Unitarianism, 1820–1850: A Study of the Life and Work of Nathaniel Langdon Frothingham* (New York: Putnam's, 1890).

The importance of Joseph Stevens Buckminster* as a cultural figure has recently been emphasized. The most valuable study is Lawrence Buell, "Joseph Stevens Buckminster: The Making of a New England Saint," *Canadian Review of American Studies*, 10 (1979), 1–29. An earlier biography is Eliza Buckminster Lee, *Memoirs of Rev. Joseph Buckminster, D.D., and of His Son, Rev. Joseph Stevens Buckminster* (Boston: William Crosby and H. P. Nichols, 1851). For Buckminster's contribution to biblical study, see Jerry Wayne Brown, *The Rise of Biblical Criticism in America, 1800–1870* (Middletown, CT: Wesleyan University Press, 1969); and for his place as a literary and cultural figure, see Lewis P. Simpson, *The Man of Letters in New England and the South* (Baton Rouge: Louisiana State University Press, 1973).

Buckminster's early death ended his leadership of the liberal movement, and that mantle fell to William Ellery Channing.* There is an enormous literature on Channing, who has been studied as a religious, literary, and political leader. For a more thorough survey of Channing scholarship, see David Robinson, "William Ellery Channing," in *The Transcendentalists: A Review of Research and Criticism*, ed. Myerson, pp. 310–16. Of the several good biographies of Channing, John White Chadwick's* *William Ellery Channing: Minister of Religion* (Boston: Houghton Mifflin, 1903) is still unsurpassed. The three-volume *Memoir of William Ellery Channing, with Extracts from His Correspondence and Manuscripts* (Boston: William Crosby and H. P. Nichols, 1848) by William Henry Channing is diffuse in organization but contains valuable excerpts from Channing's writings and conversation. Of recent biographies, Jack Mendelsohn's *Channing: The Reluctant Radical* (Boston: Little, Brown, 1971) stresses the political and social conflicts that Channing faced and ably reconstructs Channing's historical milieu. Andrew Delbanco's *William Ellery Channing: An Essay on the Liberal Spirit in America* (Cambridge: Harvard University Press, 1981) argues that Channing's coming to terms with slavery was the most dramatic event in his intellectual development. Delbanco made it clear that Channing's liberalism was a hard-won and significant accomplishment. Also useful as a survey of Channing scholarship and corrective to several interpretations of Channing is Conrad Wright's "Rediscovery of Channing," in *The Liberal Christians*. Wright noted that Channing should not be too strongly identified with either Hopkinsian Calvinism or the later Transcendentalist movement but is more correctly seen in the tradition of supernatural rationalism.

## THE TRANSCENDENTALIST CONTROVERSY, 1836–60

The literature of New England Transcendentalism, both in primary and secondary sources, is vast. A comprehensive guide to the criticism, *The Transcendentalists: A Review of Research and Criticism*, ed. Myerson, is now available. The best single resource in the field is Perry Miller's *Transcendentalists: An Anthology* (Cambridge: Harvard University Press, 1950), which includes writings by all of the Transcendentalists except major texts of Ralph Waldo Emerson* and Henry David Thoreau, along with Miller's incisive analysis. The essay by Alexander Kern, "The Rise of Transcendentalism, 1815–1860," in *Transitions in American Literary History*, ed. Harry Hayden Clark (Durham, NC: Duke University Press, 1954), pp. 245–314, is an excellent overview of the movement. A modern comprehensive history of Transcendentalism remains to be written, although Octavius Brooks Frothingham's *Transcendentalism in New England: A History* (New York: Putnam's, 1876) is well-written and insightful. There are a number of books that shed valuable light on the movement from various perspectives. William Hutchison's *Transcendentalist Ministers: Church Reform in the New England Renaissance* (New Haven: Yale University Press, 1959) views the Transcendentalist movement as an effort at ecclesiastical and theological reform rather than a purely literary or philosophical enterprise. Lawrence Buell's *Literary Transcendentalism: Style and Vision in the American Renaissance* (Ithaca, NY: Cornell University Press, 1973) traces the roots of the literary outpouring of the movement to Unitarian sermonic expression. Joel Myerson's *New England Transcendentalists and the Dial* (Rutherford, NJ: Fairleigh Dickinson University Press, 1980) is a history of the *Dial*, the major periodical of the movement edited by Emerson and Margaret Fuller.* Myerson's work contains a number of biographical sketches of contributors to the magazine.

The Transcendentalist movement may perhaps most profitably be studied in terms of the individuals who comprised it. Although there was among them something of a sense of common purpose, there was no strong and cohesive enterprise, with the possible exception of the *Dial*. Emerson was the leader of the group, and his literary stature, still growing in our century, has resulted in an enormous log of information and interpretation of him. His newly edited *Journals and Miscellaneous Notebooks*, 16 vols. (Cambridge: Harvard University Press, 1960–82), are the best single source on his thought and development. A new edition of his *Complete Works*, 3 vols. to date (Cambridge: Harvard University Press, 1971–), is in process, and his *Early Lectures*, 3 vols. (Cambridge: Harvard University Press, 1959–71), have recently been published. Ralph L. Rusk's edition of his *Letters*, 6 vols. (New York: Columbia University Press, 1939), is also an invaluable tool. Rusk also wrote *The Life of Ralph Waldo Emerson* (New York: Scribner's, 1949), and to that biography, Gay Wilson Allen's recent *Waldo Emerson* (New York: Viking, 1981) should be added. Stephen E. Whicher's *Freedom and Fate: An Inner Life of Ralph Waldo Emerson* (Philadelphia: University of Pennsylvania Press,

1953) is the best intellectual analysis of Emerson, focusing on his move from optimism to a more tempered skepticism in his career. Whicher's study can be supplemented by Sherman Paul's *Emerson's Angle of Vision* (Cambridge: Harvard University Press, 1952); Jonathan Bishop's *Emerson on the Soul* (Cambridge: Harvard University Press, 1964); Joel Porte's *Representative Man: Ralph Waldo Emerson in His Time* (New York: Oxford University Press, 1979); David Robinson's *Apostle of Culture: Emerson as Preacher and Lecturer* (Philadelphia: University of Pennsylvania Press, 1982); and B. L. Packer's *Emerson's Fall: A New Interpretation of the Major Essays* (New York: Continuum, 1982).

Although Emerson was the group's intellectual leader, it is arguable that Theodore Parker* had a more direct influence on the Unitarian denomination. Parker refused to abandon his Unitarian associations despite some pressure to do so when his radical views became controversial, and he remained a potent example to the generation of preachers who followed him. Several early biographies by later radicals in the Unitarian movement attest to that influence: John Weiss,* *Life and Correspondence of Theodore Parker*, 2 vols. (London: Longman, Green, Longman, Roberts, and Green, 1863); Octavius Brooks Frothingham, *Theodore Parker: A Biography* (Boston, J. R. Osgood, 1874); and John White Chadwick, *Theodore Parker: Preacher and Reformer* (Boston and New York: Houghton Mifflin, 1901). Parker's most significant theological work is *A Discourse on the Transient and Permanent in Christianity* (Boston: Printed for the Author, 1841), reprinted in Perry Miller, *The Transcendentalists*. His *Works* have been published in fifteen volumes (Boston: American Unitarian Association, 1906–11). Perry Miller's "Theodore Parker: Apostasy within Liberalism," in his *Nature's Nation* (Cambridge: Harvard University Press, 1967), is a superb consideration of the challenge that Theodore Parker presented to the liberal tradition in his refusal to give up the name Unitarian. Henry Steele Commager's *Theodore Parker* (Boston: Little, Brown, 1936) is the standard modern biography.

A third important member of the Transcendentalist movement is Margaret Fuller, whose work is now being reexamined because of the increasing interest in both feminist studies and the Transcendentalist movement. Selections from her works, with interpretive commentary, are available in several editions: Perry Miller, ed., *Margaret Fuller: American Romantic* (Garden City, NY: Doubleday, 1963); Bell Gale Chevigny, *The Woman and the Myth: Margaret Fuller's Life and Writings* (Old Westbury, NY: Feminist Press, 1976); and Joel Myerson, ed., *Margaret Fuller: Essays on American Life and Letters* (New Haven: College and University Press, 1978). Fuller's letters are now being edited in a comprehensive edition: Robert N. Hudspeth, ed., *The Letters of Margaret Fuller*, 2 vols. to date (Ithaca, NY: Cornell University Press, 1983–). Fuller was the subject of an early biography, Ralph Waldo Emerson, James Freeman Clarke,* and William Henry Channing,* *Memoirs of Margaret Fuller Ossoli*, 2 vols. (Boston: Phillips, Sampson, 1852), which contains much useful information on Fuller despite some very poor editorial procedures. More recent biographies are Mason Wade, *Margaret Fuller: Whetstone of Genius* (New York: Viking, 1940); Joseph Jay Deiss, *The Roman Years of Margaret Fuller* (New York: Thomas Y. Crowell, 1969); and Paula Blanchard, *Margaret Fuller: From Transcendentalism to Revolution* (New York: Delta-Seymour Lawrence, 1978). For interpretive essays on Fuller, see Douglas, *The Feminization of American Culture*; Bell Gale Chevigny, "Growing Out of New England: The Emergence of Margaret Fuller's Radicalism," *Women's Studies*, 5 (1978), 65–100; Albert J. von Frank, "Life as Art in America: The Case of Margaret Fuller," in *Studies in the American Renaissance, 1981*, ed. Joel Myerson (Boston: Twayne, 1981), pp. 1–26; and David Robinson, "Margaret

Fuller and the Transcendental Ethos: *Woman in the Nineteenth Century*," *Publications of the Modern Language Association*, 97 (1982), 83–98.

## LATE NINETEENTH-CENTURY UNITARIANISM AND UNIVERSALISM

The fact of greatest significance for liberal religion in the late nineteenth century was the formation of the National Conference of Unitarian Churches in 1865 under the leadership of Henry W. Bellows.* That story is told in Conrad Wright's "Henry W. Bellows and the Organization of the National Conference," in *The Liberal Christians*. Bellows, the outstanding Unitarian churchman of this period, is the subject of Walter Donald Kring's biography *Henry Whitney Bellows* (Boston: Skinner House, 1979). On Bellows's importance to Unitarian history, see Conrad Wright, "In Search of a Usable Past," *Collegium Proceedings*, 1 (1979), 115–36.

Other important members of what has been termed the "Broad Church" group of Unitarians are James Freeman Clarke and Frederic Henry Hedge.* Clarke was a prolific writer on religion, and among his works are *Ten Great Religions*, 2 vols. (Boston: Houghton Mifflin, 1871–73); *Self-Culture: Physical, Intellectual, Moral, and Spiritual* (Boston: Houghton Mifflin, 1880); and *Vexed Questions in Theology* (Boston: George H. Ellis, 1886). An early memoir is Edward Everett Hale,* ed., *James Freeman Clarke: Autobiography, Diary, and Correspondence* (Boston and New York: Houghton Mifflin, 1891). A modern biography is Arthur S. Bolster, Jr., *James Freeman Clarke: Disciple to Advancing Truth* (Boston: Beacon Press, 1954).

Frederic Henry Hedge deserves wider knowledge among historians than he has received. Interest in him usually evaporates after his early connections with Emerson and the Transcendentalists are noted. *Reason in Religion* (Boston: Walker Fuller, 1865) is his major theological work. George H. Williams's *Rethinking the Unitarian Relationship with Protestantism: An Examination of the Thought of Frederic Henry Hedge, (1805–1890)* (Boston: Beacon Press, 1949) argues for the importance of Hedge's insistence on historical and ecclesiastical continuity in the religious life. One recent essay on Hedge is especially notable. In "Frederic Henry Hedge and the Failure of Transcendentalism," *Harvard Library Bulletin*, 23 (1975), 396–410, Joel Myerson described the intellectual parting of the ways between Emerson and Hedge over the issue of the importance of the church. Myerson also reprinted here the letter from Hedge to Emerson in 1836 that initiated the "Transcendental Club." Opposing Bellows and the Broad Church group over the form of the National Conference were the radicals who formed the Free Religious Association in 1867. Stow Persons wrote the history of their movement in *Free Religion: An American Faith* (New Haven: Yale University Press, 1947). For a treatment of the current of modernism in American Protestantism as a whole at this time, see William Hutchison, *The Modernist Impulse in American Protestantism* (Cambridge: Harvard University Press, 1976). Hutchison situated the origins of that modernism in the Unitarian movement and stressed the work of Cyrus Bartol* and Octavius Brooks Frothingham among the Free Religionists. Frothingham is the central figure among the radicals and has written his own autobiographical work, *Recollections and Impressions, 1822–1891* (New York: Putnam's, 1891). J. Wade Caruthers's *Octavius Brooks Frothingham, Gentle Radical* (University: University of Alabama Press, 1977) is a comprehensive biography. Frothingham's most influential text is *The Religion of Humanity* (New York: Asa K.

Butts, 1873). There is a wealth of primary material on the Free Religion movement but relatively little criticism and historiography, at least as compared with the Transcendentalists. Among important primary texts are Cyrus Bartol, *Radical Problems* (Boston: Roberts Bros., 1872); Francis Ellingwood Abbot,* *Scientific Theism* (Boston: Little, Brown, 1885); John White Chadwick, *The Faith of Reason* (Boston: Roberts Bros., 1879); and idem, *Old and New Unitarian Belief* (Boston: George H. Ellis, 1894).

The currents of modernism also affected the Universalist movement as Ernest Cassara showed in his "Effect of Darwinism on Universalist Belief, 1860–1900," JUHS, 1 (1959), 32–42. Cassara discerned three stages in the impact of Darwinism on the Universalists, moving from initial "hostility" to a final "joyful acceptance" of the doctrine. One of the major figures in the growth of the Universalist denomination in the late nineteenth century is the missionary preacher Quillen H. Shinn.* Shinn's biography, including selections from his papers, is presented in William H. McGlauflin, *Faith with Power: A Life Story of Quillen Hamilton Shinn, D.D.* (Boston and Chicago: Universalist Publishing House, 1912). More information on Shinn will be included in Russell E. Miller's forthcoming volume on Universalist history after 1870.

Two women of major importance both to the Universalist denomination and American religious history are Olympia Brown* and Mary Livermore.* In addition to Hitchings and Russell E. Miller, an important source of information is "Olympia Brown: An Autobiography," edited and completed by Gwendolen B. Willis, JUHS, 4 (1963). The biography of Brown by Lawrence L. Graves in *Notable American Women* (Cambridge: Harvard University Press, 1971), 1, 256–58 is also valuable. Brown's recollections of her associates in the women's struggle can be found in *Acquaintances Old and New, Among Reformers* (Milwaukee: n.p., 1911), from which Willis drew in editing the Brown autobiography. In addition to the information in Russell E. Miller, an excellent sketch of Mary Livermore by Robert E. Riegel is presented in *Notable American Women*, 2, 410–13. Livermore also wrote an autobiography, *The Story of My Life* (Hartford: Worthington, 1897), that includes a selection of the lectures that made her so popular on the lyceum circuit.

On the western expansion of Unitarianism, see Charles C. Lyttle, *Freedom Moves West: A History of the Western Unitarian Conference, 1852–1952* (Boston: Beacon Press, 1952). Lyttle wrote with great sympathy for the radical western leader Jenkin Lloyd Jones* and his "Unity men" who led western Unitarianism in a noncreedal direction. Complementary to Lyttle's work is Arnold Crompton, *Unitarianism on the Pacific Coast: The First Sixty Years* (Boston: Beacon Press, 1957). Crompton's study is supplemented by two other items on Unitarianism on the West Coast: Earl Morse Wilbur, *Thomas Lamb Eliot, 1841–1936* (Portland, OR: Privately printed, 1937); and Henry Chamberlain Meserve, "The First Unitarian Society of San Francisco, 1850–1950," PUHS, 9, pt. 1 (1951), 24–44.

## EARLY TWENTIETH-CENTURY UNITARIANISM AND UNIVERSALISM

The chapters by David B. Parke and Carol R. Morris in Wright's *Stream of Light* provide the best guide to twentieth-century Unitarian history. Another important essay is Parke's "Liberals and Liberalism Since 1900," PUHS, 15, pt. 1 (1964), 1–25. The important leadership of Samuel A. Eliot is chronicled in Arthur Cushman McGiffert,

Jr., *Pilot of a Liberal Faith: Samuel Atkins Eliot, 1862–1950* (Boston: Skinner House, 1976).

The social mission of religion has been a central theme of twentieth-century liberal religion. Francis Greenwood Peabody,* John Haynes Holmes,* and Clarence R. Skinner have been vital to this trend. Peabody's major work is *Jesus Christ and the Social Question* (New York: Grosset and Dunlap, 1900), but he authored several other books on the social question. Peabody's *Reminiscences of Present-Day Saints* (Boston and New York: Houghton Mifflin, 1927) is a delightful blend of autobiography and biographical remembrance. Peabody's development is ably treated in Jurgen Herbst, "Francis Greenwood Peabody: Harvard's Theologian of the Social Gospel," *Harvard Theological Review*, 54 (1961), 45–69. Two of John Haynes Holmes's more significant works are *The Revolutionary Function of the Modern Church* (New York: Putnam's, 1912); and *New Wars for Old* (New York: Dodd, Mead, 1916). The first is a call for deeper involvement of the church in social issues, and the latter is an argument for pacifism. Holmes's reverence for Gandhi is chronicled in *My Gandhi* (New York: Harper and Brothers, 1953). For details of his life, see his autobiography *I Speak for Myself* (New York: Harper and Brothers, 1959); and Carl Hermann Voss, *Rabbi and Minister: The Friendship of Stephen S. Wise and John Haynes Holmes* (Cleveland and New York: World, 1964).

Some details on Clarence Skinner's contribution to Universalist social theory are contained in Emerson Hugh Lalone, *And Thy Neighbor as Thyself: A Story of Universalist Social Action* (Boston: Universalist Publishing House, 1939). Skinner's early *Social Implications of Universalism* (Boston: Universalist Publishing House, 1915) is reprinted with an introduction by James D. Hunt in JUHS, 5 (1964–65), 79–122. Skinner's *Liberalism Faces the Future* (New York: Macmillan, 1937) is a critical examination of the weaknesses of liberalism and a call for its revitalization during the reexamination of liberal values of the 1930s. His *Religion for Greatness* (Boston: Murray Press, 1945) holds out a vision of Universalism for the post–World War II era. Further information on Skinner can be found in Alfred S. Cole, *Clarence Skinner: Prophet of Twentieth Century Universalism* (Boston: Universalist Historical Society, 1956); Charles A. Gaines, "Clarence R. Skinner: The Dark Years," JUHS, 3 (1962), 1–13; and Alan Seaburg, "Clarence Russell Skinner: A Bibliography," JUHS, 5 (1964–65), 66–77.

Another significant element in twentieth-century liberal religion has been the rise of Humanism. For an able study of Humanism in a Unitarian context, devoted primarily to the thought of John H. Dietrich,* Curtis W. Reese,* and Charles F. Potter,* see Mason Olds, *Religious Humanism in America: Dietrich, Reese, and Potter* (Washington, DC: University Press of America, 1978). An enormously valuable collection of Humanist writing is Curtis W. Reese, ed., *Humanist Sermons* (Chicago: Open Court, 1927). The central document of Humanism is "A Humanist Manifesto," *The Humanist*, 13 (1953), 58–61, reprinted in Parke's *Epic of Unitarianism*, pp. 139–42. Other able expositions of the Humanist position can be found in John H. Dietrich's sermon series *The Humanist Pulpit*, 7 vols. (Minneapolis: First Unitarian Society, 1927–34); and Curtis W. Reese, *The Meaning of Humanism* (Boston: Beacon Press, 1945). One of the most eloquent opponents of Humanism within Unitarianism was William Laurence Sullivan,* whose autobiography is set out in *Under Orders: The Autobiography of William Laurence Sullivan* (New York: Richard R. Smith, 1944).

The Humanist debate can be seen as related to another debate on the capacity of human nature and thus the foundations of liberal belief, which reached prominence in Unitarianism in the 1930s. A seminal essay in that critique of liberalism was William Wallace Fenn's "Modern Liberalism," *American Journal of Theology*, 17 (1913), 509–19. A notable later essay in this context is Perry Miller, "Individualism and the New England Tradition," in *The Responsibility of Mind in a Civilization of Machines*, ed. John Crowell and Stanford J. Searl, Jr. (Amherst: University of Massachusetts Press, 1979). The doubts about the sustaining power of pure individualism raised by Miller are also forcefully stated in Conrad Wright, "Individualism in Historical Perspective," Unitarian Universalist Advance Study Paper No. 9, 1979. A leader in the critique of liberalism was James Luther Adams,* whose spiritual autobiography "Taking Time Seriously," *Christian Century*, 56 (1939), 1067–70, best captures the spirit of that critique. Some of Adams's significant essays for the important but short-lived *Journal of Liberal Religion* (1939–44) are reprinted with other material from his work in Max L. Stackhouse, ed. *On Being Human—Religiously* (Boston: Beacon Press, 1976). For assessments of Adams, see idem, "James Luther Adams: A Biographical and Intellectual Sketch," in *Voluntary Associations: A Study of Groups in Free Societies*, ed. D. B. Robertson (Richmond, VA: John Knox, 1966); George H. Williams, "James Luther Adams and the Unitarian Denomination," *Andover-Newton Quarterly*, 17 (1977), 173–83; and John R. Wilcox, *Taking Time Seriously: James Luther Adams* (Washington, DC: University Press of America, 1978).

Also influential in that debate was Unitarianism's outstanding twentieth-century leader Frederick May Eliot.* Under Eliot's leadership, the Commission of Appraisal addressed the need for renewal in Unitarianism: *Unitarians Face a New Age: The Report of the Commission of Appraisal to the American Unitarian Association* (Boston: American Unitarian Association, 1936). Eliot's own ideas have been collected in Alfred P. Stiernotte, ed., *Frederick May Eliot: An Anthology* (Boston: Beacon Press, 1959), which includes a biographical sketch by Wallace W. Robbins. For other information see Lawrence G. Brooks, "Frederick May Eliot as I Knew Him," PUHS, 13 (1960), 87–100; and Carol R. Morris, "The Election of Frederick May Eliot to the Presidency of the A.U.A.," PUHS, 17 (1970–72), 1–45. In the context of the Unitarian decline and revival in the 1930s, see the articles on Universalism by David Hicks MacPherson and Richard M. Woodman: "The Decline of Universalism, 1900–1950," JUHS, 6 (1966), 3–45.

## LATER TWENTIETH-CENTURY LIBERAL RELIGION

In "Growth and Decline: Trends and Speculations," Unitarian Universalist Advance Study Paper No. 8, 1978, James M. Hutchinson described Unitarian Universalist church growth and decline in the postwar period and offered some explanations for its causes. Hutchinson's essay can be read profitably in the context of two other denominational assessments. *The Free Church in a Changing World* (Boston: Unitarian Universalist Association, 1963) is the published result of a general appraisal of Unitarianism begun on the eve of merger with Universalism. Robert B. Tapp's *Religion among the Unitarian Universalists: Converts in the Stepfather's House* (New York and London: Seminar Press, 1973) is a study based on statistics derived from a survey conducted in the 1960s that included a final pool of more than twelve thousand questionnaires from Unitarian Universalists. Part of the phenomenon of Unitarian growth in the postwar period can be attributed to the Fellowship movement, the early history of which can be found in Laile E. Bartlett, *Bright Galaxy: Ten Years of Unitarian Fellowships* (Boston: Beacon Press, 1960). Conrad Wright's *Doctrine of the Church for Liberals* (Boston: American Unitarian Association, 1983) discusses the issue of the church in the liberal congregational tradition.

For information on the Unitarian and Universalist merger, see the various reports in the *Unitarian Register*, vols. 138 and 139 (1959–60); Carol R. Morris's discussion in Wright's *Stream of Light*; and Dana M. Greeley, *25 Beacon Street and Other Recollections* (Boston: Beacon Press, 1971). On the elections for denomination president in 1958 and 1961, see Joseph Barth,* "Contests for the Presidency: A.U.A., 1958–U.U.A., 1961," PUHS, 15 (1964), 26–65.

In the opinion of this writer, one of the leading movements in liberal religion today is process theology, emanating from the philosophy of Alfred North Whitehead but with roots in the Unitarian movement back to Channing and Emerson. Charles Hartshorne* and Henry Nelson Wieman* have been two influential process theologians. Of Hartshorne's voluminous writing, see in particular *The Divine Relativity: A Social Conception of God* (New Haven: Yale University Press, 1948) and *A Natural Theology for Our Time* (La Salle, IL: Open Court, 1967). For Wieman, see *The Source of Human Good* (Carbondale: Southern Illinois University Press) and *Creative Freedom: Vocation of Liberal Religion*, ed. Creighton Peden and Larry E. Axel (New York: Pilgrim, 1982).

# INDEX

Note: *Italic* page numbers refer to the biographical entries in Part Two.

**About the Author**

David Robinson is Associate Professor of English and Director of American Studies at Oregon State University. He is the author of *Apostle of Culture: Emerson as Preacher and Lecturer* as well as numerous articles and papers on both literary and religious topics.

ISBN 0-313-24893-1

90000>

9 780313 248931

HARDCOVER BAR CODE